"THE NILE, one of the great and storied rivers of the world, in a fascinating, engrossing book . . . history recreated with astounding vividness"
—ST. LOUIS GLOBE

*

"CONTINUOUS EXCITEMENT. . . . Man, both black and white, was the enemy of the explorer—Arab slave traders, native chieftains of incredible cruelty and savagery, who tortured people out of whim and killed them for sport. Drama, wonder and fascination"
—WASHINGTON STAR

"BRILLIANT, ADVENTURE-LOADED"
—PHILADELPHIA INQUIRER

"BLOODY, VIOLENT, EXOTIC"
—BOSTON HERALD

"MAGNIFICENT"
—CHICAGO STAR

THE WHITE NILE

Alan Moorehead

A DELL BOOK

Published by
DELL PUBLISHING CO., INC.
750 Third Avenue, New York 17, N.Y.

Reprinted by arrangement with
Harper & Brothers
New York, N.Y.

". . . of the sources of the Nile no one can give any account
. . . it enters Egypt from parts beyond."
  Herodotus, Book ii, 34

DEDICATION: To Freya Stark

First Dell printing—March, 1962
Second Dell printing—June, 1962
Third Dell printing—May, 1963
Fourth Dell printing—August, 1964
Fifth Dell printing—March, 1965

Printed in U.S.A.

CONTENTS

The Nile Valley and the Great Central Lakes

PROLOGUE

NO UNEXPLORED REGION in our times, neither the heights of the Himalayas, the Antarctic wastes, nor even the hidden side of the moon, has excited quite the same fascination as the mystery of the sources of the Nile. For two thousand years at least the problem was debated and remained unsolved; every expedition that was sent up the river from Egypt returned defeated. By the middle of the nineteenth century—barely 100 years ago—this matter had become, in Harry Johnston's phrase, 'the greatest geographical secret after the discovery of America'.

The scope of this book is limited to the years between 1856 and 1900, and so we need do no more here than mention very briefly the early history of the river. Almost certainly the ancient Egyptians knew the Nile valley from the Mediterranean as far as the present city of Khartoum, where the Blue Nile comes in from the Ethiopian mountains. Probably they knew something of the Blue Nile as well. But the further course of the parent stream, the White Nile, south of Khartoum, remained a matter of endless speculation, and it interested every distinguished geographer of this age.

This was something more than an ordinary field of exploration. In these deserts the river was life itself. Had it failed to flow, even for one season, then all Egypt perished. Not to know where the stream came from, not to have any sort of guarantee that it would continue—this was to live in a state of insecurity where only fatalism or superstition could reassure the mind.

But there is no record of the river's ever having failed. The great brown flood came pouring out of the desert for ever, and no one could explain why it was that it should rise and flow over its banks in the Nile Delta in September, the driest and hottest time of the year on the Mediterranean littoral; nor how it was possible for the river to continue in its lower reaches for well over a thousand miles through one of the most frightful of all deserts without receiving a single tributary and hardly a drop of rain.

About 460 B.C. Herodotus ascended the Nile as far as the first cataract at Assuan before turning back, having found it quite impossible to obtain definite information about the source of the river. There existed merely a vague notion that it arose from 'fountains' somewhere in the interior of Africa. The Emperor Nero sent two centurions with an expedition into the wastes of Nubia, as the Sudan was then called, but they returned unsuccessful, saying that they had been blocked in the far interior by an impenetrable swamp. Through the centuries that followed China became known to Europe; America and Australia were discovered, and the land masses and the oceans of the world were mapped and charted very much as they are today. But still, in 1856, the centre of Africa and its inner mystery, the source of the White Nile, remained almost as much an enigma as it was in the time of Herodotus.

James Bruce traced the course of the shorter Blue Nile from its source to Khartoum in the seventeen-seventies, but by 1856 even the most determined of explorers on the White Nile had not been able to get beyond the neighbourhood of the present township of Juba, on latitude 5 degrees north. At that point they were still nowhere near the source of the river. Cataracts, vast forests of papyrus reeds, malarial fever, the fierce tropical heat, the opposition of the pagan tribes—all these combined to prevent any further progress south. By now that impenetrable blank space in the centre of the continent had become filled in imagination with a thousand monstrosities, dwarf men and cannibals with tails, animals as strange as the fabulous griffin and the salamander, huge inland seas, and mountains so high they defied all nature by bearing on their crests, in this equatorial heat, a mantle of perpetual snow.

There was at least a little tenuous evidence to support

The map of Africa
taken from
Ptolemy's Map
of the World
c. A.D. 150

some of these speculations. One of the most persistent legends about the source of the Nile concerned itself with a journey that had not been made upon the river at all, but overland, from the east coast of Africa a little to the north of Zanzibar. According to this legend a man named Diogenes, a Greek merchant, claimed that in the middle of the first century A.D. he was returning home from a visit to India and had landed on the African mainland at a place called Rhapta (which might have been the site of the present settlement of Pangani in Kenya). From Rhapta, Diogenes said, he had 'travelled inland for a 25-days' journey and arrived in the vicinity of two great lakes, and the snowy range of mountains whence the Nile draws its twin sources'.

This, at all events, is the story as it was recorded at the time by the Syrian geographer Marinus of Tyre, and it was from the records of Marinus that Ptolemy, the greatest of geographers and astronomers of his time, produced in the middle of the second century A.D. his celebrated map. It shows the course of the Nile reaching directly southward from the Mediterranean to the Equator, and the river is made to arise from two round lakes. The lakes in turn are watered from a high range of mountains, the *Lunae Montes,* the Mountains of the Moon.

For 1,700 years Ptolemy's map remained a geographical curiosity, endlessly disputed yet seldom absolutely discredited. But then in 1848 Johann Rebmann, one of the earliest missionaries in East Africa, came forward with a sensational report that he himself, like the ancient Diogenes, had journeyed inland from the East African coast and had seen a vast mountain called Kilimanjaro with snow on its summit. This story was immediately ridiculed in London by a certain Desborough Cooley, a member of the Royal Geographical Society, who protested that it was impossible for snow to remain unmelted on the Equator; what Rebmann had seen was the sun shining on white rock. In the following year, however, another missionary, Johann Ludwig Krapf, claimed he had seen from a distance a second snow-capped peak, Mount Kenya, somewhat to the north of Kilimanjaro. Still another missionary, J. J. Erhardt, produced a map which showed a large inland lake which he called the 'Sea of Uniamesi'. By the early eighteen-fifties there was other evidence as well that led to a renewal of interest in Ptolemy's map: the Arab slave and ivory traders, returning to Zanzibar from the far interior, spoke of two great lakes there, one the Ujiji and the other the Nyanza. In addition there were reports of a third lake, the Nyasa, further to the south.

All this was extremely vague and confusing. Were all these lakes in reality one lake? Were Kilimanjaro and Kenya the legendary Mountains of the Moon, or was there another range further inland? And how did both lakes and mountains fit into the supposed pattern of the Nile?

It was in order to find the answer to these questions that two explorers, Richard Francis Burton and John Hanning Speke, set off for Africa in 1856. They rejected the route that followed the Nile upstream from Egypt, and decided instead to strike westward from Zanzibar into the dark interior where no white men had ever been before.

With this new expedition the great age of Central African exploration began.

PART ONE

The Exploration

Central Africa according to Krapf, Rebmann, Livingstone, and Erhardt 1849-1856

Chapter 1

ZANZIBAR 1856

THE ZANZIBAR that Burton and Speke first saw at the end of 1856 was a much more important place than it is today; indeed, it was almost the only centre of overseas commerce worth the name along the whole East African seaboard. The attempts of the Portuguese to found an empire on the mainland opposite the island had long since come to nothing, and all the country inland, the territories we now know as Tanganyika, Kenya, Uganda, South Sudan and the Congo, was very largely an unmapped, unknown void.

In a vague and general way the Sultans of Zanzibar laid claim to a part at least of this vast area, but in point of fact their power was restricted to the coastline and was not really effective even there. During the dry seasons slave and ivory caravans found their way into the wilderness that lay beyond and were gone for a year or more, perhaps for ever, but that was all one ever heard of Central Africa. It was almost as remote and strange as outer space is today.

The island of Zanzibar, however, was something of a name in the world, a regular port of call for the sailing vessels plying the Indian Ocean; and it was in one of these, a British sloop, that Burton and Speke came in on the northeast monsoon from Bombay on December 19, 1856.

Their first view of the island cannot have been so very different from the scene one sees at the present time. Then, as now, a whiff of cloves and tropical spices came out to greet the traveller from the shore, and on the shore itself a slow, oily sea of marvellous blue washed up on to white coral beaches. The jungle that began at the water's edge was green with a hectic greenness, and although occasional rainstorms and even tornadoes swept the island it was oppressed throughout the year by a deep soporific heat.

Seen from the sea Zanzibar port was an uneven silhouette of earthen hovels and large four-square buildings made of greyish coral, the only building stone on the island. One described very easily the palace of the Sultan, the houses of the consuls and the merchants, and then the minarets rising from the mosques in the town beyond. It was to one of these houses, close to the foreshore, that of Lieutenant-Colonel Atkins Hamerton, the British Agent, that Burton and Speke proposed to make their way.

The anchorage before the town was much congested. Burton counted upwards of sixty Arab dhows which, like his own sloop, had been blown across the Indian Ocean by the monsoon, and they were similar to those one sees in Zanzibar now, solid wooden hulls of anything between 50 and 500 tons with a single mast, a great lateen sail and a bowsprit that projected so far it almost doubled the vessel's length. In addition there were half a dozen square-rigged merchantmen in port, Americans from Salem, Frenchmen and Hamburgers that had sailed round the Cape from Europe. All these had come to pick up cargoes of copal, coconuts, ivory, hides, tortoise-shell, red pepper, ambergris, beeswax, hippopotamus teeth, rhinoceros horn, cowrie shells (that were called blackamoor's teeth) and anything else that was going in the bazaar. Rubbish of every kind floated by along the foreshore, and it was not unusual for a dead body to be seen among the debris. 'Here and there,' Burton wrote later, 'a giant shark shoots up from the depths and stares at the fisherman with a cool, fixed and colourless eye that makes his blood run cold.'

There was worse to come when they got ashore. The population of Zanzibar Island was about 100,000 at this time, and most of the people were living in the town itself. In the crooked dirty streets, barely 20 feet wide, a teeming procession went by of half-naked Negroes, Arabs, Indians, Persians, Swahilis and many others. Cattle and donkeys thrust their way into the crowd. Merchants, sitting cross-legged in holes in the walls, called out their wares, beggars reached up their hands to the passers-by, and over all in the stifling air hung the devastating smell of copra and decaying fish. In the bazaars piles of tropical fruits and vegetables were laid out on straw mats for sale.

In short, it was the sort of scene that is still familiar to any visitor to the East, and the only basic difference here in Zanzibar in 1856—a difference so great that it makes one feel that one is looking into another age and another world —was provided by the presence of the slaves. They roamed through every street, men, women and children, those who had been domesticated by years of captivity, and those who had just arrived from the interior and who were half mad and half dead through hunger and maltreatment—naked, bewildered creatures with teeth filed into points and cicatrices on their bodies, their whole appearance closer to that of a trapped animal than of a normal human being.

The scene had already been effectively described by Thomas Smee, the commander of the British research ship *Ternate,* which visited Zanzibar in 1811.

'The show,' Smee wrote, 'commences about four o'clock in the afternoon. The slaves, set off to the best advantage by having their skins cleaned and burnished with cocoa-nut oil, their faces painted with red and white stripes, which is here esteemed elegance, and the hands, noses, ears and feet ornamented with a profusion of bracelets of gold and silver and jewels, are ranged in a line, commencing with the youngest, and increasing to the rear according to their size and age. At the head of this file, which is composed of all sexes and ages from 6 to 60, walks the person who owns them; behind and at each side, two or three of his domestic slaves, armed with swords and spears, serve as a guard.

'Thus ordered the procession begins, and passes through the market-place and the principal streets; the owner holding forth in a kind of song the good qualities of his slaves and the high prices that have been offered for them.

'When any of them strikes a spectator's fancy the line immediately stops, and a process of examination ensues, which, for minuteness, is unequalled in any cattle market in Europe. The intending purchaser having ascertained there is no defect in the faculties of speech, hearing etc., that there is no disease present, and that the slave does not snore in sleeping, which is counted a very great fault, next proceeds to examine the person; the mouth and the teeth are first inspected and afterwards every part of the body in succession, not even excepting the breasts etc. of the girls, many of whom I have seen handled in the most indecent manner in the public market by their purchasers; indeed there is every reason to believe that the slave-dealers almost universally force the young girls to submit to their lust previous to their being disposed of.

'The slave is then made to walk or run a little way, to show there is no defect about the feet; and after which, if the price be agreed to, they are stripped of their finery and delivered over to their future master. I have frequently counted between twenty and thirty of these files in the market, some of which contained about thirty. Women with children newly born hanging at their breasts, and others so old they can scarcely walk, are sometimes seen dragged about in this manner. I observed they had in general a very dejected look; some groups appeared so ill-fed that their bones seemed as if ready to penetrate the skin. From such scenes one turns away with pity and indignation . . .'

In the forty-five years that had intervened between Captain Smee's report and the arrival now of Burton and Speke in Zanzibar a great deal had been achieved by the conscience of the world. By the eighteen-thirties slavery had been abolished in the British Empire, and the trade on the Atlantic west coast of Africa, the chief reservoir of Negroes, was already dying out. In 1845 the Sultan of Zanzibar had declared that the export of slaves was forbidden (though slavery within his dominions continued to be legal). British and French men-of-war patrolled the coast in search of Arab dhows bringing Negroes from the mainland.

But none of this had made any real difference. With a tradition of at least two thousand years of slaving behind them none of the east coast Arab dealers had as yet dreamed of giving up the trade. Slaving was in the Arab blood: no Arab regarded the trade as any more evil or abnormal than, presumably, a horse-dealer regards as evil or abnormal the buying and selling of horses today.

And so the caravans were still raiding into the interior,

the dhows, with their cargoes close-packed beneath the decks, were still successfully running the blockade of the warships; and Zanzibar market was as crowded as ever. Prices varied a good deal according to the season of the year and the supply, but in 1856 a dealer could still count on obtaining £4 or £5 for an adult male slave in Zanzibar and somewhat more for a female. Between twenty and forty thousand slaves were still imported into the island every year, about one-third of these being reserved for work on the plantations (which was still legal), and the remainder being destined, illegally, for export to Arabia, Persia, Egypt, Turkey and even further afield. There was tremendous wastage even among those slaves who had survived the journey from their villages inland to the coast: some thirty per cent of the males died of disease and malnutrition every year in Zanzibar and had to be replaced. Moreover the attempt to control the export trade had increased the hardships of the slaves. Prices were going up, and consequently it paid the dealer to cram more and more of his victims into the dhows: if just one vessel in four got through it was enough to make a profit. The ships were now built, Burton says, 'with 18 inches between the decks, one pint of water a head was served out per diem and five wretches were stowed away instead of two.'

The most desperate devices were used to keep up the supply. In Zanzibar harbour natives would be enticed on board a dhow with a bottle of rum or a decoy girl and then clapped under the hatches. A child worth a pound or two in Zanzibar would fetch up to £20 in Persia, and it was no difficult matter to hide the slaves in caves in the jungle until the dhows were ready to take them off by night. The highest prices were paid for Abyssinian girls and Circassians, who had been brought down from the north, but these last were very rare and seldom left the island: they were reserved for the harems of the rulers.

Burton's description of the market-place in 1856 indicates how little things had changed for the better since Captain Smee's day. 'Lines of Negroes,' he says, 'stood like beasts, the broker calling out *"bazar khush"*—the least hideous of the black faces, some of which appeared hardly human, were surmounted by scarlet night-caps. All were horribly thin, with ribs protruding like the circles of a cask, and not a few squatted sick on the ground. The most interesting were the small boys, who grinned as if somewhat pleased by the degrading and hardly decent inspection to which both sexes and all ages were subjected. The woman-show appeared poor and miserable; there was only one decent-looking girl, with carefully blacked eyebrows. She seemed modest, and probably had been exposed for sale in consequence of some inexcusable offence against decorum. As a rule no one buys adult domestic (as distinct from wild) slaves, male or female, for the sufficient reason that the masters never part with them till they are found incorrigible. . . . The dealers smiled at us and were in a good humour.' Then there was the prostitutes' quarter where the women had 'faces like skinned apes and lean legs encased in red silk tights'.

It was the wild slaves from the interior who, though salable, caused most of the lawlessness in Zanzibar. They roamed the streets in search of food like packs of hungry dogs and were prepared for any violence, any form of robbery. No one went about unarmed in the town and at night every door and shutter was barred against marauders in the deserted streets.

Domestic slaves, on the other hand—those who had been born or trained in Zanzibar and were more or less civilized —presented other problems. They were the laziest, the dirtiest, the most dishonest of servants; yet their Arab masters could not conceive of life without them. Often such slaves were incorporated into the family and not unkindly treated: if a concubine bore a child by her master it was at once declared free and adopted as a son or a daughter of the house. Yet drunkenness and petty thieving remained the rule among the domestics in most households, and slaves and masters alike were caught in a web of mutual distrust and even hatred.

There were at this time some 5,000 Arabs in Zanzibar, and some of them owned as many as 2,000 slaves in addition to large plantations of cloves and coconut palms, three-storey wooden houses with fine carved doorways and wardrobes of embroidered gowns and turbans. Together with the Indian dealers they controlled the ivory trade, owned ocean-going ships, loaned money at fantastic rates of interest and financed expeditions into the interior. And yet it was a listless and torpid sort of life, turning upon a monotonous and limited routine that hardly varied from one month to another. The Arab master rose at dawn, performed the morning prayer, and after a light breakfast proceeded to the bazaar. Eleven o'clock found him in his house again for lunch, followed by an hour of prayers in the mosque and a sleep. At three in the afternoon he rose, washed and again prayed. Then more visits abroad, evening prayers, dinner, a walk through the streets or a visit to the harem. Finally, towards midnight, he retired to bed. Except for the annual observance of Ramadan, a family festival or a journey, this eastern habit of life remained as steady as the heavy tropical weather itself.

Among almost all the residents of the island there was a natural tendency towards drinking and the taking of drugs, either opium or hemp, a natural decline into voluptuousness. Burton remarks that the Arabs objected to the importation of jasmine into Zanzibar on the ground that 'the scent depresses the male sex and unduly excites the feminine'. He also records that the Arabs preferred Negresses to their own wives, while their wives preferred Negroes for reasons which, he says, were 'somewhat too physiological for the general reader'.

Burton liked the Arabs. As we shall see later the full weight of his disapproval usually fell upon the Africans, whether slave or free, and from time to time upon his own compatriots. He deals briskly with the Swahilis, that hybrid chocolate-coloured race who were the product of the mixed blood of the Semites and the Negroes on the island, and who numbered about half a million at this time. He allows that they were endowed with 'an abundance of animal spirits', that they had a great fund of merriment and that they formed strong family ties. But by nature, he wrote, they were cursed by 'an eternal restless suspicion' combined with a mulish opposition to all change, a 'savage conservatism'. And they were utterly dishonest: 'when they assert they probably lie, when they swear they certainly lie.' The Swahilis were all Moslems.

In the eighteen-fifties the legitimate seaborne trade of Zanzibar was chiefly in the hands of the Americans, who in 1839 were the first foreign nation to set up a consulate in Zanzibar, and then, in diminishing importance, came the British, the Germans from Hamburg and the French. In exchange for the ivory and other products they took away, the foreign traders brought in 'merikani', the coarse American cotton cloth which was an article of barter everywhere in East Africa, firearms and ammunition, coloured beads manufactured in Venice, china, cereals, and a haphazard range of gadgets and machines from the western world.

If we are to take Burton's word, the tiny white community stationed in Zanzibar lived a miserable life. The Europeans were forever quarrelling among themselves: 'All is wearisome monotony: there is no society, no pleasure, no excitement; sporting is forbidden by the treacherous climate and strangers . . . soon lose the habit of riding and walking.

'Every merchant hopes and expects to leave Zanzibar forever, as soon as he can realize a certain sum; every agent would persuade his employer to recall him.'

The drinking water of the island was poisonous or at any rate dangerous, venereal disease was endemic, everyone was in constant danger of contracting cholera and malaria, and doctors were unknown. In consequence of this, very few white women lived at Zanzibar, most of the residents being 'contented with an Abyssinian or Somali girl'.

'I am surprised,' Burton went on in his best ironic manner, 'at the combined folly and brutality of civilized husbands who, anxious to be widowers, poison, cut the throats or smash the skulls of their better-halves. The thing can be as neatly and quietly, safely and respectably affected by a few months of African air at Zanzibar.'

He was not altogether exaggerating. One required either great fatalism or a great love of money and power to live willingly in this beautiful and exotic place. Even Hamerton, the British Agent, the one European who had outlived all the others on the island, was beginning to succumb at last. At the time of Burton and Speke's arrival he had already been for fifteen years at Zanzibar and to a very large extent the social and political life of the island revolved around him. It is extraordinary that, in an atmosphere which was remarkable for quarrels and petty jealousies, so few of his contemporaries have a word to say against this warm-hearted and genial Irishman. He was the intimate friend and adviser of the Sultan Seyyid Said, who had created this new Arab empire in the Indian Ocean; he smoothed and calmed every crisis that beset the island and he wrote very sensible dispatches to his superiors in India and London. The British Consulate under Hamerton became the recognized point of rendezvous among the foreign community. 'He kept the whole town alive,' Speke wrote, and his hospitality, like his joviality and good spirits, was remarked upon by every visitor to the island.

More than once Hamerton had been on the point of asking for his recall. His health had been undermined by malaria and other illnesses, but in this case it was neither fatalism nor money that kept the consul at Zanzibar, but rather a sense of duty, perhaps also a feeling that the island and the people in it were now his life; it was too late to make a change. Seyyid Said had died in the previous year, and had been succeeded by his third son, Majid, but still Hamerton kept on. He was now so ill that he barely survived the hot day and lived only for the night. But this did not prevent him from carrying off Burton and Speke to stay at his house, nor from busying himself with the utmost enthusiasm in launching their expedition.

There was much to do. Caravans setting off for the interior at this time usually counted on being away for a year or even two years, and all supplies had to be carried on the porters' heads. A caravan of 100 men, plus an armed guard, was regarded as quite a modest affair, and Burton actually proposed to take a complement of 170 men with him. These were to be recruited partly in Zanzibar and partly on the coast, and were to be under the general direction of the headman or guide, a half-caste Arab named Said bin Salim who was in the employ of the Sultan but had been loaned to the expedition. In addition there were two gunbearers, Sidi Bombay and Mwinyi Mabruki, who served more or less in the capacity of non-commissioned officers, and who were soon to become considerable figures in East African exploration; two Goan personal servants who cooked for Burton and Speke; and the guard which was made up partly of armed slaves and partly of Baluchis in the Sultan's service —about a score of them in all.

For the most part the caravan proposed to live off the country, either by the shooting of wild game or by the purchase of cattle, goats, milk and grain from the tribes. All other supplies (with the exception of scientific instruments, guns, medicines and so forth which were brought from England or India) had to be obtained from the Indian and Arab merchants in Zanzibar, and the list was formidable. Among many other items Burton mentions 3 rifles, 2 smooth bores, a Colt's carbine, 3 revolvers, all with spare parts, 3 swords and ammunition sufficient to last two years; a number of chronometers, prismatic compasses, thermometers, a portable sundial, sextants, barometers, a telescope, a box of mathematical instruments and '1 pocket pedometer by Dixie' for measuring, by their paces, the number of miles they marched each day.

In their camp furniture the two explorers did themselves well. They had a tent, camp beds, a portable table and chairs, 3 mats to be used as carpets, blankets, mattresses, mosquito nets, air pillows, a canteen of knives and forks, and cooking utensils. Their clothing consisted of the normal jackets, trousers and boots in which men go shooting, in addition to turbans and thick felt caps for the head. 'N.B.,' Burton adds, 'not looking forward to so long a journey, we left Zanzibar without a new outfit; consequently we were in tatters before the end, and in a climate where flannel fights half the battle of life against death, my companion was compelled to invest himself in overalls of American domestics, and I was forced to cut up blankets into coats and wrappers. . . .'

There was a small library of scientific books, stationery of every kind, sealing wax, ink, a table of the stars, sketching and painting materials, but no camera. They had a carpenter's and blacksmith's outfit, and other tools with which they hoped to assemble and rig a small portable boat on the lakes. Among the provisions were '1 dozen brandy (to be followed by 4 dozen more); 1 box cigars; 5 boxes tea (each 6 lbs.); a little coffee; 2 bottles curry stuff, beside ginger, rock and common salt, red and black pepper, one bottle each, pickles, soap and spices; 20 lbs. pressed vegetables; a bottle vinegar, 2 bottles oil; 20 lbs. sugar (honey is procurable in the country).'

Morphia and quinine were included in the medicine chest, but at this time very little was yet known about malaria— and malaria was a governing factor in all these journeys; indeed, the success of every expedition depended very largely on the explorers' resistance to the fever. Quinine had long since been discovered, but there was much uncertainty about the size of the correct dose. Burton himself preferred to place his faith in Warburg's Drops, which were compounded of sloes, quinine and opium, and in this he made an error.

The remaining miscellaneous items in the baggage included 4 umbrellas, 2,000 fishing hooks and line, 2 lanterns (policeman's bull's eye and common horn), 2 canisters of snuff, 10 steels and flints, a Union Jack and a large cargo of cloth, brass wire and beads to be used in paying the porters and in trading with the tribes. All these things were either encased in boxes or tightly wrapped in a sort of bolster which could conveniently be carried upon the porters' heads.

There was one other aspect of the expedition, and it was to play a vital part in all the unknown hazards that lay ahead. This was the personality of the two explorers themselves.

Burton, despite the plethora of books that have been written either by or about him, still remains beyond the range of ordinary definition. Above all else he was a romantic and an Arabist; he belongs decidedly to that small perennial group of English men and women who are born with something lacking in their lives: a hunger, a nostalgia, that can be set at rest only in the deserts of the East. Whatever the reason may have been—whether it was a natural revulsion from the narrow horizons and the wet and cloudy climate of England, or from the constricting Victorian

code of manners there—it was the tinkling of the camel
bell that beckoned him until the day he died. And yet with all
his amazing concentration and intelligence he remains an
amateur of the Islamic world, a devoted dilettante, more
Arab than the Arabs, but never absolutely one of them. He
returns to the East again and again like a migratory bird,
never at peace when he is away, yet never able to stay for
long without succumbing to an overmastering restlessness.
There are moments in his career when it seems that nothing
in the world can appease his almost insane hunger for ful-
fillment and excitement. Wilfrid Scawen Blunt remembers
meeting Burton once in Buenos Aires at the end of one of
his debauches, when he reappeared collarless and in filthy
clothes. He had, Blunt says, 'a countenance the most sinister I have even seen, dark, cruel, treacherous, with eyes
like a wild beast'. It was his eyes—the 'questing panther
eyes'—that everyone remembered. Swinburne, who knew
him well, speaks of 'the look of unspeakable horror in those
eyes which gave him at times an almost unearthly appearance'. 'He had,' the poet adds, 'the brow of a god and the
jaw of a devil.' Burton's wife, who was certainly not one to
criticize, describes him as being five feet eleven inches tall,
and muscular, with very dark hair, a weather-beaten complexion, an enormous black moustache, large, black, flashing eyes, long lashes and a fierce, proud, melancholy expression.

Yet beneath all this drama Burton was an intensely fastidious and scholarly man. No one else has chronicled a journey through Africa with such erudition as he has. Nothing
is beyond his observation: the languages and customs of the
tribes, the geography of the land, its botany, geology and
meteorology, even the statistics of the import and export
trade at Zanzibar. No other explorer had such a breadth
of reference, or had read so much or could write so well;
none certainly was graced with such a touch of sardonic
humour. His *Lake Regions of Central Africa* remains, possibly, not only his best book but also, in a field of writing
that was remarkably good, one of the best explorer's journals ever written.

At this time he was just 36 years of age, and we are not

here concerned with the second half of his life, with all its tumultuous journeys, its quarrels and humiliations, its fantastic outpourings of books and translations, which in the end, with the publication of his *Thousand Nights and One Night* and other Eastern erotica, were to earn for him the reputation of being a sort of intellectual rake.

Yet at 36 he was already a famous man, though not a very popular one. After an education in France and Italy and at Oxford he had served seven years in the Indian Army, had made his famous journey to Mecca and a second hardly less perilous expedition to the forbidden city of Harar in Abyssinia, and had written his books about these adventures. Never at any point in his army career in India had he proceeded in a normal, orthodox way; his way was through the interior lines and the endless subtleties and aberrations of Eastern life. He was forever disguising himself in Eastern clothes, even dyeing his face and hands, and visiting low bazaars which would have been extremely distasteful to the ordinary British officer. In consequence he knew a great deal more about Indians and their way of life than the authorities cared to know. They were no more amused by his account of vice in Karachi than by his prediction that the Indian army was on the point of mutiny. As an officer he was irascible, impatient of discipline and highly critical of his colleagues. Yet he was not altogether to be dismissed as just another British eccentric, for he was a swordsman of note, he was incontestably brave, and in his command of languages and dialects there had been few to equal him. It was said that he had discovered a system by which in two months he could learn a new language, and at the end of his life he was believed to speak and write no less than twenty-nine. At one stage he lived with thirty monkeys in order to study the noises they made, and he even succeeded in putting together a short monkey-vocabulary.

Almost too much was contained here in one man. Had he been of a sedentary disposition no doubt his life would have been easier, but there was something in his nature—perhaps inherited from his Irish parentage—that constantly drove him towards the most outlandish places and the most diffi-

cult adventures. One has the feeling that he lived in a state
of continual conflict within himself, the intellectual warring with the man of action, the methodical scholar grating
against the poet and the romantic, the fastidious hypochon-
driac fighting a losing battle with the libertine. But then he
recoils from his own unorthodoxy and struggles back to a
respectable show of things; and it was in one such recoil
that, just before the opening of this new African adventure,
he entered into an engagement of marriage with the doting
and carefully nurtured Isabel Arundell, in England. Having
become engaged to her, however, he at once abandoned her
—a thing he was to do again more than once in the long
married life that lay before them—and now he had involved
himself in another relationship which was even more singular. That this brilliant, courageous, highly-strung adventurer should have adopted as his close companion a man
who was so complete an opposite as John Hanning Speke
is, surely, as ironic a phenomenon as anything Cervantes
contrived with his Don Quixote and Sancho Panza.

Not that Speke was in any way servile to Burton. Indeed, he was the very reverse, and this in the end was to be
Burton's undoing. Burton needed a disciple and instead he
got a rival. Speke was 30, some six years younger than
Burton, and although a story was put about at one time that
he was an Anglo-Indian with mixed blood there was no
truth in it; he came from a West Country family that dated
back to Saxon times. He was tall and slender and his blue
eyes and fair hair gave him rather a Scandinavian appearance. Moreover he looked after himself; he ate a great deal
but drank very little and never smoked. The ordinary relaxa-
tions and dissipations of a young man of his age were not
for Speke; his life was in the open air, and to fit himself
for that life he was prepared to go to great lengths. Once
in Africa he even discarded his boots and walked barefoot
so as to toughen himself. He planned ahead, he set himself
definite objectives, and having once made up his mind he
proceeded with great prudence and determination. In short,
he measured up very well to the Victorian notion of what a
young man ought to be: steady, abstemious, methodical in

his habits, and respectable. But he was not entirely humourless and he had the gift of friendship. Underneath that cool and rather prosaic exterior there was a certain charm. Even Burton was prepared to admit this, though as is usual with most of Burton's judgments of people, his summing up of Speke carried a violent sting in the tail. He wrote: 'To a peculiarly quiet and modest aspect—aided by blue eyes and blond hair—to a gentleness of demeanour, and an almost childlike simplicity of manner which at once attracted attention, he united an immense fund of self-esteem, so carefully concealed, however, that none but his intimates suspected its existence.'

Like Burton, Speke had entered the Indian Army, though at an earlier age and as a cadet, and had fought in the Punjab. Like Burton, he had a taste for solitary expeditions in India, though of a very different kind; he used to go shooting in the distant Himalayas. Speke had a mania for shooting—few specimens in India and Tibet, he says, did not fall to his gun—and his various journeys on local leave took him into very remote places where, possibly, no other European had been before. This was part of the toughening-up process, and Speke was not unconscious of his own virtue in this matter. He was not like his brother officers in India, he wrote later, somewhat smugly. He never 'idled away his time or got into debt': he was away in the mountains collecting specimens and opening up the unexplored country; and the authorities approved of this.

Already in India, long before he met Burton, Speke had a great object in view; he had decided that as soon as his long leave fell due he would make a journey through unexplored Africa, travelling from the east coast to the headwaters of the Nile, and then sail downstream to Egypt. On the way he would gather specimens of rare birds and animals, and eventually he would build up a natural history museum in his father's country house in England. Of his three years' leave from the army, two were to be spent on the journey and the third year he was to recuperate at home. He saved his money, he planned, and when his ten years' service in India was up in 1854 he sailed for Aden, carrying with him £390 worth of beads and other barter goods with which he proposed to enlist the help of the natives when he crossed to the African mainland.

It was at this point—some two years before the outset of the present journey—that the two explorers met for the first time. Speke had been in Aden only a few days when Burton turned up with several other young officers on the outward journey of his Abyssinian expedition, and it was soon arranged that Speke should scrap his own plans and join forces with them.

From Burton's point of view this first African adventure had been a distinct personal success. With many manœuvrings—it was the sort of cloak-and-dagger affair he loved so well—he had first got himself in and out of the fanatical Moslem stronghold of Harar, and had then made a rendezvous with the others on the Somaliland coast. For Speke, however, the expedition had been an unqualified disaster. His side of it had accomplished practically nothing. Soon after Burton had joined the coastal party at Berbera in April 1855 a concerted rush had been made on the camp by the local Somali tribesmen at midnight, and in the desperate struggle that had ensued one of the Englishmen had been killed, Burton had been wounded in the jaw, and Speke, having been repeatedly stabbed about the legs and arms, had been taken prisoner. There had been a sharp disagreement between Burton and Speke at the height of the fray. Speke said later that he ran back under the lee of the tent to get a better view of the attackers and Burton, mistaking this action, called out to him, 'Don't step back or they will think we are retiring.' Chagrined by this Speke rushed out against the attackers, and it was then that he was speared, stunned, tied up and carried away. He was badly wounded, and would certainly have been put to death, but he managed nevertheless to escape and rejoin Burton and another of the officers who had taken refuge aboard a friendly Arab vessel. They escaped eventually to Aden and there took ship for England. One other mortification awaited Speke while he was recovering from his wounds: Burton, as leader of the expedition, considered that he had full rights to the notes taken by his subordinates, and when his *First Footsteps in East Africa* was published it was found to contain an abridged version of Speke's diary tucked away ignominiously at the end of the book.

Burton wrote a curious note about Speke's frame of mind during these early days of their acquaintance, and although it hardly squares with what we know of this clear and resourceful man one is reluctant to disbelieve it. 'Before we set out,' Burton wrote, 'he [Speke] openly declared that, being tired of life, he had come to be killed in Africa.' This of course might have been nothing more than a young man's expression of a Byronic mood. Yet one sees here a glimpse of the solitary mountaineer dreaming visions in Tibet. Perhaps he had secretly a definite and compelling need to be a hero.

But still in 1855 there had been no real grievance between the two men, and certainly no lack of courage on either side. After their Somaliland adventure both had volunteered for the campaign in the Crimea, and when the war was over they had met again in London. Burton was now full of plans for the very kind of journey upon which Speke also had set his heart—an expedition to the sources of the Nile. When Burton asked Speke to join him, Speke immediately agreed.

And so now, at the end of 1856, the two men found themselves in Hamerton's house in Zanzibar preparing for their second adventure into the African wilderness. Since Burton had obtained a grant of £1,000 from the Foreign Office and the patronage of the Royal Geographical Society he was the official leader. So far as one can make out Speke accepted this state of affairs with very good grace, and was exhilarated by the adventure that lay before them. Burton, too, was very confident. He wrote from Zanzibar to the Secretary of the Royal Geographical Society in London: 'People here tell frightful stories about the dangers and difficulty of the journey [into the interior] and I don't believe a word of it.'

The explorers were in no particular hurry to get away from Zanzibar, and in this perhaps—in the calm and leisured use of time—one sees by how much we are divided from the nineteenth century. They debated at length about their plans with Hamerton, they called on the young Sultan Majid, they bartered for further men and supplies in the bazaar, and they set off on rather a haphazard preliminary trip along the coast in order to acclimatize themselves. They were away two months, calling at the neighbouring island of Pemba (which was supposed to be the burial-ground of Captain Kidd's treasure) and travelling a short distance inland through the country that lies south of what is now the border of Kenya and Tanganyika. Burton admired the ruins of the fallen Portuguese and Persian empires at Mombasa, and the oysters on the mangrove roots in the coastal streams; and observed the crocodiles that 'waddled down, as dowagers might, with their horrid claws dinting the slimy bank, and lay upon the water like yellow-brown tree trunks, measuring us with small malignant green eyes, set deep under warty brows'.

The missionary Johann Rebmann was now the only white man living on the mainland, and they visited him at his mission outside Mombasa with the idea of getting him to join the expedition; but Rebmann declined, perhaps because Burton had agreed with the Sultan not to try and convert the Africans to Christianity. After various adventures the two explorers finally got back to their boat near Pangani so ill with malaria that Burton had to be carried on board. It took them several weeks in Zanzibar to recover. Burton, however, declared that he welcomed this first experience of fever since he believed it would 'salt' them against further attacks; and here again he was wrong.

Finally on June 16, 1857, they set off in the Sultan's corvette *Artemise* for the mainland.

Chapter 2

THE INSPIRATION

SCARCELY TWENTY MILES divide Zanzibar from the African mainland, and on a clear day you can plainly see the island from the coast. A motor launch accomplishes the journey across the straits in an hour or two and by air it is a matter of ten or fifteen minutes. Yet there is an astonishing difference between the island and the mainland shore. In Zanzibar everything is soft and beguiling; it is as relaxing as a Turkish bath. There are no hills on the island, no harsh cliffs or torrents; the plantations spread away from the forest paths with the luxuriance of a hot-house, and everywhere there is a sense of established ease, of indolence declining into sleep.

It is no less hot on the mainland, but here the wildness of Central Africa, the sensation of vast primitive space, touches the traveller directly he steps ashore; and it is a little forbidding. He sees a dry hard scrub reaching away into the distance and the native huts are as uninspiring as chicken-coops—flat-roofed, oblong boxes made of crude wooden poles and plastered mud. The only really arresting sight in the landscape are the baobab trees, which here tend to grow in groups on the plain.

There is something gnomish about a baobab tree, a quality that might have appealed to the late Arthur Rackham; it stands like a round wooden tub with antlers for branches, and its colour is the colour of an elephant's hide. It is the sort of tree that a child might make in plasticine.

And so the country continues inland for ninety miles or so until you cross the maritime plain and the mountains break into view. Then one mounts up very quickly on to the great central plateau that stretches away for hundreds of

miles into the heart of Africa. Now suddenly one realizes
how the woolly air of the coast pressed against one's lungs.
At three thousand feet—and that is the general level of
the plateau—wide plains begin to appear, broken here and
there with rough outcrops of rock, and there is never a
moment when some distant mountain is not in sight. These
are the real horizons of Central Africa. It is still not impossible to see here a troop of ostriches in the long grass,
or a herd of antelopes on the run. In the remoter parts
there is a deep silence in the bush, and if by chance an
African appears he stands quite still for a moment and
watches you with the alertness and wariness of an animal;
and then he responds with a movement of his arm, sometimes a word of greeting.

For the most part the slave route from the coast led on
from one watering place to another, and almost all the
caravans headed for Kazeh (now called Tobora) in Central Tanganyika, some 500 miles inland from the sea. From
Kazeh the paths of the caravans struck out in all directions, one directly north towards the southern shore of
Lake Victoria, another round the western side of the lake
towards the country known as Karagwe, another due westward to Ujiji on Lake Tanganyika, and still another southwards towards Lake Nyasa. Progress was extremely slow
and possible only in dry weather.

There was, however, a moment of respite at the outset
of these long journeys when travellers crossed from Zanzibar to the mainland coast at Bagamoyo. Bagamoyo
means 'Lay down the burden of your heart', and it is a
beautiful place, with a line of rustling coconut palms
on the shore and beyond them, at the right season, one of
the loveliest sights of Africa: the flamboyant trees that
spread like chestnuts and blaze with the brightest shades
of scarlet, flame and orange.

The Indian Ocean here has the texture, and no doubt the
specific gravity, of warm, very salty soup and is infested
with a thousand slimy things, broken fronds of seaweed,
livid jelly-fish, perhaps an empty coconut floating by. There
is no harbour, but a coral reef breaks the force of the
waves and the beach slopes very gently inland. At low tide

*East Africa as it was presumed to be, following the
explorations of Burton, Speke and Grant
(taken from contemporary map)*

the sea recedes for a quarter of a mile or more and all the
debris of the shore lies stranded on a wet grey plain. In
the old days it was customary for the Zanzibar dhows to
run in as far as possible on the full-tide, and the passengers were taken on to dry land on a sort of stretcher carried by native porters. Then at low-tide the boat was
propped up on either side by mango poles and lines of
slaves came slopping out through the shallows to unload
her.

At Kaole, a little to the south of Bagamoyo, are the ruins
of a coral mosque, and of graves and houses dating back
to the thirteenth century, an incredible antiquity in this
climate where every man-made thing seems destined to be

overwhelmed by nature and forgotten. A plaque set up at Bagamoyo announces that it was from here that Burton and Speke started their journey inland in 1857.

There were of course the usual difficulties in setting out. Having come ashore from their corvette at Kaole they discovered that only a fraction of the porters they wanted were obtainable and consequently asses had to be bought instead. Great haggling took place in the bazaar before thirty-six men were eventually assembled, and it was decided in the end that the portable boat and other heavy baggage would have to be left behind. Hamerton had come over from Zanzibar with the two explorers to say good-bye and to help them get away, and it was an act of singular devotion, for he was dying. He was perfectly well aware that his strength had finally run out; he confided to Burton that he expected death and welcomed it and wished to be buried at sea. On June 26, 1857, he sailed away, and he survived only a few days after his return to Zanzibar. Eleven months were to elapse before Burton and Speke were to hear in the depths of the interior that he was dead.

Speke went ahead with some of the men on June 25 on the first stage of the journey, and on June 27 Burton followed him, mounted on a camel. They marched south-westward at first so as to avoid the country of the hostile Masai tribe to the north, and there was a pause at a place called Zungomero (since vanished from the map) while they regrouped. More porters were obtained, bringing up the numbers of the caravan to 132 in all, and early August found them climbing slowly up the escarpment to the central plateau. The expedition was launched at last.

There was no particular difficulty about the route: they followed beaten paths from one village to another, and from time to time they kept passing other caravans coming down to the coast with slaves and ivory. Yet it was a progress so slow, so tortuous and disordered that one marvels that it ever got ahead at all. The day began at 4 a.m. with the crowing of the cocks, while it was still dark and very cold. Then Burton and Speke had their coffee or tea and perhaps a plate of porridge, while the Arab guard turned to the east for morning prayers. By 5 a.m. the whole caravan was stirring round the camp-fires, and a long delay ensued while the cattle and the goats were rounded up and the porters quarrelled fiercely over their loads, the weaker men usually being left to take up the heavier burdens. The last act before the departure was to set fire to the grass huts that had been built the night before. The huts, of course, might have been useful for other travellers, but one left no gifts for strangers in this hostile world.

There was a rough and ready order in the long procession when it finally got under way. In the lead went the guide, wearing a ceremonial head-dress and carrying the red flag of the Sultan of Zanzibar, and behind him marched the drummer. The cloth and bead porters came next with their bolster-like bundles on their heads, then the men carrying the camp equipment, and their women, children and cattle. The armed guard was dispersed along the line, each man carrying a muzzle-loaded 'Tower-musket', a German cavalry sabre, a small leather box strapped to the waist and a huge cow-horn filled with ammunition. Many of them were accompanied by their women and personal slaves. Burton and Speke as a rule drew up the rear, either riding the camel and the asses or, if sick, being carried in hammocks. Almost every male member of the caravan had a weapon of some kind together with an assortment of pots and pans and a three-legged wooden stool strapped to the small of his back. A continuous and violent uproar of chanting, singing, whistling and shouting accompanied the march, for it was thought important to make as much noise as possible so as to impress the local tribes. If a hare chanced to run across the track all downed burdens at once to go in pursuit of the animal, which, if caught, was eaten raw.

The final halt for the day was made at any time from 8 a.m. onwards, but usually it was about 11 o'clock when the full fierceness of the midday heat was beginning, the caravan having then covered about ten miles. If they chanced to stop in a village a rush was made to occupy the best huts, and while a tent was erected for Burton and Speke the whole caravan was gathered inside a kraal of branches and thorns. Through the midday hours the two explorers sat in the shade, taking scientific observations, writing their diaries, making sketches and conducting the general business of the march. Cloth was issued to the porters at each halt so that they could purchase grain from the local inhabitants. At 4 p.m. the Goanese cooks served dinner, which consisted of some such dish as rice and goat's meat, unless Speke had gone out and bagged a partridge or a gazelle—a diversion that Burton did not encourage: 'Captain Burton,' Speke wrote later, 'being no sportsman, would not stop for shooting.'

At night, especially if the moon was shining, the dancing began, the women in one group, the men in another. 'They are such timists,' Burton wrote, 'a hundred pairs of heels sound like one.' But then as the excitement of the dance increased, bedlam broke out, confused rushings and screamings filled the camp, until at last, towards 8 o'clock, the dancers subsided exhausted around their fires and all was peace at last.

Such might have been a normal day in the caravan's progress, but then hardly any day was normal. At every stage the local chieftains demanded their *hongo*—a tax of so many yards of cloth, so many bags of beads—before they would allow the strangers to cross their territory. Hours, sometimes days, would go by before the haggling was over, and at last a drum was beaten in the chieftain's village to announce that the caravan was free to proceed. As they got further away from the coast many of the porters deserted and had to be replaced by new ones; the asses died one after another, and disease kept breaking out in the camp. Often they were hungry to the point of half-starvation, and both white men were constantly ill; Speke indeed seems to have been in a state of continually failing health all the way to Kazeh. Often too they were swamped by unseasonable rain. But still they struggled on.

In the late eighteen-fifties the Tanganyika tribes were probably not so disturbed and brutalized as they became later on when the slave trade grew worse. The traveller was given a relatively friendly reception, and although Burton and Speke passed huge slave caravans, some of them a thousand strong, and saw the tragic aftermath of their progress—the sick men, women and children dying beside the track—both of them made the point that the hardships of the journey were not quite so bad as they were made out to be. 'Justice,' Burton wrote, 'requires the confession that the horrors of slave-driving rarely met the eye in East Africa.' On the march, he says, the slaves were seldom chained, well fed and little worked. The porters, who were free and who made the long journey down to the coast for the hire of a few shillings, had much the worst of it. Then at Zanzibar and the coastal towns a much better life often awaited the slave than the one he had left behind in his squalid and diseased village in the interior.

For a man so immersed in the study of coloured races and so avid of travel among them, Burton throughout reveals an odd and contradictory contempt for the African. 'He seems to belong,' he writes, 'to one of those childish races which, never rising to man's estate, fall like worn-out links from the great chain of animated nature.'

The African's religion is nothing but 'a vague and nameless awe', his chief preoccupation, drunkenness. Everywhere, Burton says, the drinking of *pombe,* the native beer, starts with the dawn and continues in the villages all through the day. These befuddled, ignorant, hopeless people have no code of morals: 'Marriage, which is an epoch amongst Christians, an event among the Moslems, is with these people an incident of frequent occurrence. Polygamy is unlimited, and the chiefs pride themselves upon the number of their wives, varying from twelve to three hundred.'

Unfortunately, on its inland journey, the expedition by-passed places like the Olduvai Gorge in the Serengeti Plains, where there are evidences of the extreme antiquity of life in Africa, and Burton knew nothing of the overhanging rocks at Kondoa where one can see drawings of hunting scenes with match-like figures lunging at giraffes, and abstract designs that look like fish skeletons, whirls and sprays like falling stars, and weird circles filled with dots; and the Tanganyika wells with carved stone steps leading down to the water—the work of some vanished civilization—had not yet been discovered. Burton is one of the few explorers who would have been deeply interested in these relics, but as things were he was merely oppressed by the apparent barrenness of the country's past. He wrote: 'Eastern and central inter-tropical Africa . . . lacks antiquarian interest, it has few traditions, no annals, and no ruins, the hoary remnants of past splendour so dear to the traveller and the reader of travels. It contains not a single useful or ornamental work of art, a canal or a dam is, and ever has been, beyond the narrow bounds of its civilization. It wants even the scenes of barbaric pomp and savage grandeur with which the student of Occidental Africa is familiar. But its ethnography has novelties: it exposes strange manners and customs, its Fetichism is in itself a wonder, its commerce deserves attention, and its social state is full of mournful interest.'

Even when Burton is being amusing about Africans he cannot be kind. Since his and Speke's were the first white skins ever to be seen in these regions they were the victims of 'an ecstasy of curiosity'. Natives were constantly standing in a ring around them, pressing into their tent and reaching out their hands to touch them. Burton expostulated: 'At last my experience in staring enabled me to categorize the infliction as follows. Firstly is the stare furtive, when the starer would peep and peer under the tent, and its reverse, the open stare. Thirdly is the stare curious or intelligent, which generally was accompanied with irreverent laughter regarding our appearance. Fourthly is the stare stupid, which denoted the hebete incurious savage. The stare discreet is that of Sultans and great men; the stare indiscreet at unusual seasons is affected by women and children. Sixthly is the stare flattering—it was exceedingly rare, and equally so was the stare contemptuous. Eighthly is the stare greedy; it was denoted by the eyes restlessly bounding from one object to another, never tired, never satisfied. Ninthly is the stare peremptory and pertinacious, peculiar to crabbed age. The dozen concludes with the stare drunken, the stare fierce or pugnacious, and finally the stare cannibal, which apparently considered us as articles of diet.'

And so Burton's tirade against the Africans goes on, at

times funny and at others vicious, and hardly for a moment does he pause to reflect that it was the foreign slavers in this country who were debauching and degrading these people quite as much as the *pombe* and the polygamy. In Burton's mind the Africans themselves were to blame for their own savagery, and from first to last he treats them as delinquent children with marked criminal tendencies. Speke, who suffered quite as much annoyance as Burton, did not feel this way nor did other explorers like Livingstone; indeed Burton's attitude becomes positively rabid when it is compared with Livingstone's kindness, gentleness and compassion towards Africans—as rabid as the worst racial hatred in the world today. It was perhaps not too much that one of the chieftains should have said that Burton was 'a good man but too angry'.

Yet in fairness it has to be recognized that Burton was not a shooter or a killer of Africans—and not a few such explorers were soon to appear on the scene. Probably it was more disgust than dislike that he felt towards them; and so, in this crude wilderness, where there was nothing to satisfy the requirements of a fastidious and sophisticated mind, he turned with relief to the Arabs.

When at last, after nearly five months' journey, the party straggled into Kazeh on November 7, 1857, Burton went forward to meet the Arab traders there with joy. 'Striking indeed,' he cries, 'was the contrast between the open-handed hospitality and hearty goodwill of this truly noble race, and the niggardness of the savage and selfish African—it was heart of flesh after heart of stone.' He was back with his own kind again, grave, courteous, bearded men in turbans and long white robes, cultivated men with graceful manners, and never for a moment does it disturb him that the principal preoccupation of their lives was the herding of men, women and children down to the coast, and the sale of such as survived in the slave markets of Mombasa and Zanzibar.

There were about twenty-five Arab dealers living in Kazeh at this time, and they managed to keep up an outward show of civilization. Their houses, called *tembes*, were built of mud but were quite extensive buildings enclosing

a central courtyard, with separate rooms for the domestic
slaves and the harem. Fruit, vegetables and rice had been
planted and in the bazaar most articles essential to East
African trade were on sale, though at prices about five times
higher than in Zanzibar. It was customary for the Arabs
to eat at sunrise and again at midday, but only very light
foods. Hardly any of them were healthy for two months
together, and life, though bearable, can scarcely have been
much more than a dreary round of petty bargaining and
interminable waiting. They were delighted to see the two
white men from the coast and were ready to help them in
every way. And so a month went by at Kazeh, and Burton,
at least, enjoyed himself, since he could engage in long
profitable conversations with his hosts about the unknown
country that lay before them to the west. Speke, one feels,
being ill and unable to speak Arabic, was left a little in the
cold.

Early in December, however, they set off again, and on
February 13, 1858, reached Lake Tanganyika in the neighbourhood of the Arab slaving and ivory post at Ujiji. This
was a moment of great triumph, a major discovery. Both
men were seriously ill again—Speke, who had suffered
since childhood from ophthalmia, was so blind he could
barely see the lake, and Burton with an ulcerated jaw could
take nothing but liquid food—but at least the expedition
had accomplished the first of its great objects. Speke, on
recovering his eyesight, went off in search of a boat which
would enable them to make a thorough exploration of the
region, and although he returned empty-handed two native
canoes were found at last, and in these both men set off
towards the north. It was Burton's notion that they might
find a river there which, flowing north, might well be the
source of the Nile. But in this he was disappointed: the
Rusizi flows southward into Lake Tanganyika, which in
any case is only 2,535 feet above sea-level and therefore
too low to be the origin of the Nile. 'I felt sick at heart,'
Burton wrote. They turned back to Ujiji, and here at last
a little good fortune came to them: their rearguard arrived
with supplies from the coast, and after nearly a year they
received letters giving them news of the outside world.

Burton had the sardonic satisfaction of learning that he had been quite right about India: the mutiny had broken out. In June 1858 they were back at Kazeh again.

And here, in almost a haphazard way, there occurred the beginning of a chain of incidents which was to set this journey apart from all others in Central Africa and lead on through endless bitterness and tragedy to the solution of the problem of the Nile. Burton was anxious to pause awhile among his Arab friends in Kazeh so as to refit the caravan and compile his notes upon the discoveries they had already made. Speke wanted to go off and investigate the reports they had heard from the Arabs of the 'Nyanza', a lake larger than Tanganyika, which was said to lie some three weeks' journey to the north of Kazeh. Burton willingly let him go. With Bombay and a small party of porters and Baluchi guards Speke set off on July 9, 1858.

The traveller today will find that the region between Kazeh and Lake Victoria is, at first, anything but spectacular; the eternal scrub presses around one, mile after mile, monotonously repeating itself. The few villages and clearings that occur have a poverty-stricken air, and in the dry season, when the withered grass is burnt off by the inhabitants, one sees little but vistas of blackened earth and scorched trees which would remind twentieth-century soldiers of Passchendaele in the First World War, except that here there is no mud, only the parched and listless dust. But then one gradually passes into a landscape that is altogether different. The scrub thins out and wide refreshing plains begin to sweep away to the horizon. Here and there huge rounded granite boulders, dropped probably by the melting glaciers of some former ice-age, rise up grotesquely from the ground, and from the distance they often have the appearance of the walled hilltop towns of Southern Italy. One touch of rain on this countryside and it sprouts a lawn of grass. Myriads of storks and other birds alight on the swamps and water-holes, and there is a distinct element of change in the air, a feeling, as you move along, that you are approaching a frontier of some kind, a new experience. This feeling becomes steadily more pronounced as you approach the lake. The earth grows greener, the air more humid and soon you are surrounded by shady trees, palms, emerald-green mangoes and flamboyants. Finally, near Mwanza, the lake itself breaks into view. It is much more like a sea than a lake, a tropical sea with yellow sand beaches and wooded slopes coming down to the shore. Close at hand, islands and promontories are dotted about with sailing boats moving around them, but to the north there is no visible end to the vast sheet of water. Occasionally it is ruffled up by tremendous storms with black clouds overhead, but on a normal day a light breeze blows and the white horses splash up casually on the shore. The lake takes on the colour of the sky so that it is blue in the sunshine, grey on a cloudy day and almost black in a storm. During the sunsets, and they can be astonishing at times, both sky and lake glow together in an explosion of theatrical light.

On the actual shore itself one often hears a continual crackling noise, especially where the papyrus grows, the slapping of the waves on the reeds, the whirring of countless insects, fire-flies and crickets, the slight but distinct sounds and cries made by the lily-trotters and the ibis; and the darter with his half-submerged, writhing neck looks like a snake coming through the water.

These scenes are very beautiful, and yet there is a mysterious and disturbing atmosphere about the lake. One feels here very strongly the primitiveness of Africa, its overwhelming multiplicity in emptiness. At dusk the water tends to become still, sombre and silent; there is a heavy nothingness in the hot air and yet it conjures up notions of undercurrent witchcraft and superstition, of plotting and of ambushes in the dark, and all this is made worse because there is no definite object for one's fear. The lakeside Africans are mighty drinkers of *pombe,* and when they have drunk away the oppression of the boredom and idleness of their lives they give way very easily to infantile outbursts of passion and hysteria; and then the drums and the stamping dances have a quality that is uncouth, savage and sometimes menacing.

All these things—the surrounding plains, the peoples of the lakeside, and the immense mysterious reaches of the lake itself—were of course outside the range of civilized knowledge when Speke began his march. It is, then, hardly surprising that he should have been possessed by great excitement in the early morning of August 3, 1858, when he stood on the shore near Mwanza and saw the immense stretch of water for the first time. An inspiration seized him. 'I no longer felt any doubt,' he wrote later, 'that the lake at my feet gave birth to that interesting river, the source of which has been the subject of so much speculation, and the object of so many explorers. The Arabs' tale was proved to the letter. This is a far more extensive lake than the Tanganyika, so broad that you could not see across it, and so long that nobody knew its length.'

It was a reckless and astonishing conclusion to jump to, and it was quite impossible for Speke to back it up with any scientific proof. Yet he seems to have been genuinely convinced by this one short view of a tiny section of the southern shore—he stayed only three days on the lake—that he had discovered the source of the Nile. One wishes that he could have had any other companion than Burton to share his enthusiasm. Nevertheless, he hastened back and re-entered Kazeh only six weeks after he had left it on the outward journey. The party received a warm reception: 'the Baluchis and Bombay,' Speke says, 'could scarcely be seen under the hot embraces and sharp kisses of admiring damsels,' and Speke at once acquainted Burton with his discovery. It is not difficult to imagine the scene from Burton's description:

'We had scarcely breakfasted before he announced to me the startling fact that he had discovered the sources of the White Nile. It was an inspiration perhaps; the moment he had sighted the Nyanza, he felt at once no doubt but that "the Lake at his feet gave birth to that interesting river which has been the subject of so much speculation, and the object of so many explorers". The fortunate discoverer's conviction was strong; his reasons were weak—were of the category alluded to by the damsel Lucetta, when justifying her penchant in favour of the "lovely gentleman" Sir Proteus:

"I have no other but a woman's reason.
I think him so because I think him so...."

'After a few days it became evident to me that not a word
could be uttered on the subject of the Lake, the Nile, and
his *trouvaille* generally without offence. By tacit agreement it was, therefore, avoided, and I should never have
resumed it had my companion not stultified the results of
the Expedition by putting forth a claim which no geographer can admit, and which is at the same time so weak
and flimsy that no geographer has yet taken the trouble to
contradict it.'

Speke's version of the matter is as follows:

'Captain Burton greeted me on arrival at the old house
...I...expressed my regret that he did not accompany
me as I felt quite certain in my mind I had discovered the
source of the Nile. This he naturally objected to, even after
hearing all my reasons for saying so, and therefore the
subject was dropped. Nevertheless the Captain accepted
all my geography leading from Kazeh to the lake, and
wrote it down in his book—contracting only my distances,
which he said he thought were exaggerated, and of course
taking care to sever my lake from the Nile by *his* Mountains of the Moon.'

They had already fallen out over the Mountains of the
Moon. Burton wanted to have them in one place on the
map, Speke in another, and it was a vital point since these
mountains, wherever they were, most probably provided
the first drainage for the river. So now, like an old hand
at chess, Burton neatly check-mated his opponent by
dropping the mountains on to a point of the map where
they stood fairly and squarely between the river and the
lake.

Burton himself at this time had an idea that the real
sources of the Nile lay further to the east in the general
vicinity of Mt. Kenya and Mt. Kilimanjaro. At the same
time he was not altogether satisfied that the Tanganyika
basin should be disqualified. The most he would allow for
Speke's new lake (which was now named Victoria in honour of the Queen) was that it might be a feeder of the

Upper Nile; there was also the possibility that Lake Victoria was not one lake at all, but a series of lakes.

But Burton was not adamant about any of this. He simply wished to make it clear that Speke had no grounds whatever for his sweeping assertions; it was all guesswork. Therefore in Burton's opinion it was much better in their report to the Royal Geographical Society to stick to the ground they had thoroughly investigated together, namely the Tanganyika region, and to the reports they had heard from the more reliable Arabs; and in fact while Speke had been away Burton had obtained from the dealers in Kazeh some sound information about the district of Karagwe to the west of Lake Victoria, and even about Buganda and Bunyoro which lay off the map much further to the north.

And so from this time forward we find Burton concentrating more and more upon Lake Tanganyika and Speke upon Lake Victoria; each adopted his own lake and was determined to support it against all arguments. Their quarrel may seem futile, but one has to remember that the two men had now been closeted together in the most hazardous circumstances for well over a year, and had long since begun to get on one another's nerves. Also, this issue was almost their whole world at that moment, and it seemed to them to be of the most pressing importance.

'He [Burton]', Speke wrote later to the Secretary of the Royal Geographical Society, 'used to snub me so unpleasantly when talking about anything that I often kept my own counsel. B. is one of those men who never *can* be wrong, and will never acknowledge an error so that when only two are together talking becomes more of a bore than a pleasure.'

It cannot then have been a very congenial party that set off at the end of September 1858 on the long return journey to the coast. There were 152 in the caravan now, including slaves, women and children, and many of them, having already marched 1,500 miles or more since leaving Bagamoyo, were worn out. Burton and Speke collapsed almost at once and had to be carried. Speke appears to have been suffering from pleurisy and pneumonia, and soon it was impossible for him to continue. At the height of his delirium he raved and screamed at Burton, remembering every petty, pent-up grievance—even the incident of the skirmish in Somaliland when Burton, he believed, had accused him of cowardice. These spasms passed at length and the expedition dragged itself on slowly eastward, beset by sickness and desertions. Four months elapsed before they sighted the Indian Ocean at last just north of the present town of Dar-es-Salaam. It was now February 1859 and they had been away for 21 months, but Burton had undertaken to visit Kilwa further down the coast, and with a stubbornness which seems a little pointless he was determined to keep his word. He sent a message across to Zanzibar by dhow asking the British Consul to furnish him with a boat and when it arrived the two weary, antagonistic men set sail for Kilwa. They accomplished nothing beyond their gesture; a cholera epidemic was sweeping along the East African coast and it had struck the slaving settlement at Kilwa with special force. Burton and Speke came away almost at once, and on March 4, 1859, finally reached Zanzibar.

Here everything was in turmoil; some ten thousand deaths through cholera had already occurred in the city, and the Sultan was preparing to resist an invasion which was about to be launched upon the island by his brother in Oman. The new British Consul, Captain Christopher Rigby, was an old rival of Burton's—both of them being remarkable linguists, they had competed against one another in interpreters' examinations in India—and Burton lost no time in falling out with him. The main contention between them seems to have concerned itself with Burton's failure to pay his porters all the money they expected, and when, later on, they complained at the Consulate both Rigby and Speke, to Burton's fury, supported them. He had another grievance against Rigby; he believed that he or someone connected with the Consulate had deliberately mislaid the manuscript of his book on Zanzibar since it contained criticisms of the white residents there.

For the moment, however, Burton was at the end of his tether. Those who saw him at this time describe him as wild-eyed and so gaunt and emaciated that the flesh hung in hollows on his cheeks; he himself says that the 'excitement of travel was succeeded by utter depression of mind and body'. He read French novels, avoided meeting people in Zanzibar and developed his hatred of Rigby. After barely three weeks on the island he embarked with Speke on the barque *Dragon of Salem* and they arrived at Aden twenty-five days later.

As yet there was no open breach between the two men: 'Still we were,' Burton says, 'to all appearances friends.' But Speke, the younger man, was recovering fast and was anxious to get home. It was agreed that while Burton continued his convalescence a little longer at Aden Speke should go ahead, and in mid-April he took passage in H.M.S. *Furious*. According to Burton, Speke's last word before he embarked was a promise that he would await his companion's arrival in London before revealing the results of the expedition. Upon that they parted for ever.

When Burton himself reached England on May 21 Speke had already been there for twelve days and had made good use of his time. One can explain his conduct only by remembering, as Professor Ingham of Makerere College, Uganda, suggests, 'the self-righteousness of his generation', which moved him to put 'justice before generosity'. He was filled with his conviction that he had solved the great secret of the Nile. Burton had derided his theory and washed his hands of it; therefore Speke had every right to regard his inspiration and his discovery as a personal matter, something quite apart from the official expedition.

Whether or not Speke himself used this justification is unknown, but the fact remains that, on disembarking, he went directly to Sir Roderick Murchison, the President of the Royal Geographical Society, and revealed to him the story of the expedition and his great conviction about the source of the Nile. Murchison, naturally, was intrigued, and Speke was asked to give an address to members of the Society at Burlington House; and here again he pressed his views. Within a week of his arrival word got around London that this intrepid and modest young man had made a discovery of extraordinary importance, and he was invited by the Society to go out to Africa again at the head of a new expedition. A sum of £2,500 was quickly raised to finance it, and Speke was soon at work on his plans; he proposed to strike inland again from Zanzibar along the same route as before and then work his way up the western side of the new inland sea he had discovered. On its northern coast he hoped to find its outlet which would be the source of the Nile, and then he would follow this stream northwards wherever it might lead him until he emerged at last in Egypt.

There was much enthusiasm in London for the new expedition since, in effect, Speke proposed to march straight through the blank space on the map in Central Africa, and at one stroke settle the immemorial problems of the inland lakes, the Mountains of the Moon and the fountains of the Nile.

Burton meanwhile, a lean and haggard figure, landed in England to find that he had been almost forgotten. The public was only mildly interested in his careful and scientific report on Lake Tanganyika, and he was not invited to take part in the new expedition; he was replaced by another Indian Army officer, Captain James Augustus Grant. Five years were to elapse before he was to have his full and terrible revenge.

Chapter 3

THE VALES OF PARADISE

THERE ARE no written records of Uganda—the territory that Speke now proposed to enter—before the middle of the nineteenth century. Sir John Gray describes its history as being like 'a crime to which there have been no eye-witnesses'. It seems certain, however, that at some point in the unrecorded past a superior race of cattle-owning men came south from the Ethiopian highlands, and these people set themselves up as a ruling aristocracy among the Negroes on the northern and western borders of Lake Victoria. By 1860 three separate kingdoms were established, Bunyoro in the north, Buganda in the centre and Karagwe to the south, on the western shore of the lake. Many other tribal formations existed as well, but these three little states had a certain coherency in the midst of a wilderness of utter barbarity; they formed, as it were, a tiny capsule of semi-civilization in the centre of the continent, and the outside world knew hardly anything at all about them.

A single Arab trader named Ahmed bin Ibrahim had penetrated into Buganda in the eighteen-forties, and a few others had reached Karagwe, but that was all: no white man had ever been there, no notion of other worlds and other ways of life disturbed the inhabitants. They could scarcely have been more isolated had they been living on the surface of the moon.

Normally in Central Africa it was the fate of such people to remain in a state of arrested development. In a mysterious way the light of human ambition was extinguished, the villages stayed chained to the Stone Age, and from century to century life revolved in an endless ant-like cycle of crude customs and traditions. There was no curiosity to explore, no desire for change or improvement. Every new generation gave way to the same passive fatalistic acceptance of things as they were, and reason was suffocated by habit and superstition.

But with these three puppet kingdoms it was not like this at all; they advanced marvellously. Without any precedent to guide them or any outside help they had achieved by the middle of the nineteenth century a native culture which was well in advance of any other south of the Sahara. And yet the extraordinary thing about these people is not that they should have got so far but that their progress should have been so irregular. They did well in one direction only to fail completely in another, they left enormous gaps behind them, and the most barbarous customs survived in the midst of an exceptional sophistication.

Their houses, for example, had nothing in common with the dull coffin-shaped contraptions of Tanganyika; they were large, beautifully made conical structures of tightly woven canes and reeds that often soared fifty feet into the air. These dwellings were dry and comfortable in the rain and cool in the hot seasons, and they were infinitely more attractive than any building that has been erected in Uganda in the twentieth century. The musical instruments of the tribesmen—their drums, harps and trumpets—were equally remarkable, and they travelled on the lake in immense canoes, some of them 70 feet in length.

Their basketware was so finely woven it would hold water, and they had discovered the art of making a soft and durable cloth from the bark of trees. No man attended the court of his king unclothed: in fact, in Buganda it was a criminal offence to do so; he wore sandals on his feet, his body was completely covered by a long and graceful toga, and sometimes this was surmounted by a cape of antelope skins which had been pieced together with the skill of a Parisian seamstress.

Neither men nor women disfigured their bodies with scars or tattoos like the other Central African tribes, and when they sat down to eat they washed their hands, either by squeezing a wet napkin or by pouring water over them from a jug. Domestic slaves, who were treated as part of the household like Russian serfs, served the meal, and the food was distinctly civilized: a kind of gruel made from coarse bananas, fish and meat stews, chickens, sweet potatoes, maize and wild sugarcane. Coffee beans were chewed as a digestive and they brewed their beer from bananas. Both men and women smoked.

In Buganda especially, the richest and most progressive of the three states, the power of the king was absolute, but he was advised by a group of counsellors who formed a kind of cabinet in which each man had some special duty. Thus there was the vizier or prime minister, the treasurer, the commander-in-chief of the army and the admiral of the fleet of war-canoes on the lake, the chief executioner, and others with more picturesque titles such as the chief brewer and the keeper of the drums. These men, together with the provincial chiefs, formed a hierarchy of nobles, and they were obliged to be in constant attendance on the king in his court. Here the etiquette was elaborate. No man could sit down in the king's presence, be incorrectly dressed, or speak without permission. Whenever the king appeared it was customary for the courtiers to abase themselves on the ground before him, since he was considered to be almost divine, or at all events the personification of the spirit of the race.

And yet, with all this sophistication and refinement, these people had no method of writing or counting, no means of measuring the passage of time by weeks or months or years, no mechanical contrivances even as simple as the plough or the wheel, no religion that amounted to more than the most primitive kind of superstition and witchcraft. They gave way to their passions and their appetites like spoiled and delinquent children and they were unbelievably cruel. From time to time they seem to have been seized with a wild and frantic hysteria, and it was common practice for both men and women to drink themselves into a drunken stupor.

There were strong differences between the three kingdoms, and perhaps these differences were conditioned by the geographical nature of the country. Bunyoro, to the north, is drier and harsher than the land around the shores of Lake Victoria. For months at a time no rain falls and one travels for miles through a dry hard scrub which is not unlike Central Tanganyika. The people here have a reputation for toughness and resilience; they are less sophisticated than the lakeside inhabitants, but more warlike and aggressive. These qualities were certainly reflected in their King, Kamrasi. He was a man who was both harsh and suspicious, a chieftain with the instincts of a pirate, and the absorbing hatred of his life was directed partly against Buganda in the south, and partly against a rebellious brother called Rionga, who lived on an island in the Nile.

Karagwe, on the western side of the lake, is more open country, much of it five thousand feet above sea-level, and there is a remarkable freshness and clarity in the landscape. A century ago large herds of cattle grazed across the sweeping grassy plains, and along the shores of the lake itself there are scenes that remind one of the downs in southern England: high, sharp cliffs fall sheer into the water, and except for the heat, the emptiness of land and the tropical islands off-shore this might be Folkestone or Dover. At one time this was fine country for wild animals: thousands of elephants, giraffes, buffaloes, antelopes and rhinoceroses roamed about, and even now, by night, one can watch the hippopotamuses come ashore from the lake to browse like dark lumbering ghosts on the water's edge.

Here, at a place called Bweranyange, Rumanika, the King of Karagwe, kept his little provincial court. He was a large and friendly man who had the reputation of being hospitable to strangers. Being by some way the weakest of the three kings, Rumanika took care to remain on good terms with the rulers of Bunyoro and Buganda. He sent them gifts from time to time and even acknowledged himself to be a vassal or at any rate a dependent of Buganda. Yet Rumanika had his eccentricities. He kept an extraordinary harem of wives who were so fat they could not stand upright, and instead grovelled like seals about the floors of their huts. Their diet was an uninterrupted flow of milk that was sucked from a gourd through a straw, and if the young girls resisted this treatment they were force-fed like the *pâté de foie gras* ducks of Strasbourg: a man stood over them with a whip.

Buganda, on the northern shore of the lake, has neither the dryness of Bunyoro nor the horizons of Karagwe; it is a region of jungles and broken hills and it is as lush and exuberant as Zanzibar. The climate is hot, changeable and damp, and all things spring from the earth in a blaze of exotic colour. The earth itself is red, the plantations of bananas make avenues that are filled with a warm greenish-yellowish light and the surrounding jungle is a vast aviary filled with tropical birds and flowering shrubs. These conditions create an impression of intimacy, of quickness and liveliness and of a kind of luxurious excitement, and that is the nature of the Buganda.

In 1860 Mutesa, the young king of Buganda, had only recently got his grip upon the throne and had established his capital a few miles inland from the lake on a hilltop which is not far from the modern city of Kampala. The traveller came into the town on a broad earthen road cut through the jungle and saw, scattered about the hillsides, a settlement of gracefully proportioned round huts with crowds of people moving about between them. The women for the most part went naked or wore a short cloth around their waists, but the men in their togas reminded one, Harry Johnston [1] says, of saints—they 'recalled irresistibly the conventional pictures of evangelical piety which represented the Blessed walking in the vales of Paradise'.

Mutesa's court was a compound of especially spacious huts in the centre of the town, and here he held his daily levées, sitting upon a platform of grass covered with a red blanket, and surrounded by his nobles, his pages and his wives, who numbered a couple of hundred or so. At this time he was a slim, well-built young man in his early twenties with beautiful teeth and liquid, but rather striking eyes. His tonsured hair was built up like a cockscomb on his head, his toga was neatly knotted over one shoulder, and on his arms and legs he wore broad bands of coloured beads. At his feet were his symbols of royalty, a spear, a

[1] See Notes, p. 392.

shield and a white dog. When he went walking the whole
court followed, and he affected an extraordinary stiff-legged
strut which was meant to imitate the gait of a lion. In the
manner of Queen Victoria he did not look round when he
chose to sit down; a chair was automatically placed in
readiness for him, except that in his case it was a page
crouching on his hands and knees. When he chose to speak
the courtiers listened in a strained and respectful silence
and then, in a body, threw themselves on to the ground,
uttering over and over again a curious cry that sounded
like 'n'yanzig', and was meant to indicate both gratitude
and the deepest humility. Mutesa, in short, was a very im-
pressive figure, even at this early stage of his long career,
and there might even have been a certain dignity about
him had it not been for the fact that he was very far from
being a saint in the vales of Paradise; he was a savage and
bloodthirsty monster.

Hardly a day went by without some victim being executed at his command, and this was done wilfully, casually, almost as a kind of game. A girl would commit some
breach of etiquette by talking too loudly, a page would
neglect to close or open a door, and at once, at a sign
from Mutesa, they would be taken away, screaming, to
have their heads lopped off. A roll of drums obliterated the
cries of the death-throes. Nothing that W. S. Gilbert was
about to invent with his Lord High Executioner in *The
Mikado*, nothing in the behaviour of the raving Red
Queen in *Alice's Adventures in Wonderland*, was more
fantastic than the scenes that occurred whenever Mutesa
held a court, the only difference being that here these
scenes were hideously and monstrously real. Torture by
burning alive, the mutilation of victims by cutting off their
hands, ears and feet, the burial of living wives with their
dead husbands—all these things were taken as a matter
of course. This was more than a simple blood-lust: Mutesa
crushed out life in the same way as a child will step on an
insect, never for an instant thinking of the consequences,
or experiencing a moment's pity for the pain he was in-
flicting. He felt no pain, except his own. He, and all the

people about him at his court, give the impression of playing at life, of living with an air of mad make-believe.

To be fair, it has to be recorded that it was not Mutesa himself who had invented these practices; all his ancestors (and there is known to have been a line of at least a score of kings behind him) behaved in exactly the same way, and a similar law of the jungle prevailed in all the minor tribal groups. Unless the ruler surrounded himself with an atmosphere of dread and superstitious awe he did not stay very long on his throne. Mutesa, on becoming king, had instantly put to death some sixty of his brothers by burning them alive, and this was apparently regarded as a perfectly normal precaution against rebellion.

Then too, he had other attributes besides this inherited bloodthirstiness. He was very far from being stupid: once he had seized power he had very quickly learned the arts of playing one man off against another by the careful bestowal of gifts. He knew all about the value of keeping his petitioners waiting, and he seems to have had some skill in making political appointments. One can easily see him as a sort of pantomime figure—the tribal king surrounded by his drums, his naked wives, and his black warriors—but in fact, as events were shortly to show, he was a great deal more than this. In this savage world he had the appearance and the manner of royalty, and an instinctive knowledge of politics. His foreign policy, for example, was handled with a certain crude dexterity: he left Rumanika alone in Karagwe and made war on Kamrasi in Bunyoro. It was of course not very serious war—this was still a world in which there were no firearms and still no Arab slavers to set one tribe against another—but it was a useful means of obtaining cattle and women, and Kamrasi, at least, was kept at bay.

This, then, was the strange little island of native civilization that had been left undisturbed to work out its own destiny in the heart of Central Africa a hundred years ago. It would naturally be absurd to suggest that there was any real enlightenment here; the three puppet kingdoms were still bound to a primeval way of life, and fear was the dominant factor in every man's mind. On the other hand, these people were still insulated from the abuses of civilization: there was no syphilis or smallpox, no rinderpest to kill their cattle. Mutesa's cruelties did not touch the general run of the people; they had plenty to eat and drink, and it seems not impossible that they believed themselves to be happy, or at any rate involved in an existence which was inevitable and eternal, and which they did not want to change. Only the barest echoes of other things reached them from the outside world—of the slavers coming up the Nile from Egypt and the Arab caravans from Zanzibar. Perhaps it really was a Garden of Eden of a kind, savage but fatalistic; at all events, it was still intact when Speke and his new companion, Grant, marched into Karagwe at the end of 1861, and with this the capsule was destined to burst at last.

The two explorers had taken over a year to get inland from Zanzibar, and most of the experiences of the previous expedition had been faithfully repeated; all their men save a few like Bombay and Mabruki had deserted, the local chieftains on the way had ferociously demanded their *hongo,* their goats and cattle had been stolen, and Grant had gone down with malaria. They had even failed as yet to catch a glimpse of Lake Victoria. Burton, who was now leading a separate expedition in the Cameroons on the other side of Africa, must have smiled had he heard the news. But now at last in November 1861 Speke and Grant extracted themselves from the local tribal wars to the north of Tabora and marched on into the terra incognita of Karagwe.

In Grant, Speke had found an ideal companion. The two men were of the same age and had been friends in India, where they had often gone on shooting excursions together. But Grant had another quality: he was the perfect lieutenant. He must surely be rated as the most modest and self-effacing man who ever entered the turmoil of African exploration; he never puts himself forward, he never complains, never questions any order of his leader. Burton would have found him a paragon. Grant's devotion, however, was entirely fixed upon Speke, and it was almost dog-

like in its completeness. 'Not a shade of jealousy or distrust or even ill-temper,' he says, 'ever came between us.'
Speke he describes as 'above every littleness'. General
Gordon, whose judgments about people were often rash,
thought that Grant himself was something of a bore,[1] and
just possibly he was a little dull as a conversationalist. Dull-
ness seems to be the last thing we ever hear about well-
known people in the past. Yet it would be foolish to regard
Grant as a colourless nonentity. He was a cool and very
steady man, a soldier and a sportsman well out of the ordinary, and in his own private and modest way he was a
competent artist and a genuine amateur of botany. He had
fought in a number of engagements that led up to the
Mutiny in India, and had taken part in the relief of Luck-
now where he had been awarded a medal and a clasp for
gallantry.

Rumanika was delighted to meet the two white men,
the first he had ever seen. He shook hands warmly, addressed them in good Swahili, and established them in his
best huts with an abundant supply of provisions. Speke
had a pleasant month at Bweranyange. He exchanged
presents with Rumanika, drank his *pombe,* and with a
tape measure ascertained the dimensions of his fat wives.
He did great execution among the rhinoceroses with his
gun, and made notes about even more formidable animals
which, he was told, inhabited the jungles further to the
west: 'monsters who could not converse with men and
never showed themselves unless they saw women pass by;
then, in voluptuous excitement, they squeezed them to
death.' If this was meant to be a description of a gorilla,
one of the most timid and gentle of animals, it is not accurate. But then hardly any of the things they were seeing
and hearing in this new land were very credible. Rumanika,
for example, warned Speke that he must not proceed into
Buganda until Mutesa sent for him, and that it would be
impossible for him to appear at Mutesa's court wearing his
unmentionables (Speke in his account uses this Victorian
word for trousers); he would have to obtain a gown. And

[1] Gordon, in a letter to Burton, on October 19, 1877: '. . . that old
creature Grant, who for 17 or 18 years has traded on his wonderful walk.'

so messengers were sent off to warn Mutesa of the expedition's approach and while they waited the month of December slipped by.

Grant meanwhile was having a very bad time. He was assailed by a dreadful sore in his leg, and presently the infection became so agonizingly painful he was unable to stir from his hut. Certainly he was in no condition to walk or even to be carried when, on January 8, 1862, a troop of messengers arrived from Mutesa bearing with them an invitation for the expedition to proceed. It was therefore decided that he should remain behind in Rumanika's care while Speke went forward alone. For the next three months Grant remained a prisoner in his hut, unable to go out, often in agony and without news of any kind.

It took Speke six weeks to walk to Mutesa's court, and in the course of the journey he at last came within sight of Lake Victoria opposite the Sesse Islands. More than ever now he felt that his original conjecture had been correct: the lake was a vast inland sea and somewhere on its northern shore he would find its outlet to the north—the fountains of the Nile. For the moment, however, he was forced to put his geographical work aside and prepare himself for his reception by Mutesa.

He tells us that on his arrival he unpacked his best suit, dressed his men in red blankets, and with a handsome collection of gifts got ready to present himself at the palace. But rain fell and in the best manner of royal garden parties the reception was put off until the following day. On February 20, 1862, he set forth again flanked by his red-blanketed bodyguard, with the Union Jack leading the way, only to find himself out-faced by a rival delegation which was given precedence; Speke was told to wait in the hot sun outside the palace. He stood it for five minutes and then in a fury turned round and walked back to his own hut a mile away. The courtiers who were conducting him to the King watched his retirement with consternation—evidently such a thing had never happened before—and presently they came running to say that it was all a mistake; the King would see him at once and he would be allowed to bring his own chair to sit on, an unheard-of privilege.

When Speke got back to the palace all was ready for his reception. A band playing five-stringed harps and trumpets ushered him through the outer courts where small pages were rushing around gathering their cloaks about them so as not to show their legs; and finally he came into the presence of the monarch himself. Speke set up his chair in front of the throne, erected his umbrella and awaited events. Nothing happened. For an hour the two men sat gazing at one another, Mutesa occasionally turning to his courtiers to pass a remark on the umbrella, on the bodyguard or on Speke himself. From time to time a draught of beer was handed to him. Speke simply sat and waited.

At length a man approached with a message: had he seen the King?

'Yes,' Speke answered, 'for full one hour.'

When this was translated to Mutesa he rose and walked away into the interior of his palace on the tips of his toes in his imitation of a lion. There now ensued a long wait while the King ate his dinner: as an act of courtesy, it was explained to Speke, Mutesa had refrained from eating until the meeting had taken place. Finally, at the end of the day, when they met again by the light of torches, Speke offered his presents; several rifles and guns together with ammunition, a gold watch, a telescope, an iron chair, beads, silk cloths and knives, spoons and forks. Mutesa in return sent him a gift of cattle, goats, fish, fowls, porcupines and rats, all of which apparently were regarded as suitable items of diet.

It was at a further interview that the notorious shooting incident took place. Speke was invited to display the magic of his pistols by taking a pot-shot at four cows, a feat he accomplished a little awkwardly: one of the cows, charging upon him, required a second bullet before it was dispatched.

'The king,' Speke says, 'now loaded one of the carbines I had given him with his own hands, and giving it full-cock to a page, told him to go out and shoot a man in the outer court: which was no sooner accomplished than the little urchin returned to announce his success, with a look of glee such as one would see in the face of a boy who had robbed a bird's-nest, caught a trout, or done any other boyish trick. The king said to him, "And did you do it well?" "Oh yes, capitally." He spoke the truth, no doubt, for he dared not have trifled with the king: but the affair created hardly any interest. I never heard, and there appeared no curiosity to know, what individual human being the urchin had deprived of life.'

Nothing would keep Mutesa away from his new toys after this. On fine days he would march round his capital, gun in hand, his wives, pages and courtiers following behind and the band playing; and if by luck he managed to hit a vulture on a tree he would be thunderstruck by his own magical powers, and would run forward to the fallen victim crying out 'woh, woh, woh' in infantile excitement. The court, grovelling and n'yanzigging, would fall upon the ground around him.

The women who followed Mutesa about in hordes wherever he went appeared to occupy a privileged position, but it was slavery nonetheless. 'Young virgins . . .' Speke wrote, 'stark naked, and smeared with grease, but holding for decency's sake a small square of *mbugu* (bark cloth) at the upper corners in both hands before them, are presented by their fathers in propitiation for some offence and to fill the harem.' From time to time one of these girls would be sent to Speke as a gift, and he parcelled them out as wives among his followers.

The Queen-Mother, however, whom Speke describes as 'fair, fat and forty-five', was a figure of some power in the state and kept her separate court at a little distance from Mutesa's palace. She was not often sober. Drinking, smoking and dancing to the music of her personal band were the usual occupations of the Queen-Mother's hut, and it was not surprising that she complained to Speke that she was suffering from bad dreams and illness of the stomach. He dosed her from his medicine chest and advised her to give up drinking. But she was not a good patient. Returning to her hut one day Speke found himself involved in an orgy which ended in the Queen-Mother and her attendants drinking like swine on all fours from a trough of beer.

After Speke had been for three months in these bizarre surroundings Grant finally arrived. He was still limping from the effects of the sore in his leg but otherwise restored to health, and now both men were eager to push on towards their goal. On their separate journeys from Karagwe they had crossed a considerable river, the Kagera, but since it flowed into Lake Victoria and not out of it they dismissed it as a possible source of the Nile. At Mutesa's court, however, they heard very definite reports of another stream that emerged from the lake only a short distance to the east. The lake was said to pour itself out in a wide fall of water towards the north. Speke, who had never been permitted to leave Mutesa's capital in all his three months' stay, was now determined to make his way to this spot and then follow the river downstream wherever it might lead.

Mutesa was much opposed to their going. It amused him to have the two white men at his court and he was not altogether sure that he had extracted every possible gift from them. Then, too, they were bound to enter the territory of Kamrasi, the King of Bunyoro, when they went away, and with Kamrasi he was at war. For another six weeks he prevaricated and delayed, and then at last on July 7, 1862, he let them go. The two explorers with Bombay and their caravan and a Buganda bodyguard marched out to the east. They were on the eve of the climax of their tremendous journey.

And now occurred one of the strangest incidents of the whole adventure. Their guide had led them somewhat north of the lake, and in order to reach the Nile and trace it to its source it was necessary for the caravan to turn sharply south. A conference was held, and as a result it was decided that the expedition should split once more: Speke alone was to go to the source while Grant turned north and opened up the way to Kamrasi's court in Bunyoro. One can only take the two men's word for it that they were entirely agreed upon this arrangement. From Grant we have no hint of reproach or disappointment. He had staked his life on getting to this goal, and now at the last minute, when it was within his reach, he quietly turned away from it in order to please his companion. Grant merely says that he was invited by Speke to make a flying march to the source and was forced to decline since his bad leg made it quite impossible to manage 20 miles a day. In any case, he goes on, this was not a great issue; they had seen the lake and they knew that the Nile issued from it. Just why it was necessary for Speke to dash off at the rate of 20 miles a day is not explained; but then there is so much between these two that cannot be understood unless one constantly remembers Grant's utter devotion to his leader. As with a marriage, a veil falls down between this partnership and the outside world, and no one can presume to know the intricacies of their relationship. Behaviour that might seem to us to be unfair and heartless is to them, apparently, perfectly natural. Speke, of course, was a man with an *idée fixe*; his whole being was centered upon proving that his theory of the Nile was the right one, and no doubt he was now in a state of intense impatience to get to his objective. To have hung about waiting for Grant to keep up with him—and this at a time when some accident or mischance could still wreck the expedition—was intolerable. Grant presumably felt this strongly, and with an almost feminine resignation gave way; better to stand in the reflection of Speke's glory than to strain their friendship too much.

At all events, Speke went off with his flying column and reached the Nile on July 21, 1862, at a place called Urondogani about forty miles downstream from the lake: 'Here at last I stood on the brink of the Nile; most beautiful was the scene, nothing could surpass it! It was the very perfection of the kind of effect aimed at in a highly developed park: with a magnificent stream, 600 to 700 yards wide, dotted with islets and rocks . . .' The crocodiles, the high grassy banks, the hippopotamuses, the herds of hartebeest —it was everything they had imagined, and Speke in his exaltation told his men that 'they ought to shave their heads and bathe in the holy river, the cradle of Moses . . .' Bombay soberly replied that, being Mohammedans, 'we don't look on these things in the same fanciful manner as you do: we are contented with the commonplaces of life. . . .'

They were keen enough, however, when they marched upstream and came within sight of their goal at last on July 28; all forgot their fatigue and rushed forward along the river bank. A hill blocked their view of the lake but there, at their feet, the great stream poured itself like a breaking tidal wave over a waterfall. 'It was a sight that attracted one for hours,' Speke says, '—the roar of the waters, the thousands of passenger-fish leaping at the falls with all their might; the Wasoga and Waganda fishermen coming out in boats and taking post on all the rocks with rod and hook, hippopotami and crocodiles lying sleepily on the water. . . .'

He named the place the Ripon Falls 'after the nobleman who presided over the Royal Geographical Society when my expedition was got up'.

It now remained for the explorers to keep themselves alive until they could get back to civilization to tell the story, and there was still no guarantee whatever that they would succeed. A month went by before Speke and Grant rejoined their forces (now reduced to some seventy men and four women), and together they marched into Bunyoro, where King Kamrasi received them somewhat sourly; he filched Speke's fifty-guinea gold chronometer from him before he would allow the expedition to proceed.

While they were in Bunyoro the explorers heard reports of another large lake a short distance to the west, the Lŭta Nzigé, and it seemed possible that this might be a second source of the Nile. But it was now November 1862, and they were worn out and bereft of nearly all their possessions; to have made a further detour might have settled their last chance of survival. And so they pushed on slowly to the north. They had at least one bright hope to lead them on; before leaving London Speke had arranged with the Royal Geographical Society for an expedition to be sent south from Gondokoro in the Sudan to meet them with fresh supplies and porters. It was, of necessity, a loose sort of arrangement, since it was impossible to fix a definite point of rendezvous in that unmapped country, and Speke and Grant were already a year late in keeping the appointment. But John Petherick, the British Vice-Consul at Khartoum and the leader of the relief column, was an experienced and reliable man, and the Society had provided him with a sum of a thousand pounds with which to buy boats and supplies. These were to be sent up the river from Khartoum and stationed at Gondokoro or some other suitable place to await Speke's and Grant's arrival. It was with the prospect of meeting Petherick that the two explorers now pushed on towards the north.

The journey was increasingly wearisome. In the vicinity of the present village of Masindi Port they rejoined the Nile, which they had not seen since leaving it some fifty miles below its source, and for a short distance they managed to float downstream in canoes. But they were soon forced back on to the land again. On November 19, 1862, they reached the Karuma Falls in Central Uganda, and at the end of the month they were still toiling slowly onwards through depressing scrub. As they advanced northward they found that the tribes grew increasingly more primitive; they were back in a region of naked, painted men who carried bows and arrows and who knew nothing of the arts and crafts of Buganda.

Sunset on December 3 was the moment that hope revived again. Welcoming rifle shots were heard in the distance, and presently there advanced to meet them a column of Egyptian and Nubian soldiers dressed in Turkish uniforms. A drum and fife band was playing and red flags waved overhead; it was almost the first sign of civilization Speke and Grant had seen since they had left Bagamoyo on the Zanzibar coast over two years before.

This garrison, named Faloro, was the southernmost trading post of the Egyptians on the Upper Nile, and its black commander, Mohammed Wad-el-Mek, came forward to embrace the travellers. He declared that he was the agent of Petherick and of a Maltese trader named de Bono, and that he had orders to convey them to the Egyptian stronghold at Gondokoro. Soon they were sitting down to a meal of bread, honey and mutton eaten off plates of crockery. That night they slept on genuine bedsteads; but they found soap to be the greatest luxury of all.

They were, however, not quite out of the wood as yet. Mohammed Wad-el-Mek, though friendly, was also a dyed-in-the-wool slave-driver, and was by no means ready to move north until he had plundered the district of the last available slave and tusk of ivory. It was not until January 10, 1863, that the cavalcade set out, the leaders riding cows and donkeys, the porters carrying tusks, and a disorderly mob of slaves, women, children, goats and cattle following on behind. By the time they entered the Bari country the party was a thousand strong, and the helpless tribesmen could do little more than make hostile demonstrations against them.

On February 13, 1863, nearly two years and five months after the outset of their journey, Speke and Grant marched into Gondokoro. There was no sign of Petherick, but they saw the red brick house and sheds of the Austrian Mission and a number of boats on the river; and presently a wholly unexpected figure came out to meet them. 'We saw hurrying towards us,' Speke says, 'the form of an Englishman . . . my old friend Baker, famed for his sports in Ceylon, seized me by the hand.[1] A little boy of his establishment had reported our arrival, and he in an instant came out to welcome us. What joy this was I can hardly tell. We could not talk fast enough, so overwhelmed were we both to meet again.'

The sportsman Samuel Baker and his wife had come up the Nile to look for them, and there had been others as well who had arrived at Gondokoro on the same mission, three Dutch ladies, the Baroness von Capellan and Mrs. and Miss Tinne, but they had been forced to return to Khartoum through sickness. Soon, too, three Austrian priests arrived. The two explorers could relax at last.

'Speke,' Baker says, 'appeared the more worn of the two: he was excessively lean, but in reality he was in good tough condition; he had walked the whole way from Zanzibar, never having once ridden during that wearying

[1] They had first met aboard ship when Speke was travelling from India to Aden in 1854.

march. Grant was in honourable rags; his bare knees projecting through the remnants of trousers that were an exhibition of rough industry in tailor's work. He was looking tired and feverish, but both men had a fire in the eye, that showed the spirit that had led them through.'

There was much news to give—the death of the Prince Consort in England, the outbreak of the Civil War in America—but for the moment Speke's and Grant's immediate interest was Petherick. Where was he? Why had he not come to meet them? Baker assured them that he was not far away, travelling in the West Nile district, and in fact Petherick and his wife arrived a few days later. Outwardly the little white community appeared to be an extremely friendly group and they dined together. But Speke was furious with Petherick. It was the kind of pettiness which can sometimes overtake a man who has been under a great strain, and nothing would convince him that Petherick, having taken £1,000 from the Royal Geographical Society, had not forgotten all about the expedition and instead had gone off trading for ivory in another direction. In point of fact, Petherick and his wife had spent a dreadful year struggling overland to Gondokoro and had very nearly died. But Speke would not be appeased. When Mrs. Petherick came and begged him to accept the trade goods and the boat they had brought to Gondokoro for his use Speke replied acidly that he 'did not wish to recognize the succour dodge'; his good friend Baker had supplied him with all his needs and he preferred to go down to Khartoum in Baker's boat. When Speke and Grant sailed north from Gondokoro at the end of February it was plain that they intended to speak their minds about Petherick when they got back to England; and indeed, they attacked him harshly in their reports to the Royal Geographical Society and in the books they wrote. Petherick was removed from his post as British Vice-Consul at Khartoum and was all but financially ruined when he was accused of being involved in the slave-trade. Some years elapsed before he could get a hearing for his side of the case, and his reputation is not perhaps re-established even yet.

With his own men Speke was much more generous. Of the original members of the expedition, one had died and 143 porters had deserted, hardly a bad casualty list in the circumstances. At Cairo, where Speke and Grant stayed at Shepheard's Hotel, a camp was made in a public park for the remaining 22 survivors—18 men and 4 women—and they were fêted at a round of public concerts and *tableaux vivants*. Three years' pay was given to each man, and a passage was arranged for them all to Zanzibar, where a further bonus was awaiting them.

On his way down the Nile Speke had triumphantly cabled to London: 'Inform Sir Roderick Murchison that all is well, that we are in latitude 14° 30′ upon the Nile, and that the Nile is settled'; and he had been awarded the Royal Geographical Society's Founders' Medal. Both men could look forward to a warm reception when they reached London.

But the Nile was not settled. Speke had left too many rivals and enemies in the field for anything to be settled just yet.

Chapter 4

THE COY FOUNTAINS

*'I don't wish to have any further pri-
vate or indirect communication with
Speke'*—Burton, in a letter to the secretary
of the Royal Geographical Society.

IN THE VICTORIAN AGE explorers' books exerted an extraordinary power over people's minds: they supplied the drama
and the entertainment that now very largely belongs to
the documentary cinema and television, and although such
magazines as *Blackwood's* were widely circulated, there
was as yet no illustrated press of any consequence to com-
pete with them; they had the quality of science fiction.
Few publications have captured people's imagination or
influenced political policy like Livingstone's three works on
South and Central Africa, or Stanley's accounts of his
Congo travels, or Gordon's Journals which, for a time,
focused the attention of all England upon Khartoum and
the Sudan.

These books tended to be intensely personal and were
propaganda of a kind. The author pleaded his special
cause, often with a note of religious and passionate conviction; he reached out, as it were, to his reader, arguing
with him about some such matter as the slave-trade, stirring up his sympathy and indignation. And since these appeals were interlarded with themes of bravery and high
adventure the response was enormous. There was always
the chance that the explorer might be dead before his book
came out; he might even then be lost in the wilderness or,
like a matador, be preparing to go out and meet his fate
once more. This gave an air of actuality to his work, one

suffered and lived with him. If he was attacked by jealous rivals one sprang to his defence; and in the speculative and highly charged arena of African exploration there was a great deal of jealousy. Anyone with practical knowledge of archaeological expeditions at the present time will recognize the atmosphere at once. It was as patriotic and as partisan as war.

In the 'sixties the great outpouring of these African publications began. Burton's *Lake Regions of Central Africa* appeared in 1860, and in 1863 Speke's *Journal of the Discovery of the Source of the Nile* was shortly followed by his *What Led to the Discovery of the Source of the Nile*. In 1864 Grant published *A Walk Across Africa* (a title suggested to him by Palmerston's remark, 'You have had a long walk, Captain Grant'), and Burton collaborated with the geographer James M'Queen in *The Nile Basin*. Then followed the Pethericks' *Travels in Central Africa*, Baker's *Albert N'yanza* and Burton's *Zanzibar*.

One would have thought that there was enough here to inform, confuse, and finally satiate the most besotted student of African travels, but still the public could not have enough. Perhaps this was natural, since all these books, taken together, are in the nature of instalments in a long serial story, and still no one seemed to know what the end would be.

Burton, who was first in the field with his *Lake Regions* (his account of his journey with Speke to Lake Tanganyika), said in later years that he rather regretted some of the things he wrote, but he had been exasperated by two articles which Speke had contributed to *Blackwood's Magazine* on his return to England in 1859. In these articles Speke first put forward his idea that Lake Victoria was the source of the Nile, and this seemed to Burton to make nonsense of the whole expedition. So now, at the opening of his *Lake Regions*, Burton set about putting things to rights in his own drastic fashion:

'I have spoken out my feelings concerning Captain Speke, my companion in the expedition which forms the subject of these pages. The history of our companionship is simply this:—As he suffered with me in purse and person at Berberah, in 1855, I thought it but just to offer him the opportunity of renewing an attempt to penetrate into Africa. I had no other reasons. I could not expect much from his assistance: he was not a linguist—French and Arabic being equally unknown to him—nor a man of science, nor an accurate astronomical observer. The Court of Directors (of the East India Company) officially refused him leave of absence; I obtained it for him by an application to the local authorities at Bombay. During the exploration he acted in a subordinate capacity; and as may be imagined amongst a party of Arabs, Baloch [Baluchis] and Africans, whose languages he ignored, he was unfit for any other but a subordinate capacity. Can I then feel otherwise than indignant when I find that, after preceding me from Aden to England, with a spontaneous offer on his part of not appearing before the Society that originated the Expedition until my return, he had lost no time in taking measures to secure for himself the right of working the field which I had opened, and that from that day he has placed himself *en évidence* as the *primum mobile* of an Expedition in which he signed himself "Surveyor" . . . ?'

Speke, he makes out, completely misconstrued the real nature of the expedition. They were not looking for the 'coy fountains' of the Nile at all. Their instructions from the Royal Geographical Society merely required them to investigate reports of the 'Ujiji lake' and to inquire generally into the geography and ethnography of the region. In addition they had been asked to visit the ancient slaving station at Kilwa on the mainland south of Zanzibar. All these things had been done, and that was the full extent of the matter. Speke's hallucinations about the 'Victoria Nyanza' were his own affair and were not to be confused with the practical achievements of the expedition.[1]

This was the first broadside. When it was delivered in

---

[1] Here Burton was being a good deal less than frank. The sources of the Nile had been very much on his mind, and he admitted it (perhaps unconsciously) when he wrote in his *Zanzibar* which was published some years later, that he had 'turned lovingly towards Africa—Central and Intertropical—and on April 19, 1856, I resolved to renew my original design of reaching the unknown regions, and of striking the Nile sources via the Eastern coast'.

1860 Burton, of course, was smarting from the acclaim which had been given to Speke by the Society and its relative coolness towards himself. And now here was Speke in 1863, just back from his new expedition with Grant, and more in the limelight than ever. When the two men landed at Southampton in June the town authorities were there to receive them, together with a group of enthusiastic supporters and friends, including Burton's old rival, Consul Rigby of Zanzibar. On June 22, 1863, the Royal Geographical Society gave Speke an ovation at a special meeting; so great indeed was the crowd which had come to hear the explorer lecture that several windows of the building were broken. And what had Speke got to say? 'The Nile is settled.'

To Burton, who had returned to England from West Africa about this time, it was the same old folly, the same reckless guesswork. What, in fact, had Captain Speke done? He had had a glimpse of a large sheet of water when he had visited Mwanza on the Tanganyika expedition in 1858. He had had another glimpse of another large sheet of water, 200 miles to the north, when he had visited King Mutesa with Grant in 1862. And at once he had jumped to the conclusion that the vast area between these two points—an area of some thirty thousand square miles, an area almost as large as England—was one immense lake. Had he circumnavigated this so-called lake? Not at all; he had not even bothered to visit its western shore when he was staying with Rumanika. He was entirely unable to say what rivers flowed into it or out of it.

It was quite true that he had found one outlet when he visited a waterfall (the so-called Ripon Falls), and a northward-flowing stream to the east of Mutesa's palace; but what possible excuse had he for declaring with such authority that this was the Nile? Had he followed the river downstream from the lake to Gondokoro? By no means. He had marched overland most of the way to Gondokoro, and when by chance on the journey he had caught sight of a river—any river—he had airily concluded that it was the same stream that he had seen issuing from the lake. It was much more likely that he had seen not one stream but several, not one lake but the edges of a series of lakes. Rivers, in any case, did not arise in lakes but in highlands. Speke had invested the Nile Basin 'with an amount of fable unknown to the days of Ptolemy'. His *Discovery of the Source of the Nile* and his *What Led to the Discovery of the Source of the Nile* (which was largely a reprint of his *Blackwood's* articles) both contained 'an extreme looseness of geography'.

There was quite enough logic here to convince other geographers besides Burton that Speke had left far too many questions unanswered, and that much more scientific exploration would have to be undertaken before the matter of the Nile was settled. Presently various members began to dispute Speke's conclusions at meetings of the Royal Geographical Society, and this dispute soon spread to the press. *Blackwood's Magazine* was all for Speke, but the newspapers were not so sure.

It was now evident that two rival camps were forming: Grant of course was solidly on his leader's side, and so were others like Rigby who were fired by the young man's zeal and determination. But there were others again who had fallen out with Speke or who considered themselves as rivals; and so for personal as well as scientific reasons they came down on Burton's side of the fence. The row with Petherick dragged on. It had seemed to Petherick at Gondokoro that Grant, unlike Speke, had been friendly —'throughout the gentleman'—but on his return to England Grant too had inveighed against the 'succour dodge'. He had informed the Society that the expedition had been badly let down by Petherick. Speke and himself, he said, had heard for the first time from Baker at Gondokoro that Petherick had been given £1,000 with which to supply them with goods, but when they had gone to Petherick's store they were told that they would have to purchase what they wanted like any other trader. Naturally Grant had been indignant, and now he said so. Speke in a speech at Taunton went a step further: he implied that Petherick in addition to failing to keep his word had been engaged in the slave-trade. The two explorers had now made an enemy who was every bit as implacable and bitter as Burton.

But soon a much more formidable opponent appeared, the great Dr. Livingstone himself. Livingstone, like Burton, was convinced that the true solution of the origin of the Nile was to be found well south of Lake Victoria and of the Equator. 'Poor Speke,' he wrote, 'has turned his back upon the real sources of the Nile . . . his river at Ripon Falls was not large enough for the Nile.'

Livingstone, as ever, had been firm but polite, but there were other members of the Royal Geographical Society who felt very strongly that the Speke cult had gone too far. They were out for blood. James M'Queen, in a series of reviews of *The Discovery of the Source of the Nile* published in the *Morning Advertiser*, launched an overwhelming attack. Burton was delighted, and subsequently reprinted the reviews in *The Nile Basin*. Never, Burton thought, in all M'Queen's fifty years as an African geographer, had he shown 'greater acumen or higher spirit—to say nothing of his incomparable dryness of style—than in these compositions, put forth at a time when the English world was bowing down before their latest idol'.

What Burton thought of as 'dryness of style' might seem to us today more like scurrilous and libellous abuse. Like his fellow member of the Society, Desborough Cooley (the man who scoffed at the notion of snow on the Equator), M'Queen was a talented and scholarly geographer. It was perhaps unfortunate, however, that he had practised his geography in England and had no real idea of what it was like to travel in Africa; and it was just as easy to jump to conclusions in London as it was on the shores of Lake Victoria.

M'Queen began by denouncing Speke's ungenerosity and unfairness towards Petherick, and then proceeded to demolish Speke's character. He was especially enraged by Speke's account of his dealings with the Chief Rumanika's fat wife: 'Speke was to obtain a good view of her naked, and then to measure her, upon a like reciprocity on his part. After getting her "to sidle and wriggle into the midst of the hut, I did as I promised". With bare limbs and shirt sleeves well tucked up, Speke began his measuring and, as he called it, "engineering" process, thus:—Round

the arm, 1 ft. 11 in.; chest, 4 ft. 4 in.; thickest part of
the thigh, 2 ft. 7 in.; calf, 1 ft. 8 in.; height, 5 ft. 8 in.
The height, we are told, is not quite certain, because he
could not get her laid upon the floor; "yet, after infinite
exertions on the part of us both, this was accomplished,
when she sank down again," etc. "Beside her sat her
daughter, a lass of sixteen, stark naked, sucking at a milk-
pot, on which her father kept her at work by holding a
rod in his hands. . . . I got up a flirtation with Missy, and
induced her to rise and shake hands with me. Her features
were lovely, but her body was as round as a ball."

'We believe none of our readers ever met with or ever
heard of such a piece of "engineering" as this, and we
dare say will never wish to meet with such another.'

Speke, M'Queen goes on, writes with admiration of
Mutesa and his court. But what went on there? 'Every day
saw one, two or three poor females dragged from the harem
to a cruel execution and death. In one day and at one time
no fewer than four were thus dragged forth. At page
357 [of Speke's *Discovery of the Source of the Nile*], in
proof of their modesty, Speke informs us minutely thus:—
"These twenty virgins, the daughters of Wakungu, all
smeared and streaming with grease, each holding a small
square of mbugu for a fig leaf, marched in a line before
us as a fresh addition to the harem." After this presenta-
tion, "a sedate old dame rose from the squatting mass,
ordered the virgins right about, and marched them off,
showing their still more naked reverse." '

As for Speke complaining of being lonely during his so-
journ at Mutesa's palace, this was manifestly untrue; he
was constantly accepting presents of girls and rejecting all
but the prettiest. They kept him so busy he did not even
have time to go and look at his famous lake. 'Captain
Speke was all the time mentioned amused and employed
in drinking *pombe*, courting the Queen Dowager, shooting cows, reducing to order his rebellious female intimates. . . . It is almost incredible that any man who had
come one thousand miles to see the position of the outlet
of the Nile, supposed it to be in that spot, should remain
five months within eight miles of it, without hearing or

seeing something certain about the great object of his research, or have found some means to see it. Why, he might have taken the arm of the beautiful Kariana, the wife of the courtier Dumba, with whom he was accustomed to walk arm-in-arm to teach her how to walk as he walked with the ladies in Hyde Park, shaved his beard, slipped on his or her mbugu, and instead of sitting moping and mourning, walked off in a morning walk with Kariana, got to the lake or the river, and so in one forenoon seen what he wanted, and thus relieved us and the world from all our pain and disappointment.'

One of the Queen's objects in sending Speke 'wives' as presents was to discover whether the offspring would turn out black or white. Upon this M'Queen remarks: 'The sexes mix and will continue to mix. Different colours will flow. Captain Speke is himself a most competent witness as to the process.' He would be able to reassure himself on the matter when he returned to this Garden of Eden on the Nile.

Meanwhile the reviewer wished to protest against Speke's habit of naming the places he had discovered after famous people at home: 'It is with disgust that we want proper words to express, to find the first names in Europe prostituted, and especially the name of our great and gracious Sovereign insulted and degraded, in giving names to places in this most barbarous and degraded country. We earnestly hope that the Royal Geographical Society will in future denounce with the greatest severity all such proceedings on the part of any one they patronize and employ.'

Turning next to the geography of Speke's journey M'Queen reproduces most of Burton's arguments, and with some skill manages, by using Speke's own figures, to prove that the explorer makes the Nile flow uphill. 'No correct or thinking geographer,' the reviewer went on, 'can find his way in such pages. It would puzzle the most acute Philadelphia lawyer to unravel the maze, or to derange the narrative more than Captain Speke himself has done.' What had Speke really gained and brought back?—'The sacrifice and ruin of zealous associates—a mass of intelligence, if such it can be called, so muddled and confused in everything that we really believe he himself cannot find his way in it.'

Since his return to England Speke had made a speech in which he declared that he planned to open up Central Africa by returning there and traversing the continent along the Equator from east to west. His object was, he said, 'nothing less than to regenerate Africa'.

But Speke was the last man to send back to Africa. On hearing of the project even the Prime Minister of the King of Buganda might properly exclaim, 'Woh, woh, woh, what will happen next?' Grant might be the man to go. He at least was a gentleman and was modest: 'we never find him engaged in drinking *pombe,* flirting or coquetting, and collecting harems.'

M'Queen winds up his diatribe by referring to a letter of Baker's in which, jokingly, Baker suggests that a public-house might be built on the Equator to accommodate travellers: 'Well, by all means let us have the hotel, say, thus:

THE RIPON FALLS HOTEL
SPEKE AND MUTESA
Pombe and Mbugus Always Ready.

'If such an establishment is proposed under a Royal charter, which the Government could not refuse, we will bet a new English penny coin against a royal Mbugu that the requisite capital would be obtained amongst the multitudes in this country whose heads are softer than their hearts. A hotel, a splendid Court, where flirting, intriguing and drinking *pombe* are the order of the day, would be sure to draw a fashionable array of visitors, as a railway will follow.' [1]

M'Queen's review naturally attracted great attention. It was all very Victorian, very malicious, very hypocritical, and might not have mattered tuppence had not the underlying issues been so serious. Indeed the whole quarrel might be regarded as trivial and absurd, but it was fundamental to the history of the Nile, and in the years ahead its echoes were to continue with an astonishing persistence.

[1] The railway did follow, and there is at the present time a Ripon Falls Hotel on the site.

It would have been extraordinary, of course, had it all been plain sailing for Speke. He had a fantastic story to tell, and he had been both impulsive and a little overbearing in presenting it. After all, the problem of the Nile had engrossed the most distinguished minds for thousands of years, and it was hardly likely that a young Indian Army officer of no particular qualifications had lighted on the truth where all others had failed. Moreover there was a strong tradition of scepticism in England. Nearly a century before this James Bruce had come back from Africa with a story that he had visited the source of the Blue Nile and had followed it down to its confluence with the White Nile at Khartoum; and he had been met with the greatest incredulity. His anecdotes about tribes that ate raw steaks cut from living cattle had been derided, and even the mighty Dr. Samuel Johnson had ridiculed him. Affronted by this, Bruce had retired to his home in Scotland and had waited sixteen years before publishing his *Travels to Discover the Source of the Nile in the Years 1768-73*. Speke, on the other hand, had rushed straight into print, and a public controversy had been stirred up. Clearly it was now only a matter of time before the two principal antagonists were brought face to face to have the matter out.

Eventually, in September 1864, just over a year after Speke's and Grant's return to England, a meeting was arranged at Bath of the British Association for the Advancement of Science, and both Burton and Speke promised to attend it. They were to meet on the platform on September 16 before an audience of several hundred geographers and scientists and present their rival points of view. Dr. Livingstone (who, incidentally, respected Speke but had not much time for Burton) was also to be there.

One does not know much about Speke's state of mind prior to the meeting. He was a man given to keeping his own counsel and he was not at his best in public debate. He must have been aware that Burton was a formidable rival with a command of language and a grasp of logic that he himself certainly did not possess. Burton was an intellectual, Speke was not; and there were some very damaging errors in Speke's *Journal* which as yet he had made no attempt to explain. He had not even brought a libel action against M'Queen and the *Morning Advertiser,* and some of M'Queen's statements were definitely libellous. At one point of the controversy M'Queen had actually accused Speke of condoning the slave-trade. Just possibly this might have been said about Burton, but Speke's record in the matter was absolutely clear; he was very sympathetic towards the Africans. More than once he had written that he believed that, with good government, they would soon emerge from their savage state and take their place among civilized peoples—and that was a great deal more than Burton and many other African travellers, from that day to this, would have said. But he had let all this pass by, and even Burton's worst sneers had gone unanswered. Yet Speke was a tenacious and self-confident man; so far as we know it was not in his nature to give way without a fight. He came down to the Bath meeting apparently determined to defend himself, and he stayed with his uncle John Fuller at Neston Park, near Box in Wiltshire.

Of Burton's attitude towards the meeting we know somewhat more, partly through the loving eyes of his wife Isabel, and partly through his own subsequent writings. As usual he had prepared his notes with care, and now he was not only ready to demolish Speke's theory; he was going to advance a brand new theory of his own. This, in effect, was a violent swing back to his original idea that Lake Tanganyika and its feeder streams were the true headwaters of the Nile. He had prepared a sketch map which showed the Rusizi River flowing northward *out* of Lake Tanganyika and entering the Lŭta Nzigé—that other large lake to the west of Lake Victoria which Speke and Grant had heard about when they were travelling north through Kamrasi's territory towards Gondokoro. The Lŭta Nzigé, in turn, was provided on Burton's map with an outlet which flowed on to Gondokoro. This, Burton now thought, was the true Nile. Speke's Lake Victoria he all but banished from his map, merely describing it as the 'supposed site' of a lake.

Now, as we know, Burton and Speke together had been to the northern end of Lake Tanganyika in 1858, and although they had not actually seen the Rusizi River, they had satisfied themselves from the reports of the local Africans that it flowed *into* the lake and thus could not possibly be the Nile. Burton had felt 'sick at heart' at the time. But now, upon the basis of further reflection, he felt much better. He simply reversed his previous decision and made the Rusizi flow the other way. The local Africans had misinformed them about the river: that was all there was to it. He and Speke, in any case, he declared, had been in no condition to verify matters when they were on the lake in 1858 since 'Speke was deaf and almost blind, I was paralytic, and we were both helpless'.

Burton had another and even more startling thesis to propound. He was ready to declare that the Nile, in addition to Lake Tanganyika, had a second source far over to the east. This was the Asua River, which drained from still another lake—Lake Baringo. To the south-east of Lake Baringo lay the snowcapped peaks of Mount Kenya and Mount Kilimanjaro. These Burton now dubbed the Mountains of the Moon; thus all the conditions of Ptolemy's map of the second century A.D. were admirably fulfilled.

Before the meeting took place Isabel Burton tried unsuccessfully to bring about a reconciliation between the two men. 'It is interesting *now*,' she wrote (in 1892), 'to mark in their letters how they descend from "Dear Jack" and "Dear Dick" to "Dear Burton" and "Dear Speke", until they become "Sir".' And she records that before the meeting a friend 'conveyed to Richard that Speke had said that if Burton appeared on the platform at Bath (which was, as it were, Speke's native town) he would kick him. I remember Richard's answer—"Well, *that* settles it! By God he *shall* kick me"—and so to Bath we went.'

Yet Burton was nervous as well as pugnacious about the coming encounter; he was anxious to get it over and done with. He came down to Bath with Isabel, she being elaborately dressed and almost the only woman at the conference, and they went off to attend a preliminary session in Section E (Geography and Ethnography) on the morning of September 15—the day prior to the great debate. There they saw Speke. The two men cut one another dead. It seemed to Burton that his rival looked ill and his eyesight and his hearing appeared to be troubling him again. Presently, about 1.30 p.m., Burton saw someone beckon to Speke from the bottom of the hall. Speke at once got up, and ejaculating, 'I can't stand this any longer,' left the room.

On the following morning, September 16, Burton, Isabel, Sir Roderick Murchison and several hundred other gentlemen assembled once more in the hall for the opening of the debate. 'All the distinguished people,' Isabel says, 'were with the Council. Richard *alone was excluded,* and stood on the platform—*we two alone,* he with his notes in his hand.'

One can perhaps best follow what happened next from Burton's own description: 'Early in the forenoon fixed for what silly tongues called the "Nile Duel" I found a large assembly in the rooms of Section E. A note was handed round in silence. Presently my friend Mr. Findlay broke the tidings to me. Captain Speke had lost his life on the yesterday, at 4 p.m., whilst shooting over a cousin's grounds. He had been missed in the field and his kinsman found him lying upon the earth, shot through the body close to the heart. He lived only a few minutes and his last words were a request not to be moved.'

Mr. Seton Deardon, in his study of Burton, says that 'Burton staggered visibly on the platform, then sank into a chair with his face working. "By God, he's killed himself!" he exclaimed. When he got home he wept bitter tears, repeating over and over again the name "Jack", "Jack".' Isabel also has recorded that 'when we got home he wept long and bitterly, and I was for many a day trying to comfort him'.

Burton, however, did manage to recover himself at the meeting. After Sir Roderick Murchison had delivered a moving address of condolence to Speke's relatives, Burton filled the gap in the morning's proceedings by reading a paper on 'The Ethnology of Dahomey'.

What had actually happened on the previous day was this: directly he left the hall Speke drove to Neston Park, which was six or seven miles from Bath, and there at 2.30 p.m., with his cousin George Fuller and a gamekeeper, Daniel Davis, he had gone out after partridges. In the course of the next hour he was heard by the others to fire off both barrels of his gun, which was a Lancaster breech-loader with no safety catch. About 4 p.m. Fuller, who was 60 yards away, heard a third very loud report from Speke's gun, and looking up he saw Speke himself standing on a two-foot stone wall. Then Speke fell. Fuller rushed up to discover his cousin lying on the ground with a terrible wound in his chest. One barrel of his gun had been discharged, the other was at half-cock, and it appeared that in getting over the wall Speke had drawn up his gun after him. It had gone off while he was holding its muzzle very close to his chest.

Speke was still conscious, but was bleeding profusely and it was impossible to move him—he himself said feebly, 'Don't move me.' Leaving the gamekeeper to look after the wounded man Fuller ran for help, but by the time he got back with a Mr. Snow, a surgeon of Box, Speke was already dead. He had lived only fifteen minutes and had said no more.

The body was taken to the house of Speke's brother at Corsham, and there an inquest was held on September 16 before a jury 'composed of respectable inhabitants of the place'—the solid West Countrymen of England. When Fuller, Davis and the surgeon had given evidence—the surgeon stating that the muzzle must have been held very close to the dead man's body—the coroner made a brief address in which he indicated to the jury what he thought their verdict ought to be. The jury then returned a unanimous verdict: the deceased had died from the accidental discharge of his own gun after living for a quarter of an hour.

On Monday, September 19, 1864, *The Times* devoted a leading article to Speke. The newspaper took the view that Speke had actually succeeded in discovering the source of the Nile—'the blue riband of the Geographers'—but at the same time it compared the exploit rather unfavourably with the discoveries which had recently been made by the explorers Stuart, Burke and Wills in Australia:

'A gallant soldier, who had borne himself bravely in some of the bloodiest battles in our Indian wars, and a sagacious and enterprising traveller, who had by sheer pluck and endurance solved a problem which has vexed the curi-

osity of mankind since the dawn of history, has in the full
vigour of manhood fallen lifeless in a moment, the victim
of a paltry, commonplace accident . . . We will not claim
for Speke a precedence over the genius of Stuart, or Burke
or Wills; but it was a brilliant exploit, and we were still
proud of the bold adventurer. He had won the trophy, he
was still battling for its possession against other candidates
who would fain have taken it from him. A mixed crowd of
curious and scientific folk were waiting (at Bath) with
foregone conclusions, or at least with prepossessions in his
favour, to witness a great display of fence between him and
his chief adversary.' But at that moment Speke 'lay dead
in a stubble field, shot to death by his own gun'.

The Times had decided views on how the accident had
occurred: 'His gun was found with one barrel discharged,
and the other with the hammer at half-cock. It is evident
therefore that he had laid his gun down at half-cock while
he mounted the wall, and that he had then taken it by the
barrel and drawn it up towards him with the barrels pointed
at his body.

'One of the hammers must have struck against a stone or
hitched in a bough, and the blow just lifted the hammer, and
then allowed it to fall back upon the pin of the cartridge.'

The article concluded: 'This unfortunate accident will
put an end to the controversy which was to have amused
the Geographers at Bath.'

The burial took place at Dowlish Wake church close to
Speke's family home, and it was attended by Murchison,
Livingstone and Grant. A window and a monument were
erected at the church to his memory, and later a granite
obelisk was put up in Kensington Gardens in London. The
inscription on this obelisk reads quite simply, 'In memory
of Speke, Victoria Nyanza and the Nile, 1864'—as though
we all should know the man and remember him with admiration.

Speke was unmarried and just 37 when he died, and a
strange and persistent anonymity surrounds his memory.
Where other, lesser explorers are revered, he is neglected;
while their characters and their achievements can often
seem very real to us, Speke is hardly more than a name;

and it is not even a name that is instantly and indelibly associated with the Nile as Burton's is with Arabia and Livingstone's with Africa. Burton and Livingstone have their biographers in nearly every generation; no book of any consequence has ever been written about Speke. No phrase he uttered, not even 'The Nile is settled', no idiosyncrasy of manner or oddity of behaviour has fixed him in the public mind. He remains a virtuous shade, a self-centred, pertinacious man, a keeper of the best traditions of English enterprise—but one would rather be with Burton.

Speke's very death remains obscure, since there are many who still think that he preferred suicide to facing Burton, though there is no evidence to prove it. Indeed everything we know about Speke must dispose us to think that if he contemplated suicide at all it would have been after his fight with his antagonist, not before. And yet the doubt remains.

There was a curious recrudescence of the matter in 1921. Speke's cousin, George Fuller, wrote to *The Times* as follows:

Sir,

The interesting article on Richard Burton in your issue of the 19th inst. contains a quotation written by Burton to the late W. Frank Wilson as follows:—

"Nothing will be known of Speke's death; I saw him at 1.30 p.m. and at 4 p.m. he was dead. The charitable say that he shot himself, the uncharitable that I shot him."

This is a specimen from the many heroics of Richard Burton, that is characteristic of his vivid imagination. In fairness to *The Times,* and your readers, allow me to correct these misleading points of the Author's letter.

The cause of Speke's death is well known in history; as proved at the Coroner's inquest held at this house after his death. The verdict was "Accidental death by explosion of gun".

Being now the only living eye-witness of that sad accident, and having been in company with Speke on the day of his death, I can testify that Burton could not have seen Speke on that day, and that the death occurred before 1.30 p.m.

Yours faithfully,
G. P. Fuller.

Neston Park, Corsham, Wilts.
March 20th, 1921.

This is very odd. Fuller himself gave evidence at the inquest that the death had taken place at 4 p.m. and there can be little doubt that Burton did actually see Speke about 1.30 p.m. at the preliminary meeting in Bath on September 15, 1864. One can only conclude that Fuller felt very deeply about the matter, and that in 1921, being a very old man, his memory had failed him.

There was no great remorse in England at the time of Speke's death; rather a feeling of embarrassment. *The Times,* however, was wrong in saying that the controversy was finished; Speke's opponents gained strength from his death and lost little time in still further diminishing the importance of his last tremendous journey. Grant lived on until 1892 and was eventually made a Companion of the Bath, but not for his exploit on the Nile; the distinction was awarded for some inconspicuous service he rendered in Abyssinia. Speke, of course, had had the Royal Geographical Society's medal, but some time elapsed before Queen Victoria was moved to observe that he had died 'before he had received any mark of our Royal favour'. The omission was then rectified: Speke's father was advised that he was permitted to add a crocodile and a hippopotamus to his coat of arms.

Later again a plaque was placed at the Ripon Falls. It read:

SPEKE
DISCOVERED THIS
SOURCE OF THE
NILE
ON THE 28 JULY 1862

'This source', one notes: not *the* source. But it hardly matters. The Ripon Falls have now been submerged beneath a hydroelectric dam, and somewhere in the green depths of the great river the place where Speke's plaque used to stand has been obliterated for ever.

Chapter 5

BAKER OF THE NILE

OBVIOUSLY the problem of the Nile was never going to be cleared up by learned speculation in London. The answer could be found only in Africa itself, and now the chief hopes of the geographers were fixed upon Samuel Baker and his wife, who in March 1863, following their meeting with Speke and Grant, had set off southwards from Gondokoro. It was known that Speke had confided to them the general position of the Lŭta Nzigé, which was the possible second source of the Nile, and that they had decided to go in search of it.

Baker is a kind of fulcrum in African exploration. He stands in the centre of all theories, emotions and moral attitudes, never deviating too far one way or the other. Without being in the least dull he is a practical, down-to-earth man, who knows precisely what he wants and where he is going to go. One feels with him that the fates are fighting an unequal battle; however outrageous the odds against him, things will calm down in the end and everyone will come round to his sober and sensible way of thinking. In some ways he is almost a caricature of the professional Victorian, the solid, whiskered clubman-figure who is absolutely fixed in his habits and his loyalties, but equally determined to enjoy himself. Yet he is a difficult man to define; having attached one label to him you find that you must quickly add another. Thus you might describe him as a splendid specimen of Thackeray's hunting-and-shooting Anglo-Indian nabobs, but then he writes extremely good books and is a very fair linguist; he is a prosperous member of the trading middle-class, but then he himself does not engage in business, he travels abroad on the most hazardous and daring journeys; he rears a large Victorian family and then, on the death of his wife, he marries a blonde and beautiful Hungarian girl, Florence Ninian von Sass, some fifteen years his junior; he is pompous, conservative, sentimental and stubborn, and at other times none of those things; and yet, in the midst of all this, he is not a chameleon. He is as steady as the captain of a ship. 'A magnificent and sensible man,' Stanley says of him. Grant speaks of his 'animated conversation', and even if Grant may not have been the best judge of such matters, at least he establishes a point.

Baker was born in 1821 (the same year as Burton), and he came from a line of naval captains and planters in the colonies. His father was a wealthy shipowner and the director of a bank and a railway. He was a fair, blue-eyed boy, passionately fond of shooting and the out-of-doors, and he grew up to be a broad-shouldered man of medium height, very tough and very solid; his fair hair sprouted from his chin in a massive beard. He completed his education in Germany, and then married the daughter of an English clergyman, and was off to the outposts of the world, hardly ever to return to England for very long until the end of his life. At one time Baker founded an agricultural settlement in Ceylon, and at another he was the construction manager of a railway along the Danube; but it was his obsession with big game shooting that led him on. He shot elephants in Ceylon, tigers in India, bears in the Balkans, and in the early eighteen-sixties he went over to Africa with his lovely young second wife (his four surviving children by the first marriage being safely disposed with relatives in England) to see what was offering for his gun in the wilds of the Sudan. He had, too, a second object in view; he thought he would combine a little exploring with the sport. Why not a journey up the Nile, perhaps even an expedition that would take him to the very source of the river?

As with all else in Baker's life, he prepared for this excursion with great thoroughness. He decided that first of all he would spend a year in the Sudan following up the Nile tributaries to the Abyssinian border and learning Arabic as he went along; then he would assemble his expedition in

Khartoum and tackle the White Nile itself. Baker did himself well: delicacies from Fortnum and Mason's, a battery of guns made to his own specifications by the leading gunsmiths in London, the best of camping equipment and scientific instruments. In a sense he was a new kind of explorer, since he was wealthy, he was a private traveller having no connection with the government, the Church or the scientific societies, and he was under no instructions from anybody; he was simply out to please himself. Yet a more professional explorer never set foot in Africa. The first part of his programme was followed out to the letter. Just over a year after the outset of his journey from Cairo he arrived at Khartoum, having by then a very fair command of Arabic, and having shot a large number of wild animals on the upper reaches of the Atbara River. He had been corresponding with Petherick, and at Petherick's invitation he and his wife put up at the empty British Consulate at Khartoum.

Khartoum in the eighteen-sixties had been in existence for more than forty years, and was, in its own way, as strange and as wild as Zanzibar; indeed, these two towns between them drained off the great bulk of the slave and ivory trade of East Africa, all the caravans south of the Equator going out south-eastwards to the Indian Ocean and those to the north descending the Nile to Khartoum. In a rough and haphazard fashion the Egyptians ruled the Sudan from Khartoum; but perhaps pillaged is a better word than ruled. Practically every official from the Governor-General, Musa Pasha, downwards was involved in some way in the slave-trade, and the garrison of fifteen thousand Egyptian and Nubian troops lived on the land as an army of occupation might live, except that it was far more ruthless and disorderly. Its main business was gathering taxes, and these were extorted in kind from the natives either by the use of the whip, or by armed raids on the cattle and the grain stores in the villages.

Baker and his wife loathed Khartoum on sight: 'A more miserable, filthy and unhealthy place,' he says, 'can hardly be imagined.' Beyond the river, nothing but an appalling desert; within the town itself some thirty thousand people densely crowded into huts of burnt brick that were occasionally flooded by the Nile. Dead animals lay rotting in the undrained streets and the only supply of water was a muddy fluid brought up from the river by Persian wheels with hanging earthen jars that were worked by circling oxen. There was, of course, a tax on every water-wheel. Nothing in the town could be done except by bribery; torture and flogging took place as a matter of course in the prisons; and Musa Pasha himself combined 'the worst of Oriental failings with the brutality of a wild animal'. Throughout most of the year the heat was overwhelming, and when the *haboob* blew up the sand-filled sky was black as night.

Baker describes one of these storms. 'I saw,' he says, 'approaching from the S.W. apparently, a solid range of immense brown mountains, high in the air. So rapid was the approach of this extraordinary phenomenon, that in a few minutes we were in actual pitchy darkness. At first there was no wind, and the peculiar calm gave an oppressive character to the event. . . . We tried to distinguish our hands placed close before our eyes—not even an outline could be seen. This lasted for upwards of twenty minutes; it then rapidly passed away and the sun shone as before.'

And yet, at this time, Khartoum was a fascinating place: 'the air was full of wonderment'. This was almost the last point of civilization on the edge of an immense wilderness which had hardly as yet begun to yield up the endless treasures and monstrosities it contained. Every caravan that set out was an exploration; every boat that returned down the Nile brought with it something that was phenomenal and strange: animals and birds that had not been classified as yet, wild tribesmen with outlandish ornaments stuck through their lips, ears and noses, plants and flowers that produced new drugs and perfumes, stones that might prove to contain silver or gold. The ivory trade alone was worth £40,000 a year.

Apart from the Africans, the population of Khartoum was made up chiefly of Syrians, Greeks, Copts, Armenians, Turks, Arabs and Egyptians, and many of these had taken Galla girls from Abyssinia—'the Venuses of that country'

—as their wives or concubines. About thirty Europeans were living in the town, and life for them was not intolerable. They had somewhat better and cooler houses than the general run, a monthly camel post kept them in touch with the outside world, and many luxuries such as wines, Bass's pale ale, French biscuits, soaps and perfumes were brought to them over the desert. The local Turkish and Egyptian grandees liked to entertain at long and elaborate banquets which usually wound up with a performance by African dancing girls.

But it was the slave-trade that kept Khartoum going. Any penniless adventurer could become a trader provided he was willing to borrow money at anything up to eighty per cent interest. On a normal expedition such a trader would sail south from Khartoum in December with two or three hundred armed men, and at some convenient spot would land and form an alliance with a native chieftain. Then together the tribesmen and the Khartoum slavers would fall upon some neighbouring village in the night, firing the huts just before dawn and shooting into the flames. It was the women that the slavers chiefly wanted, and these were secured by placing a heavy forked pole known as a *sheba* on their shoulders. The head was locked in by a crossbar, the hands were tied to the pole in front, and the children were bound to their mothers by a chain passed round their necks. Everything the village contained would be looted—cattle, ivory, grain, even the crude jewellery that was cut off the dead victims—and then the whole cavalcade would be marched back to the river to await shipment to Khartoum. With the stolen cattle the trader would buy ivory, and sometimes for ivory he would be willing to ransom a slave. Sometimes too the trader would turn upon his native ally and despoil him in the same way as the others; but more often these alliances were kept on from year to year, the native chieftain building up a fresh store of slaves and ivory while the trader was disposing of the last consignment at Khartoum. Every trader had his own territory and by mutual agreement the country was parcelled out all the way from Khartoum to Gondokoro and beyond.

In a good season a slaver in a small way could reckon

on obtaining 20,000 lb. of ivory worth £4,000 in Khartoum, plus 400 or 500 slaves worth £5 or £6 each—a total of perhaps £6,500. With this capital he paid off his debts, mounted a fresh expedition and year by year expanded his business.

Officially the trade was illegal, but the only effect of this was that the slaves were not sold openly in Khartoum; they were disposed of at established points of rendezvous in the desert outside the town, and thence marched off along the caravan routes to the Red Sea for shipment to Arabia or Persia or sent directly down the Nile to Cairo.

Probably nothing more monstrous or cruel than this traffic had happened in history, for it was more highly organized than the slaving in Tanganyika. Baker records the terrible facts with a juridical calm which is very effective; and yet, like Burton, and unlike Speke, he did not really take to Africans and he was no blind believer in immediate emancipation. 'However we may condemn the horrible system of slavery,' he wrote, 'the results of emancipation have proved that the Negro does not appreciate the blessings of freedom, nor does he show the slightest feelings of gratitude to the hand that broke the rivets of his fetters.' Baker had a theory that Africans were not and could not ever be equal to white men. The most he would concede was that in childhood the Negro 'might be in advance, in intellectual quickness, of the white child of a similar age, but the mind does not expand—it promises fruit, but does not ripen. . . .'

Elsewhere he attacks the Africans for the savagery and brutality of their tribal customs. 'Charming people, these poor blacks, as they are termed by English sympathizers,' he exclaims when a Nuer chief 'exhibited his wife's back and arms covered with jagged scars . . . he was quite proud of having clawed his wife like a wild beast.' And again: 'Polygamy is, of course, the general custom; the number of a man's wives depending entirely upon his wealth, precisely as would the number of his horses in England. There is no such thing as *love* in these countries . . . everything is practical, without a particle of romance. Women are so far appreciated as they are valuable animals . . . I am afraid this practical state of affairs will be a strong barrier to missionary enterprise.'

Later on Baker was to be strongly criticized in England for these views, and for his harsh treatment of the tribes. But this is merely another instance of that imperturbable equilibrium; at the very time he was being criticized he was probably doing more in a practical way to break the slave traffic than any other man in Africa. All this, however, belonged to a later day; for the moment the trade had a much more personal importance for him—it had so savaged and antagonized the tribes south of Khartoum that the whole country was in an uproar. This made it hazardous for any private traveller to proceed without a large armed escort. There was another difficulty which was even more serious: the Egyptian officials at Khartoum were by no means eager to have a stray white man roaming about in the slaving areas which were so profitable for them. They wanted no interlopers to report on their activities to the outside world. Musa Pasha therefore did all he could to prevent the Bakers from getting on. He denied them boats. He contrived to prevent their engaging an escort. He smiled and smiled and told them to come back another day.

But it would have needed a great deal more determination than Musa Pasha possessed to thwart the Bakers. On their arrival in Khartoum in June 1862 they found that they had an additional and urgent reason for continuing into the interior. A report had come in that Petherick and his wife, who had gone south some months earlier, were dead, and the Royal Geographical Society now asked Baker if he would take Petherick's place in the search for Speke and Grant. The two explorers had already been missing for over a year. Baker accepted this charge at once and privately decided that if Speke and Grant had also perished or had failed to reach their objective he himself would go on and find the source of the Nile.

After six months' persistent effort in Khartoum he acquired three sailing boats, 96 men, some of whom he armed and dressed in uniform, provisions for four months, 21 donkeys, 4 camels and 4 horses. He was also joined by a German traveller, Johann Schmidt, whom he had picked up in the Sudan. On December 18, 1862, they set sail for Gondokoro.

The Nile south of Khartoum is a complicated stream. For five hundred miles it proceeds through the desert on a broad and fairly regular course, with trees and occasional low, bare hills or *jebels* on either bank. But at the point where the Sobat comes in from the Abyssinian mountains, a short distance above the present town of Malakal, the river turns west, the air grows more humid, the banks more green, and this is the first warning of the great obstacle of the Sudd that lies ahead. There is no more formidable swamp in the world than the Sudd. The Nile loses itself in a vast sea of papyrus ferns and rotting vegetation, and in that foetid heat there is a spawning tropical life that can hardly have altered very much since the beginning of the world; it is as primitive and as hostile to man as the Sargasso Sea. Crocodiles and hippopotamuses flop about in the muddy water, mosquitoes and other insects choke the air and the *Balaeniceps rex* and other weird water-birds keep watch along the banks—except that here there are no ordinary banks, merely chance pools in the forest of apple-green reeds that stretches away in a feathery mass to the horizon. This region is neither land nor water. Year by year the current keeps bringing down more floating vegetation, and packs it into solid chunks perhaps twenty feet thick and strong enough for an elephant to walk on. But then this debris breaks away in islands and forms again in another place, and this is repeated in a thousand indistinguishable patterns and goes on forever.

Baker remarks that on the Upper Nile there are no ruins or relics of past civilizations, 'no ancient histories to charm the present with memories of the past; all is wild and brutal, hard and unfeeling . . .' And indeed this was the thing that caused a basic uneasiness among all the white men who penetrated into the South Sudan—the feeling that they were in a wilderness where life never progressed but simply turned over and over on itself in a timeless and aimless cycle. Their experiences were quite unlike those of Cortez among the Aztecs; the country was almost as barren of human achievement as Australia was at the beginning of the nineteenth century, and even more hostile to the intruder.

These effects were redoubled in the Sudd. Here there was not even a present, let alone a past; except on occasional islands of hard ground no men ever had lived or ever could live in this desolation of drifting reeds and ooze, even the most savage of men. The lower forms of life flourished here in a mad abundance, but for black and white men alike the Sudd contained nothing but the threat of starvation, disease and death. In the wet season it covered an area as large as England.

There were three main waterways through the Sudd, and all or any of them might be blocked at any time; some sixty miles beyond Malakal the Bahr-el-Zeraf, the River of the Giraffes, split off to the south; then, another fifty miles further on, there was a sheet of fairly open water known as Lake No and here the stream divided, one section, the Bahr-el-Ghazal, the River of the Antelopes, striking off in a general south-westerly direction, while the other, the Bahr-el-Jebel, continued directly south. This last, the Bahr-el-Jebel, was the main channel used by the traders. About 500 miles south of Lake No they got free of the Sudd and arrived at Gondokoro. With luck, which meant a fair wind and the ability to cut their way through the matted vegetation, they hoped to complete the journey from Khartoum in about a month and a half.

Beyond Gondokoro they could proceed no further by water; the Nile there broke up into cataracts that continued intermittently for about eighty miles. Thus Gondokoro had become the main entrepot in the interior, even though it was nothing more than a miserable collection of huts 25 feet above the river on the east bank. Already in the 'sixties it had been in existence for some twenty years, and an Austrian Roman Catholic Mission had been established there as early as 1851. But all had come to grief: fifteen out of the twenty missionaries who had been sent there had died and not a single convert had been made.

Very few of the slave and ivory traders had managed to get far beyond Gondokoro, since they despoiled their line of march and the opposition of the tribes rose up before them. A few, like the Maltese, Andrea de Bono, and his agent, Mohammed Wad-el-Mek (who met Speke and Grant), had got a little distance over the present border of Uganda at Nimule, and one of the earliest explorers, the Italian, Giovanni Miani, had carved his initials on a tamarind tree there before turning back. But in general the area beyond Nimule and the further course of the river were unknown. This region Baker now proposed to penetrate in search of Speke and Grant.

The Sudd that year was fairly clear, and Baker's little flotilla accomplished the 1,000-mile voyage from Khartoum to Gondokoro in 40 days. On the way Johann Schmidt died, others fell ill, and the whole party, both animals and men, suffered terribly from mosquitoes. Gondokoro, says Baker, 'was a perfect hell', a sort of Yukon gold-rush camp in the tropics, with six hundred traders and their men forever drinking, quarrelling and insanely shooting off their guns into the air. However, there was a moment of respite. The Bakers had been only a fortnight in Gondokoro when, as we have seen, Speke and Grant arrived from Bunyoro. In his account of the meeting Baker very handsomely covers up his disappointment at hearing that they had already reached the source of the Nile: 'At the first blush of meeting them,' he says, 'I had considered my expedition as terminated ... but ... Speke and Grant with characteristic candour and generosity gave me a map of their route, showing that they had been unable to complete the actual exploration of the Nile, and that a most important portion still remained to be determined ... a large lake called the Lúta Nzigé.'

Soon after Speke and Grant had gone north to Khartoum the Bakers set out for the lake.

The Albert N'yanza, Great Basin of the Nile, Baker's account of his next two years' wanderings, is the most readable of explorers' books. It contains indeed the ingredients of almost all African adventure stories that have been written from that day to this. Here is Allan Quartermain in his broad-brimmed hat setting forth into the jungles with a young and lovely girl at his side, and they face every hazard with marvellous determination. When wild beasts charge, Baker with his deadly aim stops them in their tracks. At the outset of the journey he quells a mutiny among his own men by striking down the ringleader with his fist. Then, as they advance, all their baggage animals die and they are forced to ride oxen, their food supplies fail and they are reduced to eating grass, fever lays them prostrate for days and weeks on end, deceitful guides mislead them, hippopotamuses overturn their boats, the slave-traders cheat them, the tribes attack with poisoned arrows, and they are never for long out of sight and hearing of the war drums and savage dancing. Through it all Mrs. Baker never flinches. 'She was not a *screamer*,' her husband says. When she hears stealthy footsteps approaching their hut at night she quietly touches him on the sleeve and he reaches for his revolver to deal with the intruder. When heavy dew drenches her Victorian skirts and they bring her to the ground she has no compunction about getting into men's clothing.

For nine months they wandered aimlessly or were beleaguered in native villages to the south-east of Gondokoro, unable to get forward because of the lack of porters. Their immediate objective was to reach the headquarters of Kamrasi, the King of Bunyoro, whom Speke and Grant had met on their journey north, but Kamrasi was still at war with his brother Rionga and he kept putting them off. And so all this time they continued in the wilderness, barely a fortnight's journey from the Lǔta Nzigé but quite unable to make any move to reach it. It baffled the Africans that they should wish to go to the lake at all. Comoro, one of the minor chiefs with whom the Bakers stayed, said to them one day, 'Suppose you get to the great lake, what will you do with it? What will be the good of it? If you find that the large river does flow from it, what then?'

This Comoro seems to have been an entertaining man. He had the cynical and fatalistic approach to life: 'Most people are bad,' he explained to Baker. 'If they are strong they take from the weak. The good people are all weak: they are good because they are not strong enough to be bad.'

By now life really did seem to the Bakers to be as dreadful as this. Both were suffering terribly from malaria and

Labels on the map:
1863-1874
Baker, 1863-73 xxxxxxxxxxxx
Livingstone, 1866-73 ....
Stanley, 1871 -----------

Gondokoro, Fatiko, Foweira, Karuma Falls, Masindi, Lake Albert [Luta Nzigé], Vacovia, Mutesa's Palace, Bahari Nzige, Mt Mfumbiro, Kivo Le, Victoria Nyanza, Muanza, Mt Kilimanjaro, Mt Kenia, Juba, Nyangwé, Kamolondo Lake, Ujiji, Tabora, Lake Manyara, Mombas, Pemba I., Zanzibar, Bagamoyo, Lake Tanganyika, L. Liemba, Monfia I., Quiloa [Kilwa], Pemba, C. Delgado, Rovuma R., Lake Bangweolo, Lake Nyassa, Chitambo's Village (Here Livingstone died May 1st 1873), Mozambique, INDIAN OCEAN

*East Africa as it was presumed to be, following the
journeys of Baker, Livingstone and Stanley up
to 1874 (taken from contemporary map)*

there were days when Mrs. Baker had to be carried on a
litter. At last, on January 22, 1864, in the company of an
Arab slaver named Ibrahim they reached the Nile near the
Karuma Falls where the river turns sharply to the west.
Here they were on the borders of Bunyoro, and Kamrasi's
tribesmen hailed them from the opposite bank. Baker's interpreter explained that he was 'Speke's brother', and had
come with rich presents for Kamrasi, but the tribesmen
feared that this was just another slaving raid, and although
they came close to the shore in a canoe they would not
land. Baker describes the scene:

' "Let us look at him!" cried the headman in the boat;
having prepared for the introduction by changing my

clothes in a grove of plantains for my dressing-room, and altering my costume to a tweed suit, something similar to that worn by Speke, I climbed up a high and almost perpendicular rock that formed a natural pinnacle on the face of the cliff, and waving my cap to the crowd on the opposite side I looked almost as imposing as Nelson in Trafalgar Square. . . . Upon landing through the high reeds, they immediately recognized the similarity of my beard and general complexion to that of Speke; and their welcome was at once displayed by the most extravagant dancing and gesticulating with lances and shields, as though intending to attack, rushing at me with the points of their lances thrust close to my face, and shouting and singing in great excitement.'

Finally Baker's party—110 of them in all—was allowed to cross the river. Mrs. Baker caused a great sensation. She chose this moment to wash her hair, and the tribesmen and their families gathered round in amazement at the sight of the long golden tresses reaching to her waist. There followed then a wearisome palaver before the local chiefs agreed to lead the party to Kamrasi's headquarters, ten days' march to the south at Mrooli, at the head of Lake Kyoga. By the time they reached their destination Baker was so ill and weak that he had to be carried into the King's presence on a stretcher and laid like a trophy at his feet. Kamrasi, surrounded by his subordinate chiefs, sat on a copper stool that had been placed on a carpet of leopard skins, and he surveyed his helpless guest with equanimity. He explained that he had greatly feared that Baker was an ally of his enemy Rionga, and had come to plunder his country. But now it was evident that he was Speke's brother, merely another impoverished traveller: he was too weak to be bad. Thus reassured, the King set about the customary business of demanding presents—shotguns, beads, carpets, lengths of cloth, everything he could lay hands on. He also insisted that Baker should repair the fifty-guinea gold chronometer Speke had given him in 1862—it had 'gone dead' after he had poked at the works with a needle to discover where the ticking came from.

It was a miserable time for the Bakers. The rain poured

down. Regularly each day Baker was seized by a violent attack of malaria, and all his quinine was exhausted. Again and again he asked Kamrasi to supply him with porters and a guide, so that he could proceed to the mysterious lake to the west, but he was invariably met with a demand for more presents. 'We shall be nailed for another year in this abominable country,' Baker wrote in his diary, 'ill with fever, and without medicine, clothes or supplies.'

The crisis came in February 1864. Kamrasi announced that Baker should go to the lake, but Mrs. Baker must remain behind: he would provide Baker with a good-looking Bunyoro virgin in exchange for her. Baker drew his pistol and pointing it at Kamrasi's chest told him he was about to shoot him dead. Mrs. Baker, meanwhile, rising from her sick-bed, rushed at the King and withered him with an outburst of furious indignation; and at this Kamrasi gave way.

On the following day porters and an escort were produced, and the travellers set off for the goal of their great adventure. They were held up almost at once by the swamp and the matted vegetation on the Kafu River to the southwest of Mrooli. 'It was equally impossible,' Baker wrote later, 'to ride or to be carried over this treacherous surface; thus I led the way and begged Mrs. Baker to follow me on foot as quickly as possible, precisely in my track. The river was about eighty yards wide, and I had scarcely completed a fourth of the distance and looked back to see if my wife followed close to me, when I was horrified to see her standing in one spot, and sinking gradually through the weeds, while her face was distorted and perfectly purple. Almost as soon as I perceived her, she fell, as though shot dead. In an instant I was by her side; and with the assistance of eight or ten of my men, who were fortunately close to me, I dragged her like a corpse through the yielding vegetation, and up to our waists we scrambled across to the other side, just keeping her head above the water: to have carried her would have been impossible, as we should all have sunk together through the reeds. I had her under a tree, and bathed her head and face with water, as for the moment I thought she had fainted; but she lay perfectly insensible, as though dead, with teeth and hands firmly clenched, and her eyes open, but fixed. It was a *coup de soleil.*'

Since there was no food to be had on the river Baker struggled forward for two more days, his unconscious wife lying on a stretcher, and on the third morning she woke demented. For a week then Baker sat with her through the day and night while she raved deliriously in a waking trance. He managed to obtain a little wild honey and a guinea-fowl or two, but they were by now half starved and still the rain poured down. At the end of a week Baker himself collapsed, but when he woke many hours later he found that his wife's brain had cleared at last, and that she was able to recognize him. After two further days to recuperate they pushed on again, following the general direction of the Kafu River to the south-west. By March 13 they had reached the 31st degree of longitude, about 25 miles north of the Equator, and their guide announced that they should come within sight of the lake on the following day.

'That night,' Baker says, 'I hardly slept. For years I had striven to reach the "sources of the Nile". In my nightly dreams during that arduous voyage I had always failed, but after so much hard work and perseverance the cup was at my very lips, and I was to *drink* at the mysterious fountain before another sun should set—at that great reservoir of Nature that ever since creation had baffled all discovery.

'*The 14th March.*—The sun had not risen when I was spurring my ox after the guide, who, having been promised a double handful of beads on arrival at the lake, had caught the enthusiasm of the moment. The day broke beautifully clear, and having crossed a deep valley between the hills, we toiled up the opposite slope. I hurried to the summit. The glory of our prize burst suddenly upon me! There, like a sea of quicksilver, lay far beneath the grand expanse of water—a boundless sea horizon on the south and south-west, glittering in the noonday sun; and on the west, at fifty or sixty miles' distance, blue mountains rose from the bosom of the lake to a height of about 7,000 feet above its level.'

Baker had long since planned to give three cheers when he reached his goal, but now he found himself overcome with emotion. He and his wife dismounted from their oxen and in a fever of excitement began to drag themselves down the steep cliff towards the water's edge. They made towards a little fishing village named Vacovia (which may be the present hamlet of Buhuka).

'I led the way, grasping a stout bamboo. My wife in extreme weakness tottered down the pass, supporting herself upon my shoulder, and stopping to rest every twenty paces. After a toilsome descent of about two hours, weak with years of fever, but for the moment strengthened by success, we gained the level plain below the cliff. A walk of about a mile through flat sandy meadows of fine turf interspersed with trees and bush, brought us to the water's edge. The waves were rolling upon a white pebbly beach: I rushed into the lake, and thirsty with heat and fatigue, with a heart full of gratitude, I drank deeply from the Sources of the Nile.'

Well, perhaps it was not *the* source of the Nile, he explains, but at any rate it was *a* source, and for the moment it was marvellous. With solemnity he named it Lake Albert in honour of Queen Victoria's husband, who had so recently died.

'It was with extreme emotion,' he goes on, 'that I enjoyed this glorious scene. My wife, who had followed me so devotedly, stood by my side pale and exhausted—a wreck upon the shores of the great Albert lake that we had so long striven to reach. No European foot had ever trod upon its sand, nor had the eyes of a white man ever scanned its vast expanse of water. We were the first and this was the key to the great secret that even Julius Caesar yearned to unravel, but in vain. Here was the great basin of the Nile that received *every drop of water* even from the passing shower to the roaring mountain torrent that drained from Central Africa towards the north. This was the great reservoir of the Nile.'

And now they faced the inevitable problem that besets all explorers—how to get home? From fishermen on the lakeshore they managed to obtain crude canoes made of

hollowed-out tree trunks, and in those they paddled northwards for the next two weeks, through fearful storms,
until they reached the point where the Nile entered the
topmost corner of the lake. Here there was another reward
awaiting them: continuing a short distance up the river to
the east, through what is now a national park for wild
animals, they came upon a spectacular waterfall. The
Murchison Falls (so named by Baker in honour of the
President of the Royal Geographical Society) are only 20
feet across and some 130 feet high, but Mr. Rennie Bere,
the director of the Uganda National Parks, has very well
described them as 'the most exciting single incident in the
Nile's long journey to the sea'. The whole pent-up volume
of the river dashes out of a ravine like a burst water-main;
it is really more of an explosion of water than a fall, and
it can exert a curious mesmerism in the mind if one stands
there and watches for a while. The pattern of thundering
water is endlessly repeated yet never for two seconds quite
the same.

The Bakers did not have much leisure to enjoy their
discovery—it was here that the hippopotamus bull charged
them and lifted their boat half out of the river. The scene
of the accident is still a favourite haunt of crocodiles and
they were lucky to be swept by whirlpools on to the bank.

They now abandoned their boat and took refuge above
the falls on the island of Patooan and there once more
they collapsed. Civil war was now raging throughout
Bunyoro, and two more months went by before the Bakers,
on the point of starvation, were able to get back to Kamrasi's headquarters. Here it was revealed to Baker that the
man whom they had previously seen before starting out
for the lake was not the King at all, but a younger brother
named M'Gambi whom Kamrasi had prudently sent in his
place in case the Bakers should prove to be dangerous.
M'Gambi or Kamrasi, it hardly mattered very much to
the two desperate fugitives—but Baker thought it advisable
to put on a show for his meeting with the real King: he
got out a kilt, a sporran, and a Glengarry bonnet from
his kit and in these presented himself at the palace. Kamrasi was sufficiently impressed to offer food to his guests

and then, in the usual way, doggedly set about relieving them of their last possessions.

And now six months went by and nothing happened. Regularly in the afternoon Baker went down with malaria, and it was not until he devised a means of distilling alcohol from sweet potatoes that he rallied a little. There was no ending to the wars—Mutesa was now attacking Bunyoro with an army from the south—and the hostilities made it impossible for unescorted travellers to get about. When Kamrasi was forced to flee to the north from the invading army, the Bakers had no choice but to go with him. By September 1864 they had all but resigned themselves to dying in Central Africa when an Arab slave caravan came in from Gondokoro bringing with it not only stores for the Bakers but mail as well. From Speke (who had died in Wiltshire just a few days before) they received a copy of the *Illustrated London News* containing his own and Grant's portraits, and also a copy of *Punch* with a cartoon on the discovery of the source of the Nile.

The Bakers now had cloth with which to obtain both food and porters, and they joined forces with the Arab caravan on its return to the north. It was a slow progress, delayed at every step by the inevitable cattle and slave raids on the villages, but finally in February 1865, after two years' absence, they reached Gondokoro. The party made a ceremonial entry, Baker and his wife mounted on oxen, guns firing, and the Union Jack flying, and they were met by a bitter anti-climax: no Europeans were there to welcome them and, worse still, there was no mail. The Bakers had long since been presumed dead.

Tragedy and misery were to pursue the explorers to the very end. Baker managed to hire a boat for the return to Khartoum for £40, but the Sudd blocked them for many weeks, and while they waited for a favourable wind, plague broke out. A number of the men, including the boy Saat who had followed them throughout, went mad and died.

They had a warm welcome from the European community when they reached Khartoum (where they heard for the first time of Speke's death), but even the normally uneventful onward passage to Cairo was hindered by near shipwreck in the cataracts and a skirmish with the Arabs. At last in October 1865, nearly five years after they had first set foot in Africa, they reached Suez, and Baker was able to indulge in a luxury which for a long time had been haunting his imagination—a tankard of iced Allsopp's pale ale. A job was found in Shepheard's Hotel in Cairo for Richarn, their last surviving follower, and they set sail for home. 'Had I really come from the Nile sources?' Baker asked himself. 'It was no dream. A witness sat before me; a face still young, but bronzed like an Arab by years of exposure to a burning sun; haggard and worn with toil and sickness, and shaded with cares, happily now past; the devoted companion of my pilgrimage, to whom I owed success and life—my wife.'

There was enough here for half a dozen film scenarios and the British public loved it. Speke and Grant in their accounts of their journeys had been a little too bizarre and at the same time pedestrian; Burton's treatises had been too sharp and too esoteric except for the sophisticated few; and Dr. Livingstone belonged to a high moral plane that was sometimes beyond the average reach. But Baker's book *The Albert N'yanza* was just right; he and his wife had the sort of reactions that everyone could enjoy and understand. One suffered and lived vicariously with this couple in the terrible African jungle just as one lived with the characters in a novel. And how brave she was. How gallant and determined he had been. They deserved their success.

There was another quality about Baker that people liked; he was not forever, like Speke, pushing on impatiently to reach the journey's end; while he was in Africa he lived there, he made a home of it. Whenever he came to a cul-de-sac he accepted the fact for the time being, and like Robinson Crusoe at once set about making himself comfortable in the wilderness. He planted vegetables, he explored the neighbourhood in search of wild game, he designed and built his own living quarters and engaged in conversation with the local chiefs like Comoro. Being an extremely practical man he would with equal facility make a boat, an alcoholic still or a suit of clothes from wild animal skins. He and his wife gathered a little group of personal retainers round them, and these were taught to cook, serve at the table and make beds like any other domestic servants. They had their pet monkeys and their pet birds who travelled with them and even their riding oxen were properly broken in and trained. Baker's observations of native life are full of interest: he notes that the White Nile, near Khartoum, is the colour of 'an English horse-pond', that the tribal drums are sometimes made from an elephant's ear, that the goods the natives brought to market were packed in fresh reeds, and that the beer gourds were covered with a lid and their contents drained through a straw. He describes just how the bark of trees was beaten into a cloth, and how the tribesmen made needles and sewed squares of goatskin into mantles 'as expertly as a French glover'. He supplies details of the vast Nile perch: one half of a fish they caught in Lake Albert (the other half having been eaten by a crocodile) weighed 150 lb.

Baker, in other words, had a pleasant intimacy with the things he found in Africa, and when he described them he wrote as Defoe might have written.

Before ever he got to England he was awarded the gold medal of the Royal Geographical Society, and his knighthood soon followed. The press was delighted with Sir Samuel and Lady Baker (now no longer a wreck but dressed in the height of fashion), and so was society in London. Presently they had the pleasure of seeing *The Albert N'yanza* run into three editions, and it was to be reprinted frequently in the years ahead. His *Nile Tributaries*, the account of his first year's shooting safari in the Sudan, soon followed and was equally successful. In 1868 Baker tried his hand at fiction, and his adventure story, *Cast Up by the Sea*, pleased the public just as well. But it was with the Nile that his name was associated in the public mind. From now on he was Baker of the Nile.

It would be unfair, of course, even facetious, to leave Baker and his reputation here. His books were much more than adventure stories and his journeys had an importance that went far beyond their popular interest. He had im-

ported something quite new into the Central African
scene; he had made it comprehensible. He formed a kind
of bridge between the original myths and legends and the
reality of what was actually to be found in the country.
Central Africa now was no longer a fantasy or a blank
space on the map: it was an undeveloped but quite habitable region, with perfectly recognizable people living in
it, and it was being exploited with the utmost savagery
and brutality by the Mohammedans. The Nile, in short,
had now become more than a geographical interest: it had
a political, humanitarian and commercial importance as
well, and Baker drove home the point that, unless England
stepped in, this promising wilderness would be utterly despoiled by the slavers and lost forever to Christianity.

Baker's books alone, of course, did not provoke a new
approach to Africa, but they certainly helped in the matter; they stimulated ideas and feelings that were already
in existence, they pointed a path which politicians, merchants and churchmen were all eager to follow. And yet
the geography remained. Until the mystery of the physical
nature of the region and its great river was cleared up it was
difficult to know precisely how to act. Despite all the
careful scientific data Baker had brought back it had to
be admitted that he had not really accomplished very
much on the Upper Nile. Compared with the journeys of
the other explorers his wanderings had taken him an astonishingly short distance (at the present time one could
easily traverse in a car his whole route south from Gondokoro within the space of a couple of days), and his discovery of Lake Albert had by no means resolved the mystery of the Nile; in fact, it was soon to become apparent
that he had only confused the issue still further. Like
Speke he had seen a large body of water and had concluded that it ran on indefinitely, perhaps for hundreds of
miles, to the south. But he had no means of proving this;
he had not circumnavigated the lake. All he could really
assert was that the stream which Speke had seen pouring
westward at Karuma Falls in Central Uganda did in fact
flow into his newly discovered Lake Albert and then out of
it again towards the north. But whether or not this was the

Nile he could not say with any authority, for he had not followed the stream northwards from Lake Albert to Gondokoro.

Another question remained, and it was vital: suppose this *was* the Nile, which lake was the true source, Speke's Victoria or Baker's Albert? If Baker's Albert stretched as far south as he thought it did, then surely it had the better claim. Baker himself left the matter in the air: Lake Albert, he said, was at least the *western* source of the river and a considerable, if not its principal, reservoir. The *full* Nile, he claimed, began only when the stream issued from it. Geographers in London saw his point but still it was not conclusive.

Speke's detractors naturally lost no time in exploiting the possibilities of Lake Albert. Surely it could be argued, they said, that this new lake might be fed by a river still further south, and if so then Speke's claims about Lake Victoria (if that lake really did exist) were nonsense. Even before the Bakers returned to England Sir Roderick Murchison felt bound to acknowledge the force of this reasoning. On May 22, 1865, he delivered a eulogy of Speke to the Royal Geographical Society, but he wound up his address by announcing that he proposed to send Livingstone out to Africa once more. His mission was to endeavour to settle once and for all the problem of the watersheds of Central Africa, and he was to pay particular attention to the area south of Lake Tanganyika. Livingstone, as all his intimates knew, believed that it was there he would come upon the true source. He was further charged with proceeding to Lake Tanganyika itself, so as to determine whether Burton's Rusizi River flowed into or out of the lake. The implication was that Burton's second thoughts about the Rusizi would probably turn out to be correct; it was expected that the river would be found to flow north and join Baker's Lake Albert; and thus Lake Victoria would be excluded from the pattern of the Nile. 'Speke,' as Professor Ingham says, 'was still on trial.'

Chapter 6

KUDOS AND BARAKA

WE TEND to think of Livingstone as an old man, but he was only fifty-two when he set out upon his last journey in 1865, and now, more than ever, he had that quality which the Arabs describe as *baraka*. In the most improbable circumstances he had the power of enhancing life and making it appear better than it was before. His mere presence seems to have conferred a blessing on everyone who met him; even the Arab slavers felt it and helped him when they could.

It was perfectly true that his Zambezi expedition [1] had been a disaster for his companions; even those who had survived had been pushed beyond all reasonable limits and had often found him self-willed and impatient of any weakness. Livingstone was never at his best when he was travelling with other white men, since he forced his own incredibly high standards upon them. But in 1865 he was on his own again, and no one had to suffer but himself. Moreover that extraordinary concentration upon Africa had not diminished in the least. The others who went there might lose faith and become confused in quarrels amongst themselves, he never. Africa by now had become an essential part of his existence, he lived for Africa, and it is only when this is understood that one can find some purpose in the apparent aimlessness of his wanderings—the 'sublime obstinacy' with which he kept on and on when there appeared to be no point in his continuing any more. The other explorers proceed, as it were, in a straight line on their African journeys, they set forth with some specific

[1] From 1858 to 1864 Livingstone had ascended the Zambezi River to the Victoria Falls and had discovered Lake Nyasa.

purpose, some definite object in mind, and when they have accomplished their missions their one desire is to return home. But Livingstone's mission begins and ends in Africa. He travels in circles. He dwells with the Africans themselves, eating their food, sleeping in their huts, and, without losing his own identity, he makes their life his own. No one understood the African Negroes and the fearful hardships to which they were subjected better than he did. Only he could have written: 'The strangest disease I have seen in this country seems really to be broken-heartedness, and it attacks free men who have been captured and made slaves.' In those few words he came to the root of the matter and they may have been just as effective as all the evidence of the atrocities and all the humanitarian outpourings that were then being broadcast from the pulpit, the House of Commons and the Anti-Slavery Society in England.

One might perhaps find some parallel between this life and the career of Doctor Schweitzer in Lambaréné at the present time, except that Livingstone was a traveller and a nomad: he had to keep on—and how clearly one sees that calm and rugged figure, with the flapped cap on his head, his walking stick in his hand, marching through the bush—because he was one of those people who cannot bear not to look over the other side of the next hill. Then too, one must remember how complete and steady men's convictions were in Victorian times. The doubts and uncertainties that have overtaken life in the twentieth century through two world wars and a plethora of political and scientific inventions, were unthinkable then. Livingstone's faith in God was absolute, and since he felt instinctively that his true approach to God was in Africa, it seems possible that he went to meet his death there rather more gladly, more spiritually content, than he would have done in any other place.

And so we can hardly think that he was serious when he said in 1865 that he did not really wish to return to Africa and would have preferred to remain on at home. Even if Murchison had not asked him to make one more effort to clear up the question of the Nile, even if the slave-trade had not existed, his twenty-two years in Africa must have drawn him back. There was so much work there still to be done. When Livingstone had first arrived in Africa in the eighteen-forties the interior of the continent had been an enormous unknown void reaching from the Kalahari Desert almost as far north as Timbuktu. He himself had done as much as and perhaps more than any other man to explore that void, but still there remained a thousand problems unresolved, including the greatest and oldest problem of all, the mystery of the Nile. Through the years of his great journeys Livingstone had developed more and more from the medical missionary into the explorer. He had come to believe that his real work in Africa was not so much in the saving of individual human souls as in the suppression of the slave-trade and in the opening up of the country so that Christianity and civilization could follow in his wake.

In 1865 there were no really urgent duties to hold him in Britain; he had no home or parish there, he had left the London Missionary Society (though he remained on the best of terms with it), and his wife had died three years before in Africa. Robert, his eldest son, was also dead; he had been impressed at Boston into the Northern forces in the American Civil War and had succumbed to wounds at the age of 18 in a prisoners' camp at Salisbury, North Carolina. As for the other children, they were being well cared for by their trustees in England.

Livingstone's books had made him the most famous of all African explorers, but he cared nothing for fame or the life of a public personality in England. His royalties had brought him in enough money to be as independent as he wished to be on his own spartan scale of living; and now there was this stimulating invitation from the Royal Geographical Society which would allow him to travel in the best of circumstances and to carry on with the work to which he had given his life; to strike one more blow against slavery and to resolve finally the great enigma of the lake and river system in the centre of the continent.

Like Burton before him Livingstone was coming round to the view that the true solution of the Nile had already been propounded by Herodotus and the ancient geographers, if not by the Old Testament itself. He was fascinated by Herodotus's description of the Nile springing from fountains of bottomless depth at the foot of high mountains somewhere in the centre of Africa. In reality this last journey of Livingstone's was a half-mystical attempt to re-discover those fountains, to find a unity with the past, a divine pattern in the geography of the river. This was to be the final achievement of his life. Of course he had to go.

Physically he appears to have been strong enough to undertake the journey. His health had not been seriously impaired by his previous work in Africa, and in any case he had been rested by a year in England. His shoulder, which had been crushed by a lion some twenty years before and had never properly set, still troubled him from time to time, but this was not a grave impediment. It may be worth while here, however, to recount in Livingstone's own words the circumstances of this accident, since it was of so much importance at the end of his life:

'. . . I heard a shout. Starting, and looking half round, I saw the lion just in the act of springing upon me. I was upon a little height; he caught my shoulder as he sprang, and we both came to the ground below together. Growling horribly close to my ear, he shook me as a terrier does a rat. The shock produced a stupor similar to that which seems to be felt by a mouse after the first shake of a cat. It caused a sort of dreaminess in which there was no sense of pain nor feeling terror, though quite conscious of all that was happening. It was like what patients partially under the influence of chloroform describe, who see all the operation, but feel not the knife. This singular condition was not the result of any mental process. The shake annihilated fear, and allowed no sense of horror in looking round at the beast. This peculiar state is probably produced in all animals killed by the carnivora; and if so, is a merciful provision by our benevolent creator for lessening the pain of death.'

The words have almost a valedictory sound.

But in 1865 there was no such shadow over the years ahead. All was confidence and hope in the new journey that

was about to start. Everyone wished him well. His attack
on the Portuguese for permitting slave-driving to continue
in their African territories had been an embarrassment to
the British government, but that had not prevented the
Prime Minister from inquiring if there was any way in
which he could serve Livingstone. And Murchison had
written: 'As to *your future* I am anxious to know what
your own wish is as respects a renewal of African exploration . . .' Did he wish to proceed by way of the Rovuma River and round the south end of Lake Tanganyika
and perhaps reach the sources of the White Nile? Such a
journey would enable him to settle 'all the great disputes
now pending'. But there was no obligation for Livingstone
to go; another man could be found to lead the expedition,
perhaps John Kirk who had been with him on the Zambezi?

Livingstone replied that he himself had been contemplat-
ing a new expedition of the very kind that Murchison suggested. '. . . If I can get a few hearty companions,' he wrote,
'I shall enjoy myself, and feel that I am doing my duty. As
soon as my book [his *Narrative of an Expedition to the
Zambesi*] is out, I shall start.'

He invited Kirk to accompany him but Kirk was about
to marry, and no doubt he felt that for the moment he had
had enough of Livingstone's formidable campaigning. Livingstone bore him no grudge at all, and instead busied himself in getting Kirk the desirable post of Surgeon and Vice-
Consul at the British Agency at Zanzibar. And so it was
resolved that Livingstone should go alone.

The Foreign Office came forward with the not overwhelmingly generous gift of £500 for the expedition
(though later they provided an additional £1,000), the
Society produced another £500, and Livingstone and his
friends found the rest. The explorer was appointed 'Consul
for Central Africa' without salary, and in August 1865 he
sailed from Folkestone. He travelled via Paris (where he
dropped off his daughter Agnes at school), Cairo and
Bombay, and at the end of January 1866 he arrived at Zanzibar.

Not a great deal had happened in Zanzibar since Burton's time. The Sultan, Seyyid Majid bin Said, had survived a revolt led by his brother Barghash and the island was being gradually drawn into the network of Western commerce and politics. Now there were half a dozen foreign consulates on the seafront, and many of the Arab and Indian merchants were growing rich. It was no longer a great event when the town drum was beaten to announce the approach of an ocean-going ship (one beat for a ship from the north and two for a ship from the south); the island was constantly visited by merchantmen and men-of-war from almost all the European powers. The traffic in slaves had grown if anything still heavier; it was now estimated that between 80,000 and 100,000 were brought down from the interior every year, and although none were supposed to go beyond the Sultan's dominions there was no real check on the dhows that sailed back to Arabia and the East in June when the south-west monsoon began to blow.

'It is the old, old way of living,' Livingstone wrote, 'eating, drinking, sleeping; sleeping, drinking, eating, slave-dhows coming and slave-dhows going away; bad smells . . . it might be called Stinkibar rather than Zanzibar. . . . On visiting the slave market I found about 300 slaves exposed for sale. . . . All who have grown up seem ashamed at being hawked about for sale. The teeth are examined, the cloth lifted to examine the lower limbs, and a stick thrown for a slave to bring, and thus exhibit his paces. Some are dragged through the crowd by hand, and the price called out incessantly; most of the purchasers were Northern Arabs and Persians.'

However the Sultan, upon whom Livingstone called, was both amiable and helpful: he gave him a *firman* to the sheikhs in the interior and loaned him a large square house that still stands on the sea wall on the outskirts of the town. It was conveniently placed for dropping stores directly down into boats in the harbour below. Kirk had also arrived to take up his new job at the Agency, and was very ready to assist in organizing the expedition.

There was a complex relationship between these two. Although Kirk was so much younger than Livingstone their backgrounds were very similar; Kirk too had come from a religious household in Scotland, he too had taken his degree in medicine and had come abroad to satisfy a craving for adventure, at first in the Crimea and then in Africa. Livingstone had taken him on the Zambezi expedition in 1858 as physician and naturalist and they had established the kind of intimacy that can develop only through a long series of shared experiences on a dangerous journey. In the end Kirk had been invalided home but they had had five years or more together in Africa, and the young man had been at Livingstone's side when he discovered Lake Nyasa. As a naturalist Kirk had shown exceptional promise and had brought home a valuable collection of African plants, some of which were entirely new to science. As a companion in adversity he had been admirable, perhaps better than any of the others, for he had just those qualities that make an ideal chief-of-staff—a shrewdness and common sense in dealing with others which Livingstone himself so often lacked. There had been differences of course. At times on the Zambezi Kirk had thought that his leader was out of his mind, and later on he had been deeply hurt when he believed (probably erroneously) that Livingstone had reported adversely upon him to the Foreign Office. Kirk had been too close to Livingstone to hero-worship him blindly. He had written to a friend, 'He [Livingstone] must have saved a good deal of money, not that I think that he sets much value on that. He would give all for a C.B. or better a K.C.B., and there will be a push made in some quarters to get it him.' This was unfriendly and yet it was probably true (even though Livingstone in the end never received any honour from the government); and there were other failings—Livingstone's whitewashing of his own brother's far from heroic behaviour on the Zambezi, for example, about which Kirk had written home very tartly at the time.

But all this was over and done with, and in any case there was no doubt whatever that Kirk's fundamental loyalty to his old leader was quite unshakable. So now they were together again for a few weeks in Zanzibar while Livingstone was assembling his caravan, and it was arranged that Kirk should act as the expedition's representative in the island; at a later stage he was to send on porters and supplies to await Livingstone's arrival at Ujiji on Lake Tanganyika.

This was a modest expedition compared with the usual thing, but Livingstone thought it lavish; he had brought a number of sepoys with him from Bombay and he now recruited others in Zanzibar, including three boys who had marched with Speke and Grant, bringing the total number in the caravan to sixty. In addition there was a small train of camels, buffaloes, mules and donkeys which were to serve as baggage animals.

Livingstone's plan was to keep well south of the usual caravan routes and to strike directly inland towards the unexplored country south of Lake Tanganyika; and with that object in view he landed in March 1866 at the mouth of the Rovuma River, which now divides Tanganyika from Portuguese East Africa. There then began that incredible series of wanderings which were to continue for seven years and to end in a failure which was also the triumph of a man's unconquerable mind.

Never can there have been a journey which was founded upon so many misassumptions as this one. It was a search for the source of a river in a region where it did not exist; it was an anti-slavery expedition that had no power whatever to put down slavery; it was the march of a man who believed that he alone, unarmed and unsupported, could pass through Africa, and that was almost impossible. But none of this made any difference. Through a series of paradoxes all comes right in the end; the march goes on— but only because the Arab slavers take care of the sick and lonely man in the wilderness. Slavery is dealt a blow from which it never recovers—not because Livingstone was able to raise a hand against it, but because he was the helpless witness of a massacre. Even the mystery of the Nile is resolved—not by Livingstone himself but because he inspired another man to go off in another direction. And to Livingstone no doubt all this was as it should have been: it was the will of God.

It it astonishing that he did not die much sooner. Quite

early in his march he lost nearly all his men and animals, and, what was just as disastrous, he lost his medicine chest as well. At the end of a year he struggled up to the southern end of Lake Tanganyika, where the Arab slavers took care of him, though at the same time they made it almost impossible for him to go on; here, as in the Sudan, they had aroused bitter hatred among the tribes, and porters were unobtainable. Yet he did manage to go on, striking out west to the Lualaba River, then south to Lake Bangweolo which no white man had ever seen before, then north again to Lake Tanganyika. In March 1869, three years after leaving the coast, he arrived at Ujiji, almost toothless and half dead with malaria and other illnesses, 'a ruckle of bones', only to find that the stores that Kirk had sent had been looted on the route up-country and hardly anything of use remained. There was no quinine and, what was almost worse, no mail. The absence of news from the outside world seems to have afflicted the explorers almost more than any other hardship. In the hope of finding mail at some outlandish spot they would rouse themselves from their illnesses and march on for weeks or even months on end; and here the deprivation was even worse since the Arab traders refused to carry Livingstone's own letters down to the coast. He had written forty-two of them, and the Arabs knew all too well that the package contained a full account of the atrocities they were committing in the interior.

So then there was nothing to be done but go on again without medicine and without supplies. Once more he headed west for the Lualaba, for he had begun to believe that it was the Nile. Now the Lualaba has nothing to do with the Nile; it is, in fact, the upper Congo River that flows north in a great westward-bending arc to the Atlantic Ocean—but Livingstone had no means of discovering this. His outward journey came to a fearful halt one morning at Nyangwe when he saw the Arab traders there open up with their rifles at point-blank range on the natives in the village.

Livingstone had enjoyed this place; he liked to watch the people coming into market, sometimes as many as three thousand of them, to barter their chickens and fruit, and the broad river flowing by into the jungle. His description of what happened on the morning of July 15, 1871, reveals, as no other incident ever has, the depths of the tragedy that occurred to the Central African Negroes when the outside world burst in upon them hardly as much as three generations ago. The Dugumbe referred to was one of the better established and therefore more restrained traders—but a slaver nonetheless—and Tagamoio who appears in the last paragraph more nearly represents the Arabs and their terrorist methods in Central Africa at the time.

'It was,' Livingstone says, 'a hot, sultry day, and when I went into the market I saw Adie and Manilla, and three of the men who had lately come with Dugumbe. I was surprised to see the three with their guns, and felt inclined to reprove them, as one of my men did, for bringing weapons into the market, but I attributed it to their ignorance, and, it being very hot, I was walking away to go out of the market, when I saw one of the fellows haggling about a fowl, and seizing hold of it. Before I got thirty yards out, the discharge of two guns in the middle of the crowd told me that slaughter had begun; the crowds dashed off from the place, and threw down their wares in confusion, and ran. At the same time that the three opened fire on the mass of people near the upper end of the market-place volleys were discharged from a party down near the creek on the panic-stricken women, who dashed at the canoes. These, some fifty or more, were jammed in the creek and the men forgot their paddles in the terror that seized all. The canoes were not to be got out, for the creek was too small for so many: men and women, wounded by balls, poured into them, and leaped and scrambled into the water shrieking. A long line of heads in the river showed that great numbers struck out for an island a full mile off: in going towards it they had to put the left shoulder to a current of about two miles an hour: if they had struck away diagonally to the opposite bank, the current would have aided them, and, though nearly three miles off, some would have gained land: as it was, the heads above water showed the long lines of those that would inevitably perish.

'Shot after shot continued to be fired on the helpless and perishing. Some of the long line of heads disappeared quietly: whilst other poor creatures threw their arms high, as if appealing to the great Father above, and sank. One canoe took in as many as it could hold, and all paddled with hands and arms; three canoes, got out in haste, picked up sinking friends, till all went down together, and disappeared. One man, in a long canoe, which could have held forty or fifty, had clearly lost his head; he had been out in the stream before the massacre began, and now paddled up the river nowhere, and never looked to the drowning.

'By-and-by all the heads disappeared; some had turned down-stream towards the bank, and escaped. Dugumbe put people into one of the deserted vessels to save those in the water and saved twenty-one, but one woman refused to be taken on board from thinking that she was to be made a slave of; she preferred the chance of life by swimming, to the lot of a slave; the Bagenya women are expert in the water, as they are accustomed to dive for oysters, and those who went downstream may have escaped, but the Arabs themselves estimated the loss of life at between 330 and 400 souls. The shooting-party near the canoe were so reckless, they killed two of their own people; and a Banyamwezi follower, who got into a deserted canoe to plunder, fell into the water, went down, then came up again, and down to rise no more.

'My impulse was to pistol the murderers, but Dugumbe protested against my getting into a blood-feud, and I was thankful afterwards that I took his advice. Two wretched Moslems asserted "that the firing was done by the people of the English"; I asked one of them why he lied so, and he could utter no excuse: no other falsehood came to his aid as he stood abashed before me, and so telling him not to tell palpable falsehoods, I left him gaping.

'After the horrible affair in the water, the party of Tagamoio, who was the chief perpetrator, continued to fire on the people there and fire their villages. As I write I hear the loud wails on the left bank over those who are slain, ignorant of their many friends who are now in the depths of the Lualaba. Oh, let Thy kingdom come! No one will ever know the exact loss on this bright sultry summer morning. It gave me the impression of being in Hell.'

After this there was no hope of obtaining boats or men to follow the course of the river.

Sickened by what he had seen and now seriously broken in health Livingstone struggled back to Ujiji unable for the moment to accomplish any more. There was little except his faith to keep him going. He had read the Bible four times on this second journey to the Lualaba, but now on his return to Ujiji after an absence of two years, he was practically reduced to begging from the Arabs in order to keep alive: and thus it was that Stanley found him when he came marching into Ujiji on November 10, 1871.

'. . . When my spirits were at their lowest ebb,' Livingstone wrote, 'the good Samaritan was close at hand, for one morning Susi came running at the top of his speed and gasped out, "An Englishman! I see him!" and off he darted to meet him. The American flag at the head of the caravan told of the nationality of the stranger. Bales of goods, baths of tin, huge kettles, cooking-pots, tents, etc., made me think, "This must be a luxurious traveller, and not one at his wits' end like me."'

Stanley's famous description of the meeting is more lively:

'Selim said to me, "I see the Doctor, sir. Oh, what an old man! He has got a white beard!" And I—what would I not have given for a bit of friendly wilderness, where, unseen, I might vent my joy in some mad freak, such as idiotically biting my hand, turning a somersault, or slashing at trees, in order to allay those exciting feelings that were well-nigh uncontrollable. My heart beats fast, but I must not let my face betray my emotions, lest it shall detract from the dignity of a white man appearing under such extraordinary circumstances.

'So I did that which I thought was most dignified. I pushed back the crowds, and, passing from the rear, walked down a living avenue of people, until I came in front of the semicircle of Arabs, before which stood "the white man with the grey beard". As I advanced slowly towards him I noticed he was pale, looked wearied, had grey whiskers and moustache, wore a bluish cap with a faded gold band around it, had on a red-sleeved waistcoat, and a pair of grey tweed trousers. I would have run to him, only I was a coward in the presence of such a mob—would have embraced him, but that I did not know how he would receive me. So I did what moral cowardice and false pride suggested was the best thing—walked deliberately up to him, took off my hat, and said, "Dr. Livingstone, I presume?" "Yes," he said, with a kind smile, lifting his cap slightly.

'I replaced my hat on my head, and he replaced his cap, and we both grasped hands, and then I said aloud: "I thank God, Doctor, I have been permitted to see you."

'He answered, "I feel thankful that I am here to welcome you." '

This then is the story of an incident which has been more frequently recalled than any other single event in African exploration. And yet a strange air of unreality remains. One is bound to wonder why it should have taken so long for help to arrive. For nearly five years now Livingstone's whereabouts had been a perennial mystery. At one time, as far back as 1868, he had been thought dead: the porters who had deserted him announced on their return to the coast that he had been killed on the shores of Lake Nyasa (which was a convenient way of explaining their desertion), and Murchison had published this news in a letter to *The Times*. But Murchison himself had not entirely believed it, and the Royal Geographical Society had sent out an expedition to discover the truth. This expedition had scarcely got under way when word reached the coast that the explorer was still alive, and soon afterwards letters were received in Zanzibar from Livingstone himself. Upon this the expedition had turned back. Thereafter a strange apathy about the explorer appears to have overtaken both officials and public alike.

From time to time vague inquiries are made, Kirk sends

up his supplies from Zanzibar but without any real assurance they will ever reach their destination; Baker keeps a general lookout from Bunyoro far away in the north; and in the Royal Geographical Society in London there are speculative discussions as to just what direction the explorer might have taken in the last twelve months or so. But for a long time no one actually makes a move to go to the assistance of the lost man. Burton, no great admirer of missionaries, affected a sardonic indifference. He wrote to a friend, when at last the hunt for Livingstone began, 'rather *infra dig.* to discover a mish'. In the twentieth century, of course, radio and aircraft have entirely altered the nature of exploration, and it requires a slight effort to remember that only fifty years ago it was nothing unusual for a ship at sea or a traveller in a distant land to be lost sight of for many months at a time; but even so it is strange that Livingstone's silence was received with so much complacency. And stranger still that it was a man like Stanley who should have come to the rescue. Even Stanley had not precisely hurried to Ujiji. Long before—actually in 1869—his employer James Gordon Bennett of the *New York Herald* had summoned him to an interview at the Grand Hotel in Paris and had said: 'I want you to attend the opening of the Suez Canal and then proceed up the Nile. Send us detailed descriptions of everything likely to interest American tourists. Then go to Jerusalem, Constantinople, the Crimea, the Caspian Sea, through Persia as far as India. After that you can start looking round for Livingstone. If he is dead bring back every possible proof of his death.'

Stanley, the most assiduous foreign correspondent who ever lived, had accomplished this programme in fourteen months. Having attended the Canal opening he had gone up the Nile and interviewed Baker's engineer, Higginbotham; he had inspected the battlefields of the Crimea and visited Persepolis in Persia, where he carved his name on the ruins; he had described the awful poverty of India and now he had arrived at Ujiji.

And who was Stanley? He was full of surprises. He was a man whose real name was not Stanley at all, but Rowlands, a Welshman who was an American, a soldier who was a sailor, and now a journalist who was leading a successful expedition into the centre of Africa. Soon the world was to know all about his picaresque background: the awful Dickensian childhood in a workhouse in Wales, his arrival as a cabin-boy at New Orleans where he took the name and nationality of a kindly American who adopted him as a son, his soldiering in the Civil War, at first for the South and then for the North, his rejection by his squalid mother on his return to England, his adventures in the American navy and in General Hancock's campaign against the Red Indians, and latterly as a journalist in the British campaign against the Emperor in Abyssinia. This was the career of a man of iron, an adventurer who was every bit as hard and ruthless as the world in which he had lived. Professor Coupland remarks pungently: 'No other famous man of his time got so high from a start so low. No one who can understand him forgets that. He never forgot it himself.'

Gaetano Casati, the Italian explorer who knew Stanley much later in life, wrote this of him: 'Stanley is a man remarkable for strength of character, resolution, promptness of thought and iron will. Jealous of his own authority, he does not tolerate exterior influences, nor ask advice. Difficulties do not deter him, disasters do not dismay him. With an extraordinary readiness of mind he improvises means, and draws himself out of a difficulty; absolute and sincere in the execution of his duty, he is not always prudent, or free from hasty or erroneous judgements. Irresolution or hesitation irritates him, disturbing his accustomed gravity: his countenance being usually serious. Reserved, laconic, and not very sociable, he does not awaken sympathy; but on closer acquaintance he is found very agreeable, from the frankness of his manner, his brilliant conversation and his gentlemanly courtesy.'

This was Stanley when he had established himself in the world. At Ujiji, however, he was only thirty years of age and still on the threshold of his success; it was the hardness, the quickness and the egocentricity in him that were uppermost. He most distinctly lacked *baraka*. In all the

world no two men could have differed so much from one
another as Livingstone and Stanley, nor could there have
been two men who, for the moment, were so beholden to
one another. Livingstone needed medicine, supplies and
news of the outside world, and his young visitor had them all.
Stanley needed fame—the 'kudos' (it was a word he was
fond of using) of having found this celebrated man, and
in fact he received a great deal more. His brief companionship with Livingstone was, Professor Coupland says,
'the supreme experience of his life. He had come close to
moral greatness, and he was startled, captivated, subjected
by it.'

At the outset of his journey Livingstone had been for
Stanley another 'assignment', another 'story', which, if
successfully reported, would help him on with his journalistic career. At Zanzibar he had behaved very much as a
newspaperman in search of a scoop. He had scented at
once the opposition of the African professionals amongst
the European officials, especially in the English colony,
which he regarded as stiff and effete, and especially Kirk.
He stayed with the American Consul, F. R. Webb, a naval
captain, and kept his plans secret from Kirk, merely giving
it out that he had come to Africa to explore some of the
coastal river districts in the hope of finding good copy for
his paper there. Perhaps Kirk found him bumptious, and
Kirk from Stanley's point of view was simply another official who feared, and therefore was hostile to, the Press.
When Stanley asked casually one day if Livingstone would
receive him should he chance to cross the explorer's path
in the interior, Kirk answered briefly that he thought Livingstone would not like it at all; he had an aversion to
publicity. This little exchange possibly explains Stanley's
cautiousness with Livingstone when he first arrived at
Ujiji. But at Zanzibar he had not been deterred by it in the
least, and he had gone about his plans very methodically.
He had engaged Bombay as his factotum, and since he
had plenty of money to spend he had bought the best of
stores and had hired the best of porters at the highest
rates. His eight months' march from the coast to Ujiji
was no bad achievement at all, considering that he had

gone down with malaria on the way, had encountered a war
between the Arab dealers and the African tribes at Tabora
and had actually taken part in the fighting himself. Two
white assistants he had engaged, Farquhar and Shaw, had
both died. And now at the journey's end there was this
comforting reception from Livingstone, this revelation of
a charitable and fascinating mind. During the long conversation that now began between the two men Livingstone
complained that Kirk had sent him only the worst of porters, men who were slaves and thieves. Stanley stored that
up for future use. Indeed, he stored up every grain of wisdom and information that Livingstone let fall, and while
Livingstone's health rapidly improved, the two fell into a
leader-and-follower relationship which was very agreeable
to them both. Soon it seemed an excellent plan that they
should make a journey together, and what better than to
go up to the head of Lake Tanganyika and settle the question of the Rusizi River? They were away three weeks on
this trip, and when Livingstone discovered that Burton
was wrong—the Rusizi flowed into and not out of the lake—
he returned more strongly than ever to his theory that the
Lualaba was the Nile. To go back to the Lualaba, however,
meant that he had to have further stores and porters, and
these, he believed, could be obtained only in Tabora, some
300 miles away. The two men walked there from Ujiji at
the end of 1871.

At Tabora few stores and no porters were to be found—
another point against Kirk—and Stanley promised to make
good the deficiency himself. It never seems to have occurred to Livingstone for an instant that he might return
to Zanzibar and civilization—he said he would not come
until his work was finished—and at the end of a month
Stanley set off for the coast alone. He left behind all he
could spare from his own supplies, and it was arranged
that Livingstone should stay on in Tabora until Stanley
could get a gang of porters up to him from the coast. In
the remarkably quick time of 54 days Stanley reached
Zanzibar carrying with him more treasure than any slave
and ivory trader had ever yet been able to get out of
Africa: all Livingstone's journals, his own notes, which

shortly were to blossom forth in his dispatches to the *New York Herald* and his first African book, *How I Found Livingstone*, and in addition to all this, a letter which Livingstone had specially written for his paper. It was in this letter that Livingstone wrote *à propos* the massacre at Nyangwe: 'If my disclosures regarding the terrible Ujijian slavery should lead to the suppression of the East Coast slave-trade, I shall regard that as a greater matter by far than the discovery of all the Nile sources together.' In this at least he was to have his wish.

Stanley had been just in time. On his way down to Bagamoyo he met a new expedition which the Royal Geographical Society had at last sent out from England to find news of the lost man, and he was able to assure them that their help was no longer needed: and so it was Stanley who, in May 1872, caused a sensation throughout the world with his description of the Ujiji meeting and of all that had since followed. He went on to a tremendous reception in England—a letter and diamond-studded snuff-box from the Queen, a medal from the Royal Geographical Society, and a round of banquets and public meetings. On the surface all this was very gratifying, but it was soon evident that the British were anything but pleased with Stanley's exploit. They did not like the idea of their greatest explorer being rescued by what was regarded as a journalistic stunt,[1] they did not like the fact that Stanley was an American citizen, and they did not much care for Stanley himself. This, at any rate, was Stanley's appreciation of the situation, and he bitterly resented it. Indeed, he had genuine grounds for complaint here—some of the rival newspapers were even referring to his journey as a hoax—and no doubt the criticism would have died down had he not, unwisely and unnecessarily, attacked Kirk. He declared that Kirk had 'let Livingstone down' by not bestirring himself more in sending up reinforcements from the coast as he had promised to do; and Stanley repeated these charges not once but several times, and not in private but in the course of public addresses, and even in Kirk's own part of the

[1] Florence Nightingale, neatly but not very sensibly, described *How I Found Livingstone* as 'the worst possible book on the best possible subject'.

country. Kirk, as an official, could not reply, but he had friends who were very ready to defend him against this journalistic outsider; and if Kirk never entirely cleared his name in this matter, Stanley also was much harmed. He created enemies who knew how to renew the attack when their chance came later on. Kirk's own reactions in Zanzibar were indignant, but private. He wrote to his friends giving the facts as he saw them, and he said to Oswell Livingstone who had come out on a Royal Geographical Society expedition: 'Stanley will make his fortune out of your father.' When Livingstone came to hear of this he made the comment, 'He [Stanley] is heartily welcome, for it is a great deal more than I could ever make out of myself.' At the same time he wrote to Kirk and soon the misunderstanding between them was explained and privately, if not publicly, forgotten.

Livingstone meanwhile was filling out the lonely months in Tabora. He was not short of stores; with the addition of those that Stanley had left him he had enough to carry on for four years. But now only Susi and Chuma and one or two other boys who had followed him from the beginning remained in his service, and they were quite inadequate for the porterage of a long journey. Thus he had to wait until the men Stanley had promised him came up from the coast. He waited five months in all, and in that time hardly an echo reached him of the acclaim that was gathering round his name in the outside world. He held his small Bible classes under the mango trees, he read Baker's *Albert N'yanza*, he prayed, he went for walks, he wrote his journal, he thought, he waited. The *tembe* in which he lived was a lonely spot, somewhat on the outskirts of the Arab settlement, and was set too low down in the scrub to command a view of the surrounding countryside. Even now there is a feeling of solitude and claustrophobia about the place. It was the usual sort of Arab trader's house, a flat earthen roof that was never absolutely proof against the rain, a 'reception room', a room for sleeping and eating, an inner courtyard where the cattle and other livestock were herded at night, and quarters for the Africans. The floors were of earth tramped down by the bare feet of the household servants passing in and out.

These were the last remotely civilized surroundings that Livingstone was to know. He was now 59, and though he had rallied somewhat in Stanley's company his health was undermined beyond all real hope of recovery. Yet if he felt that he was nearing death there is little in his journals to show it: he was filled with hope about his theory of the Nile and perhaps by now in his loneliness the river had begun to assume for him a religious significance. This last effort was to be more than a journey to the lost fountains. It was to be a revelation and a justification of everything he had lived and prayed for, a proof of himself and of his humble faith in God. However shaken he was by fever— and there must have been days when he was delirious and unable to move from his bed—there was at least no weakening in the extraordinary steadiness of his mind. The notes and letters he sent down to the coast from time to time were written in a firm and flowing hand. Often they dealt with very practical details. If, he writes, a chronometer can be lent him by the Navy without detriment to the service it will be of very signal benefit to his exploration. He signs himself, 'David Livingstone, H. M. Consul, Inner Africa'.

At the same time he kept dreaming of the day when he would return home: he wrote to a friend asking him to look out for rooms on Regent's Park in London which he could share with his daughter Agnes.

In August 1872 the fifty-seven porters sent by Stanley finally arrived, and within a few days Livingstone led his caravan out into the bush. He was very clear about his direction, for by now he had made up his mind that the source of the Nile would prove to be a stream running into Lake Bangweolo, which he had discovered four years before; and so he marched slightly south of west, and, having reached the shores of Lake Tanganyika about its centre, he turned directly south. By the end of April 1873, eight months after leaving Tabora, he was working round the south of Lake Bangweolo, still hoping to come on some feeder stream which would flow on through the lake into the Lualaba and perhaps join Baker's Albert Nyanza far away to the north in Uganda. He had some uneasy doubts that just possibly the Lualaba might turn out to be the Congo and not the Nile; but he hated that idea and turned away from it. He had fixed his heart upon the Nile.

It was dreadful country. The little column waded about through an interminable swamp and close to the village of a chieftain named Chitambo Livingstone became so weak he had to be carried in a litter. In the early hours of May 1, 1873, his boys came into his hut and found him dead. He was kneeling across his bed in prayer.

However often the story is told of Susi's and Chuma's journey to the coast with Livingstone's body it remains incredible, and perhaps it was a miracle of a kind, since such devotion among primitive and uneducated men can hardly have been inspired by any ordinary emotion. They cut out the heart and viscera, and dried the body in the sun for a fortnight. It was then wrapped in calico and placed in a cylinder of bark taken from a tree, and this in turn was sewn into a sheet of sailcloth and lashed to a pole so that it could be carried by two men. In the middle of May, Susi, Chuma and sixty odd men who had remained faithful to the end, set out for Zanzibar. Well over a thousand miles divided them from the Indian Ocean, and it was not really feasible that such a strange burden could be carried over that distance in the heart of Africa where so many tribes were out to despoil every wayfarer who came by. Nevertheless the journey was accomplished in eleven months. During that time two more expeditions set out from England in search of Livingstone, one of them intending to strike inland from the west coast of Africa, and the other from the east coast. Susi and Chuma met the east coast party led by the naval officer, Lovett Cameron, when they reached Tabora in October 1873. Cameron then continued on to Ujiji (where he salvaged a quantity of Livingstone's papers) and eventually emerged on the Atlantic coast two years later. Susi and Chuma meanwhile went on to the Indian Ocean, and when they walked into Bagamoyo on February 15, 1874, H.M.S. *Vulture* was waiting to take the body across to Zanzibar. Here for a time it was placed in Hamerton's old house on the seafront, which was still the British Consulate, awaiting transshipment to England. There could be no doubt about the dead man's identity; when a surgeon came to open the improvised coffin the mark of the old lion wound on the shoulder was plainly visible.

A special train was sent to Southhampton to take Livingstone on his last journey to Westminster Abbey on April 18, 1874, and on that day England went into mourning.

In London the body had remained overnight in the Map Room of the Royal Geographical Society in Savile Row, and when the cortège set out in the morning the streets were lined with silent crowds. Admission to the Abbey could be obtained only by ticket and the building was crammed. Stanley, Grant and Kirk were among the pallbearers who carried the body to the grave.

Today if one enters the Abbey by the main door and continues down the nave one comes first upon the tomb of the Unknown Soldier and then, a little beyond it, Livingstone's grave, with its epitaph inscribed in brass lettering on the grey stone. It reads, 'Brought by faithful hands over land and sea here rests David Livingstone, missionary, traveller, philanthropist, born March 19, 1813 at Blantyre, Lanarkshire, died May 1, 1873 at Chitambo's village, Ulala.

'For 30 years his life was spent in an unwearied effort to evangelize the native races, to explore the undiscovered secrets, to abolish the desolating slave trade, of Central Africa, where with his last words he wrote: "All I can add in my solitude is may Heaven's rich blessing come down on everyone, American, English or Turk, who will help to heal this open sore of the world." '

Even before he wrote those words Livingstone's great power over men's minds had reached out from Central Africa. The sources of the Nile eluded him at the end, but his description of the massacre at Nyangwe had raised a storm of indignation which had forced the Sultan of Zanzibar to close the slave market on the island forever.

Chapter 7

LE BRISEUR D'OBSTACLES

A CURIOUS COMBINATION of hatred and love drew the explorers back to Africa. They were like men who make a life at sea; having once committed themselves to its hazards they feel impelled to go back again and again even if Africa kills them. At one time or another most of them rail against the country and its inhabitants, declaring them to be ugly, brutal, scheming, debauched and finally hopeless. It is extraordinary in the accounts of their journeys how seldom they are touched by the beauty or the grandeur of the landscape, the tremendous plains of the central plateau with the blue mountains in the distance and the herds of wild animals roaming there 'to the explorers it is all basically hostile, incomplete, not to be regarded with an aesthetic eye until it is reformed and reduced to order by civilization and Christianity.

Dr. Schweinfurth, one of the calmest and most self-sufficient of explorers on the Upper Nile, remarks, 'The first sight of a throng of savages, suddenly presenting themselves in their naked nudity, is one from which no amount of familiarity can remove the strange impression; it takes abiding hold upon the memory, and makes the traveller recall anew the civilization he has left behind.'

In other words, there is here a sort of Rousseauesque attraction, a nostalgia for simplicity, which nevertheless is constantly being upset by the lonely traveller's remembrance of the comfortable, reassuring world at home.

Recoiling from the savagery of Africa, Schweinfurth returned to Europe. But he found he could not remain there; within a year or two Africa called him back. It was the same with all the others, whether they were missionaries like Livingstone, scholars like Burton, soldiers and collectors like Speke, or sportsmen like Baker.

All of them in their books claim that they are in Africa because they have a mission there; they want to resolve the geographical problems and they want to reform the country, to convert the untilled land into useful farms, to open up commerce and to lift the natives out of their animism and savagery into a higher way of life. And yet one cannot help feeling that there is still another reason for their journeys: a fundamental restlessness, a simple absorbing curiosity in everything that is strange and new. To satisfy that curiosity they are prepared to put up with anything, even the prospect of death itself.

Joseph Thomson, the young Scottish explorer who was the first to cross Kenya to the great lakes, was quite frank about this. Just before he died he wrote: 'I am doomed to be a wanderer. I am not an empire-builder. I am not a missionary. I am not truly a scientist. I merely want to return to Africa to continue my wanderings.' The others may not have approved of this at all, and yet this basic nomadism was certainly a part of all their natures and may even have been a governing factor in their lives.

Now Stanley does not fit into this scheme of things at all easily. He is a new kind of man in Africa, a modern man who at the same time has many of the attributes of a *condottiere* in Renaissance Italy. You might call him a businessman-explorer, not in the sense of his wanting to trade in Africa, but in the extremely logical, sensible and efficient way in which he went about the problem of setting up an expedition and getting it to the journey's end. It may have been ruthless but it was also expert, and one must never lose sight of the fact that he was very determined and very brave. Perhaps he resembles Speke more than any of the others, but not even Speke was as concentrated as Stanley was. Stanley was not in Africa to reform the people nor to build an empire, and he was not impelled by any real interest in such matters as anthropology, botany or geology. To put it bluntly, he was out to make a name for himself, and it must be judged as the supreme irony of African exploration that in the end he should turn out to be the greatest empire-builder and explorer of them all. He was even able to open up the field for the missionaries and the scientists rather more effectively than anyone who had gone before. A recent study of the explorer by Jean-Jacques Laufer has been well entitled *Stanley, Briseur d'Obstacles*.

Naturally this brusque and philistine irruption into Africa was not very endearing to an educated public in England who had been following the exploits of its own favourite explorers for years past; and the *condottiere* side of his nature made things worse. Here was a man, it was felt, who would take on any adventure for the sake of publicity and under any patronage, an interloper who had changed his nationality once and might do so again (as in point of fact Stanley did; he reverted later to his British citizenship). Baker and Gordon might serve foreign masters such as the Khedive in Egypt and the Manchus in China, but it was not quite the same thing; in the end, one believed that they would remain basically loyal to Britain. But with Stanley you never knew; if he worked for Mr. Gordon Bennett of the *New York Herald* he could just as easily go running off to someone else like the King of the Belgians and change his loyalties in the interests of his career.

All this was very unfair, but then Stanley was a man who attracted prejudice almost as strongly as Livingstone attracted love. His only course was to baffle his enemies with his achievements and this he resolutely proceeded to do. Fortunately he had no need of friends to put his case for him. He was the most readable of authors; his books have a pace and an excitement which not even the purple passages and the occasional pomposities can subdue, and the facts he had to give were incontrovertible facts based upon his own close and hard-won observation.

So now in 1874 he set about the arrangements for his new journey, which in many ways was his greatest, with a dispatch and far-sightedness that even Baker could hardly have equalled. He tells us that, on Livingstone's death, he decided to go back to Africa and complete his work; somehow or other he would finally elucidate the problem of the

Nile. The emphasis is on Livingstone, one notices; twelve years had now elapsed since Speke was in Africa, but Speke's reputation had not recovered with time, it had sunk almost to its lowest ebb. In Dr. Schweinfurth's book, *The Heart of Africa*, published in 1873, Speke's great Victoria Nyanza is obliterated from the map and replaced (much to Burton's satisfaction, no doubt) by five small lakes.

Stanley set himself three objectives: he planned to circumnavigate Lake Victoria and thus establish whether or not it was one great lake and whether or not the stream pouring out at Ripon Falls was its only outlet. Next he proposed to put Burton's theories to the ultimate test by sailing around Lake Tanganyika in the same way. Finally he planned to take up Livingstone's unfinished work on the Lualaba: he was resolved to get a boat on the river and follow it downstream wherever it led until he reached the mouth. In short, he was going to make a last settlement, not only of the Nile, but of the whole pattern of lakes and rivers in Central Africa.

As a first step towards this extraordinarily bold design he managed to get the *New York Herald* to combine with the London *Daily Telegraph* in financing him (a thing which they did handsomely) and then in England he settled down to reading every scrap of information about East and Central Africa he could find; he purchased, he says, 130 books. The companions he chose to take with him on the journey were distinctly unusual, in fact they were not companions at all, but rather hired assistants who came from working-class families and who knew nothing whatever about Africa. There were two young sons of a Kentish fisherman, Francis John Pocock and Edward Pocock, and a clerk named Frederick Barker who had happened to catch Stanley's eye at the Langham Hotel in London. All three were much younger than Stanley and were chosen, one fancies, for their toughness and sense of discipline—the sort of qualities that make a good sergeant in the army. None of them was in the least likely to come home and write books about his adventures or to dispute Stanley's views in the Royal Geographical Society. When five dogs

had been purchased the little party was complete and it
sailed for East Africa in August 1874.

The expedition that set out from Zanzibar early in the
following November was the largest and best equipped
explorer's caravan that had ever been seen in East Africa.
They had with them a forty-foot wooden boat, the *Lady
Alice,* which had been built in sections for porterage, eight
tons of stores and 356 men. It was an unwieldy procession
that stretched out for half a mile along the forest paths
and by the time Stanley got it on to the shores of Lake Victoria three and a half months later, Edward Pocock
was dead of typhus and a hundred men had been lost
through desertion, sickness and skirmishes with the local
tribes. Such was to be the pattern of all Stanley's marches:
the quick advance, the shooting down of any African
tribes that opposed him, the heavy loss of life among his
own men and the final attainment of the objective. For
anyone to accompany Stanley on an expedition in Africa
was rather like being in the *corps d'élite* of a successful
general—you triumphed and you died. Anything less like
Livingstone's journeys cannot be imagined.

They reached the south shore of Lake Victoria at a little
Arab village slightly to the west of Mwanza where Speke
sixteen years before had first seen the great stretch of water
and had indulged in his guess that it was the source of the
Nile. Stanley was not a guesser. He was here to find facts
and he at once assembled the *Lady Alice* on the shore.
Leaving the two surviving Englishmen and the bulk of his
expedition behind him, he set sail with a picked band of
eleven Africans on March 8, 1875. They travelled up the
eastern shore, and in three weeks' hard sailing and pad-
dling arrived at Speke's Ripon Falls. Presently a dignitary
in a red robe came forward to meet them with gifts of
bullocks and other presents; and on April 5, 1875, Stanley
was conducted into Mutesa's presence.

Great changes had taken place in Buganda since Speke's
day. Its population had risen to something like three millions, and the little kingdom stretched for about 150 miles
along the north-western shore of the lake. Mutesa was now
in his early forties, and Stanley describes him as 'a tall,

*East Africa as it was presumed to be following
Stanley's expedition of 1874–1877
(taken from a contemporary map)*

clean-faced, large-eyed, nervous-looking thin man', clad in
a tarbush, a black robe and a white shirt belted with gold.
He seemed to be completely at ease. He shook hands
warmly with his visitor, addressed him in fluent Swahili,
and invited him to take a seat on an iron stool. The capital, now moved to a different site nearby called Rubaga,
was a considerable settlement that covered the hills for
several miles around, and there were splendid huts for
visiting caravans. Guns had become a commonplace in
Buganda, and Mutesa could now deploy a force of 150,000
warriors in addition to his fleet of war canoes on the lake.
His personal retinue had grown larger than ever—Stanley
estimated the horde of wives at 200 or more—and all manner of manufactured objects were to be seen about the pal-

ace, bales of cotton cloths, wooden stools to sit on, steel knives and other tools and ornaments of Venetian beads. There was no longer any evidence of murders and other atrocities taking place about the court.

Stanley was enchanted. It was quite impossible, he declared later, to reconcile Speke's description of Mutesa and his brutalities with this intelligent and affable man. Mutesa had been taking an interest in Mohammedanism, and Stanley resolved at once to change all this; he declared that the king must be converted to Christianity, and he actually began a series of Bible-readings at the court. Mutesa listened very willingly.

Now in fact no radical change had taken place in Mutesa's nature, but his nineteen years on the throne had done a great deal to polish his natural talents as a politician. He had long since realized that there were other powerful states outside his own little world in Central Africa, and that there was every advantage to be had in befriending them; they could supply him with the guns and ammunition with which to fight off Kamrasi in Bunyoro and his other enemies. Their inventions and their ideas could be very useful in Buganda. As far back as 1869 he had received a caravan with a present of eight bullocks from the Sultan of Zanzibar, and had replied by sending to the coast a gift of 150 tusks and a baby elephant. Since then a further gift had arrived from Zanzibar of a quantity of gunpowder, guns, soap, brandy and gin. Within the past year he had also had a visitor from the north: a white man named Chaillé-Long had arrived on horseback from the Sudan, declaring that he was the emissary of a certain 'Gordoom Pasha', who had taken the place of Baker there. Mutesa had welcomed him to Rubaga and had slaughtered thirty human beings in his honour (an incident he was wise enough not to mention to Stanley), and now Gordoom Pasha was sending him another envoy who was expected any day.

And so, for the moment, all was peace and friendship at the court. The King and the explorer had their daily meetings in an atmosphere that was increasingly cordial, and presently Colonel Gordon's new envoy turned up. This was a likeable and courageous young Frenchman named Linant de Bellefonds, who, like the American, Chaillé-Long, had taken service under Gordon with the Khedive of Egypt, and was reconnoitring the land south from the Sudan with a view to its future annexation. He had come straight from Gondokoro and was able to regale Stanley with *pâte de foie gras,* Bologna sausages, sardines and other delicacies which were just the sort of thing, one feels, that an intelligent Frenchman ought to have had about him in Central Africa. De Bellefonds, being a Protestant, was very willing to promote Stanley's plan for the Christianization of Buganda, and offered to take back with him a dispatch of Stanley's to the London *Daily Telegraph* urging that missionaries should be sent out from England. Upon this the two men parted: de Bellefonds to report to Gordon at Gondokoro, and Stanley to continue his voyage round the lake.

On May 6, 1875, Stanley was back at his starting-point at Mwanza after a voyage of 1,000 miles and 57 days, and the first of his great objectives was accomplished: it was now proved beyond all doubt that the Victoria Nyanza was a single lake. Speke had been right and his detractors hopelessly wrong. Moreover, this voyage had established that the lake had only one major outlet—at the Ripon Falls—and only one major intake—the Kagera River that flowed in on the west coast to the north of Karagwe.

'. . . Speke,' Stanley wrote, 'has now the full glory of having discovered the largest inland sea on the continent of Africa, also its principal affluent as well as its outlet. I must also give him credit for having understood the geography of the countries we travelled through better than any of those who so persistently opposed his hypothesis. . . .'

One observes that Stanley is not yet quite ready to concede that Speke's Nile is the true Nile; still, he is beginning to approach that conclusion and soon he was to go the whole way towards it.

There now lay before him the second objective: to explore the Tanganyika Lake thoroughly and to discover just what connection it had, if any, with Baker's Albert Nyanza and any other lakes that might lie in the unexplored country on the Equator. In July 1875 he put the whole of his expedition into canoes on Lake Victoria, and with the *Lady Alice* in the van, sailed north again to Buganda. His force was much depleted—Frederick Barker, the clerk from the Langham Hotel, had died at Mwanza, and others had deserted or fallen ill—but Mutesa had promised to supply him with reinforcements.

First, however, he had a score to settle with the natives on the island of Bumbire, which lies off the western shore of the lake, somewhat south of the present town of Bukoba. On his journey south from Buganda in the *Lady Alice* he had been roughly handled by these natives, and now, coming into sight of the island again, he had his revenge. He was fortunate to be joined just at this moment by a fleet of Mutesa's war canoes which had come south looking for him. Between 2,000 and 3,000 Bumbire spearsmen unwisely exposed themselves on the shore, and Stanley, bringing his little fleet of canoes into position, delivered a broadside with his guns. Those of the enemy who were not killed or wounded scattered and fled.

Continuing northwards again Stanley joined Mutesa himself at the Ripon Falls, where a second battle was fought against another mutinous island.

There is something naïve about all Stanley's dealings with Mutesa, and one pauses here to wonder why it was that he got so heavily involved with a man who was at once so savage and so crudely cynical. Perhaps he was bound to seek Mutesa's alliance in order to complete his circumnavigation of the lake, and because he needed a Buganda escort for his forward journey, but the attack on Bumbire was a piece of senseless and revengeful folly, and the reward Stanley received for his intervention in the Buganda wars was as empty as Mutesa's profession of interest in Christianity: the promised reinforcements naturally bolted at the first opportunity, leaving the explorer to continue on his own.

One must remember of course that Stanley was still only 34 and that Livingstone's brief spell of influence upon him had to contend with all the experience of his earlier years in which he had found the world a harsh and ruthless place. Yet when he came to write about the Bumbire massacre—and he had ample time to reflect before doing so—he related the story almost with truculence, almost with an air of defying the reader.

'. . . The savage,' he wrote, 'only respects force, power, boldness and decision . . .'

No one was going to dispute the fact that life *was* very tough in Central Africa, and that often violent methods were needed if the explorer was going to survive; but it was not wise to make a virtue of this, and most of Stanley's protestations about the white man's duties in Africa and the need for Christian influence there ring a little hollow. To many people in England it seemed that the relationship he had with Mutesa was similar to that which might have been established by any Arab slaver, and that the Bumbire incident bore a strong resemblance to the massacre Livingstone had witnessed at Nyangwe; and it was an additional cause for offence that he had gone into action in these skirmishes carrying the Union Jack as his banner. Only the most insensitive of men could have failed to see that all this was going to cause an outcry in England. But then insensitiveness was part of Stanley's strength; he simply did not care. And certainly in his plain work of exploration he was superb.

He accepted with equanimity the loss of the escort which Mutesa had given him, even though this meant that he failed to determine the extent of Baker's Albert Nyanza and of Lake Edward, which lies just below the Equator, and instead he turned south into Karagwe. Here he spent a month with Rumanika at Bweranyange. Rumanika was growing old—indeed, Stanley was the last white man to see him alive, for he died soon after this. Apparently his mind became overwhelmed by the death of a favourite son and by the misery caused by an infliction in his eye, and he committed suicide.

Rumanika flits through the Central African story as a genial but not insubstantial ghost. One has the feeling that one knows him very well. He had been kind to Speke and Grant, and now once again he received Stanley with every form of hospitality. It was with some pride that he produced the gun which Speke had given him so many years before, and it is not difficult to picture him standing there holding it in his hand, a giant of a man, well over six foot in height, dressed a little pathetically in a red blanket. It was not easy to make the jump out of the Stone Age into the nineteenth century. Rumanika had been cruel enough in his time, in destroying other claimants to his throne, but he was less scheming and less brutal than Mutesa (whom he never met), and he possessed a dignity that did not depend upon his strutting about in imitation of a lion.

Restored by his month's rest in these surroundings, Stanley pushed on southwards to Lake Tanganyika, and he was intrigued, on arriving at Ujiji, to find that the water level had risen; the three palm trees that had stood in the market place when he was there in 1871 were now under water, and the sandy beach on which he used to walk with Livingstone was 200 feet from the shore. This appeared to argue that no sizable river flowed from the lake.

In June 1876 he launched the *Lady Alice* at Ujiji, and in under two months was back again bringing with him certain evidence that the lake had no outlet which could possibly be described as the source of the Nile. With this, Burton's theories finally collapsed, and Speke at last was master of the field.

There remained now the third and final matter to clear up: what was Livingstone's Lualaba River and where did it flow? If it was not the Nile, then how did it fit into the great pattern of the Central African rivers? In August 1876, two years after he had left the coast, with his expedition reduced to less than half its original size, Stanley set out on this last and greatest adventure of all.

The story of Stanley's voyage in the *Lady Alice* down the Lualaba and the Congo to the Atlantic is one of the great epics of African adventure. For many months he had no notion of where the river was eventually to take him—it might have been northwards into Egypt or anywhere into the vast unexplored regions to the south—but having once started he had to go on. Stanley's account of the voyage in *Through the Dark Continent* reads like some chronicle of the early Spanish conquistadors in South

America, for he was overtaken by every possible disaster: shipwreck and starvation, the attacks of the riverside tribes and the loss of all his supplies, and finally the drowning of his last surviving white companion, Frank Pocock. Nine hundred and ninety-nine days after leaving Zanzibar the survivors emerged like ghouls from the jungles at the mouth of the Congo, and here a little community of European traders brought them back to life again. Of Stanley's original 356 followers only 114 remained (including 13 women and their children) and these were taken back by sea to Zanzibar.

Prior to Stanley's journey the course of the Nile from the Ripon Falls to the present border of the Sudan had been plotted by Gordon's lieutenants. Chaillé-Long had gone down from the source as far as the Karuma Falls in Central Uganda, and had discovered Lake Kyoga on the way, and the Italian, Romolo Gessi, had circumnavigated Lake Albert and had followed its outlet to the north as far as the border at Dufilé.

But Stanley's had been by far the main achievement. All the essential questions had now been answered: the Lualaba joined the Congo and flowed across Africa into the Atlantic. The Nile rose in Lake Victoria and flowed north to Egypt and the Mediterranean. The blank space on the map was a blank no longer. It could still be argued, of course, that the ultimate source of the Nile must be at the headwaters of the main stream that feeds Lake Victoria—the Kagera—and in fact there is a just perceptible drift of water from the mouth of the Kagera across the north-western corner of the lake to the Ripon Falls (or rather what used to be the Ripon Falls before the hydro-electric dam was constructed there in the nineteen-fifties). And if we follow the Kagera and its tributaries upstream for some hundreds of miles we find that its ultimate beginning lies in mountains over 6,000 feet high to the north of Lake Tanganyika. Thus Burton was very nearly right when he argued that the true source of the river would be found in these regions. But surely this is too fine a definition: if the argument were carried to its logical conclusion it must be admitted that the river begins in the rains of the sky itself and that Homer was right when he spoke of the 'Jove-descended Nile'. For ordinary purposes it would seem most sensible to accept the side of the Ripon Falls as the source, since it is only from there that the mighty river confines itself to a definite course, at first northward through Lake Kyoga to Central Uganda, then westward over the Karuma and Murchison Falls to Lake Albert, then generally northwards again through the rapids of Equatoria, the swamps of the Sudd and the deserts of the south Sudan to its junction with the Blue Nile at Khartoum; then on again for thousands of miles through a vast waste of sand until it reaches the pyramids and green delta of Egypt.

With Stanley's return to Zanzibar in 1877 it could be said that the exploration of the White Nile was virtually ended. It remained now to be seen what the political and religious forces of the world were going to do with this new eldorado that had been put into their hands.

PART TWO

The Exploitation

Chapter 8

BEGGAR ON HORSEBACK

BY THE END of the eighteen-sixties the Khedive Ismail of Egypt had arrived at the crest of his highly prosperous career. He looks out at us from the photographs taken at the time with the quickness and complacency of a sleek and shining seal. His black frock-coat is of that peculiar type which was known in the Near East as a Stambouli, his fez is perched slightly sideways on his head, his reddish-sandy whiskers harmonize splendidly with the decorations on his plump chest, and he sits, a little incongruously, cross-legged on a divan. Behind him there is a carved lattice-work which no doubt gives on to the inner rooms in the palace, and it conveys a suggestion of harems and oriental banquets. And yet he is not entirely oriental; you might just conceivably describe him as a new type of ruler, an occidentalized oriental potentate. In 1869 he was 39 years of age, and now, after six years in power, he was the absolute monarch of Egypt. Technically he was still a vassal of the Sultan in Constantinople, and Egypt was still a part of the Ottoman Empire, but in fact Ismail had unquestioned authority over the Nile Delta, and he was as rich as only a new-made multi-millionaire can ever hope to be.

He felt rich. He spent his borrowed piastres in billions. In the manner of Pope Leo X Ismail might have exclaimed, 'Since Allah has given us the vice-royalty let us enjoy it.' Sir Evelyn Baring might have found him 'utterly uneducated' and 'an astute but superficial cynic' (by which he probably meant that Ismail was both superficial *and* a cynic, not just a novice in cynicism), but Sir Evelyn was also bound to agree with everybody else who knew the Khedive that he had remarkable charm and an energy in handling his affairs which was unique in the East and even astonishing in a man who had been brought up as a spoilt child in Paris.

Most Europeans who served under Ismail liked and admired him, at any rate in the early stages of his reign. Both Baker and General Gordon trusted him and believed that he was sincere when he said he meant to abolish the slave-trade. Admittedly both Baker and Gordon were politically naïve, and neither knew Ismail as well as Baring did, but at least he touched a spark of enthusiasm in their natures and he treated them very well. They were excellent agents for the great design he had in view: the westernization of Egypt and the creation of a new Egyptian empire in East Africa.

When Ismail succeeded his uncle Mohammed Said in the vice-royalty in 1863 Egypt was financially sound and even prosperous. The American Civil War had caused a sharp rise in the price of cotton, and the Egyptian crop had increased in value from £5,000,000 to £25,000,000. Ismail transferred his private debts to the state, increased the taxes, and got to work. He spent money with an abandon which eclipsed anything the oil sheikhs of the Middle East have achieved in the twentieth century. It was not only honest men like Baker and Gordon who were attracted to his service; a plague of speculators descended upon Egypt as well and they easily contrived to get rid of Ismail's money even faster than he borrowed it. In round figures the Egyptian national debt was £3,000,000 at Ismail's accession, and before long he managed to convert this into a deficit of £100,000,000—and this at a time when the pound was worth two or three times what it is today. Egypt in short was bankrupt, and Ismail the Magnificent was also known as the impecunious millionaire.

By 1869, however, when disaster was still some years ahead, Ismail already had a good deal to show for his money. His westernization of Egypt included every kind of internal reform, new canals and water-works, the remodelling of the customs system and the post office, the creation of a new sugar monopoly and a dozen other commercial enterprises. He maintained a new and expanding army and Cairo itself was partly rebuilt. In place of the foul streets and the rickety wooden houses a new commercial and residential quarter built of stone grew up around the Abdin Palace—the palace itself just one of the new residences which Ismail had constructed for his own use. A theatre and an opera house appeared, and the Bedouin were treated to the wonderful sight of a railway train steaming across the desert. Ismail's personal spending was equally sumptuous: with the gift of a steam yacht, a diamond-studded dinner service and a large sum in money he got a *firman* from the Sultan in Constantinople by which he became Khedive or Viceroy and virtually independent; and then there were his lavish trips abroad (he was received by Queen Victoria in 1867), his enormous households of women and slaves, his jewels, his *objets d'art* and his furniture brought from France.

In 1869 he was ready to make his greatest display of all. The Suez Canal was finished and he was determined to celebrate the opening with a series of entertainments which would establish Egypt's reputation as a new and important power in the world. The canal, of course, was not an Egyptian enterprise, but the Khedive was heavily involved in it. Ferdinand de Lesseps had formed his Compagnie Universelle du Canal Maritime de Suez in 1854, and had obtained from Mohammed Said a concession that was to run for 99 years from the opening date (after which time the canal was to become Egyptian property). From the beginning de Lesseps had run into difficulties on every side. The project itself was believed to be impossible, despite the fact that more than one such canal had existed on the site in ancient times. Napoleon had ordered a survey to be made at the time of his invasion of Egypt in 1798, and his engineer had estimated that there was a difference of 33 feet in the sea-levels of the Mediterranean and the Red Sea; an absolute obstacle to the construction of a canal. (In fact there is practically no difference at all in the sea levels.) The expenses of the undertaking—in the end, 287,000,000 gold francs—proved to be far higher than the original estimate, and ten years were needed to complete the work instead of six. British investors would have nothing to do with the scheme and the money was obtained mostly from French and Turkish sources, Egypt receiving four-tenths of the shares.

Then, too, there was massive opposition to the canal on political grounds, chiefly from Britain. Palmerston disliked French intervention in the Near East, and believed that British shipping interests would be affected. Even in France itself it was argued that the canal was not really necessary, since the existing method of crossing the Egyptian isthmus worked very well; travellers coming from the Mediterranean disembarked at Alexandria and took the new railway to Suez where they boarded another vessel in the Red Sea, with similar arrangements for the reverse direction. It was also claimed that if a canal were to be built it would immediately become a political target and a battlefield—a point, incidentally, that has been all too amply demonstrated in the last fifty years.

But de Lesseps' pertinacity was endless. He got his money, he drew up his plans (a canal 100 miles in length with a depth of 8 metres and a bottom width of 22 metres, with a secondary fresh-water canal coming in from the Nile), and the Khedive supplied him with an army of forced labourers. Many technical difficulties had to be overcome as the work went forward; it was found, for example, that wet dredging—first flooding the sand and then scooping it out with dredges—was better than dry digging. A cholera epidemic held up the work and there was a fearful death-roll caused by the hardships of life in the eastern desert of Egypt, one of the worst deserts in the world. But at the end of 1869 the main structure of the canal was completed, and most of its critics had fallen silent. It was apparent now that no maritime nation could afford to ignore or boycott the enterprise, least of all the British. The journey from Western Europe to India and the Far East had been reduced by one half, both in time and distance, and this was a vital economy now that coal-burning steamships were everywhere replacing sail. The cutting out of the long journey round the Cape of Good Hope also meant that the whole pattern of the British

Empire's defence was altered, since troops and men-of-war could now so quickly be transferred from the Atlantic and the Mediterranean to the Indian Ocean.

It was apparent too that the breadth and depth of the canal would affect shipbuilding design, and that all kinds of neglected territories would be opened up to Western civilization. Stanley's newspaper, the *New York Herald,* made the editorial comment: 'The ... Suez Canal brings all these late discoveries around the equatorial sources of the Nile of Speke, Grant, Baker, Burton, Livingstone within a convenient distance for English colonization.'

There was one other point: the canal was part of the French bid for power in Egypt, and of their general campaign to dislodge the British from their position of increasing influence in East Africa and the Near East. A Frenchman had built the canal, French money had financed it, and the French were now determined to exploit their advantage to the full. Henceforth they could claim that they had a vital stake in Egypt and an established right to intervene in Egyptian politics.

Ismail's arrangements for the opening, which was fixed for November 17, 1869, had the Haroun-al-Raschid touch. The festivities were to continue for four days, and were to take place both at Cairo and on the Canal itself. In Cairo he built his opera house, and Verdi was commissioned to write *Aïda* for its inauguration (although, in fact, the opera was not performed in Egypt until later on). Plots of land were sold off in the centre of the city to raise money, and the pyramids were illuminated with magnesium light. At Port Said three pavilions were built, one for the more illustrious guests, one for the Moslem hierarchy, and another for the Christians. An arsenal of fireworks was prepared for an opening salute, and 500 cooks and 1,000 servants were imported from France and Italy to cater for six thousand guests. The best of wines and the most expensive food were of course provided without stint.

At Ismailia, the half-way point on Lake Timsah, a new town was built with a palace, hotels and kiosks; it was here that the fleet carrying the chief guests from Port Said was to meet a smaller flotilla sailing north from Suez, and thus the Mediterranean and the Red Sea were to be joined for the first time.

Such lavish preparations could not have been expected to go off without a hitch, especially in such a country as Egypt; at Port Said the fireworks dump blew up and very nearly demolished the town; and at the last moment a ship became grounded and blocked the canal. De Lesseps galloped off to the scene and had the vessel blown up.

The morning of November 17, however, found all ready for the start, with a great assembly of ships at Port Said, and both town and ships bedecked with bunting. The canal was blessed by Moslem, Greek Orthodox, Coptic and Roman Catholic priests, every available cannon and gun was fired off, twenty military bands struck up, and through the drifting smoke of gunpowder the Empress Eugénie of France in the imperial yacht *Aigle* led the way into the canal. She was followed by Ismail aboard the *Mahrousa* (his royal scimitar blazing with jewels), the Emperor of Austria (in white tunic, scarlet pantaloons and a cocked hat with a green feather), and a number of minor royalties and officials aboard two Austrian and five British ironclads, a Russian sloop-of-war and a great number of ships partly under steam and partly under sail—an armada of some 70 vessels in all.

At Ismailia the flotilla coming from Suez was met at sunset, and amid great ceremony Africa was now declared to be an island. The guests went ashore to attend a banquet, a fireworks display, and a ball illuminated by ten thousand lanterns. During her stay at Ismalia the Empress Eugénie had the excitement of riding a camel while the local Bedouin tribesmen fired off their muskets, and the fleet then steamed on to the Red Sea.

The British Royal Family were absent from this spree, but in fact they had anticipated it; some months beforehand the Prince and the Princess of Wales (who more than thirty years later were to become King Edward VII and Queen Alexandra), had come out to Egypt on an official visit and had been present when the sluices had been opened into the Bitter Lakes towards the southern end of the canal.

It had been something of an occasion for a naturalist, since great quantities of fish from the Mediterranean swept in with the tide, while all the fish from the fresh-water canal, which there joined the lakes from the Nile, were instantly killed. Thereafter Their Royal Highnesses had gone off for a trip up the river to Luxor.

It was this visit that brought Samuel Baker and his wife back to Africa. Baker, with his knowledge of Arabic and of Egypt, was invited to accompany the tour as an interpreter. At a fancy dress ball given by de Lesseps, Ismail drew the explorer aside and put before him a momentous proposition: he had decided, he said, to mount a military expedition which was to annex the Upper Nile to Egypt and suppress the slave-trade there. Would Baker take command?

The terms were generous, even for Ismail. Baker was to become a pasha, a lord of the Ottoman Empire, and a major-general. He was to choose his own staff and he himself was to have a salary of £40,000 spread over the four-year tenure of his office. The force he was to command was to consist of some 1,700 men, and Baker Pasha was to be given a free hand in the purchase of their equipment.

A more politically minded man than Baker might, of course, have regarded these proposals with a certain scepticism. It was extremely doubtful, for instance, that Ismail was sincere in his wish to abolish the slave-trade. He himself was one of the largest slave-owners; the fellaheen who worked on his enormous estates, and the hordes of servants in his palaces might have been given the appearance of free men, but in fact they were tied to their jobs as completely as any Russian serf, and Ismail exercised the power of life and death over them. As for the slavery in the Sudan, Ismail was perfectly well aware that all his officials there were deeply involved in it, and he himself had actually given state contracts to private traders authorizing them to exploit the Upper Nile. In Egypt as in Zanzibar slavery was part of the Moslem way of life and the government benefited very greatly from it.

But the abolition of the traffic had now become the great political cry in both Europe and America, and Ismail realized that he would have to make at least an outward show of joining the anti-slavery campaign if he was to continue to receive the support of the Western world. That support was quite essential to him. He needed more money from Europe, and he needed political backing for the larger aims he had in view: the extension of his power through the South Sudan, East Africa and Abyssinia. All was to be done under the banner of civilization; the new Egypt was to bring the blessings of the modern world to these savage areas in the south.

And who could object to this expedition? No other state was proposing to pacify and civilize these regions, and Ismail surely, being so near at hand and so Western-minded, was the logical ruler to undertake the work. It was only reasonable that his good faith should be accepted until things were proved otherwise. So, at all events, it seemed to Samuel Baker, and no doubt the Prince of Wales and the British Government as well. Baker accepted the commission and threw himself into the arrangements with method and gusto—and, it may be added, without much regard to the cost.

His first journey up the Nile had turned him from a big game hunter into an explorer. Now the explorer was to develop into the soldier and the administrator.

The European staff was to number ten: Baker's nephew, Lieutenant Julian Baker, R.N., was engaged at a salary of £500 a year to act as personal assistant to the commander; then there were Dr. Joseph Gedge, the physician, two engineers, Higginbotham and McWilliam, Marcopolo, the storekeeper and interpreter, and Jarvis, the shipwright, with four assistants. Lady Baker was to be the only white woman to accompany the expedition.

Next, the entire force had to be organized on a proper military basis. There were to be two regiments, one of Sudanese soldiers and the other of Egyptians (who turned out to be mostly felons from the Cairo gaols), and from these Baker later selected a personal bodyguard of forty-eight sharpshooters. He put them into fezzes and scarlet uniforms and called them the Forty Thieves. In addition, there was to be a contingent of 200 cavalry and two batteries of artillery.

Next, the equipment, and it was to be of the best. In England Baker ordered the construction of a flotilla of boats all of which could be taken to pieces so that they could be dragged or carried by camels across the desert and then reassembled and launched on the Nile above the cataracts. The largest of these was a 100-foot paddle-boat of 251 tons and 20 horse-power, and in addition there were two smaller twin-screw steamers, one of 108 tons and the other of 38, and two 10-ton lifeboats.

At a cost of £9,000 general stores were also bought in England and were expected to last four years: four galvanized iron sheds 80 feet long and built in sections, 200 Hale's rockets and 50,000 rounds of Snider ammunition, medicines, uniforms, 'Manchester goods', several saw-mills, tools and camping kits of every kind—'anything from a needle to a crowbar, or from a handkerchief to a boat's sail'—and finally, to impress and amuse the natives, toys, drums, musical boxes and a magnetic battery.

The main body of the expedition was to go up the Nile in relays while Baker himself and his wife travelled ahead to Khartoum on the Red Sea route (which meant crossing to the river from Suakin), and the transport arrangements were formidable. Hundreds of camels were engaged and in the end a fleet of nine steamers and fifty-five sailing boats was required to bring the soldiers and their equipment up from Cairo. Such a force had never been seen or even dreamed of in Central Africa before.

Naturally there were delays: quite apart from the normal apathy that overtakes all things in Egypt there was a strong desire among the slave interests to prevent the expedition's ever getting under way at all. The Suez Canal festivities also made it difficult for Baker to requisition boats.

It must be regarded as something of a marvel therefore that by February 1870, hardly a year after receiving his commission, Baker had assembled the bulk of his force at Khartoum and was ready to set out for Gondokoro, which was to be his main base of operations. It was apparent at once at Khartoum that his presence was desperately needed. The slave traffic had been bad enough at the time of his earlier expedition and now it was ten times worse. The whole country was in ruins. Khartoum itself had been so taxed and despoiled by the Egyptian officials that the population of 30,000 had been reduced by half. In the surrounding villages the Africans had given up the hopeless work of tilling the land only to see their crops seized from them, and now there was desolation everywhere along the river, nothing but idle water-wheels and fields that had lapsed back into desert. Some 50,000 slaves were being brought down from the Upper Nile every year, and a gang of at least 15,000 Arabs was engaged in the trade. Some of these dealers had become as independent and powerful as robber barons in the Middle Ages; a certain Agad, for example, had a government contract giving him trading rights over an area of 90,000 square miles and a small private army was under his command. All these people looked on Baker as their enemy. There was nothing he could do to touch them in the vicinity of Khartoum since his commission gave him no powers there, but he was bound for the Upper Nile which was the main source of the slave supply, and there the Khedive had conferred on him absolute authority. He could stop a slaving boat on the river, release the victims stowed away between decks and arrest the dealers regardless of whether they were officials or not. He could exercise summary justice and even impose the death penalty. On February 8, 1870, he sailed south from Khartoum with well over a thousand armed men, and they were strong enough to deal with any opposition they encountered on the river.

But it was the river itself that was Baker's real enemy now. In the five years that had elapsed since he had been on the Upper Nile nothing had been done to keep a clear channel through the Sudd, and by 1870 the stream at many places had disappeared beneath a spongy mass of tangled vegetation. For two dreadful months Baker's soldiers hacked a channel into this morass, but they succeeded in penetrating only a few miles. Islands of floating debris kept closing round behind the boats so that they looked 'as though frozen in an ice-drift in the Arctic'. Meanwhile the level of the river, unseen beneath the reeds, was rapidly falling. At the beginning of April Baker decided to back out and establish a base camp on hard ground near the present town of

Malakal, while he waited for the annual flood to come down again at the end of the year.

The next seven months were spent profitably enough trapping slave-boats on the open river north of Malakal, and in reconditioning the expedition, and by the beginning of December 1870 Baker was ready to try again. The river was now in flood, a strong breeze blew from the north, and 59 vessels with 1,600 men and women and Lady Baker on board struck out once more for the hateful swamp. Two months later they were still creeping forward yard by yard along the Bahr-el-Jebel and the same monotonous scenes were repeated every day: the reluctant soldiers wading about in the bog, some of them hacking with billhooks at the matted barrier of reeds, others hauling on ropes to get the vessels through and others again working with shovels in the clinging mud. The heat was appalling and many collapsed with fever and sunstroke. One after another the sailing boats sank or were stranded on the mud, and by night there was no escape from the mosquitoes unless the men landed and slept in the smoke of fires. But for the most part they could not land: there was no land, only the endless billowing maze of papyrus, with the swamp beneath. Nowadays the Bahr-el-Jebel channel has been cleared, and the Nile paddle-steamers pass through this part of the Sudd in less than three days, but even so this journey is a tedious and oppressive business. To have lingered there for months on end in that claustrophobic green prison with no certainty that one would ever emerge must have been an experience to test the sanity of any ordinary man.

Towards March 1871 even Baker's nerve was beginning to fail. 'It is quite impossible to say where we are,' he wrote in his diary; and then again he records that there appeared to be no hope—the Egyptian soldiers had now ceased to care whether they lived or died. And many did die. Gedge, the doctor, had long since collapsed and had been sent off to Khartoum, and now there was no one to treat the hundreds who came down with malaria and dysentery. Baker himself and his wife seemed miraculously to be the only ones who were able to remain in health. Early in March the Nile began to fall again at an alarming rate, and on March

9 Baker records that the entire fleet 'was hard and fast aground'. But it was on that same day that, in a light reconnaissance boat, he went ahead and reached the clear water where the Bahr-el-Jebel comes in to join the Bahr-el-Zeraf from the north. This was a tremendous moment, and Baker summoned his exhausted men to make one more effort. 'I at once determined,' he says, 'to make a dam behind the vessels so as to enclose the position in which we lay like a millpond. Common sense assured me that this must succeed in raising the level, provided we could construct a dam of sufficient strength to bear the pressure of water. I had a great quantity of fir timber in the shape of beams and rafters for building purposes. I therefore directed Mr. Higginbotham to prepare two rows of piles which were to be driven across the river.'

For the next two days 1,500 men were employed in filling sacks with sand and clay and in tying together large fascines or bundles of reeds. All this material, at a given signal, was to be packed around the piles so as to form a continuous barrier across the river, and by March 13 everything was in readiness.

'I stood on one of the stranded boats only a few yards from the row of piles,' Baker says. 'The buglers and drummers stood upon another vessel ready to give the signal. At the first bugle every two men lifted the sacks of sand and clay. At once all the drums and bugles then sounded the advance, and 500 heavy sacks were dropped into the row of piles, and firmly stamped down by the men. The troops now worked with intense energy... while some stamped frantically and danced upon the entangled mass, all screaming and shouting in great excitement, and the bugles and drums kept up an incessant din. A double line of men formed a transport corps, and passed a never-failing supply of fascines to the workers who stood in the water and kneaded firmly the adhesive mass. At 2.15 p.m. the river was completely shut in, and the people with increased energy worked at the superstructure of the dam, which now rose like a causeway for about one hundred and ten yards from shore to shore. At 3.30 the water had risen to an extent that obliged men in some places to swim. The steamer that had been hopelessly stranded, and the entire fleet, were floating merrily in the pond.'

Now at last their troubles were over. One by one the boats were sailed out into the clear water, and a month later they were tying up on the banks below the ruined Austrian mission house at Gondokoro.

The place if anything was more dismal than ever, but Baker at once set about landing his stores and building a fort there. It was enough to revive hope just to be out of the Sudd at last, and by the end of May an orderly line of huts had sprung up and these were surrounded by vegetable gardens and newly-sown fields of maize. On May 26, Baker indulged himself in a ceremony which might have been pathetic had it been conducted by any other man. He paraded twelve hundred of his men in clean uniforms, ran up the Ottoman flag on an 80-foot pole, and solemnly annexed the surrounding country to Egypt. Henceforth it was to be known as Equatoria, and Gondokoro, the little capital, was renamed Ismailia in honour of the Khedive. There was no one to record the scene for the outside world, and none to watch except the naked Bari tribesmen, who presumably understood nothing of what was going on and preferred instead to make nightly raids upon the camp. But Baker and his friends were reassured by their little gesture of formality in the wilderness. That night they had a dinner of roast beef, Christmas pudding and rum.

There remained now two years of Baker's contract to run and the story of these two years is, very largely, a story of colonial warfare. This had ceased to be an expedition; in a small way it was a military campaign that was designed to 'pacify' the country—and that word 'pacification' had sinister connotations. In the eighteen-seventies it was already recognized by many people as a self-righteous euphemism which was meant to cover up the brutal facts of military operations against primitive and almost helpless people. Strong liberal and humanitarian feelings were stirred up in England when the details of Baker's campaign became known. And yet it is difficult to see how, having once embarked on this adventure, he could have acted in any other way. He was caught up in a pattern of expansion which has since become labelled with the word 'colonialism'—the exploitation of the weak by the strong, an aspect of human behaviour which Baker's friend, Chief Comoro, thought he understood very well when he said 'only the weak are good; they are good because they are not strong enough to be bad.'

But it would be wilful and sentimental to dismiss colonialism in these terms, especially in Central Africa. Here was a vast area that supposedly had been left untouched through the centuries, and perhaps it might have been well to have left it so; the local tribes had worked out a Stone Age system of life which was perfectly valid despite its brutality, uncertainty and suffering. But it had not been left untouched; Arab traders had gone in with no other object but private gain and they had grabbed out of Africa both animals and human beings in the same way as a miner will take rock out of the ground. By 1870 this primitive Eden had become soiled, debauched and finally vile. To Baker and men like him it seemed that it was a moral duty for civilized governments to restore order once again, to throw out the ruthless foreign slavers and to teach the natives to live in peace and on a far higher standard than they had had before. The natives naturally found all this very confusing. Baker appeared to them to be merely another kind of trader and invader, and consequently they made war on him; and the more they made war the more Baker deemed it necessary to pacify them for their own good. Eventually, he found that he had to occupy the ground and impose good laws by force. And so, willy-nilly, another new colony was formed.

A great deal depended, of course, upon what means were used to achieve these worthy objects; clearly a wise, strong and patient commander could handle the difficult period of transition with far less brutality than a pugnacious empire-building soldier who was out to make a name for himself. And Baker undoubtedly, within himself, was wise, strong and patient; it was simply his misfortune that he entered the colonizing process in Central Africa under the dubious patronage of the Khedive, and at its roughest and crudest moment. His expedition had to fight for its life and that made all the difference; unless he used strong-arm tactics he not only failed, he died.

And so when the Bari tribes attacked him at Gondokoro with poisoned arrows he drove them off with guns; when they refused to sell him cattle and grain he went off on raids and seized the food he needed for his men. None of this was very simple or easy. The Arab traders, notably one Abu Saoud, joined forces with the Baris against him and soon they were able to stir up mutiny within the Gondokoro garrison itself. The Egyptian gaolbirds in Baker's little army were not men of great moral fibre. Baker came back to Gondokoro from one of his raids one day to find that 1,100 of them had seized thirty of his sailing vessels and had decamped down the river to Khartoum. This disaster left him with barely 500 men. However, he decided to push on into Bunyoro, the kingdom of Kamrasi. The Forty Thieves had become an efficient bodyguard, the Sudanese soldiers were loyal, and by now they had amassed a store of grain and large herds of cattle and sheep—an ample supply of food for the journey. A small garrison was left behind in Gondokoro under the command of an Egyptian officer, Raouf Bey, and this man was instructed to keep an eye open for Dr. Livingstone and to look after him well if he turned up during Baker's absence. Livingstone at that moment was hundreds of miles away to the south on Lake Tanganyika, but Baker had had no news of him or indeed of anyone for a year or more.

It was a steady and well-organized march. They set out on January 22, 1872, Baker, his wife and the nephew, Julian, leading the way on horseback, and having by-passed the long series of rapids south of Gondokoro, they arrived on the frontier of Bunyoro in the middle of March. Everywhere along the route, even so far south as this, the slave-trade had created desolation, and Fatiko, the outpost which the Bakers had visited in 1864, had now expanded into a compound covering at least thirty acres. A healthy young girl was valued at 'a single elephant's tusk of the first class' (worth from £20 to £30 in England but of course very much less in Bunyoro). She could also be purchased for a new shirt or for 13 English sewing needles, and these things were so much desired that parents frequently sold their children.

Baker made no attempt to investigate the unexplored reaches of the Nile, but pushed on steadily southwards, and now with his little army he had no need to ask permission of the king to enter Bunyoro. On April 25, 1872, he arrived at the capital, and saw 'some thousands of large beehive-shaped straw huts' on the site of the present town of Masindi. Kamrasi was dead and Baker did not care for his successor: 'This,' he says, 'was Kabba Rega, the son of Kamrasi, the sixteenth king of Bunyoro, of the Galla conquerors, a gauche, awkward, undignified lout of twenty years of age, who thought himself a great monarch. He was cowardly, cruel, cunning and treacherous to the last degree.'

The young King advanced on Baker's camp, walking like a giraffe, at the head of a horde of some 2,000 of his followers, and Baker did not like his demeanour at all. He says that Kabba Rega was drunk most of the day except for a couple of hours when he conducted business in the early afternoon, and that the capital was a bedlam of dancing, shouting, horn-blowing and drinking all through the night.

Kabba Rega, or Kabarega, is of some importance in the Central African story, and Baker's judgement upon him can certainly not be taken as the last word. From the first Baker seems to have expected to find qualities in the young King which would have been exceptional in any African chieftain at that time, and there can be no doubt whatever that Baker's own behaviour was designed to precipitate a crisis in Bunyoro. He made no pretence at all of what he had come to do, and that was to dominate Kabarega, by friendship if possible, and if not, by force.

He pitched his tent under a huge banyan tree and then proceeded to build himself, close by, a 'government house, and a private dwelling adjoining for myself'. Only the barest outlines of these structures remain today among the green lawns and the jacaranda trees in Masindi, but we have Baker's description of them and it is given with some justifiable pride: the government house was of one room, measuring 18 feet by 14 feet with a roof 20 feet high, the walls being made of canes and hung with red blankets. A remarkable gallery of pictures was displayed on these walls to impress the Africans—photographs of Queen Victoria and the Princess of Wales, coloured fashion-plates of 'very beautiful women, with very gorgeous dresses', and a number of sporting prints. The musical box was unpacked and rugs were spread on the floor. In these surroundings Baker Pasha, the new viceroy of the Khedive, prepared to receive official visits. Later on, a circular fort of heavy upended logs with an earthen roof and a surrounding ditch was constructed beside Government House. Gardens of cucumbers, melons, pumpkins and cottonseed were planted, and if Kabarega was still in any doubt about the strangers' motives the position was made absolutely clear to him on May 14, 1872; on that day Baker publicly annexed Bunyoro to the Khedive.

Now Kabarega, even at this early stage of his career, was a great deal more than a drunken lout. He had had to fight for his throne on the death of his father two years before, and already he had shown signs of those qualities which, later on, were to make him the most resourceful guerrilla leader in Central Africa. At this stage he was very inexperienced and very greatly in need of good advice, but one can hardly blame him for resenting Baker's intrusion into his kingdom. It was all very well for Baker to protest that he had come here in friendship. In this savage world no strong man went anywhere simply in friendship—he conquered the countries he invaded and automatically turned their inhabitants into vassals. And that surely, *au fond*, was what Baker had set out to do. Kabarega must have seen this very clearly. It was quite evident to him that he would have to get rid of Baker if he was going to remain King of Bunyoro, and because he was rash and aggressive he decided to set about the business at once. The drum-beatings and horn-blowings that Baker heard through the night, and even the drinking bouts, were not merely a savage debauch, they were the primitive man's way of working up his spirit for war. It was childish and barbaric, even a little pathetic, but it was also a real expression of tribal feeling; all of Kabarega's warriors and minor chiefs were behind him in the matter. Many were armed with guns and they were ready

to follow him anywhere. They had an overwhelming desire
for war and Baker was not the first or the last Englishman
who has failed to recognize in crude rioting the seeds of a
genuine popular rising.

Through the last days of May, while Baker pushed on
with the building of his fort, Kabarega's threats increased,
and on June 8 the Battle of Masindi broke out. It was preceded by a little strategy of Kabarega's which immediately
distinguishes him from the general run of other African
chiefs, and might well have been applauded by the ancient
Greeks; he sent over a gift of poisoned cider to Baker's
troops, and many of them were feeling desperately ill when
the fighting began.

The Battle of Masindi lasted just an hour and a quarter,
and Baker describes it very vividly:

'Suddenly,' he says, 'we were startled by the savage yells
of some thousand voices, which burst unexpectedly upon
us .. ! "Sound the taboor!" Fortunately I gave this order to
the bugler by my side without a moment's delay. The Forty
Thieves had just the time to grab their rifles and open up a
point-blank fire upon the mass of Africans charging down
on them through the cover of the tall grass.' Perhaps for a
few minutes Kabarega might have had a chance of success
but it was gone directly Baker got his 'blue lights'—the
Hale Rockets—into play. Before long he was able to lead
his men into the enemy camp and set fire to the straw buildings there.

'In a few minutes the conflagration was terrific, as the
great court of Kabarega blazed in flames 70 or 80 feet high,
which the wind drove in vivid forks into the thatch of the
adjacent houses. We now followed the enemy throughout
the town, and the Sniders told with sensible effect where-
ever they made a stand. The blue lights continued the work
of vengeance; the roar of the flames and the dense volume
of smoke, mingled with the continued rattle of musketry
and the savage yells of the natives, swept forward with the
breeze, and the capital of Bunyoro was a fair sample of the
infernal regions.'

Soon 'not a house remained of the lately extensive town;
a vast open space of smoke and black ashes, with flames

flickering in some places where the buildings had been consumed, and at others forked sheets of fire where the fuel was still undestroyed, were the only remains of the capital of Bunyoro. The enemy fled. Their drums and horns, lately so noisy, were now silent.'

With so many dead and wounded Africans lying about in the thick grass it was impossible to arrive at an estimate of Kabarega's losses, but Baker heard reports that nine chiefs had been killed and 'a larger number of common people'. He himself had lost only four men. The vultures in hundreds settled down around the ruined town.

But this was merely the first round of an affair that grew steadily more serious for the little expedition. The Bunyoro did not retire, they kept skirmishing about Baker's lines from the heavy cover of the grass, and presently it became obvious that it was impossible for him to stay where he was. Every day there were losses and no hope of reinforcements. Food was beginning to run short. In brief, the invaders had won the battle but lost the war.

On June 13 Baker decided that there was no help for it but to beat a retreat to Foweira, a traders' station on the Nile some sixty miles to the north-east, and there regroup so that he could return and fight Kabarega on another day. There were, of course, no longer any local porters available, and a great part of his stores which had been carried all the way from Cairo, over 3,000 miles away, was burned. The return march began in drizzling rain on June 14 and the horrors of the next ten days can be compared (with due allowance for the tropical heat and the perhaps farcical nature of the comparison) only to Napoleon's retreat from Moscow.

Day by day Baker's wretched men were harried by spearsmen, every other swamp and turn in the track was an ambush, and the war drums continued relentlessly all around them throughout the night. Lady Baker, as can be imagined, was magnificent throughout this disaster, but the native wives were a terrible hindrance to the march, since any who fell behind could face only instant death. The horses and donkeys were soon all dead, and the wounded had to be carried on stretchers. Presently it became necessary to abandon the cattle together with a further quantity of stores, and each man was rationed to forty rounds of ammunition. Baker's chief worry was to prevent his soldiers from firing off their rifles at the first sign of danger in the surrounding bush, and indeed it was remarkable in every way that on June 24 he was able to lead the remnants of his exhausted and wretched column into Foweira. Their losses on the march were ten dead and eleven wounded. Of the advance guard 200 strong which had gone to Masindi, only the three Europeans, 97 men and 51 women and servants remained.

Foweira did not prove to be much of a haven for the expedition, since the fort there had been burned down and the banana plantations were deserted. But here at least they were troubled no more by Kabarega's warriors, and soon Baker was able to strike up an alliance with Rionga, the traditional enemy of the Bunyoro Kings, who lived a little further up the river. August 1872 found Baker back at Fatiko, and here, after more fighting, he decided to establish his main headquarters.

It was an admirable place to choose, and from the moment he settled in, Baker's fortunes began to improve. Before the end of the year he was even strong enough to attack Kabarega from the north and eventually put him to flight. This seems to have been the signal for a general collapse of the opposition of the tribes south of Gondokoro. For the last six months of his tenure of office Baker was able to concentrate without disturbance upon the building of his fort at Fatiko, and from here, in a rough and ready fashion, he was able to rule, by the mere threat of his presence, the little kingdom he had conquered. Half of it, including the Nile valley itself, was still unexplored, all of it was still savage, but while Baker remained it was at least in peace.

By the time he and his wife and nephew came to leave in March 1873 he was able to write:

'In the end every opposition was overcome: hatred and insubordination yielded to discipline and order. A paternal government extended its protection through lands hitherto a field for anarchy and slavery. . . . The White Nile, for a distance of 1,600 miles from Khartoum to Central Africa, was cleansed from the abomination of a traffic which had hitherto sullied its waters. Every cloud had passed away, and the term of my office expired in peace and sunshine. In this result, I humbly traced God's blessing.'

A garrison of soldiers under an Egyptian officer was left behind at Fatiko and the Bakers reached Cairo in August 1873. By the end of the year they were safely ensconced in England where the untouched salary of £40,000 was awaiting them in the bank.

Fatiko was the chief monument Baker left behind in Africa, and even today the place still bears the stamp of his rugged and determined personality; it is an admirable expression of Victorian England in the heart of Africa. Except for a few African farmers no one lives there now, but the general outlines of the fort have been maintained more or less as they were in Baker's time. One reaches the site on a side road about 17 miles north of the present town of Gulu, and it can be discerned from quite a long way off by a sharp outcrop of rock that rises some hundreds of feet above the level plain. From here the African bush, with its immemorial stillness, spreads away: to the west, just visible to a practised eye, the green valley of the Nile; to the north, the road to Gondokoro; and to the south and east the vast plain that gently rises to the great lakes and the mountains of Ethiopia. Baker loved this country and dreamed of the creation of a great civilization here. But things have not really altered very much in the past ninety years. A few primitive fields of cotton and a few villages and roads have tamed the landscape a little and driven most of the wild animals away, but this is still a world of thatched huts and silence, and the general impression is one of enormous space and enormous emptiness.

The fort itself is a large square compound with a surrounding ditch, and it is anchored on the Nile side to a huge pile of rounded granite boulders. Upon these Baker built his storehouses of broken stone, using the local anthills for cement, and the visitor at the present time will find there a plaque which reads:

Fatiko
1872–88
Founded by
Sir Samuel Baker
Occupied by
Gordon and Emin

The strange myopic figure of Emin we have yet to meet, but the name of Gordon, here as everywhere in Central Africa, evokes an instant sense of gallantry and adventure, and it is pleasant to know that he followed Baker here, and that both men, no doubt, often looked down from these battlements towards the Nile, which was so strong a theme in their lives, and that they heard, as one hears now, the rustling of the borassus palms beside the fort and saw, in the evening, these same flat-topped acacia trees which spread in the plain below and make a convenient perch for the migratory birds settling down there for the night.

Chapter 9

TO GO IN PEACE

CENTRAL AFRICA had no part in the great migrations that poured out of Europe through the middle of the nineteenth century. The push of the potato famine and the pull of gold brought hundreds of thousands of immigrants to Australia, California and other distant parts of the world, and having once arrived at their new homes most of these people turned their backs upon Europe for ever. But up to the end of the eighteen-seventies nothing of the kind had happened in Central Africa. It had remained explorers' country and no one, with the exception of the missionaries who were preparing to enter the field, dreamed of making a permanent life there. It was thought that the opening of the Suez Canal would lead to a great expansion of trade along the eastern seaboard of the continent, but no such movement took place: most of the ships continued on to India, the Far East, Australia and New Zealand, and it was left to the only two local powers of any consequence, Egypt and Zanzibar, to struggle against each other for the possession of the vast hinterland. It was not a struggle which could continue for very long—the European powers were bound eventually to step in and take charge of the situation—but in the eighteen-seventies the Khedive of Egypt and the Sultan of Zanzibar still had a few more years of independence to run, and Central Africa continued as an arena for purely African politics.

Zanzibar, of course, was much the weaker of the two states, and her little population of half a million had been badly hit, at first by another cholera epidemic in 1869, and then by a hurricane that all but levelled the city and the port in 1872. Yet the Sultan was still undisputed master of the three islands of Zanzibar, Pemba and Mafia, and of about a thousand miles of the coastline on the mainland. The slave-trade was beginning to feel the pressure of the international blockade, but other exports such as indiarubber were proving even more profitable. The clove harvest, which was sent largely to Java (where the fruit-buds are still used to give a flavour to cigarettes), brought in an increasing revenue: and places like Dar-es-Salaam, Mombasa and Lamu on the mainland were developing into considerable towns.

In 1870 the Sultan Majid had died, and had been succeeded by Barghash, the same man who, with the aid of a pro-French party, had raised a revolt some years before. It was a move for the better, since Barghash was a robust and forceful man. The photographs of him now in the little museum at Zanzibar reveal a plump and genial Henry the Eighth in the ceremonial robes of the East, and they suit him. He is not soft like his powerful antagonist to the north; where the Khedive is urbane, Barghash has a more simple dignity, and he carries about him still the atmosphere of the rocks and the hard spaces of Oman.

When Barghash was asked one day what determined the succession in Zanzibar, he replied with some truth, 'the length of one's sword'; and yet he was a great deal more than a swashbuckler and an adventurer; he was a shrewd and skilful negotiator and a man who kept his word. The British disliked and distrusted him at first; indeed, H. A. Churchill, the British Agent of the time, was driven almost frantic by his hostility and his prevarications. But then Churchill sailed away to take up another post, and Kirk was left in charge of the Agency with the rank of acting consul. Kirk was already proving himself to be the ablest British representative on the island since the death of Hamerton. He liked Barghash. He realized that a reformed rebel, like a high-spirited horse that has been broken in, is likely to make the best partner in the long run, and at once patched up relations between the Agency and the Palace. There then began that intimate relationship between the two men that was to continue for the next sixteen years and was to lay the foundations of British power in East and Central Africa.

It was never an easy relationship, because in the very nature of things the two men were obliged to be opponents; Barghash wanted to rule his little empire in his own way, and that included the continuance of slavery, while the British were determined upon abolition. The issue came to a head over Livingstone's revelations of the horrors being committed by the Arab traders in the interior, and Kirk's handling of it was masterly. Ostensibly it was Sir Bartle Frere who conducted the negotiations, but there is no doubt that Kirk was the man who was responsible for their success. Frere came out to Zanzibar at the head of an official British mission in 1873, and although he was a seasoned diplomat there was nothing he could do to persuade or intimidate Barghash. Barghash's stand was quite simple: if you kill slavery you kill me and the whole state as well. Again and again Frere put up to him the terms of a new treaty under which the slave-market in Zanzibar was to be closed and the shipping of slaves anywhere inside the Sultan's dominions was to be abolished. But Barghash twisted and turned and would not sign. Not even the threat of a naval blockade would move him, and matters still stood in an ominous deadlock when Frere left the island, deciding that for the moment he could do no more. It was Kirk then who brought Barghash round. Tactfully and firmly—but always keeping the threat of the blockade in the background—he persuaded him that he had no choice in the matter, and in the end Barghash gave way and put his signature to the hated document.

In point of fact the new treaty was not at once effective: the Zanzibar slave-market was closed in June 1873 and a new Christian church rose on the site, but slaving still went on as before on the mainland and the smuggling of human cargoes across the Indian Ocean continued as relentlessly as ever. Yet this treaty was a public and official declaration against the idea of slavery, and it made it possible for the British to take more definite action later on.

Barghash, who had been defeated and somewhat humiliated by the affair, could reasonably expect some *quid pro quo* in return. What he got was Kirk's determination to keep his little empire intact. From this time forward the new consul (Kirk was confirmed in the office after Frere's departure) turned all the force of his patient logical mind upon the work of persuading the British Foreign Office that Barghash must be supported against all encroachments from outside, especially from Egypt. Kirk was ready to go to the limit in this matter. He was even willing, illogically, to support the slave-traders in Central Africa since they were to some extent the agents of the Sultan, and could serve a useful purpose there in keeping the Egyptians at bay. In particular, though not of course very publicly, he made a friend of Mohammed bin Sayed, who was the greatest trader of them all. Mohammed bin Sayed, who was generally known as Tippu Tib (a nickname that referred to an affliction in his eyes that made him blink), is not a character who can be understood in Western terms, for he was a gangster of the most brutal kind with all the attributes of a scholarly and distinguished gentleman. He was tall, darkskinned, black-bearded and very good-looking, an authoritative figure, beautifully dressed, intelligent to talk to, a pirate of considerable charm and delicacy.

This gentle ruffian—and we shall see his kind repeated later in the Sudan—was a man of immense wealth, and his splendid house in the centre of Zanzibar (which still stands) was the terminus of a network of caravans that were already working up to the borders of the Congo and beyond. He was not normally in Zanzibar, however; he was more often to be found on the shores of Lake Tanganyika and on the Lualaba River, and there he behaved like a robber-baron in his own right. In the past he had been one of the slavemasters who had saved Livingstone from destitution in the interior, and he had furnished Stanley with porters on his march across Africa. And now, provided his own pocket was well lined, he was quite ready to put his resources at the disposal of Barghash and Kirk in their struggle against Egypt.

It must have been a curious little community on the island at this time, at once intimate and antagonistic. Bishop

Steere, of the British Universities Mission to Central Africa, was at work designing and building his new cathedral on the site of the old slave-market, a remarkable structure with an unsupported roof made of ground-up coral and cement that has survived intact to the present day. The crucifix on the pillar at the left-hand side of the chancel is made from the wood of the tree which marked the place where Livingstone died south of Lake Bangweolo, in Central Africa. The Moslems of Zanzibar must have hated this citadel of the unbelievers, but the Bishop was never molested in his work. Kirk had his chapel and his house on a little promontory just outside the town, and there he indulged himself in his passion for planting exotic flowering trees. They rise up splendidly now in the heavy scented silence of the island: the frangipani with its starlike, waxy flower, the purple jacaranda, the flamboyant and the cannibal-tree which sucks insects into its lurid pink and yellow blossoms and which, perhaps, might be taken as a symbol of the brutality and the beauty of the island as it was nearly a century ago.

Then there were Barghash's various palaces and kiosks, with his retinue of wives, relatives, slaves and hangers-on; and the narrow hectic streets running down to the port; and, in the port itself, the brigs of Salem, the dhows, the India merchantmen, and the new steamers with their paddle-boxes and their thin vertical funnels sticking up like chimney pots among the rigging.

Despite the cholera epidemics and the restrictions upon slavery the town had grown busier and more prosperous in recent years. A group of shops had sprung up behind the palace: coppersmiths, goldsmiths and ivory-dealers with their piles of tusks. The wealthiest people of all were the money-lenders who charged enormous rates of interest. There was no one coinage: Indian rupees, English pounds, American dollars, French francs, and Egyptian piastres were all in circulation, but the Maria Theresa Austrian dollar, worth about five shillings, was the chief currency. Great caravans setting out for the interior made a constant stir of movement on the waterfront, and throughout the day coolies kept up a monotonous chant as they trotted with their burdens between the dhows and the godowns on the docks. Every well-to-do Arab, riding forth on his donkey, had a slave running before him to clear a way through the dense, quarrelling crowds. There was a lively business in drugs and narcotics, and any open space served as a school where Arab boys, sitting in a circle, droned through the words of the Koran.

It was a complex little beehive of widely differing manners, religions and politics, the East struggling against the West, Islam against Christianity, the worst of poverty surviving under the utmost luxury, and it was all too fragile and too disordered to last. Yet in the early eighteen-seventies Zanzibar was capable of making one more effort to maintain its independence, and Barghash and Kirk between them were still a match for the Khedive in Egypt.

Cairo through these years was becoming very grand. The days when travellers like Kinglake could speak of the open market of slave-girls, of unpaved streets, of no fine buildings other than the mosques, and of lions tied up like dogs in the citadel, were gone, or at any rate, rapidly going. The opening of the canal had brought a great influx of Western ideas into the capital. We have Winwood Reade's description, written about 1873: 'Cairo, like Rome and Florence, lives upon tourists, who, if they are not beloved, are welcome; the city is lighted by gas; it has public gardens in which a native military band performs every afternoon; an excellent theatre for which Verdi composed *Aïda*; new houses in the Parisian style are springing up by streets, and are let out at high rents as soon as they are finished. No gentleman wears a turban ... Already there is telegraphic communication between Cairo and Khartoum, and a railway is about to be commenced. As for the Soudan, it was formerly divided among a number of barbarous chiefs almost incessantly at war. It is now conquered and at peace, and trade is seldom disturbed ... The traffic in slaves is abolished ...' He goes on to describe the Khedive, now in his early forties, as possessing 'marvellous intelligence and energy'.

Perhaps Cairo really did seem like this to a passing tourist in the eighteen-seventies—and there is certainly no cause to doubt Reade's description of the physical appearance of the city—but to anyone who knew the real facts about the Khedive and the Sudan his account is absurd. The Sudan was not at peace, trade there was on the point of ruin except in one department—the traffic in slaves, which was flourishing more strongly than ever; and in Cairo the Khedive was using all his remarkable intelligence and energy in the desperate pursuit of money.

He quadrupled the land-tax, gathered one-fifth of Egypt's arable land into his own hands and extorted money from the fellaheen with the use of the whip; but still it was not enough to keep pace with his own spending or to satisfy his creditors. With the ending of the Civil War in America the price of cotton fell, and this still further increased his difficulties. Then, too, in every enterprise Ismail was swindled by his own officials, and although he was everywhere installing machinery and modern, Western devices he was actually getting less out of the land than he had done at the opening of his reign. Egypt was becoming bankrupt, and in 1875 he was driven to the expedient of selling his Suez Canal shares to Britain for £4 million. The canal was a great success; in the first year after its opening 500 vessels passed through, but from now on Egypt received very little financial benefit from it.

None of these difficulties however deterred Ismail from his plans for the conquest of the valley of the Nile.

'The audacity manifested in all these projects of empire,' Stanley wrote, 'is perfectly marvellous—almost as wonderful as the total absence of common-sense.' But then common-sense had never been a mainspring at the Abdin Palace; Ismail was out for the full, rich life, and if his course led downhill he was still determined to proceed at speed. With Baker's return to Europe he cast about for another European who would take charge of his campaign into Equatoria and the regions round the sources of the Nile, and his choice fell on Colonel Charles George Gordon of the British Royal Engineers.

Gordon was 41 and already a famous man: he had served with great bravery in the Crimean War, and had led the Ever Victorious Army through its hazardous adventures in China. Even the six anonymous years he had just passed in garrison duty at the mouth of the Thames in England had not really diminished his reputation as an eccentric adventurer and Bible-soldier, one of the long line of British military mystics that leads on to such generals as Orde Wingate in the last of the great world wars. We have, therefore, to consider him here, not as he was in his early struggles, but in the last ten years of his life.

One of the strangest aspects of Gordon is the changing nature of the reputation that has overtaken him since his death. He dies as a national hero more loved and pitied than any other figure in the Victorian age, not even Livingstone excepted. There can seldom have been, at any one time, such a widely read book as his posthumous *Khartoum Journals*; they were known to every literate adult in England and established a legend which seemed to his contemporaries to be as noble as the classic heroism of St. George. Then, most unexpectedly, a quarter of a century after his death, a homosexual intellectual revives the story, and all at once Gordon takes on a new reputation in Lytton Strachey's detached and ironical essay in *Eminent Victorians*. Here we have Gordon as the pious toper who likes a 'b. and s.' for breakfast, and then again more brandy and more soda when he retires, sometimes for days on end, into his tent in a fit of melancholy depression. This Gordon is still brave, still the mystical man-of-action, still quixotically generous and kind, still an erratic sort of saint, but definitely a little mad.

For a later generation, however, this brilliant denigration of the hero will not do at all. We are told that Strachey was all wrong about the b. and s., and that the stories of his drunken bouts of black depression were nothing but libels put about by Chaillé-Long who was an unreliable person, and whom Gordon certainly despised. The character that now emerges is a man with a reputation such as Field-Marshal Montgomery might have had, especially if he had died at the height of his battles: a concentrated and highly efficient soldier, a man of great piety and simplicity who put aside all the normal distractions and comforts of life in order to serve his fellow-men. There is something scout-masterish about this figure, with his spartan life, his deep interest in the welfare of boys, his proficiency in playing games and his emphasis upon duty; and if he is a little too vain, a little too fond of publicity, then this is only part of his flair for leadership and his genuine, courageous faith in himself.

The comparison, of course, will not stand too close a scrutiny, since Montgomery married and Gordon did not, Gordon undeniably was a heavy smoker and was well known at least to take a drink from time to time, while the Field-Marshal has always been a total abstainer; and there are other more important differences besides. But there is enough similarity in the lives of the two men to establish a relationship between them, and perhaps this third and latest character given to Gordon comes closer to the truth than the other two.

Yet who will ever understand General Gordon? No matter how much evidence is compiled, both for and against him, an elusive quality remains, and it is strange that, being so unlike other men, he yet should strike such an instant chord of recognition in our minds, so that we laugh with him at his most reckless jests, and feel that we comprehend something of his mystical strivings. When he is being most diffi-cult and hobgoblinish in his dealings with officialdom, we are, irrationally, nearly always on his side. He does what we feel we ourselves would have done had we the same icon-oclastic courage and individuality. He can switch his loyalties in twenty different directions and still he seems to us to be utterly loyal to the fundamentals of his own nature and to mankind; he worships in no church but he is an intensely religious man just the same. It is no wonder that almost without exception everyone who served him loved him. He was a most moving man; he could charm the birds out of the trees with those bright blue eyes in the sunburnt face, with his boyishness (despite the touch of grey in his hair) and his absolute sincerity. It is useless for him to protest that he loses his temper at times and gives way to occasional at-tacks of 'the doles'; useless for him to say, 'Talk of two na-tures in one! I have a hundred, and none think alike and

all want to rule;' and again, 'No man in the world is more
changeable than I am.' We know him very well (which is not
quite the same thing as understanding him); he is the man
who is completely selfless, who is always interested in us
no matter who we may be, and who always wants to help.
Here is *baraka* a hundredfold.

Gordon was at Constantinople in 1872 when Nubar
Pasha, the Egyptian Prime Minister, met him in the British
Embassy and asked him if he could recommend a man to
replace Baker as Governor of Equatoria. Gordon replied
that he himself would accept the post if he could obtain
leave from the British army, and the matter was finally settled on his return to England in the following year. On January 28, 1874—the same day that the news of Livingstone's
death was received in England—he set off to take up the appointment, and arrived in Cairo ten days later. Gordon liked
the Khedive at their first meeting, and the Khedive, on his
side, was delighted to find that Gordon entirely approved of
his plans for expanding the Egyptian empire to the great
lakes in the centre of the continent. The details of the appointment were quickly settled: Gordon was to establish a
chain of military stations down the White Nile from Gondokoro to the source of the river in Buganda, to annex
Buganda itself and then to launch Baker's steamers upon
Lake Albert and Lake Victoria. The usual worthy clause
about abolishing the slave-trade was added to his instructions and he was to acknowledge in a general way the authority of Ismail Pasha Ayoub, the Governor-General of
the Sudan, who had his headquarters in Khartoum.

Gordon must have seemed a rare bird in the predatory
world of the Cairo officials, and they can hardly have approved of him. He rejected Baker's salary of £10,000 a
year—£2,000, he said, was all that was necessary—and
there was a brisk and authoritative air about the way he
made his arrangements. The selection of his staff presented
no particular difficulty; from every part of the world at this
time adventurous young men were making their way to
Egypt in the hope of obtaining employment with the Khedive or of getting themselves attached to one or other of the

expeditions setting out for the interior. There were Americans like Chaillé-Long, Colonel Prout, Major Campbell and Lieutenant-Colonel Mason, whose zest for action had not been satisfied by the Civil War in the United States; young Englishmen like Lieutenant Chippindall and Gordon's nephew, Willy Anson, who had caught Gordon's eye in the past and who now eagerly accepted his invitation to join the expedition; Frenchmen like Auguste and Ernest Linant de Bellefonds, and the Italian Romolo Gessi, who were already familiar with Egypt and the Middle East; and a number of others, naturalists, botanists, anthropologists and geologists, upon whom Africa cast a spell because they hoped to make discoveries which would open up a new world for science.

Then there were in addition the native Turks, Egyptians and Sudanese who provided the bulk of the officers and men for the expedition, and who followed the European and American leaders to the south, not out of any great love of adventure, but because they were ordered by the Khedive to go. Gordon was a rapid and spontaneous chooser of men. Baker, in England, observed with indignation that one of the principal posts on the staff was to be given to the notorious slaver, Abu Saoud. But everyone was grist to Gordon's mill; if he thought he could use a man he believed he could reform him; and he argued that Abu Saoud, in the manner of a poacher turned gamekeeper, would have a valuable knowledge of the local conditions, and would help him to deal with the Arab slavers on the Nile.

Some of these men were already in the Sudan, others were to join Gordon later, and for the moment it was decided to split the force into two halves; while the Italian Gessi and one or two others remained behind to organize the stores and bring them up the Nile to Khartoum, Gordon and Chaillé-Long were to go ahead by the Red Sea route and make contact with the garrisons Baker had left behind in Equatoria. Gordon required just two weeks to complete these arrangements and then he was off at that breakneck pace which was to characterize all his journeys in Africa. He travelled by sea from Suez to Suakin and then, mounting a camel for the first time, he rode across the Nubian desert, arriving at Khartoum in the record time of twenty-one days. Strachey describes his reception:

'On his way up the Nile, he was received in state at Khartoum by the Egyptian Governor-General of the Sudan, his immediate official superior. The function ended in a prolonged banquet, followed by a mixed ballet of soldiers and completely naked young women, who danced in a circle, beat time with their feet, and accompanied their gestures with a curious sound of clucking. At last the Austrian Consul, overcome by the exhilaration of the scene, flung himself in a frenzy among the dancers; the Governor-General, shouting with delight, seemed about to follow suit, when Gordon abruptly left the room, and the party broke up in confusion.'

Gordon delayed only nine days in Khartoum before embarking by steamer for his capital at Gondokoro, a thousand miles away in the south. He was fortunate to find an open channel through the Sudd, and after a voyage of twenty-five days the *Bordein* brought him to his destination. A year had now elapsed since Baker had left Equatoria, and the province had gone to ruin. At Gondokoro the garrison had long since lost all discipline; the soldiers were paid either in spirits or slave-girls shipped up the river to them from Khartoum, and the old corrupt control of the Egyptian officials governed all. Within five days Gordon reached a series of drastic decisions: the officials he found dealing in slaves were dismissed, Chaillé-Long was dispatched to Buganda to make contact with Mutesa, and he himself sailed directly back to Khartoum. Here he demanded of the Governor-General that Equatoria henceforth should be separated from the rest of the Sudan and treated as an independent state. When Ismail Pasha Ayoub naturally refused, Gordon got through on the telegraph to Cairo and obtained the Khedive's consent. Next, with a boat-load of Austrian dollars (with which he proposed to pay his soldiers in lieu of their spirits and slave-girls), he sailed north to Berber, where he met Gessi and the remainder of his staff coming up the river. By the end of May he had his whole party together, and he sailed south once more for Gondo-koro with four steamers and their attendant barges.

Now finally Gordon began to realize that he had embarked upon an enterprise that was infinitely more hazardous than anything he had undertaken in China. South of Gondokoro the river had never yet been navigated or mapped, and much of the territory he proposed to invade was still unexplored. His Egyptian soldiers had antagonized the tribes for miles around with their ruthless pillaging and no traveller could move in any direction except with an armed guard. The climate was unbearable; to avoid the mosquitoes it was necessary to go to bed before seven in the evening, and one after another the Europeans succumbed to malaria and the fearful heat. Before the end of the year three of them were dead, others were ill and others again had to be invalided home. Gordon alone remained miraculously unscathed—perhaps because he never allowed himself for a moment to be idle.

In these terrible circumstances—and it is safe to say that no modern traveller in Africa can have any inkling of how bad they were—the true nature and capability of his companions soon began to reveal itself. Chaillé-Long went down with fever on his return from Buganda and had to be sent to Khartoum to recuperate. Gordon cannot have been sorry to see him go, for he was proving to be a braggart and a complainer. Abu Saoud by natural instinct returned to his slave-dealing and his treachery the moment he reached Gondokoro, for he knew no other way of life, and Gordon was forced to get rid of him. Ernest Linant de Bellefonds, whose brother had already died, was the next to go. He had, as we have seen, replaced Chaillé-Long at Mutesa's capital in Buganda and had met Stanley there. But he had hardly returned to Equatoria before he was speared in an action against the Bari tribe. In the same skirmish Baker's Forty Thieves, the corps d'élite of Gordon's little army, were practically wiped out. Of the other officers on his staff only Gessi seemed to be able to rise above the appalling hardships which oppressed and unnerved them all from time to time.

It is strange that Romolo Gessi is not better known either in Africa or in his own country (a street has been named after him in Ravenna, but there is little else in Italy to recall his memory), for he is the greatest of Italian pioneers on the Nile. Of all Gordon's lieutenants Gessi was the toughest, the most cheerful, the most determined and the best. Gordon described him thus: 'Italian subject, aged 49 [in 1881]. Short, compact figure; cool, most determined man. Born genius for practical ingenuity in mechanics. Ought to have been born in 1560 not 1832. Same disposition as Francis Drake. Had been engaged in many petty political affairs. Was interpreter to Her Majesty's Forces in the Crimea, and attached to the headquarters of the Royal Artillery.'

Gessi, who had been born of an Italian father and an Armenian mother in Constantinople, was almost the same age as Gordon, and the two men had much in common; while Gordon was leading the Ever Victorious Army in China, Gessi was fighting with Garibaldi for the liberation of Italy, and they had served together in the Crimea. Both were at their best in irregular guerrilla warfare, for by nature they remained cool and steady in the most bizarre and dangerous of circumstances, and neither of them had much time for the regular peacetime soldier's world of parades, uniforms and promotions. In sum, they were men of the commando type, and they complemented one another very well: where Gordon was sensitive, solitary and ascetic, Gessi was warm-hearted and gregarious, and both were impulsively brave. They were equally prone to violent outbursts of anger, but that too may have been a bond; for it cleared their differences like a sudden thunderstorm, and always in a crisis they were loyal.

Now, however, amid the strains and setbacks of the opening of his expedition, Gordon felt it was necessary to send this most reliable of all his men back to Khartoum so that he could hasten the dispatch of his steamers up the river. Thus he was left almost alone with his native soldiers to open up the route to the south.

'I have been a good deal worn,' Gordon wrote to a friend at the end of 1874, 'and I fear my temper is *very*

very bad, but the people are trying and it is no use unless one is feared.'

It was during these early days that he gave way to his fits of melancholy. According to Strachey (who picked up the story from Chaillé-Long), he sometimes sat in his tent 'with a hatchet and a flag placed at the door to indicate that he was not to be disturbed for any reason whatever; until at last the cloud would lift, the signals would be removed, and the Governor would reappear, brisk and cheerful'. In one such crisis Chaillé-Long says that he nerved himself to enter the tent and there he found Gordon silently sitting with an open Bible and a bottle of whisky.

Whether or not these stories be true (and their implication that Gordon was a drunkard is certainly a lie) they cannot affect the fact that Gordon, during these early years on the Upper Nile, accomplished far more than he ever did in his last fatal stand in Khartoum eight years later. The Bible was opened in the morning, the text was read, and then, inspired and uplifted, he emerged to grapple with the problems of the day. He did not proceed as his predecessor Baker had done; he was not a shooter of Africans and he made raids upon the tribes only under the direst necessity. He admired their resistance to this violent intrusion from the outside world and their refusal, at first, to deal with him. He envisaged them as saying, 'We don't want your cloth and beads, we do not want to see your chief. . . . we want you to go away.' He coaxed and persuaded the African chiefs, he infused the blaze of his energy into his own men, and he was adamant; he simply would not accept defeat.

One of his first acts on his arrival in Equatoria was to move his headquarters from Gondokoro to a healthier climate some miles further downstream at Lado. Next he tackled the problem of the river itself. A little above Gondokoro it broke into rapids, followed by a fairly smooth stretch of some thirty miles, then again more rapids that came racing down through steep, heavily-wooded banks from regions that were quite unknown. Even today no steamer attempts to make the passage through this dan-

gerous and turbulent section of the river—and it runs for
about a hundred miles from the present-day town of Juba
to Dufilé on the Uganda border—but in 1874 Gordon
believed he could manage it. He had three steamers, the
251-ton paddle-boat *Ismailia*, which Baker had left behind
in sections in Khartoum and which Gessi was now assembling in the dockyards there, the 108-ton *Khedive*, a still
smaller vessel the 38-ton *Nyanza*, and two steel boats. In
Gordon's phrase he 'prayed' these vessels up the river, and
a fantastic amount of ingenuity and of physical labour was
involved. He himself went ahead carefully mapping the
stream and establishing military outposts at regular inter-
vals along the banks. The *Khedive* was the first vessel to
come up behind him, partly sailing under her own steam,
and partly being winched up by gangs of natives towing
on long lines from the bank. By September 1875, she had
covered barely half the distance to Dufilé and then one
day she broke from her moorings and stuck fast upon a
rock. The prospect of even worse disaster lay ahead; advancing up the Nile Gordon for the first time came in sight
of the Fola Falls which are the last and most serious obstacle in the Nile before Dufilé is reached. 'It is all over,'
he wrote. '. . . I fancied for some time I heard a voice like
thunder, which increased as we approached the river. At
last we stood above it on a rocky bank covered with vegetation, which descended abruptly to the stream, and there
it was appalling to look at, far less to think of getting anything up or down, except in splinters . . . it boiled down,
twisting into all sorts of eddies, while the banks, steep
and precipitous, prevented a great length of view. These
shoots last two miles.'

He resolved now to abandon the *Khedive* for the time
being and to send for Gessi, who was to bring up the
smaller vessel, the *Nyanza*, and the two steel boats as far
as possible under their own power. Below the Fola Falls
they were to be dismantled and a thousand men were to
carry them in pieces over land to Dufilé, where they were
to be put together again. Gordon himself meanwhile
pushed ahead on foot to establish more stations to the
south and to complete his conquest of Buganda. Walking

at the rate of 16 miles a day in intense heat he made first towards Baker's old outposts at Fatiko and Foweira. Baker had been in ecstasies about the beauty of this country. Gordon described it, 'A more dreary, weary set of marches you cannot conceive. The country is quite uninhabited—a vast undulating prairie of jungle grass and scrub-trees . . . Everything relating to this country has been much exaggerated.'

Dropping off soldiers at Fatiko and Foweira he continued on again to the south, and in a final forced march of thirty miles reached Mrooli, which is about ten miles east of the modern Masindi Port on Lake Kyoga, and here still another outpost was set up. There had been occasional skirmishing with the natives along the way, but Kabarega had fled before Gordon's advance, and now at last the expedition was within reach of Lake Victoria and the source of the Nile. Nuehr Aga, one of the best of Gordon's native officers, was sent on with a force of 160 men to establish a base in Buganda, while Gordon himself turned back to see how things were progressing at the rapids. He reached Dufilé on February 8, 1876, after covering 400 miles in 40 days. Here he learned that the *Khedive* had been floated off the rocks but was far down the river, and the *Nyanza* was still in the process of being reassembled above the Fola Falls. However, the two steel boats, each of ten tons, were afloat at Dufilé, and Gordon decided to dispatch them up the river to explore the unknown section that presumably led on to Lake Albert.

This was a moment of great triumph, for it seemed now, with the sailing of these two boats, that the conquest of Central Africa lay clear before them. Gordon, of course, would not permit himself the pleasant and exhilarating experience of taking charge of this voyage himself; that would have been self-indulgence. He handed over the command to Romolo Gessi and Carlo Piaggia, another Italian explorer who had just arrived, and wrote, perhaps a little too sententiously, in a letter to one of his correspondents, 'I wish to give practical proof of what I think regarding the inordinate praise which is given to an explorer.' On March 6, 1876, Gessi and Piaggia sailed away on that green and beautiful stretch of the Nile that runs to Lake Albert, and Gordon walked back to Lado, a hundred miles away, to await their return.

Gessi was back at the end of April, to be followed soon afterwards by Piaggia, and they had news that was both exciting and disturbing. Above Dufilé the Nile, they had discovered, did in fact lead on to Lake Albert without rapids or obstacles of any sort. At the entrance to the lake Gessi had continued around its shores and had discovered it to be much smaller than Baker had thought, while Piaggia had struck out eastwards in canoes, carrying them around the Murchison and Karuma Falls, and had reached Lake Kyoga. All this was a solid geographical gain, but the disturbing thing was that both men claimed that on their journeys they had discovered new branches of the Nile; Gessi said that he had seen a stream flowing out of the river to the west a few miles above Lake Albert. Piaggia declared there was a similar river flowing out of Lake Kyoga to the north-east. What then was the true course of the Nile; which was the main stream?

Gordon decided now to investigate the matter for himself, for he was determined to map the river accurately from Gondokoro to its source. The *Nyanza* was now afloat at Dufilé, and on July 20, 1876, he went on board and steamed to the south, towing the two steel boats. He soon established that Gessi's new river, north of Lake Albert, was a fiction, and then steamed east as far as the Murchison Falls, where he disembarked and continued on foot along the bank of the river until he reached Foweira for the second time in six months. It was now clear that he had no hope whatever of getting the steamers up the river past the Murchison Falls, and in a further journey to the south as far as Lake Kyoga he discovered that Piaggia's alternative outlet to the north-east failed to exist. A further disappointment was awaiting him; at Foweira Nuehr Aga met him with the news that, far from his having annexed Buganda, Mutesa had virtually imprisoned the Egyptian garrison there. Gordon wrote grimly in his journal, 'Mutesa has annexed my soldiers; he has not been annexed himself,' and another officer was sent south to extract the garrison from Buganda.

Nor was this all. Another and even more ambitious plan of Gordon's for the conquest of the great lakes had come to nothing. There is a reference to it in one of the letters Gordon wrote at this time. 'I see,' he wrote, 'that the Khedive withdrew his troops from Juba by the command of the British government.' This had been a strange business. Early in 1875 Gordon, in the midst of his difficulties on the Nile, had conceived that it might be possible to find a better route into Central Africa by striking inland from Jubaland on the east coast of the continent, and he had written, 'I have proposed to the Khedive to send 150 men in a steamer to Mombaz [Mombasa] Bay, 250 miles north of Zanzibar, and there to establish a station, and then to push towards Mutesa. If I can do that, I shall make my base at Mombaz and give up Khartoum and the bother of the steamers etc. . . . The Centre of Africa would be much more effectually opened out, as the only valuable parts of the country are the high lands near Mutesa, while south of this [i.e. south of Lado] is wretched marsh. I hope the Khedive will do it.'

This was a really spectacular notion, for it entailed nothing less than the encirclement of Abyssinia (with which Egypt was already at war) and the invasion of Barghash's dominions on the east coast of Africa. Once a route from Mombasa to the Great Lakes was established the Khedive would be in a position not only to control the whole valley of the Nile but large sections of Central and East Africa as well. The smallness of the force that Gordon proposed to land indicates that, as yet, he knew very little of the geography of the regions he was invading, and still less about the politics of Africa. It was hardly likely, for example, that Barghash and Kirk in Zanzibar would look on this adventure in a very kindly light. Gordon indeed did anticipate some slight trouble from that quarter, but he brushed it aside. In the course of a letter he wrote to Burton inquiring about conditions on the Somaliland coast he remarked, 'You must know nothing would delight the

Zanzibar Consul better than to have the thwarting of such a scheme inasmuch as it would bring him into notice and give him the opportunity to write to the F.O.' This was uncharitable, and it was also greatly underrating Kirk.

The Khedive, however, had liked the idea very much indeed. He already had in his service a Captain H. F. McKillop who was on loan from the British Royal Navy, and this officer was now placed in command of the enterprise. Chaillé-Long, on his return from Equatoria, was also enlisted, together with 550 Egyptian soldiers who were to carry out the operations on land. In September 1875 they sailed from Suez in four warships, and this, the craziest of all African adventures, opened with a certain *panache*. The first landing was made at Barawa, which was a northern outpost of Barghash's on the coast of what is now Somaliland. There was no opposition. Barghash's flag was hauled down on the fort and replaced by the Egyptian banner, and in order to ingratiate themselves with the natives the European commanders of the expedition announced that slaving (which had been made a criminal offence by Barghash two years before) was legal once more. A hundred men under an Egyptian officer were put ashore as a garrison, and the expedition sailed on to Kismayu. Here Chaillé-Long landed with the remainder of the force. Once again there was no bloodshed; four hundred of Barghash's soldiers surrendered and the town collapsed. A third landing was then made at Lamu, still further to the south.

It is hard to see what Chaillé-Long and McKillop imagined they were next to do. They had succeeded in raising a commotion along the whole coast; the wildest rumours flew from town to town and everywhere, even as far south as Mombasa, it was reported that the rule of the Zanzibar sultans was broken at last: Egypt had taken command and the great age of unmolested slaving was to begin anew. But where were Chaillé-Long and his 550 men supposed to go? They had no camels or transport animals of any kind, and Gordon was in the centre of Africa hundreds of miles away towards the west. They could not hope to command the coast with so minute a force, they could not even stay where they were; they had no supplies and no coal for their ships. Moreover Kirk was now aroused.

Directly Kirk heard the news of the landings he boarded H.M.S. *Thetis*, which happened to be in Zanzibar just then, and sailed north at speed to Barawa. At first when he attempted to land he was met by armed Egyptians who forced him back on board, and it was only when he threatened to bombard the town that the Egyptian commander let him come ashore. Kirk soon saw, however, that there was nothing to be done on the spot—this was an international affair that had to be settled in London and Cairo—and he returned in haste to Zanzibar, where he sent off a strong protest to the Foreign Office. This was supported by a similar message sent by Barghash to the Khedive.

Meanwhile, the position of McKillop and Chaillé-Long was becoming ludicrous; made desperate by their lack of supplies they sent a ship into Zanzibar to obtain coal. Barghash was with some difficulty restrained by Kirk from capturing the ship, and instead he handed over the coal to the Egyptians with a polite note for McKillop: 'I send you the coal you desire, also fruit. The latter may serve to keep you in good health, the former to take you away from my country. Go, and peace be with you.'

If there had ever been the ghost of a chance of the expedition forcing a *fait accompli* upon Barghash it was now gone. The Foreign Office was disposed to support him since he had capitulated over the anti-slavery agreement of 1873, and there was, in addition, a large and influential group of people in England who had no wish to see the Khedive push his corrupt rule down into Central Africa. The missionary societies were against him, the liberal press took up the cry, and Grant, who was now regarded as an expert on African affairs, added his voice.

In Cairo the Khedive saw that the game was up—indeed, it had been a farce from beginning to end—and McKillop was ordered to re-embark his troops and return home. The whole adventure had occupied only three or four months.

So now in Central Africa, where the news of these happenings penetrated at last in 1876, Gordon was forced to admit that he had made a mistake. He wrote to Lord Derby, the Prime Minister, in England saying that he, personally, was to blame for the whole affair, and in a further letter to Kirk he made an apology of a kind. He assured him that he now had no further designs on Buganda, and that his garrison was being withdrawn from Mutesa's capital.

Gordon had now been for two and a half years in Central Africa, and if he had failed in his grand design—the annexation of the Nile from Gondokoro to its source and the launching of his steamers on Lake Victoria—he had only just failed. The river was accurately mapped and explored for the first time to within sixty miles of its source, the *Nyanza* was afloat on Lake Albert and the *Khedive* was soon to join her there; the Arab slavers had been driven out of Equatoria, and his military forts held a secure control from one end of his province to the other. Even more important, perhaps, than all this, he had prevented his own soldiers from pillaging the inhabitants, and had converted the tribes along the river from enemies into friends. It was now possible for a single traveller to move about armed with nothing more than a walking stick. That was something of a marvel for Central Africa.

The forts alone had been a remarkable achievement. Already they had begun to take on the appearance of settled townships. There were about a dozen of them in all and they formed a connected chain stretching for 600 miles from Fashoda on lat. 10 N. almost as far south as the Equator, the principal ones being Lado, the new capital of the province, Dufilé and, later, Wadelai, on the Upper Nile to the north of Lake Albert. These places were very much alike. Each enclosed an area of about half a dozen acres at some convenient spot on the river bank where there was a good crossing, free of papyrus, and a clear line of vision both upstream and down. One side was open to the river, and here, as a rule, a landing stage and a little shipbuilding yard were constructed so that the steamers could be assembled and repaired. The other three sides consisted of a high, thick, earthen embankment surrounded by a ditch. From the river's edge neat streets of straw huts ran inland, and in the centre of the fort were the brick buildings of the principal officers, the storehouses and the ammunition dump. Cannon were posted round the embankment and the Khedive's red flag floated overhead. Normally a little shade would be provided by the borassus palms and the flat-topped acacia trees, but the forts were always hot and humid places infested by mosquitoes and subject to malaria. The grass and scrub outside the embankments were cut down so as to give a clear line of fire and to provide space for vegetable gardens and cotton and cassava plantations.

Gordon had imposed his own strict notions of discipline on the garrisons: a bugle sounded reveillé at 5.30 a.m. when the day was breaking—a strange sound in this wilderness. (The tribesmen remembered it in after years; in the Murchison Game Park in Uganda there is still a place called Bugili. It stands on the river opposite the ruins of Gordon's old fort at Magungo, and was so named by the natives because a man standing there could hear the sound of the garrison bugles, and thus be warned that he was getting too close for comfort.)

The streets were then swept and the soldiers turned their women out to work in the fields through the day. At 8 p.m. the gates of the fort were locked for the night and the evening meal was cooked and eaten.

It was a monotonous existence, of course, since the steamers and the supplies and letters they brought were the lifestream of the garrisons, and often weeks and months would go by before the sound of a distant whistle would send everyone rushing to the river bank. But then Central Africa, like any other tropical place, had its own torpid methods of enhancing life. It was always possible that the tribesmen might attack. The brilliant birds and the wild animals were always about them, the hippopotamuses and the crocodiles in the river, the elephants and the rhinoceroses (the rare white species in these regions) in the surrounding bush. The soldiers fished for the Nile perch and the tilapia, they brewed their native beer, they found wives among the local tribes, they danced at the full moon, and they turned towards Mecca for their daily prayers. If the

steamers failed then there were always couriers passing
along the jungle paths that linked one garrison with the
next, and in their isolation in this green world of the river
they produced their own gossip and their own crimes. It
was an intimate, organized, ant-heap sort of life, and at
least it provided security where there had been nothing
but uncertainty and savagery before.

But Gordon was tired. In all his two and a half years
on the Upper Nile he had never taken so much as a day's
holiday, and he had driven himself to the utmost. Although
he had never been seriously ill he had been surrounded
from the beginning with the sickness and death of his men,
and the unrelenting climate of the Nile had, for the moment, undermined his strength. Often too he had been in
physical danger, and it is a sign of his exhaustion that
about this time he quarrelled with Gessi: it was the quarrel of two men who had been strained too much.

According to Gessi's son, who wrote an account of the
incident many years later, Gessi was aggrieved because the
other officers on Gordon's staff received higher rewards
than he did. Matters came to a head when Gessi returned
from his circumnavigation of Lake Albert and Gordon,
delighted with his achievement, was incautious enough to
remark, 'What a pity you are not an Englishman.' At that
Gessi took off his cap, threw it on the floor, and gave in
his resignation.

This obviously is not the whole story, but there is no
doubt that some such scene took place, and Gessi certainly
departed. However, they must have made things up soon
afterwards because Gordon, too, was determined to resign,
and the two men made their way down to Cairo together
at the end of 1876.

Perhaps Gordon's very success had disheartened him,
for his work in Equatoria had revealed the enormity of
the problem of the whole Sudan. Gordon, in short, was
like a surgeon who, in performing a local operation, dis-
covers that the whole body of his patient is diseased.

In Cairo he told the Khedive that he did not want to go
back, and although Ismail persuaded him to reconsider
the matter he went off on leave to England full of misgiv-

ings; and from England he sent in his definite resignation. It was something more than the gesture of a tired and disillusioned man; he was oppressed by an overwhelming sense of his own inadequacy. 'I have a sort of wish,' he was to write later to his sister, 'that I could get rid of Colonel Gordon'.

Chapter 10

THE CAMEL RIDER

'I am the chisel which cuts the wood:
the carpenter directs it.'—General Gordon.

THE SUDAN covers an area of nearly a million square miles, and in the eighteen-seventies it still possessed no towns of any size except Khartoum and El Obeid, the capital of Kordofan, virtually no railways, no roads, no means of transportation other than the boats on the Nile and the caravans of mules and camels in the desert. Almost the only link with the outside world was provided by the newly-made telegraph line that ran from Khartoum to Cairo. It was estimated that nine million people lived in this enormous space, but it may have been a million more or less, since it was impossible to count them, and no one as yet had defined the borders of the country. There were no borders. To the east a sort of boundary was provided by the Red Sea and the mountains of Abyssinia, and it was generally conceded that the northern frontier with Egypt lay somewhere in the neighbourhood of Wadi Halfa, just south of the Tropic of Cancer. But to the west the unmapped plains spread away into the wilderness which came to be known as French Equatorial Africa, and to the south Gordon's forts had established only a rough and ready border on the Nile above Buganda.

The Sudanese were a mixed race, an intermingling of the Arabs with the black indigenous tribes. Apart from the pagan Negroes on the Nile most of the people were Moslems. A network of Egyptian military garrisons, most of them many hundreds of miles apart, was established in the country, but whenever there was trouble the soldiers were hardly more than prisoners within their own forts. It was like the sea: the desert kept the inhabitants constantly on the move in search of pasture and water for their animals, and every trading-post was a kind of port where the caravans rested for a while and then went on their way again.

Outside Khartoum the Egyptian government had no real authority. The tribes and the slave and ivory traders made their own law, and it was the law of force. Equatoria, of course, was now in a different case, but then Equatoria was only a small corner of the Sudan, and the authority that Gordon had established there had very little hope of surviving so long as an Egyptian governor-general sat in Khartoum. Until that official was supplanted by an honest and efficient man and the whole Egyptian system was uprooted, there was no hope for the Sudan. Gordon had seen this very clearly. That was why he had resigned.

Once again the real issue was slavery. Baker had been altogether too optimistic, if not downright misleading, when he declared that he had abolished slavery from the Nile: all he had been able to do was to drive the traffic off the river, and now it was flourishing more strongly than ever in the open desert. The traders had found very little difficulty in developing new overland routes to Egypt and the Red Sea, and in the provinces of Bahr-el-Ghazal, Darfur and Kordofan a vast manhunt was going on. At least 5,000 traders were operating there. Gessi estimated that since 1860, when the traffic began, more than 400,000 women and children had been taken from the area to be sold in Egypt and Turkey, and that many thousands more had died. Baker, he thought, had done very little to improve the situation: his second expedition had cost half a million pounds and had achieved 'no important result'. Gessi also asserted that Baker's methods had been unnecessarily harsh.

This was a cry that had already been taken up in England. On Baker's return home in 1873 he had been attacked as a dupe of Ismail's, and there had been a hot correspondence upon the matter in the columns of *The Times*. McWilliam, the engineer of the expedition, accused his leader of cruelty in his treatment of the tribes on the Upper Nile, and the nephew, Julian Baker, had written strongly in reply. These charges against Baker were not altogether fair, but Julian Baker was not the best man in the world to defend his uncle, for he had very little love for the Africans himself. In his journal he writes of 'the treachery of these brutes of niggers'.

Dr. Schweinfurth, the Baltic explorer and naturalist, was perhaps the most reliable witness of what had been happening, for he had been travelling for years in the remote Bahr-el-Ghazal province and he had no axe to grind for anybody. The picture he gave of the slaving there was appalling. He said that the traders who had been driven off the Nile swarmed through the region, and they ranged from the small man who went about the country on a couple of donkeys buying up three or four slaves at a time, to great merchant princes who dealt with their victims in tens of thousands. The Egyptian officials, Schweinfurth thought, had only made matters worse, since they promoted the slave-trade instead of controlling it; unless something was done the African tribes would be entirely wiped out. 'The kindest thing that the enlightened ruler of Egypt can do for these lands,' Schweinfurth wrote, 'is to leave them alone.'

It was a complex situation, for it was hard to say who was an official and who was a private trader. The case of Zobeir Pasha was really spectacular. Zobeir was the Tippu Tib of the Sudan, and he lived upon an even grander scale than the Zanzibar nabobs. Like Tippu Tib he was a man of distinguished appearance and courtly manners. When Winston Churchill, as a young man on his way to the Battle of Omdurman, met him in Cairo many years later he was dressed in a frock-coat and shiny boots, and he dispensed an air of great wealth and political authority. The huge spaces of Bahr-el-Ghazal and Darfur were his hunting ground. Here, in the dry clear antiseptic air of the desert and the Marra mountains, he disposed of a private army of Arab horsemen whose faces had the beauty and the predatory cruelty of hawks. They raided like Mongols for hundreds of miles into the interior and spread that special sort of terror which is fanatically Moslem, and absolutely ruthless. By 1874 Zobeir could fairly claim that he had conquered all Darfur and no one—certainly not the Egyptian officials—would have dreamed of contesting his authority. Schweinfurth visited his headquarters: 'Seebehr [Zobeir],' he writes, 'had surrounded himself with a court that was little short of princely in its details. A group of large well-built square huts, enclosed by tall hedges, composed the private residence; within these there were various state apartments before which armed sentries kept guard day and night. Special rooms, provided with carpeted divans, were reserved as ante-chambers, and into these all visitors were conducted by richly-dressed slaves, who served them with coffee, sherbet, and *tchibouks*. The regal aspect of these halls of state was increased by the introduction of some lions, secured, as may be supposed, by sufficiently strong and massive chains.' The master himself reclined on a couch behind a curtain in the inmost hut, outside which fakirs sat murmuring prayers, and domestic slaves stood waiting to be called.

About the time of Gordon's resignation Zobeir had left his young son Suleiman in charge of his slaving empire, and had gone down to Cairo to claim from the Khedive a *firman* which would establish him as the legal governor of Darfur.

Ismail, as ever, was in a difficult position. He had poured money into the Sudan, and except in Equatoria everything had gone wrong. The McKillop fiasco had been followed by two unsuccessful campaigns against the Negus of Abyssinia on the Red Sea littoral. In Khartoum the Egyptian Governor-General, Ismail Pasha Ayoub, had developed a system of bribery and extortion that was wonderfully complete, even by Egyptian standards. And here was Zobeir wanting to set himself up in Darfur as virtually an independent ruler who would take good care that precious little of his wealth would find its way down to Cairo.

It was too late for Ismail to retrench. Too much money had been expended on the Sudan, and too much prestige was involved for him to abandon the country altogether. He was like a man who has expanded his business far beyond his resources, and who faces bankruptcy in the midst of apparent prosperity; and so he must somehow go on and hope that the tide will turn one day. Even if the profits of the slave-trade were eluding him there were other natural resources in the Sudan which could be made to pay. Nominally he had a monopoly in the ivory trade, and although the elephants had been butchered in tens of thousands there were still further hunting fields to be exploited. The inexplicable craving of the outside world to have billiard balls, piano keys and statuettes of ivory was just as strong as ever, and nobody cared how many elephants were destroyed.[1] The ostrich-feather and gum-arabic trade also brought in a revenue, and there were other commercial products in the Sudan as well.

But how to manage all this? How to collect the revenue, come to terms with Abyssinia, clean up Khartoum, keep Equatoria going, and at the same time put Zobeir in his place? There was one man who might just conceivably accomplish all this, and that was Gordon.

In Gordon, Ismail had found a paragon, a governor who really governed and who was spectacularly uncorrupt. Gordon of course would make difficulties over the slave-trade, but even if he destroyed that valuable business or at any rate a large part of it, Gordon was still worth employing. He was the one available soldier who could conquer the Sudan and bring it under the direct control of the Abdin Palace. He, more than any other man, could prevent the bribery and wastage among the Egyptian officials on the Nile and guide the taxes safely back into the viceregal treasury. But would Gordon come back?

Ismail knew his man. On January 17, 1877, he telegraphed to Gordon in London: 'I refuse to believe that, when Gordon has once given his word as a gentleman, anything will ever induce him to go back on his word.' The telegram was signed, 'Your affectionate Ismail.'

Gordon's exploits on the Nile had been enthusiastically described by the newspapers in England, and he was once

[1] An exception was made of the Indian elephant which, unlike the African species, could be trained. The Khedive imported 6 animals from India and sent them to the Sudan—they walked the whole 2,000 miles from Cairo and swam the Nile 6 times—but they failed to be of any use.

more in the public eye. *The Times* had proposed that he should be appointed 'Governor of Bulgaria'—the country was then in the midst of its struggle for independence—and there was an alternative plan (which Gordon himself favoured) that he should lead an expedition against slavery inland from Zanzibar. But Ismail's telegram was compulsive, and after barely a month in England Gordon returned to Cairo. He arrived in February 1877 and named his terms: he must have the governor-generalship of the whole Sudan—all the million square miles of it—he must have full powers to treat with the Negus of Abyssinia and to suppress the slave-trade. Ismail agreed at once. Gordon describes the interview in the laconic style that presently the world was going to know so well: 'Then I began, and told him all; and then he gave me the Sudan, and I leave on Saturday morning.' The salary of the Governor-General of the Sudan was £6,000 a year. Gordon reduced it to £3,000. He did, however, accept a present of a fine gold-lace coat worth £150, and it proved most useful in impressing the tribesmen in the Sudan.

Sir Evelyn Baring (the future Earl of Cromer), who had just taken up his career as a British representative in Cairo, remarks dryly, 'Even assuming that Ismail Pasha was sincere in his desire to suppress slavery and to govern the Sudan well, nothing is more certain than that he was powerless to do so.'

Yet there is at least an air of sincerity in Ismail's dealings with Gordon. He had made things easier for him in Darfur by putting Zobeir under a form of house-arrest in Cairo. He gave him all the arms and men he wanted. He even wrote to the new viceroy as he was setting off to take up his post, 'Use all the powers I have given you. Take every step you think necessary; punish, change, dismiss all officials as you please.'

That was precisely what Gordon intended to do.

First he travelled down the Red Sea to Massawa, and there came to an agreement with the local Abyssinian chieftains for a suspension of hostilities. A long camel ride through the Red Sea provinces of the Sudan brought him to the Nile, and he burst in upon Khartoum on May 4, 1877.[1] There had been some apprehension about his coming, and the whole town was waiting on the river bank to receive him. He did not keep them waiting long. 'With the help of God,' he declared, 'I will hold the balance level.'

There then followed a stream of new statutes and decrees that were aimed at breaking up the power of the officials and making life more bearable for the poor. Flogging in the prisons was abolished, taxes upon the peasants were lightened or remitted altogether, a box for petitions was set up at the Palace door, the privileges of the Ulema (the Moslem teachers) were stopped, and the worst of the army officers and civil servants were sent packing to Cairo.

Gordon through these days presents himself at his best. He has not yet given way to the mood that was to make him write, 'When you have got the ink that has soaked into the blotting paper out of it, then slavery will cease in these lands.' He really believes that he can do something. The doles disappear, the slight crankiness in his character evaporates, and he is not at all dismayed by the corrupt and lethargic administration he has inherited from his predecessors. He is very firm and very patient. He speaks little Arabic but it does not matter; interpreters and secretaries are available, the orders go out, and presently Khartoum begins to learn something of the direct approach, of power exerted steadily and persistently from one central and unbribable source.

The Governor-General lived alone in his Palace on the Nile, and he was to be found there at all hours of the day receiving callers, a trim and alert figure in his red fez and his white uniform, his secretaries at his side, and the inevitable tobacco jar close to his hand. One of his contemporaries describes him as 'a strange little unpretending man with eyes like blue diamonds', and others speak of his 'superhuman energy', his marvellous resistance to the fatiguing climate.

It had always been Gordon's way to be generous and to keep nothing for himself. The Manchus in China had of-

[1] Ismail Pasha Ayoub had left before Gordon arrived, and in a rage at his dismissal his sister had smashed all the palace windows—some 130 of them—and cut the divans to pieces.

fered him a large sum of money and he had refused it. The gold medallion with which they had presented him had long since been sold to provide funds for charity in England, and most of his army pay had gone the same way. But now as Governor-General he had a great deal to give in the way of rewards and promotions for his staff, and every traveller arriving at Khartoum refers to his hospitality and kindness. Dr. Junker, the German explorer (a rather engaging figure amongst all these determined men—he had great difficulty in getting up in the morning), is invited to take all his meals at the Palace, and Gordon is concerned to give him a supply of Warburg's 'fever tincture' before he proceeds to the malarial districts to the south. A party of British missionaries is provided with transport and stores to take them to Uganda, and Gordon pays all the expenses. European officials arrive to take up the vacant places on the staff, and one and all are enchanted by the new Governor-General. It is true that the meals at the Palace are very frugal and very fast—ten minutes is the usual time allowed for lunch—but Gordon is a lively and amusing host, and of his private anxieties the casual caller sees no sign whatever.

He was not, however, very often in Khartoum. The true picture of Gordon at this time is not that of an administrator in an office, but of a soldier riding on a camel. His journeys are prodigious. He covers distances which would make quite a respectable excursion for a modern car. He rides on and on for weeks and months at a time until it becomes second nature for him to be perched up there on the hard hump, nothing but the empty desert around him, with the brilliant stars by night and the pitiless sun by day, and no doubt it is a wonderful background for those solitary musings upon the Bible which are the obsession of his life.

Whenever a crisis occurs his immediate impulse is to get on a fast camel and ride to the scene of the disturbance at once. He astonishes them all with his sudden appearances, and there is something about his bearing so absolutely confident that he manages to impose his will where he might just as easily get a bullet through his brain. At one moment he is off to Darfur, accompanied only by an interpreter, to settle an insurrection which is brewing with Suleiman, Zobeir's son; then he is up in the Berber and Dongola provinces in the North Sudan; then again in Abyssinia, travelling as far as Harar to treat with the Negus; next he is back in Cairo to preside over a financial conference, and within a matter of months we find him once more in Darfur. It is bewildering, and the results are bewildering too.

Trade flows again, and Khartoum with its new shops and buildings begins to look like a modern city; it reminded Gessi of Milan. A channel through the Sudd is cleared, and Baker's steamer, the *Khedive,* is dragged in parts to the head of the Fola Falls where it becomes the flagship of the little fleet on the upper reaches of the river. Abyssinia is quiet and Darfur remains the only serious centre of disturbance. Even with Darfur Gordon is fortunate, for he finds the one man who is supremely fitted to lead an expedition there: Gessi had returned in 1878.

Gessi was still aggrieved. He came back to the Sudan at the head of a private expedition which was to explore the Sobat River up to its source in the Abyssinian mountains, and presently we hear of him complaining that the new Governor-General is refusing to give help to private expeditions. Gessi was wrong there. Gordon received him very kindly, offered him *carte blanche* to go wherever he wished, and soon charmed him back on to the staff again.

Gessi was by no means eager to go off fighting against the Arab slavers, but Gordon managed to persuade him. Perhaps it was the very magnitude of the undertaking that attracted him, for by the summer of 1878 the situation in Darfur and in Bahr-el-Ghazal had become extremely dangerous. Suleiman was in secret correspondence with his father in Cairo, and had raised a force of Arab chieftains against the government. He retreated south through Darfur into Bahr-el-Ghazal beyond the reach of the Egyptian soldiers—and in fact the soldiers had no reach, they preferred to remain locked up in their garrisons and to wait there passively until help arrived. Gessi sailed south from Khartoum in the *Bordein* with a contingent of Government

troops, and fought a series of pitched battles against Suleiman in Bahr-el-Ghazal. In the end he ambushed the young
man and put him to death with all his leading sheikhs. Ten
thousand slaves were released. It was a fast and brilliant
operation, the first of the great guerrilla battles in the Sudan, and the only one in which the European commander
showed any real understanding of the nature of war against
the Arabs. Its effects were remarkable. For the first time in
twenty-five years the Western Sudan was freed from the
tyranny of Zobeir and his family, and for the moment at
least the wholesale traffic in slaves was checked. Gordon,
following up in Gessi's rear, mopped up the isolated pockets of resistance, and it seemed that at last he was in
sight of bringing the whole of the Sudan under his control.

By now a new staff had been established, and the provinces were parcelled out among them. Gessi was appointed
Governor of Bahr-el-Ghazal, with the rank of Pasha, and
a young Viennese officer named Rudolf Carl von Slatin
was sent to Darfur.[1] Frank Lupton, an Englishman who
had been serving as first officer on a cargo boat in the Red
Sea and had been recommended by the missionaries as a
steady man who did not drink, was being trained at Khartoum; and there were others as well, Egyptians and Arabs
among them, whom Gordon had picked up at random on
his travels and had liked and trusted. Equatoria after Gordon's departure had been governed in turn by the two
Americans, Prout and Mason, but their health had failed,
and they were now replaced by a German doctor named
Eduard Schnitzer who had already been for some years
in the Turkish service. Schnitzer had travelled widely
through the Middle East, and had become so enamoured
of it that he had adopted the Moslem faith and had changed
his name to Emin, which means 'The Faithful One'. These
men seem without exception to have been devoted to Gordon, and Emin was probably speaking for them all when
he wrote in a letter from Equatoria that the province was
at peace—'thanks to Gordon Pasha's eminent talent for

[1] Gordon previously had offered Darfur to Burton, but Burton had replied: 'I could not serve under you, nor you under me.'

organization, thanks to his three years of really superhuman exertions and labours in a climate which very few
have hitherto been able to withstand, thanks to his energy
which no hindrances were able to damp. . . . Only one
who has had any direct dealings with Negroes . . . can
form a true estimate of what Gordon Pasha has accomplished here.'

Thus it went all the way down the river, past the Fola
Falls to Gondokoro, and on through the Sudd and the
desert to Khartoum and the Egyptian border. East of the
Nile to the Red Sea, and west to Darfur, another network
of outposts and trading routes was spreading out, and
everywhere the new governors were making it possible
for the inhabitants to live without war. Gordon was probably justified in writing, as he did later on, 'No man could
lift his hand or foot in the land of the Sudan without me.'
The country was being better governed than it had ever
been before.

And yet, in the midst of all this success, strange evolu-
tions were taking place in Gordon's mind, and they were
soon to make it impossible for him to continue. There was
something in his nature that impelled him to find disillusionment and failure at the heart of all his best achievements. With him, every arrival is another departure, his
reach forever exceeds his grasp, and nothing in this world
can fulfil his hunger for perfection. He seems to have
no inner peace within himself as Livingstone had, and
his endless self-questionings can be put at rest only when
he is surrounded by difficulties and hardships. A sense of
guilt envelops him. 'Nothing shocks me,' he cries, 'but
myself.' And so, all at once, his enthusiasm evaporates,
he detests the object he has been so desperately striving
for, he sees another point of view and rushes away into
the most bewildering complications and contradictions.
This happened to him now in the Sudan.

It is clear from Gordon's letters and journals that about
this time he began to hate his own Egyptian soldiers. They
were ruthless with the Negroes, just as ruthless as the
Arabs were, and in using them Gordon felt he was bringing, not progress, but perfect misery to the Upper Nile.

'Baker,' Blunt wrote, 'had been brutal to these poor blacks; Gordon's heart went out to them.' And yet he had to 'pacify' the blacks somehow or they would make slave and cattle raids on one another; and at any rate he could argue that his methods were more humane than those of the Egyptian governor-general who had preceded him.

The time was to come, of course, when Gordon was to give his life for these same Egyptian soldiers, but now in 1879, after five years in the Sudan, he was discovering that many things about the country were more complicated than he had imagined. The Arab slave-dealers, for example, were not quite so heinous as they had been made out to be. There were even virtues to be found in Islam. 'To me,' he wrote, 'it appears that the Mussulman worships God as well as I do, and is as acceptable, if sincere, as any Christian.' And again: 'I like the Mussulman, he is not ashamed of his God. His life is a fairly pure one. Certainly he gives himself a good margin in the wife line, but at any rate he never poaches on others'. Can our Christian people say the same?' It was a question too as to whether or not you could really abolish slavery in a Mohammedan country, since it was a fundamental of the Moslem way of life, and on closer acquaintance it was not all bestiality: many of the slaves did very well for themselves and would not have exchanged their masters for freedom. Suddenly to uproot the system could lead only to chaos. Men like Zobeir might be villains, but they knew how to govern their territories better than the Turks and Egyptians who had come into the Sudan from Egypt and who committed their own brand of atrocities in the name of civilization. But then by the very terms of his appointment as governor-general he had been bound to destroy men like Zobeir. And so he goes on and on turning over these points in his mind, and this is a dangerous business because Gordon, unlike other men, cannot quietly accept a compromise, he has to act and say precisely what he thinks.

A further disillusionment had overtaken Gordon in Cairo. Ismail's financial dealings were now entering their final downslide into ruin; there was an £80 million debt owing to European creditors and a board of inquiry had been set up to discover means by which Ismail could pay the next instalment of interest at 7 per cent. De Lesseps was on this board, and so was Baring. In March 1878 Ismail had had the strange notion of bringing Gordon up to Cairo to preside at the meetings of the board. He knew he could be sure of Gordon's loyalty, and at the same time he hoped no doubt that Gordon's reputation in the world would help to smooth things over. On the other hand, Gordon knew very little about finance, and it had never been his way to get things done through committees.

Now there was only one way for the Khedive to raise more money, and that was to extort it from the peasants with the use of the whip, and the peasants had already been taxed into abject beggary. It seemed to Gordon (and of course to the Khedive) that the only rational thing to be done was for the European creditors to forgo their interest for the next few months. He also wanted to exclude from the board of inquiry the representatives of the European creditors, since they were interested parties. On both points he met implacable opposition: the European investors were adamant and they were not concerned to know how the money was to be raised provided they got it. Baring, de Lesseps and the others were also quite determined that the representatives of the European creditors should be present at the inquiry so that they could keep an eye on the proceedings and also, probably, upon Gordon himself.

Inevitably Gordon quarrelled with them all. Baring he disliked on sight: 'He has,' he wrote, 'a pretentious, grand, patronizing way about him. We had a few words together. I said, "I would do what His Highness asked me." He said, "it was unfair to the creditors," and in a few moments all was over. When oil mixes with water we will mix together.' Ink in the blotting pad, oil and water, slavery in the Sudan and the greed for money in Europe—where was there any hope for mankind in all this? The Europeans in their own way were just as ruthless as his Egyptian soldiers and the slave-drivers in Africa. He resigned from the inquiry and returned to Khartoum.

By now he was suffering increasingly from nervous exhaustion, and the campaign against Suleiman that followed his return from Cairo had drained his last reserves of energy. The hot summer months in Khartoum in 1879 must have been a misery to him, and one catches here a glimpse of the momentous tragedy that lay ahead. He was aware of a growing hostility. It mounted up against him from the officials he had dismissed and from the slave-traders he had ruined. In Cairo as well as Khartoum the Egyptian Pashas were his enemies. Zobeir was not likely to forget the death of his son. And then there was Baring.

Baring certainly was not an enemy, but at that first meeting with him in Cairo Gordon had had a sharp and chilling reminder that, when all the crises are over, it is officialdom that really rules the world, and Baring *par excellence* was an official. Baring was seven years younger than Gordon and not nearly such a great name with the public, but he represented a force which Gordon had recognized at once and from which he instantly recoiled.

Nowadays we would say that Baring was a member of the Establishment (which Gordon certainly was not). He represented the *status quo,* and by breeding and instinct he defended it with a steady, unemotional discipline. The eccentricities of a man like Gordon were not at all likely to dismay him, and he was prone neither to hero-worship nor to jealousy. In a world of untidy, adolescent enthusiasms he stood for precision and the middle course, and in a detached and desiccated way he threw out an air of privilege and of adult firmness. Wilfrid Scawen Blunt, being a poet and an impassioned Arabist, disliked this composed, methodical man much more than Gordon did, and he reminds us that Sir Evelyn was a member of the banking family, Baring Brothers, and was 'of Dutch' and, 'it is generally said, of Jewish origin'. Thus he 'belonged from the beginning of his career to the inner ring of high finance in Europe'.

At first, however, he had been trained in the army, and it was not until he was 31 that he was sent out to India as private secretary to his cousin, the Viceroy, Lord Northbrook. His ability was then quickly recognized and now eight years later he was on the verge of his tremendous career as the virtual ruler of Egypt. A reputation for rudeness held him back, and Blunt says he had very little real knowledge of the East—he spent his mornings at his desk dealing with official papers and his evenings in the European society of Cairo. Naturally he was a target for his less inhibited colleagues and one of them wrote,

> *'The virtues of Patience are known,*
> *But I think that, when put to the touch,*
> *The people of Egypt will own, with a groan,*
> *There's an Evil in Baring too much.'*

There was envy in all this, and prejudice as well. Baring was a great deal more than a stuffed shirt, and any balanced judge of him in his dealings with Gordon will admit that, throughout the tumultuous years that lay ahead, it was he and not Gordon who was fair, patient, loyal and very sensible. Spontaneity Baring lacked, and perhaps also Gordon's flair for seeing into the simple truth of things—his was the official's world of caution and the safe negative—but he was a remarkable administrator and he was not afraid. In all honesty one ought not to take Gordon's side in this dispute, and yet one does.

Already Gordon's wings had been clipped by just such a man, though rather a lesser one, during the McKillop affair, and now in 1879 it is a little painful to see him being rebuffed again in Cairo. Between Kirk in Zanzibar and Baring in Cairo, two of the greatest British civil servants of the age, the lonely figure in Khartoum did not stand much of a chance.

And it was Gordon's loneliness that was gaining on him now. The young governors he had appointed were far afield, and in Khartoum there was no one to confide in. Gessi just possibly might have helped him, but then Gessi was too impulsive and too ignorant of politics, and in any case was involved in his own problems in Bahr-el-Ghazal.

There is a certain pent-up desire for understanding and communication in Gordon's correspondence at this time. He rages against 'official dinners' in society in London, what bores they are, what a waste of time. Again and again he declares that he is 'dead to honours and riches'. Marriage he rejects: 'What a blessing it is that one was never married! Marriage spoils human beings, I think: if the wife is willing the husband is not, and *vice-versa.*' Apart from his great interest in the training and activities of boys (which was certainly innocent) there is no evidence that he had homosexual inclinations; rather, he is a neuter. But still he must communicate; and so he turns to religion and finds perhaps a palliative to his loneliness in the universality of human suffering. Unlike Baring he cannot approach the world's miseries through the filter of official papers and reasoned judgements: he has to attack them with all the passion of his warm and generous nature. They are his personal responsibility. And of course he exhausts his strength, arouses jealousies, makes enemies and finally recoils upon himself. Hence the 'doles', the sudden rages, the recourse to the occasional 'b. and s.' and the inevitable self-disgust. All these things now beset him once again at Khartoum, and he was much less able to withstand them than he had been when he first came to the Sudan in 1874. Five years in that climate had made a very great difference. It needed only a small additional set-back to push him to the end of his resources, and presently that set-back was supplied. In June 1879 word arrived that Ismail, the friend to whom he had been able to 'tell all', the man who had 'given him the Sudan', had been deposed.

Ismail, after sixteen years of glorious spending, had had one final spree. After the failure of his board of inquiry he had engineered a military riot against European interference with his affairs, and had set up an autocratic government of his own. It had sailed along dizzily for a few months, but then the tide of debts had washed over him again. Baring and his colleagues, with the backing of their European governments, had supervised the final sinking of the Khedive with diplomatic skill. The Sultan in Constantinople, who was still the nominal overlord of Egypt, was induced to send Ismail a telegram in which he addressed him as the 'ex-Khedive' and informed him that his eldest son Tewfik had succeeded to his place.

Ismail had departed in much the same way as he had

come in the beginning; he had cleaned out the cash in the treasury, gathered together his valuables, and with a sum of about £3 million had boarded his yacht *Mahrousa* and had sailed away. He was to console himself for the remainder of his life in a palace on the Bosphorus, and cannot have been too much saddened by his fall.

But to Gordon his going was a deep and final break; the only Sudan he knew was the one that Ismail had given him and he did not wish to continue there under any other master. He did not like Tewfik, and he said so; he did not care for the ruling cliques of pashas in Cairo nor for the European officials who would now inevitably take the power into their own hands. Even with Ismail he was disillusioned, and he wrote in one of his letters, 'Do not fret about Ismail Pasha—he is a philosopher and has plenty of money. He played high stakes and lost . . . I am one of those he fooled but I bear him no grudge. It is a blessing for Egypt that he is gone.'

Now finally Gordon was disgusted. 'I may indeed say,' he wrote, 'I have lost every desire in a material way for the things of this life, and I have no wish for eating, drinking, or comforts. If I have a wish for anything it would be for a dreamless sleep.'

In July 1879 he decided to resign his governor-generalship. His last act before returning home was to make another of his prodigious rides into Abyssinia—he had now travelled in all some 8,000 or 9,000 miles on the back of a camel—in an attempt to obtain a final settlement between Egypt and the Negus. The Abyssinians, however, arrested him and ignominiously turned him out, and after a terrible forced march he struggled back to Cairo on January 2, 1880. Hardly anyone in authority was sorry to see him go. 'Some,' Blunt says, 'thought him mad, others that he drank, and others again that he was a religious fanatic;' and for the moment there was no place for such a man in either Europe or Africa. General Gordon was too headstrong and too erratic.

It was also thought typical of this difficult man that he should have chosen to make still another powerful enemy on his way home to England. Passing through Paris he told the Ambassador, Lord Lyons, who had the ear of the British cabinet, that unless the British found a successor for the governor-generalship of the Sudan he would go to the French and suggest that they should fill the place. Lord Lyons demurred, and Gordon wrote to him: 'I have some comfort in thinking that in ten or fifteen years' time it will matter little to either of us. A black box, six feet six by three feet wide, will then contain all that is left of Ambassador or Cabinet Minister, or of your humble and obedient servant.'[1]

Lord Lyons was not amused; surely this man was mentally unhinged.

Soon too another link between Gordon and the Sudan was broken: Gessi was dead. He had hung on for a year or more in Bahr-el-Ghazal after Gordon's departure, but the Nile had killed him in the end, and perhaps the ingratitude of the Egyptians also had a hand in it. Gessi was one of the best servants the Egyptians ever had, but they recalled him in 1881 and degraded him from the rank of governor to the status of a minor official. On his way downstream to Khartoum he was blocked for three frightful months in the Sudd, and most of the 400 men in his escort died of starvation; some of them had even been reduced to cannibalism before they were rescued. Gessi himself survived only long enough to reach Egypt.

Gordon wrote to his sister, 'Gessi! Gessi! Gessi! how I warned him to leave with me! When at Toashia how I said, "Whether you like it or not, or whether I like it or not, your life is bound up with mine." He knew me to the depths. I almost feared this in one way. However Gessi is at rest. It is God's will.'

But Gessi could no more have divorced himself from Africa than Gordon could have done. They had suffered too much there to put the country out of their lives; like Livingstone they had to continue in Africa to the end. It

[1] Sir C. Rivers Wilson in his *Chapters from My Official Life* gives a slightly different version of this: 'Anyhow, it matters little; a few years hence a piece of ground six feet by two will contain all that remains of ambassadors, ministers and your obedient humble servant, C. G. Gordon.'

required, however, a major catastrophe to get Gordon back; but then catastrophies were never absent from the Nile for very long, and the one that overtook the river in the eighteen-eighties was fundamental and drastic in the extreme.

PART THREE

The Moslem Revolt

Chapter 11

SUEZ 1882

THE BRITISH INVASION of Egypt in 1882 bears a depressing resemblance to the abortive Anglo-French campaign on the Suez Canal in 1956, except that the earlier adventure was handled so much more efficiently and was successfully carried through. In 1882, as in 1956, the cry of Egypt for the Egyptians was raised, and Colonel Arabi, like Colonel Nasser, emerged from the obscurity of the Egyptian army to become the leader of the nation against the Western invader. Then, as later, Britain was divided against herself except for a short time when the hostilities were joined, since there were many people in England who abhorred the whole affair. In similar circumstances too, pride became as quickly involved. It was the familiar pattern; all at once the national blood mounts up on either side, the national honour is engaged, and a thousand reasons are discovered for military action. In Egypt the British become rapacious bullying monsters. In England the Egyptians are described as 'terrorists' who break all pledges and murder innocent European civilians, and it becomes an imperative necessity that troops must be landed to restore law and order. And so the crisis sweeps on from riots to ultimatums, and finally to war.

Sir Evelyn Baring has given a calm and reasoned account of the political events which led up to the 1882 invasion, and he concludes that it was both justifiable and inevitable: had it not happened, he says, Egypt would have been given over to anarchy. If we do no more than follow the facts as he sets them out—the diplomatic exchanges, the political tensions between France, England and Turkey, the intrigues of the army and the palace in

Cairo itself—we must conclude that he is right. But the axiom that war is the failure of diplomacy still holds, and it seems very possible that in this case the conflict would have been avoided had the diplomacy been better exercised. Baring almost, but not quite, concedes this point when he says, 'Mistakes were, without doubt, committed. The true nature of the Arabi revolt was misunderstood. It was more than a mere political mutiny. It partook in some degree of the nature of a *bona fide* national movement.'

This is the fundamental point. The Egyptian grievances were very real and they were not all of their own making. After the removal of Ismail it should not have been difficult for the British and the French to have given the country a breathing space so that it could recover from its bankruptcy. But the European creditors still demanded their interest, and only the smallest efforts were made to reduce taxes upon the fellaheen. Turks and Circassians still held a privileged position in the government and the army, and no real parliamentary reform was attempted because it was believed that the Egyptians were not fit to govern themselves. Tewfik's every move was overlooked and guided by Baring and de Blignières, the French representative in Cairo. These two men controlled the revenue and the expenditure, and although for a little time they did succeed in improving the administration they were resented as foreigners and infidels. Perhaps they might have avoided the crisis had they possessed European troops to enforce their decrees, or even if they could have been sure of the support of their own governments at home, but both those factors were lacking. Thus they were given responsibility without power, and the way was open for the ancient animosity of the East towards the West to flare up again.

Since Napoleon's invasion at the end of the previous century Egypt could look back upon hardly anything but defeat and humiliation at the hands of the Christians. At the first sign of trouble British and French warships were sure to appear at Alexandria, and the possibility of outright invasion was always in the air. In May 1881 the French took possession of Tunis, and that was one more stronghold of Islam in Africa that had collapsed. This steady encroachment was bound to arouse hostility. Even as early as 1868 Schweinfurth had noticed that everywhere, even in the depths of the Sudan, the Franks (a term that applied to other Europeans besides Frenchmen) were detested, and in the years that had elapsed since then this xenophobia had increased. It had been kept underground, its spirit had faltered because of the natural lethargy of the Middle East, but still it continued to expand.

In Paris and in London politicians had begun to talk of a dangerous Pan-Islamic conspiracy, a resurgence of fanatical Mohammedanism. In Cairo it seemed to the Egyptians that things were the other way about: they were being encircled by a Pan-Christian movement that was becoming more menacing every day.

No one was really content with the situation. The Cairo pashas resented Tewfik's subservience to his European advisers; the *Ulema,* the religious leaders in the mosques, resented the influence of the Christian religion; the Egyptian soldiers resented their Turkish officers; the slavers resented the Western interference with their business, and the fellaheen were simply miserable.

The crisis began, as Middle Eastern crises often do, at the height of the summer, when the Nile comes down in flood, and the humid, oppressive air is a wonderful stimulant to exasperation. A group of young Egyptian army officers had been becoming increasingly restless and defiant of discipline, and on September 8, 1881, they were ordered to take their regiments out of Cairo. Instead they marched their men to the Abdin Palace. Tewfik capitulated at once and completely. He agreed to the formation of a nationalist ministry, and Ahmed Arabi, the leader of the mutinous officers, was soon installed as secretary of state for war. Arabi does not quite resemble his reincarnation in Colonel Nasser seventy years afterwards, for he was a rather slow and rustic figure, and as things turned out not a very aggressive soldier; yet he was a good public speaker, he was undoubtedly sincere and—what was more important—the masses were more than ready to support him. They wanted a hero, a man who would symbolize and express their dislike of the foreigners, and they found it in this tall impressive-looking soldier who had been born the son of a sheikh in the provincial town of Zagazig forty-two years before.

Even if Arabi did not at first know where he was going, events soon decided the matter for him. The British and the French protested at his appointment, and that was bound to make him more popular than ever. Presently it was announced that a plot to take his life had been discovered; it was said, probably with little truth, that some forty Turkish and Circassian officers were behind it, and these men were tried in secret and sentenced to exile in the Sudan. When Tewfik refused to confirm this sentence the conditions for revolt were nearly everywhere fulfilled. The army was in a state of near-mutiny, Europeans were spat on and insulted in the streets of Cairo and Alexandria, and throughout the Delta Arabi was acclaimed as a national leader. A group of Egyptian sympathizers in England had by this time come out in open support of the insurgents, and they did nothing to ease the tension by warning Arabi in a telegram that he must keep the government and the army together or 'Europe would annex Egypt'.

The British now resorted to the course of action which had served so well in the past: the Mediterranean Fleet, under the command of Sir Beauchamp Seymour, was ordered to Alexandria, and Tewfik was presented with a joint Anglo-French note which demanded the resignation of the national government and the expulsion of Arabi. On May 27, 1882, the government resigned, only to find itself reinstated again at the head of a popular rising in Cairo. Arabi's position was now that of a dictator in a country where all the usual forms of government were disintegrating. There was panic in the European community. All who could leave packed up their belongings and made for Alexandria, where some twenty-five warships of the Western powers were waiting to take them on board. By June about 14,000 had been embarked, and 6,000 more were preparing to follow.

Through the first week of June conditions on shore became steadily worse. Agitators ran through the streets calling out, 'O Moslems, kill the Christians.' The vernacular press took up the cry for the regeneration of Islam and an independent Egypt. And Arabi, who was surrounded by a violent and persistent clamour wherever he went, began to prepare for war. Gangs of workmen started to set up gun emplacements around Alexandria harbour, and on June 11 savage rioting burst out in the town. By the end of the day several hundred people had been killed or wounded, some fifty Europeans among them. The British Consul, Sir Charles Cookson, was badly hurt, and a mob was running through the streets, looting shops and setting European houses on fire. At Benha and one or two other centres in the Delta further riots took place through the following days, and although some effort was made at the end of June to get a peaceful settlement it was now apparent that it was war or nothing.

Gladstone in England had done all he could to put off the evil day. He had chopped and changed and delayed. He had foreseen that as soon as war broke out British and French interests would come into collision in Africa, and he had declared, 'My belief is that the day which witnesses our occupation of Egypt will bid a long farewell to all cordiality of political relations between France and England.' He did not want to take responsibility for Egypt, he did not want to enter the Sudan and he wanted no commitments whatever in East Africa. But Gladstone could no more keep England out of Africa than he could cause the Nile to dry up. The British explorers and missionaries had already committed him there with their hue and cry against the slave-trade. Disraeli with his purchase of the Suez Canal shares had committed him still further, and so had the people who had invested money in Egypt and were determined not to lose it. And now with this rioting and the murder of British subjects he had reached the point of no return, and in the worst of circumstances: the French would not join him, neither would the Italians, but the British public pressed him on.

On July 10 Admiral Seymour sent a message to the commandant of the Egyptian garrison in Alexandria saying that unless the shore batteries were dismounted he would open fire on the following morning. The Egyptians replied that they were prepared to make a partial demolition, but it was late at night before their messenger managed to find the Admiral, and Sir Beauchamp, in any case, was not satisfied with the offer. At 7 a.m. on July 11 he gave the order for the action to commence, and the bombardment continued until five in the evening. By that time all the Egyptian batteries were silenced (though they had managed to get seventy-five hits on the British fleet), and most of the inhabitants of the town were streaming in confusion into the desert. On the following day the mob which had remained behind took over, and a great part of the city was pillaged and burned. It was not until late on July 13 that a small party of marines and bluejackets was landed to start the work of restoring order again.

Arabi meanwhile retreated with his army towards Cairo, declaring that he would blow up the Suez Canal and cancel Egypt's foreign debt.

The ensuing events can be quickly described. In mid-August General Sir Garnet Wolseley landed in Egypt with a force of about 20,000 men, and he proceeded at once to occupy the Suez Canal. He then struck inland from Ismalia, and after a series of skirmishes brought the Egyptian army to battle at Tel-el-Kebir, about sixty-five miles from Cairo, on September 13. The action was over in an hour or two, and the Egyptians scattered over the desert, leaving some thousands of dead and wounded on the field. Arabi, who had not commanded his troops himself, reached Cairo on horseback but was captured there when the British entered the city on the following day.[1] On September 25 Tewfik, who had taken refuge in one of his palaces outside Alexandria, returned to the capital.

As a military operation it had been a resounding success, and it committed Britain to a political position the end of which no one had as yet begun to see. Having opposed the building of the Suez Canal she was now the

---

[1] Later he was condemned to death, but was subsequently exiled to Ceylon.

master of it. Having used every expedient to control Egypt
without the use of force she was now obliged to occupy
the country with her army, and to rule it with a government of her own choosing. France, as Gladstone had foreseen, had been turned from a partner into an enemy, for
she was intensely jealous of this sudden expansion of
British power in the Near East. 'From that moment [the
Battle of Tel-el-Kebir],' Baring wrote, 'until the signature
of the Anglo-French agreement in 1904, French action in
Egypt was more or less persistently hostile to England.'
Baring could speak with authority on this matter, since he
was the man who was selected to govern Egypt.

There remained still another problem, and that was the
valley of the Nile itself. Did the conquest of Egypt mean
the conquest of Egypt's possessions as well? Had the Sudan
also to be occupied? This was a question that was answered
very directly by the Sudanese themselves: they rose in the
name of Islam and threw the foreigners out.

Even today the traveller on the Nile must be struck
by the power of Islam in the North and Central Sudan. It
would seem that there is little enough to thank God for in
these appalling deserts, and yet the poorest and most
wretched of the inhabitants will be seen throughout the
day to prostrate themselves upon the sand with a simple
concentrated fervour that is hardly known in the green
delta of Egypt. No village lacks its minaret even if it be
nothing more than a ramshackle scaffolding of poles, and
the muezzin, calling the people to prayer, at once brings
to a halt all sound and movement on the ground below.
Here every precept of the Prophet, every injunction that
governs the great fasts and feasts, appears to be observed
to the letter.

Perhaps it is the very austerity of life in these arid wastes
that predisposes the people to worship. Mecca lies only a
short journey away across the Red Sea, and the Prophet
Mohammed himself lived and received his inspirations in
just such an environment as this. An immense silence
possesses the surrounding desert. The heat is so great it
stifles the appetite and induces a feeling of trance-like de-

tachment in which monotony dissolves into a natural time-lessness, visions take on the appearance of reality, and asceticism can become a religious object of itself. These are ideal circumstances for fanaticism, and a religious leader can arouse his followers with a devastating effect. All at once the barriers are swept aside, revolt becomes a holy duty, and it can be a shocking and uprooting thing because it makes so sharp a break with the apathy that has gone before. The long silence is broken, the vision is suddenly translated into action, and detachment is replaced by a fierce and violent concentration.

In the very nature of things, then, the revolt in the Sudan was bound to be at once more drastic and more fundamental than the rising in Egypt. It was a religious, rather than a political, movement, and although the events in Egypt undoubtedly affected the Sudan, it was a spontaneous explosion. Had Gordon been able to continue as Governor-General it might have been another story, but directly he went the authority of the government disintegrated and revolt became inevitable. Emin continued in Equatoria, Slatin continued in Darfur, and Frank Lupton, the British sailor, replaced Gessi in Bahr-el-Ghazal, but there was nothing really effective these white men could do to hold the Sudan together so long as an Egyptian Governor-General ruled in Khartoum—and Raouf Pasha, the man who followed Gordon in that office, was the worst possible choice. Gordon had actually dismissed him from the Sudan service because of his inhumanity to the Africans. Raouf, like a good party boss, lost no time in restoring his old cronies to office, men of the calibre of Abu Saoud, who had swindled both Baker and Gordon in his day, and in very little time bribery once more became the normal method of conducting business in Khartoum, flogging and torture were resumed in the prisons, and the slave-traders everywhere took heart again. In 1882 Abd-el-Kader, the soldier who had once commanded Baker's Forty Thieves, succeeded Raouf as Governor-General, and he was a better man. But by then it was too late: the Sudan was ready for chaos.

Hatred of the Egyptians was the first motive of the

rebellion. There were about 28,000 of them stationed in the various garrisons throughout the country, and their behaviour towards the Sudanese had become unbearable. Taxes were gathered with extreme harshness, and every Egyptian official was known to be corrupt. A British officer sent up from Cairo to investigate the garrisons after Gordon left wrote in his report: 'Their general conduct and overbearing manner is almost sufficient to cause a rebellion. When to this conduct cowardice is added, it is impossible for me to avoid expressing my contempt and disgust.' Gordon himself had foreseen trouble, even as far back as 1879, when he wrote, '... If the present system of government goes on, there cannot fail to be a revolt of the whole country.'

Early in 1881 the general air of unrest in the Sudan began to crystallize around the name of a strange personality who had appeared on Abba Island in the Nile, about 150 miles upstream from Khartoum. This man was said to have set himself up as a new religious leader, a Mahdi. The Sudan, he declared, was to be purged of the corrupt Egyptians, and her people were to be brought back to the austerities of the true faith.

There was no great alarm at first. Abu Saoud and a force of 200 men were dispatched to Abba Island with instructions to bring the rebel into Khartoum for punishment. But it was soon apparent that the Mahdi was something more than another provincial fakir with visions of glory. His followers on the island obeyed him with a fanatical reverence. They butchered Abu Saoud's soldiers with terrible ease, and presently there was news that the Mahdi, retreating into the deserts of Kordofan, had raised the cry for a Jihad, a Holy War.

Mohammed Ahmed Ibn el-Sayyid Abdullah, the Mahdi, follows the true tradition of the warrior-priests of Islam. Like a sandstorm in the desert he appears, suddenly and inexplicably out of nowhere, and by some strange process of attraction generates an ever-increasing force as he goes along. Confused accounts were given of his origins: some said that he came from a family of boat-builders on the Nile, others that he was the son of a poor religious

teacher, others again that he was the descendant o
of sheikhs. It was generally accepted, however, t
was born in the Dongola province in the North Sudan in
1844 (which would make him 37 years of age at this time),
and that quite early in life he had achieved a local reputation for great sanctity and for a gift of oratory that was
quite exceptional. His effects, it seemed, were obtained
by an extraordinary personal magnetism. To put it in
Strachey's phrase: 'There was a strange splendour in his
presence, an overwhelming passion in the torrent of his
speech.' He was a man possessed. Mohammed had promised that one of his descendants would one day appear
and reanimate the faith, and Abdullah now declared, with
an unshakable conviction, that he himself was that man.
His hatred of the Egyptians was intense.

We have several first-hand descriptions of the Mahdi, the
best of which perhaps is that given by Father Joseph Ohrwalder, the Austrian priest who for seven years was his
prisoner. 'His outward appearance,' Father Ohrwalder says,
'was strangely fascinating; he was a man of strong constitution, very dark complexion, and his face always wore
a pleasant smile.' He had 'singularly white teeth, and between the two upper middle ones was a vee-shaped space,
which in the Sudan is considered a sign that the owner
will be lucky. His mode of conversation, too, had by
training become exceptionally pleasant and sweet.'

Slatin, the Governor of Darfur, who spent an even
longer period as the Mahdi's prisoner, bears this description out. The Mahdi, he says, was a powerfully-built man,
with broad shoulders, a large head, sparkling brown eyes,
a black beard and three tribal gashes on his cheek. He
was forever smiling. He smiled when he prescribed the
most brutal tortures for some wretch who had blasphemed
or had taken a glass of liquor. He was a smiler with a knife.

Wingate, the future Governor of the Sudan who made
an exhaustive study of the subject, came to this conclusion: 'There is no doubt that until he was ruined by un-
bridled sensuality, this man had the strongest head and
the clearest mental vision in the two million square

miles of which he more or less made himself master before he died.'

There is an element of fantasy in the progress of this inspired and highly gifted man, and even now, after the passage of eighty years, it is difficult to assess him. Certainly he was not an adventurer in the ordinary sense. Even if it is assumed that he was not sincere, that his religious protestations were simply a bogus cover for his personal ambition, it still has to be admitted that his followers worshipped him; they never, now or later, questioned his authority, they thought him semi-divine, and from the most powerful Emir to the humblest water-carrier they were ready to die for him. He was lifted up on a wave of religious adoration, and he was able to exact from his wild followers a sense of duty and of discipline that was utterly lacking in the Egyptian ranks. His success was astonishing. To begin with, in Kordofan his men were hardly armed at all, except for spears and sticks, and yet they routed a column of Egyptian soldiers sent against them, and in August 1882 (the same month that the British landed on the Suez Canal) they laid siege to El Obeid, which was a town of 100,000 people, protected by a strong Egyptian garrison. The Egyptians knew that they could expect nothing but death from these madmen, and so they held on for six months. Famine defeated them in the end; it was so frightful that every rat and dog was eaten by the garrison, and a single camel fetched the price of two thousand dollars. In January 1883 the city fell, and when the ensuing massacre had subsided it was found that a large store of arms and a sum of money equal to about £100,000 had fallen into the Mahdi's hands. From this point onward the revolution became a civil war.

The tyranny of the Mahdi in the desert in the eighteen-eighties followed a pattern that was not altogether dissimilar from dictatorship in Europe in the nineteen-thirties. It was merely cruder and more violent; atrocities here were committed not in the name of patriotism, but of God.

At the centre stood the Mahdi, the new reincarnation of

the Prophet, and he was attended by his inner ring of disciples: the three Khalifas who were his principal lieutenants. Beneath these were the Emirs, the Mukuddums, and the leaders of the tribes. Finally came the wild horde of tribesmen themselves, with their camp followers and their herds of domestic animals. They had their uniform—a *jibbeh* with square patches sewn on it as a mark of virtuous poverty, and a turban; their emblems—the flags of the Emirs inscribed with texts from the Koran, and the green flag of the Mahdi himself; and their military parades —usually a headlong cavalry charge across the open desert.

The following proclamation was published by the Mahdi from his new residence at Government House in El Obeid:

'Let all show penitence before God, and abandon all bad and forbidden habits, such as the degrading acts of the flesh, the use of wine and tobacco, lying, bearing false witness, disobedience to parents, brigandage, the non-restitution of goods to others, the clapping of hands, dancing, improper signs with the eyes, tears and lamentations at the bed of the dead, slanderous language, calumny, and the company of strange women. Clothe your women in a decent way, and let them be careful not to speak to unknown persons. All those who do not pay attention to these principles disobey God and His Prophet, and they shall be punished in accordance with the law.

'Say your prayers at the prescribed hours.

'Give the tenth part of your goods, handing it to our Prince, Sheikh Mansour [the new governor of El Obeid], in order that he may forward it to the treasury of Islam.

'Adore God, and hate not each other, but assist each other to do good.'

These precepts were ferociously enforced. Flogging to death and the cutting off of the hands were the penalties for the most trivial offences. Marriage feasts and festivities of every kind were abolished. No man might swear, or take an alcoholic drink, or even smoke, unless he cared to face the instant pain of death. There was but one honourable way to die and that was in battle in the holy service of the Mahdi.

After the fall of El Obeid, Father Ohrwalder says that the Mahdi was venerated almost as the Prophet himself. The very water in which he washed was distributed to his followers who hoped in drinking it to cure themselves of their ills. No one doubted the success of his mission any longer, and his nightly dreams and visions were regarded as a direct revelation from God. When all the Sudan had fallen, the Mahdi declared, he would take Egypt and proceed to the bloodiest of all battles outside Mecca. Next he would advance on Jerusalem where Christ would descend from heaven to meet him, and Islam thereafter would conquer the whole world.

The Mahdi's notions of the world were extremely sketchy, but this was of no consequence in these early days of his crusade; the desert was the only world these people knew. The Mahdi smiled and a sublime confidence radiated from him. He was not at all dismayed when he heard, in the summer months of 1883, that an Egyptian army commanded by a British general was advancing upon him from the Nile.

Egypt had taken a full year to bestir herself. From month to month it had been hoped that the Governor-General in Khartoum would have been able to handle the situation with the soldiers already under his command. But with the fall of Kordofan, the richest province in the Sudan, it had become plain that a military expedition would have to be sent from Cairo if the revolution was to be suppressed. But who was to raise this expedition? The British would have no part in it. In England a reaction had set in after the Battle of Tel-el-Kebir. Gladstone wanted no more conquests in Africa, and would no doubt have retired the British soldiers from Egypt had Baring been able to rule the country without them. It remained then for the Egyptian government to find the arms and the men, and in this, miraculously, they succeeded. The command was given to Colonel William Hicks of the Bombay Army, who was yet another of the footloose soldiers who had joined the Egyptian service, and he had with him a staff of over a dozen Europeans, including a correspondent of *The Times* and another from the London *Graphic*. When the force was finally assembled and despatched up the Nile to Khartoum it numbered some 7,000 infantry, 1,000 cavalry, and the usual horde of camp followers. More than 5,000 camels were required to carry supplies into the desert, and the equipment included both mountain and machine guns with a million rounds of ammunition. On paper it was a formidable array, but there were ominous weaknesses. Many of the soldiers were men who were serving terms of imprisonment because they had taken part in the Arabi rebellion—they were actually sent off in chains to Khartoum—and Colonel Hicks was a long way from being another Gessi. He was a thorough-going British officer who was not at all lacking in courage, and he might have done very well had he been leading an expedition in Europe. But this was Africa. 'In three days,' the *Times* correspondent wrote from Khartoum, 'we march on a campaign that even the most sanguine look forward to with the greatest gloom.'

There is no need to linger over the painful details. After a series of preliminary skirmishes the expedition ascended the Nile as far as el-Dueim, about 100 miles south of Khartoum, and then marched westward across the dry plains towards El Obeid. The guides either deliberately or through carelessness lost their way, the commissariat was hopeless, the soldiers unwilling, and the supply of water virtually non-existent. It was a wonderfully obsolete cavalcade. Despite the terrible heat some of the wretched soldiers were wearing chain armour and antique helmets, which looked as though they might have dated from the times of the Crusaders. In battle they were ordered to form a square with their guns pointing outwards from each corner while their camels were herded together with the baggage in the center. Each soldier carried with him a contraption made of four iron spikes known as a crow's foot, and this he threw down in front of him on the sand so as to make a barrier against the charges of the enemy.

From El Obeid the Mahdi and the Khalifas watched the approach of this cumbersome and helpless column with a predatory joy. Long before the inevitable end there was a despairing note in the dispatches which Hicks sent back to Khartoum: the water has failed, in increasing numbers his men and his camels are dying every day, the Mahdi's horsemen have cut off his line of supply to the Nile and he does not know where he is. On November 5, 1883, the expedition was wandering in the depths of a dry forest thirty miles to the south of El Obeid when 50,000 Arab warriors burst upon it. No one knows the exact details of the battle, since the Arabs kept no written records and few if any prisoners were taken. Of the original ten thousand two or three hundred men may have survived, and Hicks and his European staff were not among them. Two weeks elapsed before the news of the disaster filtered through to Khartoum and the outside world, and months were to go by before its full implications were realized.

In the Sudan it was as though a dam had burst. In a tremendous wave the cult of Mahdism swept outward, and there was hardly a corner of the huge country that was not engulfed. In Khartoum a panic began and many of the wealthier families fled down the Nile to Egypt. In Darfur Slatin was completely cut off. He fought a series of hopeless battles with the Arabs and then surrendered. In Bahr-el-Ghazal Frank Lupton hung on desperately into the New Year, and then he too collapsed. Emin in Equatoria retreated up the Nile. And far away to the east a Turkish-Sudanese slave-dealer named Osman Digna rose for the Mahdi on the Red Sea coast. Here and there, at strongholds like Sennar and Kassala, an Egyptian garrison remained like an island above the tide, but they were islands of sand rather than of rock.

At the end of 1883 it might then have been argued that the honours in the struggle between Islam and Christianity were fairly equal. The British had won Egypt but they had lost the Sudan. Gladstone no doubt would have been glad to have left the matter at that—in fact, he was determined to do no more. Khartoum, he declared, must look out for itself, and the Egyptians in the Sudanese garrisons must fend for themselves as best they could. But there were others in England who believed that nothing as yet had been settled, that all that had happened to date was merely a prelude to a much more intensive struggle on the Nile. These people believed that, having gone so far in Africa, England could not go back, and they began in the winter of 1883 to look about for a man who would force the government into action. They found him in General Gordon.

Chapter 12

SARAWAKING THE SUDAN

'If you want some out-of-the-way piece of work to be done in an unknown and barbarous country, Gordon would be your man.'
Sir C. Rivers Wilson in a conversation with Lord Salisbury.

NOTHING VERY SATISFACTORY had overtaken Gordon since his retirement from Khartoum in 1879. Ill and exhausted as he had been, he had plunged, one of his contemporaries says, into 'a series of abortive undertakings, accepted in haste and repented of at leisure'. For some months after his return to England he had busied himself with the Sudan question and had written anonymous articles and reports for the Anti-Slavery Society. But he had refused to be lionized. He declined an invitation to dine with the Prince of Wales and when an equerry came to his lodgings to ask the reason the following conversation is said to have ensued:

Equerry: 'But you cannot refuse the Prince of Wales.'

Gordon: 'Why not? I refused King John [of Abyssinia] when he invited me to go with him to his hot spring in the mountains—and he might have cut off my head for refusing. I am sure His Royal Highness will not do that.'

Equerry: 'Well then, let me say you are ill.'

Gordon: 'But I am not ill.'

Equerry: 'Give me some reason, then, that I can give the Prince.'

Gordon: 'Very well then, tell him I always go to bed at half-past nine.'

Eventually, however, he accepted an invitation to lunch.

In the spring of 1880 Gordon paid a brief visit to the King of the Belgians in Brussels. It was Stanley's idea that he and Gordon between them should govern the newly discovered Congo under Leopold's patronage, and Gordon told the King he was very ready to fall in with the plan if it ever came to maturity. Then Lord Ripon, the new Viceroy of India (after whom the falls at the source of the Nile had been named), had wanted him as a private secretary, and so he had gone off to Bombay, only to resign after three days because he could not tolerate his lordship's habit of saying that he had read his letters when he had not actually done so. Gordon, one feels, would never have made a really satisfactory private secretary. But now China was in the news again—there were rumours of her going to war with Russia—and so within two days he was off to Pekin. Then he was back in England offering to help the South African government in its campaign against the Basutos. Eventually he went to Mauritius for a year in command of the Royal Engineers, and before he returned to England he contrived to have a quarrel with the South Africans.

In 1882 he was in the strange position of being promoted to the rank of major-general with no employment, and he applied for a year's leave of absence so that he could go to Palestine and there immerse himself in the study of the Bible. Palestine naturally was not the end of the journey. He wrote to his sister from Jaffa on July 1, 1883: 'I have moved down here [from Jerusalem] and have taken a pretty good house for six months. This place is well situated for going in all directions.' More especially, he might have added, to Africa.

All through these years he had been thinking of the Sudan; again and again in his correspondence he refers to the subject, often with a feeling of anger and regret at what was happening there. At the end of 1883, however, King Leopold offered him definite employment in the Congo under Stanley, and Gordon decided to accept. On his journey back to Europe he disembarked at Genoa and proceeded overland to Brussels. The arrangements with Leopold were soon made, and on January 7, 1884, he arrived at his sister's house at Southampton determined to resign from the British army. It was then that he discovered that the Sudan had blown itself up into a political storm in Whitehall and that he himself was in the thick of it. He could hardly have arrived at a better moment.

The Hicks disaster, Gladstone was discovering, was not an event that could be conveniently forgotten, nor was it really possible to abandon Khartoum and the Egyptian garrisons to their fate. His own Cabinet was divided on this issue. Both Lord Hartington, the Minister for War, and Lord Granville, the Foreign Secretary, were in favour of some form of intervention, and so was Samuel Baker, who was now living in retirement in the country but was still regarded as an authority on the Nile. On January 1, 1884, Baker had written a strong letter to *The Times* suggesting that British or Indian troops should be sent to the Sudan to fight the Mahdi and that Gordon should have command. *The Times* had backed this up in a leading article and a day or two later the *Pall Mall Gazette* (which had hitherto favoured evacuation) also came out for a much stronger hand in the Sudan.

The *Pall Mall Gazette* was edited by William Thomas Stead, who was the most vigorous political journalist of his day, and it was not in his nature to let a split in the Cabinet wither away to nothing. He himself had introduced the 'interview' into British journalism, and he saw here an opportunity for an interview of the most effective kind. He took a train to Southampton and nobbled Gordon at his sister's house. What, he asked, did the General think about the Sudan? The General thought very strongly indeed about it. There could be no question of getting out. The Mahdi, who was he? Simply another Arab rebel who could be dealt with just as Zobeir and his son Suleiman had been dealt with in their time. But unless he was dealt with, he could be very dangerous. Khartoum must be held at all costs, and perhaps it might be useful to have a couple of million pounds to put the Egyptian army in the Sudan on to a proper footing. All that was really needed was the presence of a strong commander on the spot.

Gordon had some very effective things to say upon the

central issue of the conflict of Christianity and Islam in the Near East: 'The danger to be feared is not that the Mahdi will march northward through Wadi Halfa; on the contrary, it is very improbable that he will ever go so far north. The danger is altogether of a different nature. It arises from the influence which the spectacle of a conquering Mohammedan power, established close to your frontier, will exercise upon the population which you govern. In all the cities in Egypt it will be felt that what Mahdi had done they may do; and as he has driven out the intruder and the infidel, they may do the same. Nor is it only England that has to face this danger. The success of the Mahdi has already excited dangerous fermentation in Arabia and Syria. Placards have been posted in Damascus calling upon the population to rise and drive out the Turks. If the whole of the Eastern Sudan is surrendered to the Mahdi, the Arab tribes on both sides of the Red Sea will take fire. In self-defence the Turks are bound to do something to cope with so formidable a danger, for it is quite possible that if nothing is done the whole of the Eastern Question may be reopened by the triumph of the Mahdi.'

Stead published these views together with a leading article in which he said, 'Why not send General Gordon with full powers to Khartoum to assume absolute control of the territory, to relieve the garrisons, and do what can be done to save what can be saved from the wreck in the Sudan?' In Sarawak, on the northern coast of Borneo, James Brooke had been given a free hand in somewhat similar circumstances. Could not the same procedure be adopted with Gordon on the Nile? Stead called it 'Sarawaking the Sudan'.

Up to this point it had been difficult to know whether the agitation over the Sudan had come from Fleet Street itself or whether it had been inspired by the 'Imperialistic' group in Cabinet—the Granvilles, the Hartingtons and all those who had already favoured a tough line in Egypt. But after the publication of Stead's interview with Gordon there could be no doubt about the way the public's mind was drifting: it wanted action of some kind, some gesture that would at least assuage the humiliation of the Hicks defeat.

Gordon could hardly be accused of blowing his own trumpet—in his talk with Stead he had suggested that Baker, and not himself, was the best man to Sarawak the Sudan— but it was now clearly desirable that the two men should meet. The rendezvous took place very quietly in Devon. Gordon, by arrangement, went by train to Newton Abbot station where Baker was waiting for him in his carriage. They lost no time in getting down to business. As they drove along the country lanes to Baker's house, Sandford Orleigh, near Exeter, Baker urged Gordon to forget about the Congo and the King of the Belgians and to return to the Sudan instead. We are told that Gordon was silent, but that his blue eyes gleamed with elation. That night he wrote Baker a letter in which he set out once more his views for intervention, and Baker passed this letter on to *The Times*. It appeared on January 14.

With the publication of this letter it was not politically possible for Gladstone to ignore the matter any longer. Granville, the Foreign Secretary, was urging him to change his mind, both Hartington and Wolseley at the War Office thought something had to be done, and most of the London papers were in full cry. There was one man, however, who kept his head, and that was Baring in Cairo. When Granville sounded him out on the possibility of using Gordon in the Sudan, Baring replied that the General was 'quite unfit'. He said he had talked to both Tewfik and to the Egyptian Prime Minister, and neither of them wanted Gordon. Baring still held his ground when Granville pressed him a second time.

But now opinion in London was running far ahead of Gladstone and his minister in Cairo. Gordon's name was everywhere. In Whitehall, in Fleet Street, in the West End clubs and in the provincial cities, it was suddenly apparent to everyone who took an interest in the matter that Gordon was the perfect man to employ. Why on earth had they not thought of him before? He knew the Sudan intimately, his authority there was very great, he had the necessary dash, he was available, he knew what was wanted, he would cut the red tape and put an end to this ridiculous indecision.

But how to persuade Gladstone? Lord Granville and his friends at the War Office believed they knew a way: Gordon would go out to the Sudan not as a military commander or as a governor but merely to report. Once on the spot he would be in a position to advise them about getting the garrisons out, and perhaps through his personal influence he could bring about a peaceful settlement of the whole affair. And so, without expense, without really involving the British government, you would put an end to the public clamour and everyone would be satisfied.

It was an absurd notion, for it was based upon a wishful ignorance of both Gordon and the Mahdi. Anyone who thought that Gordon, once out of the range of Whitehall, would be content to sit still and passively make 'a report' simply did not know him. There was nothing in the General's past which could give the government the slightest confidence in holding such an opinion. The underestimation of the Mahdi in London was even more serious. Gordon himself was just as deluded as everybody else; he was quite unable to see that in the four years that had elapsed since he had been in the Sudan the situation had entirely changed. The Mahdi was not another local agitator with a rabble of lawless tribesmen at his back. He was the leader of a national religious rising and he was very dangerous. There was only one way of dealing with him, and that was the way that Arabi had been dealt with in Egypt: by sending out a properly organized military expedition from England. Yet the idea that Gordon could go out to the Sudan and work miracles was very attractive in London at this moment, and Gladstone himself was finally drawn—or perhaps inveigled is the better word—into the general delusion. He agreed that Gordon should be brought to London and sounded out upon his willingness to go, but only of course as a 'reporter', nothing more.

It has been suggested by some contemporary observers that Granville and the imperialistic group in the Cabinet were under no real misconception about the consequences of sending Gordon. They saw that Britain would be committed directly he arrived in the Sudan; that, one way or another,

his presence in Khartoum would eventually force the British
to send out a military expedition, and that the Sudan would
be conquered just as Egypt had been conquered. But this
seems to be premature. Nobody wanted war at this stage.
What was wanted was the security of the Suez Canal and a
peaceful settlement of the question. Surely the Gordon ex-
periment was worth trying even if it had but the smallest
chance of success? If Gordon failed—well then the matter
could be raised again in a more forceful way.

It was Wolseley who interviewed Gordon in the War
Office on January 15, and Gordon at once said he was ready
to go. Granville now felt he could put a little pressure on
Cairo. He sent a third telegram urging Baring to reconsider
the appointment, and Baring saw that he could resist no
more. In his *Modern Egypt* Baring says that he never thereafter ceased to regret that he gave his consent to Gordon's
mission to Khartoum. He says he yielded simply because
everyone was against him. Even at that time he made very
definite stipulations in the reply he sent to Granville; Gordon was to take his orders from Cairo (that is, from Baring
himself). Gordon was to make it clear that he understood
perfectly that his duties were to report on the Sudan and
get the garrisons out if he could, but that was all. Baring, in
brief, did not trust Gordon. Granville saw the point and
agreed.

One is constantly astonished at the precipitancy with
which political action is taken in Victorian England. There
may be enormous and often fatal delays while the argument
goes round and round for months or even years on end.
But then, abruptly, a decision is taken, special trains and
ships are pressed into service, the Cabinet assembles, and
within a matter of hours there is another fateful traveller
with a half-packed bag and a dispatch-case of hurriedly
written instructions departing from Charing Cross Station.

On January 16 Gordon went over to Brussels and got
Leopold to agree to the postponement of his Congo appointment. On January 17 he was back, and on the following
day he had his first and final meeting with the Cabinet.
Gladstone was ill and did not come to the meeting: in fact,

it was attended only by Granville, Hartington and one or two others who had been urging an active policy all along. Gordon's account of what took place is as follows:

'At noon he, Wolseley, came to me and took me to the Ministers. He went in and talked to the Ministers, and came back and said: "Her Majesty's Government want you to understand this. Government are determined to evacuate the Sudan, for they will not guarantee future government. You will go and do it?" I said: "Yes." He said, "Go in." I went in and saw them. They said: "Did Wolseley tell you our ideas?" I said: "Yes, he said, 'You will not guarantee future government of Sudan, and you wish me to go and evacuate it.'" They said: "Yes," and it was over, and I left at 8 p.m. for Calais.'

So all was decided and everyone was delighted. The press the following day acclaimed the decision, Whitehall was satisfied, Gladstone acquiescent. The Prime Minister after this, Blunt says, 'was powerless to draw back, and, putting a good face on the matter as long as the sun shone, he went in for the gamble with the rest'.

Gordon was off within a few hours of his meeting with the Cabinet. Wolseley, Granville and the Duke of Cambridge were at Charing Cross Station to put him in the train at 8 p.m., and they were joined on the platform by Colonel J. D. H. Stewart, who was also to make the journey as Gordon's second-in-command. At the last moment it was discovered that Gordon had only a few shillings in his pocket, and Wolseley pressed upon him his own spare cash together with his watch and chain. Then the train was off, carrying him out of the London winter into the sunshine of the Mediterranean. The Brindisi Mail took him down to Southern Italy, and from there he went on to Egypt in the S.S. *Tanjore*.

On the voyage down the Mediterranean Gordon was hardly able to contain the cataract of ideas and plans that came whirling through his brain. No traveller was ever so beset with anticipations about his journey's end. He had a sudden memory of his old enemy Zobeir. Zobeir was dangerous. He might be in communication with the Mahdi. Gordon sent off a message to Granville suggesting that

Zobeir should be watched and, if possible, removed from Cairo to Cyprus. Next there was the question of his getting across the desert to Khartoum. He would by-pass Cairo, he decided, and proceed directly down the Red Sea to Suakin and then strike inland to the Nile on camels. And the Sudan itself? What was the best way to settle the country once one had got the garrisons out? Why should not the Sudanese sheikhs be set up as nominally independent rulers when the Egyptians had gone? That was the system that had been adopted with the maharajas in India. He wrote a memorandum about it. But first the Mahdi had to be dealt with. Well, he had had a way of handling rebels in the past, and why should he not put it into practice again? He would ride off to see the Mahdi in his stronghold in the desert and there he would reason with him, persuade him to get his tribesmen to disperse. And then his own future? Once his mission was accomplished he would not return to Europe, or stay in the British army. Could he not sail one of the Khartoum steamers to Equatoria, where Emin was still holding out, and take over the province? If England did not want it then perhaps the King of the Belgians would be interested—Equatoria could be attached to the Congo. One final thought: if he was to carry out his mission in Khartoum successfully he must have an official position of some kind. Tewfik must appoint him Governor-General once again. But then he had quarrelled with Tewfik. All the more reason then for him to avoid Cairo—Baring could arrange the matter.

The *Tanjore* took but three days to carry its impatient passenger down the Mediterranean, but that was time enough for Baring to become aware of some, at least, of the plans that were coursing through Gordon's mind. He liked hardly any of them. He was prepared to have Zobeir watched and he had nothing against Gordon resuming the title of Governor-General, but he emphatically did not want the General to go riding off into the desert to see the Mahdi; if he did so he would probably never be heard of again. Gordon's plan for sailing up to Equatoria was equally dangerous; he had much better stay in Khartoum. There at least he could be controlled through the telegraph. As for his planning to proceed directly to Khartoum by the Red Sea route, that was impossible: the Mahdists under Osman Digna had overrun the territory between the coast and the Nile, and no one could get through. The only way to reach Khartoum was to proceed up the Nile from Cairo. He must have a talk with Gordon, Baring decided; that was absolutely essential.

When the *Tanjore* arrived at Port Said a messenger came on board with a letter for General Gordon: he was requested to come at once to Cairo. Since he was under Baring's orders he could hardly refuse. He set off in a special train, a small solitary figure in a black overcoat, without servants and with practically no baggage, and a few hours later he was with the Consul-General. Nearly seven years had elapsed since their last meeting, and both men were prepared to make a fresh start. Certainly they had no time to indulge their mutual distrust of one another, even if they had wished to do so, and Baring, who was suffering from a sore throat at the time and could hardly speak, was anxious only to help. The events of the next forty-eight hours were bizarre. First there had to be an official call on Tewfik, and it passed off very well: Gordon apologized for the criticisms he had made in the past and was confirmed in his appointment as Governor-General. Next it was necessary for them to draw up the precise terms of his mission. A good deal had happened in the short period—it was barely a week—that had passed since Gordon had left London. From a mere 'reporter' he had become a Governor-General, and in London as well as Cairo it had gradually become apparent that the mere business of reporting would not meet the case at all; there had been reporting enough already. The time had arrived when the garrisons had to be got out of the Sudan at once or not at all, and Gordon, presumably, was the man to manage the evacuation. But he could not simply abandon the Sudan to the Mahdi: some form of government had to be left behind. To resurrect the ancient sheikhdoms and tribal leaders was hardly a sufficient solution: someone in authority would have to bind them together into a sort of confederation. Who should it be? Gordon now came forward with a proposal which, for the moment, left them all aghast: why not Zobeir?

But was not Zobeir Gordon's sworn enemy? Had he not described him as 'the greatest slave-hunter who ever existed'? Had he not wanted him removed to Cyprus? The General waved these points aside. He explained that an extraordinary phenomenon had happened and now everything was changed. Purely by chance he had come face to face with Zobeir in the course of one of his official visits in Cairo, and at once he had been overtaken by a mystic feeling that he could trust him. 'I cannot,' Gordon wrote to Baring, 'exactly say why I feel towards him thus, and I am sure that his going (with me) would settle the Sudan affair to the benefit of Her Majesty's and Egyptian Governments, and I would bear the responsibility of recommending it.' He suggested that Baring and Nubar Pasha, the Egyptian Prime Minister, should join him in another meeting with Zobeir and see if they felt the mystic feeling too.

'I have no confidence in opinions based on mystic feelings,' Baring wrote in his account of this meeting. Nevertheless he was not absolutely opposed to Zobeir who, apart from Gordon, was incomparably the ablest administrator who had ever been in the Sudan, and on January 26, 1884, the meeting took place. The occasion must have been painful for all of them, since Gordon had been responsible for the execution of Zobeir's son, and Zobeir, indeed, refused to shake Gordon's hand. Baring was even moved to write, 'The scene was dramatic and interesting. Both General Gordon and Zobeir Pasha were labouring under great excitement and spoke with vehemence.' Zobeir denied absolutely that he had incited Suleiman to revolt; Gordon declared he had the proof of it in a letter taken from Suleiman's body. Eventually Zobeir left the room, and it was decided to defer the question of his employment for the time being. In the meantime his place on Gordon's staff was taken by another sheikh who was living in exile in Cairo, the Emir Abdul-Shakour. The Emir was very far from being another Zobeir, for he was a soft and unintelligent man, somewhat given to drink, but at least his political record was clean. He was a descendant of the original sultans of Darfur, and it was proposed now that he should be set up in the province as the first of the independent rulers. He was supplied with £2,000, an embroidered coat and the largest decoration that could be found in Cairo.

Gordon's second-in-command, Colonel Stewart, was a Scottish soldier who had already served in the Sudan. Blunt admits that Stewart was energetic and able, but describes him as 'a smart young cavalry officer of the Hussars, the 11th, with all the English officer's contempt for "natives".' Baring, on the other hand, found him admirable, a cool and patient man, with a very clear understanding of Moslem politics; in short, an ideal foil for Gordon. It was arranged that Stewart should report separately to Baring in Cairo.

The remaining arrangements were quickly settled. Gordon was given a credit of £100,000 and a promise of more if he needed it. Two *firmans* were drawn up: one announcing his appointment as Governor-General, and the other proclaiming the Khedive's intention of evacuating the Sudan; 'We have decided,' it read, 'to restore to the families of the kings of the Sudan their former independence.' It was left to Gordon's discretion as to when or if at all these *firmans* should be published to the Sudanese. Finally Gordon repeated his assurance that he approved of the policy of evacuation and that he would carry out such instructions as might be given him by Baring and the Egyptian government. The Red Sea route was abandoned. Instead he was to leave Cairo by special train for the south and then continue up the Nile valley by boat and camel until he reached Khartoum.

That same night, January 28, he was off, having spent just three days in Cairo. There was a moment of farce at the end. It was cold and the dim lanterns on the station gave very little light. Extra carriages had to be attached to the train to accommodate the Emir Abdul-Shakour's twenty-three wives and their baggage, and further delay was caused by the disappearance of the embroidered coat. At last it was found, and the train with its oddly-assorted passengers rolled away into the desert.

But Gordon out of sight, Baring discovered, was not Gordon out of mind. The telegraph was a two-edged weapon. It could be useful for issuing instructions to the new Governor-General, but then it also exposed one to the Governor-General's responses; and these were tumultuous. Gordon used the telegraph as most men use conversation. Hardly a thought danced through his brain without his dashing off yet another telegram to Baring. He would do this, he would do that, he would do the other thing; and then again he would do nothing at all and all his earlier messages were to be forgotten. The party had hardly left Cairo before the first of these telegrams began to arrive and presently they began to number from twenty to thirty a day. Wearily, Baring let them pile up from early morning until afternoon, and then, with his other work finished, he opened all together, setting aside those that flatly contradicted one another, answering those that seemed to need an answer, passing on to London such fragments as he deemed worth saving from the torrent. After one particularly hard day he wired to Gordon, 'I am most anxious to help and support you in every way, but I find it very difficult to understand what it is you want. I think your best plan will be to reconsider the whole question carefully, and then state to me in one telegram what it is you recommend, in order that I can, if necessary, obtain the instructions of Her Majesty's government.' Stewart did his best to stem the flood. He wrote to Baring, 'Yesterday, I told Gordon that his numerous communications might tend to confuse you, but he replied that he was merely giving you different aspects of the same question.'

And yet, as Baring himself admits, there was often a good deal of simple truth and foresight immersed within the spate of Gordon's words, and often, too, he had important and even startling information to convey.

The party reached Korosko, close to the Sudan border, on February 1, 1884; Berber, beyond the great loop of the Nile, on February 11, and Khartoum a week later. At every staging-post there were crises. Before they had even reached the Sudan Gordon had quarrelled with both Stewart and with the Emir Abdul-Shakour. Stewart felt bound to stay on, but the Emir in a huff had disembarked with his wives at Assuan and was left behind. Eventually he struggled on to the Dongola province, but he soon retired to Cairo and was heard of no more.

The issue that arose at Berber was more serious. Berber was still holding out against the Mahdi, and it was a vital point of communications on the Nile. To keep Berber loyal was a first consideration, especially since the surrounding tribes were known to be wavering in their allegiance to Egypt. They needed encouragement and a firm declaration of Gordon's intention to resist the Mahdi. Instead he chose to assemble the leading sheikhs and take them into his confidence. He announced that Egypt was going to evacuate the Sudan, and at the same time he made it known that he would do nothing more to interfere with the slave-trade. 'Whoever has slaves,' he declared, 'shall have full right to their services and full control over them. This proclamation is a proof of my clemency towards you.'

According to Stewart, Gordon pondered all night before taking this drastic step, and he had his reasons—he believed that the sheikhs would be delighted at receiving their independence and would consequently be stiffened in their resolve to fight the Mahdi. The gesture about slavery was thrown in as a *bonne bouche* because it cost Gordon nothing—at this moment he was quite powerless to do anything to stop the traffic anyway —and at the same time he hoped that by his condoning it the sheikhs would be still further disposed towards him.

In actual fact, however, the effects were very different. The tribes had no wish to be exposed to the vengeance of the Mahdi when the Egyptians had departed. They knew the power of the Mahdi (which Gordon at this stage did not) and they now began to gravitate towards him while there was still time.

Gordon, meanwhile, continued on to Khartoum, and he entered the city on February 18. He was received with fervour. Five years' absence had done nothing to efface the people's memory of his firmness, his liberality and the magnetism of his name. In this one respect the British government had been right in sending Gordon to Khartoum: no other man on earth commanded such influence in the city. He installed himself in the Palace once more, and it was as if the last five years had suddenly rolled away. Power, the British Consul in Khartoum, telegraphed to Baring: 'Gordon arrived here this morning, and met with a wonderful demonstration of welcome on the part of the population. The state of affairs here, since it was heard that Gordon was coming, gives every promise of the speedy pacification of this portion of the Sudan. His speech to the people was received with the greatest enthusiasm.'

The gates of the city were flung open and all those who wished to leave and join the Mahdi were invited to do so. Arrangements were set in hand for the evacuation of the first batch of Egyptian soldiers and a messenger was sent off to the Mahdi offering peace. In a second telegram to Baring, Power reported further good news. Gordon had formed in Khartoum a 'Council of twelve Notables, Arabs, to sit with him. Burned all old records of debts against people, and instruments of torture in Government House. Colonel Stewart at prison striking irons off all prisoners of war, debtors, and men who have long ago served their sentences. . . . Everything is now safe here for troops and Europeans. He is giving the people more than they expected from the Mahdi.' Gordon himself had telegraphed a few days earlier, 'I believe you need not give yourself any further anxiety about this part of the Sudan. The people, great and small, are heartily glad to be free of a union (with Egypt) which only caused them sorrow.'

This then was the hopeful situation in Khartoum in February when the weather as yet was not too hot, and Gordon in the first flush of his arrival had instilled confidence everywhere. The Mahdi made no move—and that surely was a good sign in itself, perhaps even an indication that he realized that he had met his match at last and would come to terms. But then as February turned into March there was a less encouraging note in the telegrams that piled up on Baring's desk in Cairo. Gordon was beginning to have second thoughts about the policy of evacuation. Could you really abandon these people to the anarchy that would certainly ensue if they were left without a ruler? Was that humane? Was it wise? Directly he left the Sudan, the Mahdi would descend upon Khartoum and then it would be in his power to menace Egypt. The chances of coming to an agreement with the Mahdi no longer seemed quite so bright as they had been before. 'If Egypt is to be kept quiet,' Gordon now wrote, 'the Mahdi must be smashed up. Mahdi is most unpopular, and with care and time could be smashed. Remember that once Khartoum belongs to Mahdi the task will be far more difficult; yet you will, for safety of Egypt, execute it. If you decide on smashing Mahdi then send up another £100,000, and send up 200 Indian troops to Wadi Halfa, and send officer up to Dongola under pretence to look out quarters for troops. . . . I repeat that evacuation is possible, but you will feel effect in Egypt, and will be forced to enter into a far more serious affair in order to guard Egypt. At present it would be comparatively easy to destroy Mahdi.'

Fourteen years were to elapse before the prophecy contained in these words was to be made manifest.

For the moment, however, all depended upon how they were to get through the present crisis without leaving a vacuum (or a chaos) in the Sudan. Once again Gordon returned to the plan of employing Zobeir. Was he not the ideal man to succeed as Governor-General? His ten years' exile in Egypt must surely have done something to reform him. He still had a greater following in the Sudan than any other man in Egypt. Why could he not govern the Sudan, or at any rate a large part of it, as a vassal of the Khedive?

Baring was inclined to agree. He put the matter to Granville in London and received the curt reply that 'public opinion in this country would not tolerate the appointment of Zobeir Pasha'. This might have been an end to the matter had Baring been a mediocre official, but he was very far from being that, and nothing better illustrates the tenacity and the fairness of his character than the fight he now made on Gordon's behalf with the British Cabinet. It was perfectly admirable. Baring's own position in the affair was very weak. He had opposed the employment of Zobeir in the beginning, and now he had to admit he had come round to Gordon's point of view. It was a proposal that involved the greatest risk: who was to guarantee that Zobeir would not go over to the Mahdi's side, or that on his arrival in

Khartoum he would not find some way of injuring Gordon, whom he hated? Baring was not a man who courted risks, but he was prepared to take this risk because he saw more clearly than anyone in England that the situation was becoming desperate. It was absolutely essential to maintain the loyalty of the tribes to the north of Khartoum, or the city would be cut off, and Zobeir was the one man who had a following among the sheikhs in those areas. Winston Churchill, much later on, summed up the matter very well when he wrote: 'The Pasha was vile, but indispensable.' On personal grounds Baring had no reason to take Gordon's side. He continued to regard Gordon with a kind of detached mental distaste, and Gordon of course was no help to him at all at this crucial moment. The telegrams became more agitated than ever. Reckless phrases like 'smashing up the Mahdi' were bound to antagonize the British Cabinet, but still they continued to pour out of Khartoum, and presently Gordon was declaring that he would resign unless he got what he wanted. Patiently Baring sifted out the argument and put the case once more before the Cabinet. Again he was rebuffed and once again he returned to the attack. 'I venture to think,' he wired to Granville, 'that any attempt to settle Egyptian questions by the light of English popular feeling is sure to be productive of harm. . . .'

Perhaps in the end Baring might have won the day. Gladstone said that he was prepared to take a chance with Zobeir, even though he was bound to face a vote of no confidence in the House. Queen Victoria was consulted and approved. But the other members of the Cabinet were much alarmed; already the public had been asked to swallow Gordon's proclamation legalizing slavery in the Sudan and now it was altogether too much to expect them to accept the employment of 'the greatest slave-hunter who ever existed'. There would be an outcry. No government could hope to survive it. One might as well have asked Gladstone to advocate a policy of legalized prostitution in England.

And yet it was not impossible that the public might have come round to the appointment once the reasons for it were explained. Up to this point the correspondence about Zobeir had been kept secret, and it would have been a matter of no great difficulty to have introduced the proposal carefully through the House of Commons and the Press.

Gordon chose this moment to undo all Baring's tactful and persistent work. In a rage at the delay he sent for Power, who was the correspondent of *The Times* as well as the British Consul in Khartoum, and he laid before him the whole story of the Zobeir negotiations. Within a matter of hours the storm broke in England.[1] The Anti-Slavery Society was unanimous—the employment of Zobeir by the British government would be 'a degradation for England and a scandal to Europe'. The Conservative opposition was not slow to see here a marvellous chance of attacking the government. And to Zobeir in Cairo it was apparent that he might strike a hard bargain with Baring, now that he had become so important in the world. Baring's pleadings with the Cabinet were now useless. On March 16 they returned to him a final and decisive No. The first real shadow of the coming tragedy had fallen on Khartoum.

There was another reason for intransigence in London. Fighting of a minor but extremely bloody kind had broken out between British soldiers and the tribesmen led by Osman Digna on the Red Sea coast of the Sudan. It was a confused and altogether unsatisfactory affair. Inland from Suakin an Egyptian garrison was cut off by the forces of Osman Digna, and in December 1883 a small detachment of some three thousand untried and untrained Egyptian soldiers had been sent down from Cairo to liberate them. The leader of this force was General Valentine Baker, a younger brother of the explorer. He was the type of man who could hardly have appeared anywhere except in Victorian England. To his brother's capabilities and passion for adventure he added another quality of his own—he was high-spirited to the point of recklessness. As a hard-riding cavalry officer, at first in the Lancers and then in the Hussars, he had fought in both South Africa and the Crimea, he had commanded his regiment in England (where he

---

[1] Bernard M. Allen, in his *Gordon and the Sudan*, makes the point that the Consul in a dispatch to *The Times* had revealed a week before this that Zobeir's employment was being considered and that the matter was already being violently debated in England. But there is no doubt that the interviews with Gordon had a decisive effect.

hunted four days a week), he had made a tremendous journey through Central Asia, and at the age of 47, when he was rising to the top of the army, his career was suddenly and dramatically ruined. He was convicted of an indecent assault on a young woman in a railway carriage. In the dock Baker spoke no word in his own defence, and his punishment seems to have been unnecessarily harsh: he was fined, sent to prison for a year, and dismissed from the army.

On his release Baker went off as a soldier of fortune to Turkey and there he did so well in the war against Russia that he was appointed Governor of Armenia. In 1882 he arrived in Cairo to take command of the newly formed Egyptian gendarmerie, and it was a part of this force that he now led down to the Red Sea.

Baring had naturally scented danger in this expedition. He knew that Baker was out to reinstate himself with the British army, and he knew that Baker hoped to do this by carrying out some desperate feat of arms. Consequently he sent for the General before he left Cairo and impressed upon him very emphatically that he was not to involve them all in another Hicks disaster. These instructions flew to the winds once Baker arrived at Suakin. The little force of terrified Egyptians was marched out to battle with the tribesmen, and at the first shock of the Arab charge they laid down their arms They were methodically butchered within a few minutes, and Baker almost alone cut his way out. This was on February 4, 1884, two weeks before Gordon arrived at Khartoum, and the public's attention, already focused upon the Sudan, suddenly took a turn towards belligerence. It was bad enough for the Sudan to be in revolt, but it was altogether worse for the Red Sea route to India to be endangered. Admiral Hewett was ordered to take his squadron to Suakin and make a landing there, and he was soon followed by a British force of 4,000 men under General Sir Gerald Graham. Graham's two battles against the Arabs achieved a terrible revenge—Osman Digna himself was wounded and several thousands of his tribesmen were killed—but with this the spark of resolution died out in London. Gladstone aroused himself. He declared that

he would have no more battles in the Sudan. The enemy on
the coast was defeated and that was enough: General
Graham must post an Egyptian garrison at Suakin and
then withdraw.

Gordon in Khartoum was not much perturbed by these
events. He had hoped naturally that a route might have
been opened up between Suakin and the Nile at Berber, but
on the whole, he wrote to Baring, Khartoum could be very
little affected by what happened on the Red Sea. The
Zobeir affair preoccupied Gordon's mind, and in his exasperation he began to canvass a plan for abandoning Khartoum and for evacuating his force to Berber. In his heart
Gordon had no real intention of carrying out this design; it
was simply another device with which to *épater* Baring and
the deluded politicians in England. But then on March 13
there was a development that made it unnecessary for any
of them to concern themselves with Zobeir any more, and
even the question of occupying Berber went by the board:
the tribes north of Khartoum rose for the Mahdi and
blocked the Egyptian traffic on the river. The telegraph
went dead. Khartoum was cut off.

Chapter 13

A ROOF WITH A VIEW

FROM MARCH 1884 until January in the following year—a period of ten months—a steadily deepening silence fell on the Sudan. It was known that Gordon was still in Khartoum, and that the town had not fallen, since he managed to send out native runners from time to time. But the messages they brought were written on tiny scraps of paper and gave only the briefest information. Presently it became known that Slatin in Darfur and Lupton in Bahr-el-Ghazal had surrendered to the Mahdi, and had escaped execution only by professing the Moslem faith. Father Ohrwalder and a group of priests and nuns who were attached to the Austrian Mission in Darfur were also believed to be prisoners of the Mahdi, together with a number of Greek traders who had been overrun in the distant outposts. Emin was still holding out in Equatoria, and so were the Egyptian garrisons in Kassala and Sennar, close to the Abyssinian border, but in May Berber fell and the Mahdi's empire now covered an area as large as all France, Spain and Germany combined.

Gordon's plight in Khartoum was not absolutely desperate. He had with him in the town about 34,000 people, of whom some 8,000 were soldiers, not really reliable soldiers perhaps, but they were armed with rifles and they had in addition twelve pieces of artillery and nine armed paddle-boats that were able to keep up a running fight along the river. Two million rounds of ammunition had been stored in the town before it was cut off, and the arsenal was capable of producing another 40,000 rounds every week. In March Gordon estimated that he had sufficient food to last six months, and with the Nile flowing by there was naturally no problem about water. The treasury was soon reduced to the equivalent of a few thousand pounds in cash, but Gordon printed a new paper currency of his own.

Khartoum was by no means an impossible place to defend. To the north it was protected by the Blue Nile, and to the west by the White Nile—and the White Nile, even at low water, was half a mile wide. By keeping to the centre of the stream the paddle-steamers with their light armour-plating were in no great danger from the Arab riflemen on the bank. A strong Egyptian garrison was posted in Omdurman Fort on the west bank of the White Nile, and the surrounding country was held by the Shaigiya tribe which was still hostile to the Mahdi. The weak point in the defence was, of course, in the south where the town was exposed to the open desert, but here a deep semicircular trench four miles long had been dug from the White Nile to the Blue. From the first Gordon concentrated his attention upon this southern flank. Primitive landmines were sown in the sand, along with thousands of crows' feet and broken bottles—the Arabs had bare feet—and dyed cotton was used to imitate earthworks while new trenches and fortifications were being constructed further back.

After March some 30,000 Arabs laid siege to the town, but the bulk of the Mahdi's forces remained scattered through the Sudan, and through the hot summer months no serious attempt was made to break through the defences. The tribesmen were content merely to keep up a desultory rifle fire, and the raiding parties that Gordon sent out were often able to bring in cattle and maize. His steamers sailed as far north as Berber, and messengers were constantly passing through the lines. It was not exactly war nor was it peace, and there is almost a mediaeval flavour in the letters that passed between the besieged and the besiegers. On March 22 the Mahdi rejected Gordon's offer of peace. His envoys, on being admitted to the Palace in Khartoum, presented the General with a *jibbeh* and invited him to become a follower of the Mahdi. Gordon threw the bundle of clothing on the ground and declared he would never surrender. Later we find him sending out gifts of soap and other rarities to the Emirs who were encamped outside

Khartoum. There is no hunger as yet, very few think of deserting to the Arabs, and the daily life in the town continues in a muted and fatalistic way but without real tension or alarm. Neither Gordon nor anyone else imagines that the situation can continue indefinitely; either they will have to be rescued by an expedition sent up from Egypt or they will be forced to surrender. But for the moment the expectation of rescue is very strong, and Gordon, who is forever on the move about the town, radiates a confidence which inspires them all, from the glummest merchant to the most miserable Egyptian soldier asleep on sentry duty in the lines. He promotes captains to majors, doles out special rations for the feast days, rewards the more daring soldiers with double pay, imprisons criminals and settles disputes with an air of absolute authority that nobody can deny. Gordon Pasha is now something more than the Governor of Khartoum, he is the will of Khartoum itself, and when he reads out to his Council of Notables the Mahdi's call for their surrender they unanimously and enthusiastically reject it. And so the long stifling days of April, May and June go by and no one has lost hope as yet.

In London meanwhile the government was becoming uncomfortably—and perhaps even indignantly—aware that they were being subjected to a form of blackmail by the Governor-General in Khartoum. Just conceivably, even at this late stage, it might have been possible to abandon the Egyptian garrisons to the Mahdi, but to abandon Gordon was altogether different; he was a public figure, he had gone out to the Sudan with the aura of a Christian knight-errant about him, and it was practically certain that the Press would raise an outcry unless something was done to rescue him. Even as early as March 24 Baring had seen this very clearly. He had telegraphed to Granville: 'The question now is how to get General Gordon and Colonel Stewart away from Khartoum.' Queen Victoria, who understood the emotions of her subjects rather better perhaps than any member of the Cabinet, was even more emphatic. 'It is alarming,' she wrote in a telegram to Lord Hartington. 'General Gordon is in danger; you are bound to try and save him . . . you have incurred fearful responsibility.'

Nor was it long before the public took up the cry. By May mass meetings were being held to protest against the 'betrayal of General Gordon'. Funds were raised for his rescue, prayers were said for him in the churches. But neither Gladstone, nor Granville at the Foreign Office was prepared to admit that their gamble had failed as yet. After all, Gordon was still perfectly safe in Khartoum and it was still quite possible for him to leave if he chose to do so.

There is an undertone of irritation in the telegrams which Granville now began to send out to Cairo. He asks repeatedly for information. What is General Gordon doing? Is Khartoum in any real danger? General Gordon must be made aware that 'we do not propose to supply him with Turkish or other force for the purpose of undertaking military expeditions, such being beyond the scope of the commission he holds, and at variance with the specific policy which was the purpose of his mission to the Sudan; that if with this knowledge he continues at Khartoum, he should state to us the cause and intention with which he so continues.'

In other words, Gordon was invited to make his way back to civilization as best he could, and let the garrisons fend for themselves.

Months elapsed before the General's reply was received, and it was tart: 'You ask me to state cause and intention in staying at Khartoum knowing government means to abandon Sudan, and in answer I say, I stay at Khartoum because Arabs have shut us up and will not let us out.'

It was not quite true of course. Gordon himself was able to escape even as late as September, but he was wholly unwilling to leave his soldiers behind; either the garrison came with him or he stayed. This was precisely the point that the government would not accept. Gladstone was quite determined upon this issue. He declared that he would not send a military expedition, and he turned down a proposal of Baring's that a dash across to Berber should be made by the British forces on the Red Sea coast. Replying to a vote of censure in the House in May he stated calmly that he was not at all prepared to admit that General Gordon was cut off or in any real danger. He was 'hemmed in' for the time being perhaps, but that was all. There was no cause for alarm.

But this was merely playing for time. As the weeks went by Gordon's messages became fewer and fewer like a voice growing fainter in the distance, and by July the feeling of indignation in England began to take a much stronger hold. It was Lord Hartington who precipitated the crisis. At the end of July he told Gladstone that he would resign unless an expedition was sent to Khartoum. It was 'a question of personal honour and good faith,' he said, 'and I don't see how I can yield upon it.' Hartington's resignation was enough to bring the government down, and Gladstone gave way at last. On August 8 it was announced that an expedition would be sent to the Sudan and Parliament voted a sum of £300,000 to defray the expenses. Lord Wolseley, the victor of the Battle of Tel-el-Kebir, was appointed to the command.

There is a fated quality about the events of the next six months, an air of pure and certain tragedy that lifts the story out of time and space so that it becomes part of a permanent tradition of human courage and human helplessness. It can be repeated just as a Shakespearean tragedy can be repeated, and it never alters. The values remain the same in every age, and the principal characters are instantly recognizable; we would no more think of their playing different roles from the ones they actually played than we would dream of withholding death from King Lear or of rescuing Hamlet from his hesitations. Each of the three main protagonists—Wolseley coming up the Nile with his soldiers, Gordon waiting and watching on the Palace roof in Khartoum and the Mahdi with his warriors encamped in the desert outside the town—behaves precisely as he is destined to do, and it is wonderfully dramatic that these three men, who were so perfectly incapable of understanding one another, should have been thrust together in such desperate circumstances and in such an outlandish corner of the world. Each man is the victim of forces which are stronger than himself. The Mahdi, having raised a holy war, is bound to assault Khartoum. Gordon, having committed his word to the people in the town, is bound to remain there to the end. And Wolseley, the soldier, having received his orders, is bound to try and rescue him. None of these three really controls events, none of them can predict what will happen. From time to time they feel hope or despair, confidence or uncertainty, but in the main they simply hold on to their predestined courses and they are like the pilots of three ships in a fog that are headed for an inevitable collision.

Wolseley arrived in Cairo on September 9, left Shepheard's Hotel with his staff for Wadi Halfa on September 27 and finally joined battle with the Mahdi's forces north of Khartoum in January 1885. It was not a very rapid progress, but it does not compare badly with the British march into the Sudan twelve years later. After all, Wolseley had to convey 7,000 men and their equipment 1,500 miles into the desert, and the memory of the Hicks disaster was very recent. The news Wolseley got from Khartoum did not indicate that Gordon was in such straits that an extra week or two would make a vital difference. Admittedly this news was very sparse, and eventually ceased altogether, but Wolseley's intelligence staff was not unhopeful. An energetic young major named Herbert Kitchener had gone ahead of the column into the desert, and as early as August had established himself at Debba on the loop of the Nile, barely 200 miles away from Khartoum. From this outpost Kitchener was able to send runners into Khartoum with news of the expedition's approach, and to receive the messages that Gordon sent out.

Nor was the Mahdi on his side to be greatly blamed for delaying his assault on Khartoum. El Obeid had fallen to him because he had starved out the inhabitants, and he had every reason to believe that the same fate would overtake Khartoum. It would have been the height of rashness to have launched his warriors on to the town's defences earlier than the New Year, since Gordon's guns and rifles were much superior to his own and the Egyptian garrison had not yet become demoralized by starvation.

As for Gordon himself, he had no choice; being who he was he had to hang on, using every conceivable device to keep up the morale of his people because the alternative—

surrender—was unthinkable. Surrender meant massacre. The Mahdi's tribesmen took no prisoners in battle except women and young boys and girls, and all of these were destined for slavery.

Yet Khartoum, or more especially Gordon himself, remains the real focus of this tragedy. He occupies throughout the centre of the stage, and the final scenes he dominates entirely. It is fortunate, therefore, that through his journal we know exactly what he thought and felt, we know all about his daily hopes and fears, and Khartoum in its death throes is almost as real to us as a catastrophe that has taken place in our own lives. The journal is an astonishing document. No other English soldier has revealed his heart so emphatically, so simply or so movingly as Gordon does in these wild jottings, sometimes written on telegraph forms and flimsy scraps of paper, sometimes heavily underscored or crossed out, sometimes decorated with oddly exact little maps and ribald caricatures, sometimes pathetic, ironical or recklessly unfair, but always absolutely honest.

By September (when, unknown to Gordon, the relief expedition was beginning to form up in Egypt), the situation in Khartoum was becoming critical. The supply of food was still holding out; indeed so many cattle had been captured by raiding parties that the price of meat had fallen from ten shillings to two shillings a pound. But the Egyptian soldiers were every day more lethargic, and on September 4 a serious reverse occurred: over eight hundred men were killed in a skirmish outside the town, and it was apparent that from now onwards the garrison must remain entirely on the defensive. But it was the absence of news that was the really undermining factor—the feeling that they had been abandoned and that there was nothing definite to look forward to. Each successive day was a little more oppressive than the last, and even Gordon was forced to admit that unless help arrived within a month or two the town would fall.

He decided to send the steamer *Abbas* down the river with an Arab captain who was to take with him dispatches appealing for immediate help. It was a dangerous undertaking but it was not at all impossible that the boat could get through; once beyond the Mahdi's stronghold at Berber the crew would find themselves among friendly tribes who, no doubt, would agree to send on the messages by camel to Kitchener and Cairo.

There had remained with Gordon in Khartoum only a small group of Europeans—Stewart, his second-in-command, three consuls, Power the Englishman, Herbin the Frenchman and Hansal the Austrian, and a number of Greeks and others of European extraction. Directly it was heard that the *Abbas* was to sail applications were made to the Palace for permission to go with her. Herbin came first, and Gordon says he jumped at the offer: Herbin might be able to get the French government to move. Then Stewart offered to go provided that Gordon exonerated him from the charge of desertion. Gordon told him that he would not actually order him to go, since there was too much risk involved in the journey, but he would certainly give him an official letter which would make it clear that there was no question of desertion; indeed, Stewart could perform a valuable service by going. He could reveal the true situation in Khartoum, and make a personal appeal to the European powers for assistance. Gordon had another idea; if England would not help perhaps others could. He wrote out an appeal to the Pope in Rome and another to the Sultan in Constantinople.

Power, the British Consul, now said that he too would join the party. Hansal, the Austrian, elected to remain behind.

There are some curious aspects about this matter, and they have never been satisfactorily explained. Among the papers which the party was to take down was the cypher that was used to decode official messages from Egypt. According to Gordon he let the cypher go because he feared that it might fall into the hands of the Mahdi if it remained in Khartoum. This meant presumably that he and all of them expected Khartoum to fall, and thus Stewart and the two consuls cannot altogether escape the charge of desertion. It is also a little difficult to understand just why Gordon would not order Stewart to go. Stewart had a long interview with Gordon before he left and pressed him to give the order. Gordon's explanation that he would not give the order because of the dangerous nature of the journey does not ring altogether true. He must have known that without the order to leave Stewart would have some trouble in clearing his name. Nor was it true, as Gordon later attested in his journal, that Stewart was serving no useful purpose in Khartoum. The plain fact was that Gordon very badly needed the assistance of another white officer, especially so experienced an officer as Stewart. It was simply impossible for one man to control so large and so reluctant a garrison without at least one reliable assistant. Nevertheless, he rejected Stewart's services now just as, for other reasons, he rejected Slatin's services later on.

The only conclusion that one can draw from all this is that Gordon wanted to be alone. He wanted them all to leave, and he would have liked Hansal to have gone as well. He did not like Hansal. The Austrian Consul was that same man who, if we can believe Strachey's story, had disgusted him so many years before when he had first arrived at Khartoum by flinging himself into an orgy of naked girl dancers at an official banquet. In his journal Gordon now wrote, 'I hear Hansal, the Austrian Consul, is disposed to go with his *seven female attendants* to the Arabs. I hope he will do so.' It seems unlikely that Hansal ever had any such intention. He had large properties and business interests in Khartoum, he had lived there many years, and no doubt had succumbed to the inertia of the place—these probably were his real reasons for staying: and no doubt by staying he clouded somewhat Gordon's subconscious wish for solitary martyrdom. If the two men were ever intimate during the last months of the siege there is no record of it in Gordon's journals; indeed he is at pains to say that he has no friends in the town, no one whom he can trust.

On September 10 all was ready for the others to go. They boarded the *Abbas* together with a party of Greeks and a small bodyguard of soldiers, and with two other steamers to escort them beyond Berber they set sail down the river to the north. The pilot of the *Abbas* was one of the most experienced men in the Nile service, and he was especially enjoined to gather firewood for the ship's engine only at deserted places outside the territory of the hostile tribes. Gordon watched them run the gauntlet of the Arab rifle fire beyond the limits of the town, and then, alone, turned back to his endless vigil on the lines and his solitary communings in the Palace.

'The Mahdi is still at Rahad [near El Obeid, about 200 miles from Khartoum],' he wrote in his journal that same day, September 10, and once again he allowed his mind to brood over the troublesome question of Slatin. He himself had enlisted Slatin in the Sudan service—that young, good-looking officer from Prince Rudolf's regiment, a Roman Catholic and a gentleman; he had written to him in Austria inviting him to join the Sudan service, had trained him, promoted him and had sent him off to Darfur. And now Slatin had surrendered to the Mahdi and had become a Moslem. 'It is not a small thing for a European, for fear of death, to deny our faith; it was not so in old times, and it should not be regarded as if it was taking off one coat and putting on another. If the Christian faith is a myth, then let men throw it off, but it is mean and dishonourable to do so merely to save one's life if one believes it is the true faith. . . . Treachery never succeeds, and however matters may end it is better to fall with clean hands than to be mixed up with dubious acts and dubious men.'

But then who was really brave? 'During our blockade, we have often discussed the question of being frightened, which, in the world's view, a man should never be. For my part I am always frightened, and very much so. I fear the future of all engagements. It is not the fear of death, that is past, thank God; but I fear defeat, and its consequences. I do not believe a bit in the calm, unmoved man. I think it is only that he does not show it outwardly. Thence I conclude no commander of forces ought to live closely in relation with his subordinates, who watch him like lynxes, for there is no contagion equal to that of fear. I have been rendered furious when, from anxiety, I could not eat. I would find those at the same table were in like manner affected.'

Now, at least, there was no danger of his private life

being overlooked too closely. Except for his servants he lived alone at the Palace. He ate his meals alone. He watched the antics of his favourite turkey-cock in the court-yard, and the hawks flying by along the river. He stepped out alertly in the morning on his round of the forts, the arsenal and the ship-building yard, the barracks and the storehouses. He spent hours on the flat roof of the Palace with his telescope—'by far the best glass I ever saw'. It was made by Chevalier's in Paris and he had bought it in Khartoum for £5. One could see so much from the roof; the wide sweep of the river to the north whence one day the relief expedition must arrive (Stewart must surely be past Berber by now); the great ocean of sand that lay around the town, and, moving across it, the Arab horsemen, the Arab tents and huts, the enemy. They were forever prostrating themselves in prayer. 'Another church parade,' he notes in his journal.

Then there was the question of those nuns with the Austrian Mission to Darfur; there was a rumour that they had been married to the Greek traders who had also been captured by the Mahdi. 'What a row the Pope will make about the nuns marrying the Greeks. It is the union of the Greek and Latin churches.'

It was strange stuff for him to be writing in what was supposed to be an official dispatch to the War Office in London, and yet he could not prevent his mind from running on. Nuns, Greeks, turkey-cocks, apostasy and Arab tribesmen praying on the sand—it was all part of this forgotten little world on the Nile, but it was worth recording for in the end human beings forgot everything. 'It is curious how quick the people forget their disasters and losses,' he wrote on September 14; 'it is only ten days ago that we lost in killed nearly one thousand men, yet no one speaks of it now; it takes about four to six days to obliterate the bitterness of a disaster.'

By the last week in September Gordon had definite news that the expedition was on its way. A native runner came in from Kitchener at Debba with a message saying that Lord Wolseley had left London, and that already in

August (the message took nearly a month to reach Gordon) the vanguard of the column was moving out of Wadi Halfa into the Dongola province.

Gordon made the most of these tremendous tidings. All the forts were ordered to fire their guns in celebration, and presently pictures were pasted up in the streets showing British and Indian soldiers on the march. The men had the stamp of victory and success on their faces. Along the Blue Nile houses were rented for the incoming English officers, and a great to-do was made over the engagement of servants and the purchase of furniture and water jars. Contracts were signed with the Khartoum butchers and bakers to supply the soldiers when they arrived.

Gordon also learned from Kitchener's dispatch that Baring had temporarily gone to London and that his place at Cairo had been taken by a Mr. Edwin Egerton. Kitchener appended a message from Egerton: 'Tell Gordon steamers are being passed over the second cataracts, and that we wish to be informed through Dongola exactly when he expects to be in difficulties as to provisions and ammunition.'

It was a relief, of course, to know that at last something was being done. But oh, those dunder-headed officials in Cairo! 'I am sure I should like that fellow Egerton,' Gordon wrote in his journal. 'There is a light-hearted jocularity about his communications, and I should think the cares of life sat easily on him. . . . Now I really think if Egerton was to turn over the "archives" (a delicious word) of his office, he would see we have been in difficulties for some months. It is as if a man on the bank, having seen his friend in the river already bobbed down two or three times, hails, "I say, old fellow, let us know when we are to throw you the life buoy, I know you have bobbed down two or three times, but it is a pity to throw you the life buoy until you are really *in extremis,* and I want to know *exactly* for I am a man brought up in a school of exactitude. . . .!" '

Other telegrams as well arrived, but they were in cypher and Gordon, having no means of decoding them, could only speculate about their contents. Speculations now filled half his day. Where was Stewart? By now he ought to be across the loop of the Nile and possibly in touch with Kitchener. Where was the Mahdi? When was he going to bring the main bulk of his army up to Khartoum?

On the whole Gordon was inclined to think that the Mahdi would wait until the Nile began to fall towards the end of the year before he made his assault. Would the expedition reach Khartoum before then? It depended upon how well Wolseley understood the tactics of fighting in the desert. Gordon's own notions on this matter were precise. 'I cannot too much impress on you that this expedition will not encounter any enemy worth the name in a European sense of the word; the struggle is with the climate and destitution of the country. It is one of time and patience, and of small parties of determined men, backed by native allies, which are got by policy and money. A heavy lumbering column, however strong, is nowhere in this land. Parties of forty or sixty men, swiftly moving about, will do more than any column. If you lose two or three, what of it—it is the chance of war. Native allies above all things, at whatever cost. It is the country of the irregular, not of the regular. If you move in mass you will find no end of difficulties; whereas, if you let detached parties dash out here and there, you will spread dismay in the Arab ranks. The time to attack is the dawn, or rather before it (this is stale news), but sixty men would put these Arabs to flight just before dawn, which one thousand would not accomplish in daylight. This was always Zobeir's tactics. The reason is that the strength of the Arabs is their horsemen, who do not dare to attack in the dark. I do hope you will not drag on that artillery: it can only produce delay and do little good.'

Let them remember Hicks. Better still let them remember Cambyses and his army that was swallowed up in the desert. Gordon looked up the relevant passage in Herodotus and pasted it into his journal.

There is a note of firmness and hope in these entries, but as September passed into October the mood begins to change. He is constantly wondering what has happened to Stewart. He is worried about his armed steamers, his only lifeline with the outside world: 'My beautiful steamers, which used to be comparatively sweet, now stink like badgers.' Perhaps he will sail one of them up to the White Nile into Central Africa and have done for ever with London and its hypocritical politics, its clubs and its frightful dinner parties. He would sooner live like a tribesman with the Mahdi, he declared, than go out to dinner every night in London. 'It is one of my joys that I never have to see Great Britain again. I hope to get out of this affair, and either go to the Congo, via Equatorial Province or by Brussels.' Perhaps he might make a deal with the Mahdi— the Mahdi should have Khartoum and the steamers and the ammunition as well provided he allowed the garrison to return unharmed to Egypt. On the other hand, he himself would never surrender—this was a matter of 'national honour'.

Next he turns his thoughts once more to the hawks on the wing outside the window and a mouse—obviously a female 'judging by her swelled-out appearance'—that shares his solitary meals: 'A mouse has taken Stewart's place at table; she . . . comes up and eats out of my plate without fear.' Then there is the turkey-cock that has become 'so disagreeable that I had to put his head under his wing and sway him to and fro till he slept'. And then again, when will the British column arrive? 'It is, of course, on the cards that Khartoum is taken under the nose of the expeditionary force, which will be *just too late*. The expeditionary force will perhaps think it necessary to retake it; but that will be of no use, and will cause loss of life uselessly on both sides. It had far better quietly return, with its tail between its legs.'

Towards the middle of October there was a sudden flurry of activity. News reached the Palace that a group of sixteen leading men in the town were planning to raise a revolt and go over to the Mahdi. With misgivings Gordon put them under arrest. 'I confess,' he wrote, 'I am more perplexed about these arrests than I like: is it a good thing? Or is it not? If I could be sure that the majority wished to go to the Mahdi, I could make up my mind at once what to do: it would be an immense relief to me, but does the mass wish it?' No one could give him an answer as yet.

The mass of the people in the town were becoming seriously hungry at last and could think of nothing but food. The long siege had broken their power to take decisions of any kind. Gordon himself was the one solid factor in their lives and what he willed they willed. They held on now because he held on.

About Slatin, however, Gordon had no hesitation whatever. On October 16 he wrote: 'The letters of Slatin have arrived. I have no remarks to make on them, and cannot make out why he wrote them.' In these letters, which had been brought into Khartoum from the Mahdi's camp, Slatin said that he had heard that Gordon had taken a harsh view of his surrender and he begged the Governor-General to listen to his explanation. He had merely professed to be a Moslem, while he was still fighting the Mahdi, he says, in order to gain the confidence of his troops: 'Whether by my conversion I committed a dishonourable step is a matter of opinion—it was made more easy to me because I had, perhaps unhappily, not received a strict religious education at home.' As for his surrender, he had had no choice; when his soldiers capitulated he was bound to follow suit. 'Does your Excellency believe that to me, an Austrian officer, the surrender was easy? It was one of the hardest days of my life.

'By submission and obedient behaviour,' he went on, 'I have attained a certain degree of confidence amongst the local magnates, and have thus received permission to write to you, because they are of the opinion that by these lines I am requesting your Excellency to surrender. Should your Excellency not despise my feeble services and small knowledge of tactics, I beg to offer you my help, with no desire for a higher post of honour, only from devotion and friendship for your Excellency and the good cause. I am ready with or under you, for victory or death. My few faithful ones here, my fortune, etc., all—all will I gladly desert to die, if God so please, an honourable death.'

When this had gone unanswered Slatin had written again:

'Your Excellency, I have fought twenty-seven times for the government against the enemy, and they have beaten me twice, and I have done nothing dishonourable, nothing which should hinder your Excellency from writing me an answer, that I may know what to do. . . . If there are letters from Europe for me at the post I beg you to send them me, because it is almost three years since I have had any news of my family. I entreat your Excellency to honour me with an answer.

Your devoted and obedient servant
Slatin.

P.S. I and Seid Gjoma, Mudir of Fascher, are seeking occasion to enter Omdurman to remain with you. Pray, Excellency, do your best to give us permission, because we are always in fear of spies. I pray God that He may give you success in the siege.

P.S. If your Excellency has perhaps understood that I have done anything contrary to the honour of an officer, and if that hinders you writing to me, I pray you give me a chance of defending myself, and judge according to the truth.'

'He evidently is not a Spartan. . . . If he gets away I shall take him to the Congo with me, he will want some *quarantine*; one feels sorry for him.' Next day he returned to the subject: 'I shall have nothing to do with Slatin's coming in here to stay, unless he has the Mahdi's positive leave, which he is not likely to get; his doing so would be the breaking of his parole, which should be as sacred when given to the Mahdi as to any other power, and it would jeopardize the safety of all those Europeans, prisoners of the Mahdi.' He did however offer to ransom Slatin and the other Europeans from the Mahdi for a sum of 10,000 guineas. There was no reply.

But it was not Slatin who occupied Gordon's attention at this moment; another, much more disturbing matter had come up. In his second letter Slatin had declared that the *Abbas* had not got through; it had been captured below Berber, and Stewart had been put to death. Gordon had heard a similar report from another source only a few days before, but had refused to believe it. He reassured himself that such rumours were always flying about and they were always unreliable. And yet, on October 21, he confesses, 'I am very anxious about the *Abbas*: it would be terrible, if it is true, that she is captured.' Then on October 22, a letter from the Mahdi himself arrived. It was written on a single, very large sheet of paper to which had been affixed the Mahdi's square seal, and it began:

'In the name of God the merciful and compassionate: praise be to God, the bountiful Ruler, and blessing on our Lord Mohammed with peace.

'From the servant who trusts in God—Mohammed the son of Abdullah.

'To Gordon Pasha of Khartoum: may God guide him into the path of virtue, amen!

'Know that your small steamer, named *Abbas*—which you sent with the intention of forwarding your news to Cairo, by way of Dongola, the persons sent being your representative Stewart Pasha and the two consuls, French and English, with other persons, has been captured by the will of God.

'Those who believed in us as Mahdi, and surrendered, have been delivered; and those who did not were destroyed—as your representative afore-named, with the Consuls and the rest—whose souls God has condemned to the fire and to eternal misery.'

There followed a long and exact catalogue of all the papers and documents that had been taken from the dead men—Stewart's journal, the cypher, the appeals to the Pope and the Sultan, the statements which gave details of the amount of food and ammunition remaining in Khartoum, copies of all the telegrams that had passed between Gordon and Cairo, a census of the number of soldiers remaining in the garrison and of their arms, and Gordon's letters repeatedly asking for help.

'We have now understood it all,' the Mahdi wrote, and once again he invited Gordon to surrender before it was too late: 'For, after the beginning of the battle were you to surrender, it would be from fear, and not willingly, and that will not be accepted.'

A dispatch was enclosed from the Mahdi's commander in the south and it revealed that the Bahr-el-Ghazal province had fallen.

So Stewart was really dead and Lupton had surrendered. But no, it could not be true. The documents the Mahdi had seen must have been copies which he had sent out by an agent before the *Abbas* sailed. Perhaps one of the Greeks who went down the river had read Stewart's papers and had turned traitor.

Perhaps—but he put the sinister Arabic scrawl away from him: 'As for these letters, I cannot make head nor tail of them, so I leave them to the Arabic scholars of the Universities.'

To the Mahdi he replied: '. . . to me it is all one whether Lupton Bey has surrendered or has not surrendered. And whether he [the Mahdi] has captured twenty thousand steamers like the *Abbas,* or twenty thousand Stewarts Pasha; it is all one to me.

'I am here, like iron, and hope to see the newly-arrived English. . . .' It was impossible, he added, for him to have any more dealings with the Mahdi; from now on they had better communicate with bullets.

Yet the news was true, and within a few days Kitchener smuggled through a message to confirm it. Again and again Gordon asked himself how it could have happened. The *Abbas* was strong enough to ward off any Arab attack so long as she continued in the middle of the river; she could hardly have hit a rock and sunk for she was fitted with buffers. Only treachery could explain it; some traitorous sheikh must have led them into a trap while they were in search of wood for fuel on the bank.

'I can see in imagination the whole scene,' Gordon wrote, 'the sheikh inviting them to land, saying "Thank God the Mahdi is a liar"—bringing in the wood—men going on shore and dispersed. The *Abbas* with her steam down, then a rush of wild Arabs, and all is over!' There follows in the journal page after page of self-recrimination. Why had he let them go? What other precautions should he have taken for their safety?

What had actually happened was that on September 18 the *Abbas* had struck a rock and had been disabled when she was 60 miles below Abu Hamed and only 100 miles from Kitchener's outpost. Believing that they were beyond enemy territory Stewart went ashore and there met Suleiman Wad Gamr, the chief of the Monasir tribe, and other sheikhs. The Arabs were immediately friendly and when they offered to provide camels to take on the party overland Stewart presented them with two swords and an embroidered cloak. The sheikhs then pressed the Europeans to pass the night ashore and the invitation was accepted. In the night there was a rush of wild Arabs and all was over. Having massacred Stewart, Herbin and Power the sheikhs went on board the *Abbas* and killed all but fourteen of her remaining passengers and crew.

On October 21, the Mahdi, heartened by the information he had received from the *Abbas* papers, moved up to Khartoum with the main bulk of his forces and established himself in two camps close to Omdurman on the western bank of the Nile. He announced his intention to attack Khartoum in a letter to Gordon: '...I have taken pity on some of my men and allowed them to die so as to obtain ... paradise.' The final stage of the siege had begun. In the Palace Gordon calculated his chances. He was not seriously worried about his ammunition—his arsenal continued to produce some forty thousand rounds a day—but the question of food was urgent. 'If they (the British troops) do not come before 30th November the game is up, and Rule Britannia. In this calculation I have given every latitude for difficulties of transport, making forts etc., and on the 15th November I ought to see Her Majesty's uniform.' He speculated very closely on the expedition's advance: having reached Debba or Merowe further upstream, Wolseley must send one column up the river to attack Berber while another struck directly across the desert to Metemma, a little over 100 miles north of Khartoum. Here Gordon could help his rescuers, for he still commanded the river thus far. He dispatched five of his steamers to Metemma with instructions to the captains that

Map reproduced from *Gordon and the Sudan*
by Bernard M. Allen (Macmillan & Co.,
London, 1931) based on map
in Wingate's *Mahdiism*

they must remain there until the vanguard of the British column appeared, and then they were to bring it on to Khartoum.

Early in November a batch of letters arrived and they included one from Samuel Baker and another, six months old, from Stanley in the Congo. Baker's letter had an official note written on the envelope, *'Communications avec le Soudan interrompées'*, which gave Gordon a certain grim pleasure. 'I should think the communications were interrompées!!!' Kitchener had wrapped these letters in a newspaper, the London *Standard* of September 15, which Gordon's servants threw away in the Palace yard, and it was only by chance that he recovered it. He read it eagerly, for it was the first news of the outside world he had had for many weeks, but one report drove him into a frenzy: 'Lord Wolseley seen off at Victoria Station, for the *Gordon relief expedition*!!! NO! for the relief of the Sudan garrisons. . . . *I declare positively, and once and for all, that I will not leave the Sudan until every one who wants to go down is given the chance to do so, unless* a government is established which relieves me of the charge; therefore if any emissary or letter comes up here ordering me to come down, I WILL NOT OBEY IT BUT WILL STAY HERE; AND FALL WITH TOWN, AND RUN ALL RISKS.'

Why could they not understand this? Baring was to blame. Baring had failed to get him soldiers when he asked for them. Baring was responsible for every disaster that had overtaken them. He wrote pages about Baring, tore them out of his journal and then again returned to the attack on a later day. There was a message from Tewfik saying that Baring was coming up with Lord Wolseley—presumably on a camel. 'There was a slight laugh when Khartoum heard that Baring was bumping his way up here, for so we read Tewfik's telegram—a regular Nemesis'.

His attacks on Granville were equally bitter. 'Eh what?' he makes the Foreign Secretary exclaim. 'We will have to go up to Khartoum? Why, it will cost millions, what a wretched business! What! Send Zobeir? Our conscience recoils from *that*, it is elastic, but not equal to that, it is a pact with the Devil . . . Do you think there is any way of getting

hold of HIM [Gordon] in a quiet way?' Elsewhere he pictures Granville opening his copy of *The Times* and discovering with dismay that Khartoum was still holding out.
'Why, HE *said distinctly* he could *only* hold out *six months*,
and that was in March (counts the months). August! Why,
he ought to have given in! What *is* to be done? They'll be
howling for an expedition . . . It is no laughing matter:
that abominable Mahdi.'

It was childish, it was petty, it was unfair—and just possibly, as with nearly everything that Gordon wrote or
fancied, there was a grain of truth in it. At all events such
outbursts helped to relieve the strain of these crushing and
wearisome days when there was nothing to distract his
tired mind from its endless anxiety. To be in Khartoum
now was to have the feeling that one was held in a steadily
tightening vice.

If Gordon had known the terms of Wolseley's orders he
would have been even more furious with Baring and Granville. These orders had been drafted in Cairo and were
as follows: 'The primary object of the expedition up the
valley of the Nile is to bring away General Gordon and
Colonel Stewart from Khartoum. When that object has
been secured, no further offensive operations of any kind
are to be undertaken.' So now, in overpowering heat, the
long cumbersome column was slowly making its way up the
Dongola province to rescue one man who was dead and
another who did not wish to be rescued—not at any rate
on these terms; not until the garrisons were got away and
some reasonable form of government was set up in the
Sudan.

Gordon began to give his mind more and more to this
question of the future government. Zobeir of course was
still the best solution. Set him up as Governor-General
and let Gordon himself look after Equatoria. Failing that
let the Turks come in and rule the Sudan. Failing that
find some other competent man who would take control
with a subsidy from Egypt. He had a new idea. Why not
this fellow Kitchener? Kitchener, it was true, had made
an awful mess of his intelligence service—hardly any

of his runners got through to Khartoum—but Baker in his letter had spoken very highly of him. Baker had said:

'The man whom I have always placed my hopes upon, Major Kitchener, R.E., is one of the few *very superior* British officers, with a cool and good head and a hard constitution, combined with untiring energy . . .'

Well then, let them make this young officer Governor-General. Gordon sent off a letter to Kitchener himself suggesting the appointment.

This was an extraordinary piece of intuition, for Kitchener was by some way the most promising soldier, not only in Wolseley's force, but in the whole British army. He was aged 34 at this time, a man six feet two inches tall with piercing bright blue eyes, and already he had a reputation for cold, determined, machine-like precision. He was a good horseman—he had raised a force of 1,500 irregulars on the Sudanese border earlier in the campaign—and there was a touch of daring in the young man that is hardly recognizable in the awesome figure of the general he was later to become. Being a friend of Stewart's he had pleaded for permission to make a dash through Arab territory so as to meet the *Abbas* at Berber, and had been incensed when Wolseley held him back. The staff knew him as a diligent officer who was interested in archaeology, who spoke French, Arabic and some Turkish, and as a man who was indifferent to women. It was hardly Kitchener's fault that Gordon got more messages out of Khartoum than he received—men could always be found who were willing to leave the besieged city, but few wished to go there—and Kitchener ran exceptional risks in trying to maintain the correspondence; he ventured far into the enemy's ground, sometimes in Bedouin disguise and carrying with him a bottle of poison so that he could commit suicide if he was captured. When, about this time (November 1884), his exploits were revealed in the Press, an aura of romantic glamour attached itself to his name; it was the sort of reputation that was later to overtake Lawrence of Arabia.

So now, divining the importance of this young soldier whom he had never met, Gordon writes in his journal:

'Whoever comes up here had better appoint Major Kitchener Governor-General, for it is certain, after what has passed, *I am impossible*. (What a comfort.)'

Then again his mind returns to Baring. 'If Baring does bump his way up here as British Commissioner, I shall consider that he has expiated his faults and shall forgive him. We seldom realize our position. In ten or twelve years' time Baring, Lord Wolseley, myself, Evelyn Wood [the British General in Cairo], etc. will have no teeth, and will be deaf; some of us will be quite passé; no one will come and court us; new Barings, new Lord Wolseleys will have arisen, and who will call us "bloaks" and "twaddlers". "Oh! for goodness' sake come away, then! Is that dreadful bore coming? If once he gets alongside you, you are in for half an hour," will be the remark of some young captain of the present time on seeing you enter the Club. This is very humiliating, for we, each one, think we are immortal. That poor old General who for years vegetated at the end of —— Street close to his Clubs! who ever visited him? Better a ball in the brain than to flicker out unheeded, like he did.'

Should he commit suicide then? He had thought of it. He had actually placed explosives under the Palace so that in an instant it could be blown up with himself inside. But he rejected the idea, for it was, in a way, 'taking things out of God's hands'.

Gordon now spent more and more of his time on the Palace roof. From that perch above the desert he could see into every part of his fortress, even as far as Omdurman Fort on the opposite bank of the river, and—what was just as important—his soldiers could see him. They were quite incorrigible, these soldiers, he reflected—not perhaps the Sudanese, but certainly the Egyptians. Unless they saw he had his eyes upon them sentries fell asleep at their posts, orders were forgotten, and every one lied. 'The North Fort hate my telescope; day and night I work them.' Yet still they found ways to circumvent him. 'I certainly claim to having commanded, more often than any other man, cowardly troops, but this experience of 1884 beats all past experiences. . . . A more contemptible soldier than the Egyptian never existed. Here we never count on them; they are held in supreme contempt, poor creatures. *They* never go out to fight; it would be perfectly iniquitous to make them.'

He packed off as many of them as he could in the steamers that he sent to Metemma and gave orders that, under no circumstances, were they to be brought back.

As for his own servants in the Palace they were hardly any better. 'You cannot do anything with them while in these fortresses, *eating, saying prayers, sleeping or sick,* and they know it. You would be a brute if you did (which I fear I often am). You want to send an immediate order, and there is your servant bobbing up and down, and you cannot disturb him. It is a beautiful country for trying your patience. It is very curious, but if I am in a bad temper, which I fear is often the case, my servants will be always at their prayers, and thus religious practices follow the scale of my temper; they are pagans if all goes well.'

And yet, poor devils, they had never asked to be put into this mess—to be abandoned like this. 'Oh! Baring. Baring. Baring.'

By November 12 the Mahdi had got his guns into position, those same guns that he had captured from Hicks, and the shelling of Khartoum began. It was erratic and did hardly any harm, but it had a demoralizing effect upon people who were now suffering from malnutrition, and presently events began to take a more ominous turn: one of the best of the steamers that had remained at Khartoum ran aground under the enemy shellfire and had to be abandoned. At the same time the Mahdi's forces closed in around Omdurman Fort and cut it off from Khartoum and the river. Gordon was still able to signal to the Egyptian commander there with bugle calls. But the Mahdi also had a bugler who knew the signals, and when Gordon sounded 'Come to us. Come to us,' from the Palace roof, he was answered ironically from the Arabs' camp, 'Come to us. Come to us.' There was, in any case, no hope for Omdurman Fort—unless of course the expedition arrived in time. Early in November there had been recovered a large haul of grain which had been stolen and secreted by merchants in Khartoum, and that gave the garrison a brief reprieve. But on December 13 Gordon estimated that they could hold out only another ten days.

Whenever he went out of the Palace now a crowd of women gathered round him calling out for food; every day the shelling and the rifle-fire grew a little heavier. The Arabs had a gun trained upon the Palace, and the shells crashed loudly but usually harmlessly on to the heavy stone walls.

'One tumbles at 3 a.m. into a troubled sleep;' Gordon wrote. 'A drum beats—tup! tup! tup! It comes into a dream, but after a few minutes one becomes more awake, and it is revealed to the brain that *one is in Khartoum*. The next query is, where is this tup, tupping going on. A hope arises it will die away. No, it goes on, and increases in intensity. The thought strikes one, "Have they enough ammunition?" (the excuse of bad soldiers). One exerts oneself. At last, it is no use, up one must get, and go on to the roof of the Palace; then telegrams, orders, swearing, and cursing goes on till about 9 a.m.'

Somehow he kept the ship-building yard going and his engineers actually produced a new steamer to replace the one that had been lost. 'The town wanted to call it after me, but I said, "I have put most of you in prison and otherwise bullied you and I have no fear of your forgetting me".' The vessel was named the *Zobeir*. He could still occasionally be as light-hearted as this, could still refer to the Mahdi as 'his holiness', but then the frightful weight of uncertainty returned. '. . . There is not one person on whom I can rely. . . . I am weary of my life, day and night, day and night, it is one continual worry.'

The river was now beginning to fall and the drying mudbanks brought the enemy very near.

On December 13 he wrote, 'NOW MARK THIS, if the Expeditionary Force, and I ask for no more than two hundred men, does not come in ten days, *the town may fall*; and I have done my best for the honour of my country. Good-bye.

C. G. Gordon.

'You send me no information, though you have lots of money.

C. G. G.'

This was almost the last communication received from General Gordon. He bundled up the papers of his journal—the telegraph forms, the pieces of tissue paper, the little maps he had made and the pen and ink sketches—sewed them up in a cloth and wrote on the wrapper, 'Events at Khartoum. General Gordon's Journal. No secrets as far as I am concerned. To be pruned down if published. C. G. Gordon.'

The packages were handed to the captain of the *Bordein*, and on December 15 the vessel, under heavy fire, left for Metemma.

Chapter 14

THE FALLING NILE

BY THE END of December 1884 the advance guard of the expedition had reached the Nile at Korti, midway between Debba and Merowe, and was in a position to start the final advance on Khartoum. It was decided that Gordon's plan should be adopted: one column was to follow the course of the river on its great eastward loop past Abu Hamel and Berber, while the other column, under Sir Herbert Stewart,[1] marched directly across the desert to Metemma, where it was known that Gordon's steamers would be waiting. Wolseley had been forbidden by the British government to lead the advance guard, and remained behind at Dongola to assemble the bulk of his forces. There still appeared to be no cause for desperate haste. On December 30 one of Gordon's runners came into the camp at Korti with a message written on a piece of paper the size of a postage stamp. It said: 'Khartoum all right. 12.12.84. C. G. Gordon.' The runner, however, reported verbally that he had been instructed to say that the supplies of food in Khartoum were running very low and that the expedition should come on as quickly as possible. It must be remembered that up to this time no one had read the last batch of the journals, which were on board the *Bordein* at Metemma, 160 miles away.

On the morning of December 30 Sir Herbert Stewart began his advance with 100 British troops and 2,200 camels, and on January 2 he reached Jakdul Wells, 98 miles away. Here he gave orders for an outpost to be set up while he himself returned to Korti to bring on a further contingent of 1,600 men and 2,400 camels. On January 13 the whole

[1] No relation of Colonel Stewart who had just been killed by the Arabs.

column was united and the advance was continued until the evening of January 16, when it was reported that strong forces of Arabs lay ahead. They were encamped round the Abu Klea Wells and were clearly prepared for battle. Sir Herbert Stewart bivouacked for the night about three and a half miles away, and on the morning of January 17 he advanced to the attack. The Arab horsemen charged with the utmost recklessness, and succeeded in breaking into the British square where fierce hand-to-hand fighting took place among the camels. It was all over in five minutes. The Arabs drew off, leaving 1,100 dead on the ground, and the British casualties were under 200.

That same night the British took possession of Abu Klea Wells and at 4 p.m. on the following day the column resumed its march towards Metemma, 23 miles away. They continued all night, and soon after dawn on January 19 came within sight of the Nile. Their path to the river, however, was blocked by the enemy and once again the Arabs attacked out of the scrub and thick grass. The British soldiers had now been without sleep for more than forty-eight hours, but they managed to drive off the attack with a further loss of 111 men killed and wounded, and finally reached the bank of the river a little to the north of Metemma. Sir Herbert Stewart was mortally wounded in this skirmish, Burnaby, his second-in-command, had already been killed at Abu Klea, and thus the command of the column fell to Sir Charles Wilson, an officer of the Intelligence service who had not led troops in battle before.

On the morning of January 21 four of Gordon's steamers appeared, and the journals were now opened and read together with a letter dated December 14 in which Gordon declared that he expected Khartoum to fall within ten days. Still later news was brought in by a runner who carried another message written on a minute scrap of paper, and it read: 'Khartoum is all right. Could hold out for years. C. G. Gordon. 29.12.84.'; but Gordon apparently had sent this message simply as a gesture of confidence which, if intercepted by the Arabs, would deceive them. It was evident, therefore, that for at least three weeks Khartoum had been in the greatest extremity, and Wilson had every reason to push on without delay. Yet three days went by while the steamers' engines were overhauled and a reconnaissance was made along the river, and it was not until January 24 that he was ready to proceed. Wilson himself led the way in the *Bordein* with ten redcoats of the Royal Sussex regiment and 110 Sudanese troops. The *Tell Hewein* followed with ten more soldiers of the Royal Sussex, and 80 Sudanese, and she towed a lugger with a heavy cargo of maize and fifty more native troops. The crews were men of the Shaigiya tribe whom Gordon had sent down from Khartoum.

The Nile had now fallen very low, and the little convoy got into difficulties almost at once. On the second day out the *Bordein* struck a rock in the Sixth Cataract, and it was not until the morning of January 27 that the steamers were able to go on again. Further delays were caused when the firewood for the boilers ran out and more had to be gathered from the river bank. As the steamers neared Khartoum they were obliged to face an increasingly heavy rifle fire from the shore, and it seemed for a time that they would not get through. The Shaigiya tribesmen on board, whose families were in the town, wanted to desert to the Mahdi at one stage, and the captains of the two steamers agreed to go on only when they were promised a bonus of £100 apiece. On three separate occasions Arabs called out to the British from the bank that they were too late, that Khartoum had fallen and that Gordon was dead. But this was disregarded, and at last on the morning of January 28 the *Bordein* under incessant artillery fire steamed up to the junction of the Blue and White Niles and came within sight of the town. The help which Gordon had been calling for since March in the previous year had finally arrived.

At this point let us turn back and see what had been happening in Khartoum since Gordon had sent out his last messages in December. By the end of that month the supply of maize had failed almost entirely, and soon every living animal—donkeys, dogs, monkeys, even rats—had been eaten. Most of the women had long since sold their jewels for food. All that was now left for soldiers and civilians alike was palmtree fibre and a species of gum which contained very little nutriment and caused violent pains a few hours after it was eaten. Five thousand of the more disaffected citizens were sent out to the Mahdi with a message from Gordon that he should be merciful to them, but still the hunger increased. Father Ohrwalder declared later that Khartoum during the final days of the siege was not reduced to the same degree of starvation that faced El Obeid before its surrender, yet the shortage of food must have been acute; the dead lay in hundreds in the streets, and those that remained alive were too weak and too dispirited to bury them. On the barricades the soldiers, according to one witness, 'stood like pieces of wood' or went about their work in a sort of mechanical trance hardly knowing what they were doing any more. On January 5 the commander of Omdurman Fort signalled that he could hold out no longer, and Gordon was forced to agree to his surrender. The Arabs now closed in upon the town from every side.

Gordon still found means, however, to keep his people going. Rumours were spread about the town that messengers had come in from the expedition; it was due to arrive on the following day, and if not then, certainly it would come on the day after that. The soldiers were promised a year's pay for every day they hung on. Labourers on the docks were set to work preparing anchorages for the incoming steamers.

These measures were sufficient to keep a flicker of hope alive, but the town was now under continual bombardment through the day and night, and by the middle of January both Egyptian and Sudanese soldiers as well as civilians were deserting to the Mahdi. Gordon was approaching his fifty-second birthday, and there is a quality in the figure that emerges through these last days of the siege that seems rather to belong to legendary tragedy, to some incident of history as it is imagined in a fresco or painting, than to life itself. The trim, alert officer vanishes, the crankiness evaporates, and now at last all inner uncertainties are resolved. He knows precisely what he has to do, even though events may bring him to the breaking point. No doubt his sense of guilt remained, but that was a secret thing, and it must have diminished under hardship; it was his resolution, his complete acceptance of responsibility, that his soldiers and the townspeople saw. To them he appeared to be a remote and frightening figure, not unjust or rigid—he was too warm for that—but a man utterly indifferent to ordinary weakness. He may have been respected, perhaps even venerated, by these thousands of dying Moslems at this desperate moment, but he was also very much feared. Officials who called upon him were seen to tremble when he came into the room, and there were some whose hands shook so badly they were unable to light a cigarette.

Bordeini Bey, a Khartoum merchant who survived the siege, has given an intimate picture of Gordon in his Palace at this time. 'In spite,' he says, 'of all this danger by which he was surrounded, Gordon Pasha had no fear. I remember one night some of the principal men of Khartoum came to my house and begged me to ask Gordon Pasha not to light up the rooms of the Palace, as they offered a good mark for the enemy's bullets. When I mentioned this to Gordon Pasha he became very angry, saying, "Who has said Gordon was ever afraid?" A few evenings afterwards I was with Gordon in the Palace, and as the rooms were still lighted up I suggested that he should put boxes full of sand in front of the windows to stop the bullets. Gordon Pasha was then more enraged than ever. He called up the guard. and gave them orders to shoot me if I moved; he then brought a very large lantern which would hold 24 candles. He and I then put the candles into the sockets, placed the lantern on the table in front of the window, lit the candles, and then we sat down at the table. The pasha then said, "When God was portioning out fear to all the people in the world, at last it came to my turn, and there was no fear left to give me; go, tell all the people in Khartoum that Gordon fears nothing, for God has created him without fear." '

On January 20 the garrison was startled by a salute of 101 guns from the Mahdi's camp, and it was thought at first that this was to celebrate a victory over the oncoming expedition. But in fact the salute was a stratagem of the

Mahdi's to cover up the defeat at Abu Klea, and Gordon guessed as much when he saw through his telescope the Arab women weeping on the opposite bank of the river. He now redoubled his promises to the garrison that help was on the way, while in secret he laid a mine in the arsenal so that it could be blown up if the town fell. The steamer *Ismailia*, which was anchored below the Palace, was ordered to stand ready to take on board as many passengers as she could. At a given signal she was to escape with them down the White Nile to the south.

A meeting was then called of a group of the principal officials in the town, and was informed by Gordon's secretary, Giriagis Bey (Gordon himself did not attend), that when the first of the expedition's steamers approached Khartoum they were to put on their full uniform and come to the Palace. It was probable, Gordon said, that he alone would be asked to go aboard the steamer, in which case the officials were to protest violently to the British commander that they would not permit him to leave Khartoum. Whether the expedition arrived in time or not, Gordon added, he had no intention of going away.

It was one more attempt to keep the garrison firm, and it was not successful. By Saturday, January 24, all hope had been abandoned in the town.

Bordeini Bey gives this last picture of Gordon:

'At last, Sunday morning broke, and Gordon Pasha, who used always to watch the enemy's movements from the top of the Palace, noticed a considerable movement in the south, which looked as though the Arabs were collecting at Kalakala (one of the forts on the ditch to the south of the town). He at once sent word to all of us who had attended the previous meeting and to a few others to come at once to the Palace. We all came but Gordon Pasha did not see us. We were again addressed by Giriagis Bey, who said he had been told by Gordon Pasha to inform us that he had noticed much movement in the enemy's lines, and believed an attack would be made on the town; he therefore ordered us to collect every male in the town from the age of eight even to the old men, and to line all the fortifications, and that if we had difficulty in getting this order obeyed we were to use force. Giriagis said that Gordon Pasha now appealed to us for the last time to make a determined stand, for in twenty-four hours' time he had no doubt the English would arrive; but that if we preferred to submit, then he gave the commandant liberty to open the gates and let all join the rebels. He had nothing more to say. I then asked to be allowed to see the pasha, and was admitted to his presence. I found him sitting on a divan; and as I came in he pulled off his fez, and flung it from him, saying, "What more can I say, I have nothing more to say, the people will no longer believe me, I have told them over and over again that help would be here, but it has never come, and now they must see I tell them lies. If this, my last promise, fails I can do nothing more. Go and collect all the people you can on the lines and make a good stand. Now leave me to smoke these cigarettes" (there were two full boxes of cigarettes on the table). I could see he was in despair, and he spoke in a tone I had never heard before. I knew then that he had been too agitated to address the meeting, and thought the sight of his despair would dishearten us. All the anxiety he had undergone had gradually turned his hair a snowy white. I left him, and this was the last time I saw him alive.'

The Mahdi and his Emirs were very well aware of what was going on in Khartoum. With the fall of Gordon's fort at Omdurman all supplies had been cut off from the town and deserters brought him the latest news of its ordeal every day. Yet still the Mahdi hesitated. He had an extreme fear of the British soldiers and Father Orhwalder asserts that the mere appearance of twenty British redcoats at Khartoum would have entirely undermined his resolution. When the news of the defeat at Abu Klea reached Omdurman there was something like panic in the Arab camp. The Mahdi himself, Ohrwalder says, was in favour of retreating at once to Kordofan, and actually declared that he had had a vision in which he had been adjured, like Mohammed himself, to make a Hegira—to flee. The more aggressive of his Emirs, however, pointed out that the perfect moment for attack had arrived; the mud of the falling Nile had filled in a part of the ditch on the southern side of the town, and Gordon's soldiers were too weak to build new earthworks there. Let the tribesmen cross the White Nile by night and then rush this gap in the darkness. If they failed in this assault they could still retreat to Kordofan, while if they succeeded and the town fell the British expedition was bound to retire.

Throughout the third week of January there was a continuous council of war in the Mahdi's camp, and January 25—that same day that Gordon was making his final appeal to the garrison and Wilson in the *Bordein* was struggling up through the Sixth Cataract—the Mahdi overcame his anxieties at last. Orders were given for the assault to be made in the early hours of the following morning, and at once large parties of warriors began to cross the Nile. The Arabs went into the attack without the fear of death. In a final oration to his followers the Mahdi reminded them that paradise lay before them if they died, and no doubt they were not unmoved by the prospect of looting the richest town in the Sudan.

The moon set early that night. In silence some 50,000 Arabs crept up to the defences, especially concentrating at the point where the mud had filled in the ditch and a ridge of dry land opened a way into the town. It was found to be firm enough to bear their weight. At 3 a.m. on January 26 the town was awoken by a wild yelling on the lines, and the sound of heavy rifle and artillery fire. Those on the barricades who survived remember the Arabs rushing towards them crying 'Kenisa! Saraya!'—to the Church! to the Palace!—and then all was lost in confusion. The soldiers seem never to have had a chance of defending themselves. Before any sort of resistance could be organized the streets were filled with a tide of screaming fanatics who hacked with their spears at every human being in their path. No wild animals ever behaved as the Arabs did in that one short hour before the dawn; they killed their victims regardless of whether or not they surrendered, and without distinguishing between men, women and children. Most of the inhabitants naturally barricaded themselves in their houses, but the doors were soon bashed in, and fires, springing up everywhere, drove them into the streets again.

Barely three miles separated the Palace from the point where the defences were breached, and it was still dark when the first of the tribesmen came rushing into the Palace yard. Gordon, according to Bordeini Bey, had sat up writing until midnight on the previous night, and had then slept for two or three hours. He was woken by the sounds of the battle on the lines, and at once went up to the roof in his night clothes to try and make out what was happening. There was a gun on the roof and in the dawn light he began firing down on the thousands of Arabs pressing forward to the Palace. When he could no longer depress the gun at a sufficiently sharp angle to keep the mob back from the building he went to his room and changed into his white uniform. He then took up a revolver and a sword and went to the head of the stairs, 'standing in a calm and dignified manner, his left hand resting on the hilt of his sword'. The Arabs meanwhile had been hanging back, fearing that mines had been laid around the Palace, but now four men, bolder than the rest, rushed forward, and at once they were followed by hundreds of others. Some made for the roof where the Palace guard was stationed, and all were massacred. Others ran up the stairs to Gordon, and one of them called out, 'O cursed one, your time has come.' Gordon is said to have made 'a gesture of scorn' and to have turned away. Within a few seconds he was speared to death. It was just before sunrise.

Later his head was cut off and taken away in a handkerchief to Omdurman to be displayed before the Mahdi. The body remained all day in the Palace yard where every passing tribesman jabbed his spear into it; and eventually it was flung into a well.

There are several other versions of the General's end—some witnesses asserted that he did defend himself and actually fought his way down into the garden before he was overwhelmed—but it is at least certain that the death did occur somewhere about the Palace in the very early hours of the morning, and Slatin, sitting in chains in Omdurman (he had been imprisoned when his correspondence with Khartoum had been discovered) saw the head being carried by to the Mahdi's tent later in the day. Afterwards the head was fixed to a fork in a tree, and all who passed by cursed it and threw stones at it.

The General's death was a disappointment to the Mahdi, for he had hoped to make a prisoner of Gordon, and to chain him like Slatin until he professed the true faith. There was, too, a certain admiration for Gordon among the Arabs. According to Ohrwalder it was a common saying with them that, had he been a follower of their faith, he would have been a perfect man.

For six frightful hours the looting and the massacre went on until, in the end, some four thousand people were dead. Hansal, the Austrian Consul, was killed in his house. Numbers of women who had cut off their hair and put on men's clothes were captured, stripped and raped. Merchants and householders were flogged until they revealed the places where they had hidden their jewellery and their money, and in many cases servants saved their own lives by betraying their masters. The rage of the Arabs to destroy was just as great as their desire for loot, and so in every house mirrors and crockery were smashed, furniture was overturned and hangings were stripped from the walls and carried away. Human beings were the chief loot, but there was a great wastage of them at first. Men and women alike were stripped naked and then taken across the river to Omdurman where they were herded into compounds. Many died of thirst there under the blazing sun. The more attractive women and young girls received better treatment: they were placed in three enclosures, one for unmarried girls who were young and fair, one for married women who were still good-looking, and one for black slave girls. Under the rule of the Mahdi all loot, whether slaves or property, was placed in the *Beit-el-Mal*, the treasury of Islam, to be shared out according to each man's status and his prowess in battle. So now the Mahdi came to the women's enclosures and selected for himself all the younger and fairer girls of the age of five and upwards, and then it was the turn of the three Khalifas and of the Emirs.

In Khartoum meanwhile there was a confused scramble among the principal Arabs to obtain possession of the best dwelling-houses along the river. Gordon's garden was

seized by Abdullah, the chief Khalifa, and before long every
building of any size was the headquarters of some Emir
and his retinue of wives and followers. For the moment
all thoughts of austerity were forgotten, and in the midst of
the shambles of Khartoum triumphal feasts and entertainments continued through the night. For two days the general pillaging of the town went on, and there was a constant passage of small boats carrying loot and prisoners
across the river to Omdurman, but at length the Mahdi
reasserted his authority; the workshops were re-opened,
some attempt was made to clear the streets, and once more
Khartoum began to resemble an armed camp, with Arabs
instead of government soldiers manning the entrench-
ments and the guns. Here and there a fire still burned with
a pall of smoke above it, and along the banks of the river
the wrecked buildings lay deserted and roofless under the
sun.

This then, was the situation in Khartoum on the afternoon of January 28, Gordon's 52nd birthday, when Sir
Charles Wilson and his little flotilla appeared before the
town. They were met by intense artillery and machine-
gun fire from either bank, and when they came within
sight of Government House they saw that no flag was flying on the roof. The ruined buildings and the enemy shooting from every side made it clear beyond all doubt that
Khartoum had fallen, but to make absolutely sure Wilson
ordered the *Bordein* to the bank, and here he heard from
Arabs on the shore that all the defences had collapsed.
The steamers had now been under fire for four hours,
and were in imminent danger of being sunk. Wilson gave
the order to put about, and in the early evening they ran
downstream under a furious barrage from either shore.
Like most such retreats from disaster the return journey of
the two boats has been very largely forgotten, but it was
something of a miracle of its kind. Even after the British
had cleared the limits of the town a hundred miles of hazardous navigation still lay between them and their base at
Metemma, and now the Arabs, seeing them retreat, feared
nothing from the redcoats and their guns. From dawn onwards they were harried by rifle fire from the shore, and at

one stage the *Bordein* was reversed, and lowered on winches, stern-first, through a gorge. Eventually both steamers stuck fast and were abandoned.

It was while the British were trying to extract themselves from this impasse that the Mahdi sent Wilson a message:

'In the name of God, the merciful, the compassionate, praise be to the bountiful Lord, and blessings be upon the Lord Mohammed, and on his family. From the servant who stands in need of God, and on whom he places dependence, Mohammed, the Mahdi, son of Abdullah, to the British and Shaigiya officers and their followers: God direct them to the truth. Surrender and be spared . . . as you have become a small remnant like a leaflet within our grasp, two alternatives are offered to you'; they could send an envoy to see for themselves that Khartoum was destroyed, and that Gordon was dead, and then offer their own surrender; or they could try to fight on and face inevitable death and torment in the next world.

They decided to go on. In the end, with the aid of the other steamers that Gordon had sent down the river they reached Metemma.

It seemed to Wolseley, when he heard the disastrous news, that his only possible course now was to advance on Berber and there build up his forces for a counter-attack in the autumn. But when he applied to London for permission to proceed with this plan he was ordered to return. The expedition fell back in some disorder down the Nile.

For some months prior to the fall of Khartoum Gordon's name had been a household word, not only in England but throughout the rest of the world as well, and it evoked the extremes of pity and admiration almost everywhere. From one end of Britain to the other the public had anxiously and eagerly followed the story of Wolseley's advance, and had debated Gordon's chances of holding out. Towards the end of January hopes had run very high. *Punch* had actually anticipated the rescue by publishing at the beginning of February a full-page cartoon which showed the General at the gates of Khartoum welcoming the expedition into the city. The caption was 'At last!' The following week the magazine was obliged to make a painful and humiliating retraction. It printed another cartoon showing an agonized Britannia with her arm over her eyes and in the background the Mahdi riding with his hosts into Khartoum. The caption this time was 'Too late!'

Queen Victoria's feelings have been described by Sir Henry Ponsonby, her private secretary: 'The Queen was in a terrible state about the fall of Khartoum, and indeed it had a good deal to do with making her ill. She was just going out when she got the telegram and sent for me. She then went out to my cottage, a quarter of a mile off, walked into the room, pale and trembling, and said to my wife who was terrified at her appearance. "Too late!" '

The following letter in the Queen's handwriting reached Gordon's sister in Southampton:

'*How* shall I write to you, or how shall I attempt to express *what I feel*. To *think* of your dear, noble, heroic Brother, who served his Country and his Queen so truly, so heroically, with a self-sacrifice so edifying to the World, not having been rescued. That the promises of support were not fulfilled—which I so frequently and so constantly pressed on those who asked him to go—is to me *grief inexpressible*! Indeed it has made me ill ... would you express to your other sisters and your elder Brother my true sympathy, and what I do so keenly feel, the *stain* left upon England, for your dear Brother's cruel, though heroic fate!'

Miss Gordon replied by sending the Queen one of Gordon's Bibles, and it was placed in a glass case in Windsor Castle.

There were some dissenting voices, however. Wilfrid Scawen Blunt was in the centre of a little party which, though sympathetic to Gordon himself, detested the whole conception of British aggression in the Sudan. These people believed that the Mahdi, like Arabi in Egypt before him, was the leader of a popular rising, and that the Sudan should have been left to work out its own destiny. It had been wrong to send Gordon in the first place, wrong of him to stay in Khartoum and criminally wrong of the government to send a military expedition. Even as late as

December 1884 Blunt and his friends were describing Wolseley and his men as 'butchers', and were agitating for peace negotiations with the Mahdi. The news of the fall of Khartoum reached London on February 5, 1885, and Blunt recorded the event as follows: 'Unexpected and glorious news of the fall of Khartoum . . . I could not help singing the way down [to the country] in the train.'

Most of Blunt's contemporaries, however, were absolutely and passionately opposed to him in this matter. The British public felt every bit as deeply as their Queen. Sir Philip Magnus, in his recent study of Kitchener, speaks of 'a mood of hysteria which lasted about three weeks, drew crowds every day to Downing Street in the hope that they might have a chance to hoot and jeer at the Prime Minister'. It was thought particularly unfeeling of Gladstone to have gone to the theatre on the evening of the very day the news of Gordon's death was received, and he was hissed by the crowd in St. James's Street.

It was all very well for the House of Commons to vote a sum of £20,000 to Gordon's family; to the public it seemed that the General's death could not be compensated by money. The stain on England was ineffaceable and who was to blame for all the shilly-shallying and delay if not the Prime Minister himself? Where now was all Gladstone's fine talk about Gordon being merely 'hemmed in' and there being no cause for alarm?

There were other lesser scapegoats as well; had the soldiers in the relief column been resolute enough? Could they not have pressed on a little faster? When the details of the campaign came out and it was realized that the expedition could certainly have saved Gordon if it had got the steamers up to the town just two days sooner, there was a particular feeling of wrath towards Sir Charles Wilson. Why had he delayed three days at Metemma when he could have started in the *Bordein* for Khartoum on January 21—five days before the garrison fell?

Wilson's reply to this was that he had questioned the Egyptian officers who had come down to Metemma from Khartoum and none of them had believed the town was about to fall, none had thought that there was any special need for haste. And so he had followed sound military principles by securing his base near Metemma and by reconnoitring the river before he proceeded. Then too, there had been many unexpected delays on the journey upstream; it had been constantly necessary to gather fuel from the banks, often wrong channels were taken, and the steamers, going astern, ran aground. It had also to be remembered that his force consisted of only one battalion and that his orders were not to relieve Khartoum but merely to make contact with Gordon, pending the arrival of the full expeditionary force in March.

Before the end of the year Gordon's journals were handed over to his brother, Sir Henry Gordon, and were published in two volumes that became best-sellers overnight. Some of Gordon's more outrageous abuse of Granville was deleted, but most of the references to Baring remained. It was not until his retirement in 1907 that Baring, by then the Earl of Cromer, was able to make his reply in his *Modern Egypt*. It was a dignified performance. He pointed out that in 1885 a 'Gordon Cultus' took hold of England and silenced every criticism of him. Yet there was, in fact, a good deal to criticize. At Khartoum Gordon had forgotten all about his instructions, and, by remaining there, had forced the British government to send an expedition for his relief. Gordon, Baring said, 'was extremely pugnacious. He was hot-headed, impulsive, and swayed by his emotions. . . . He was liable to fits of ungovernable and often of most unreasonable passion. He formed rapid opinions without deliberation and rarely held to one opinion for long. . . . He knew nothing of English public life, or generally of the springs of action which move governing bodies. He appears to have been devoid of the talent, so valuable to a public servant in a distant country, of transporting himself in spirit elsewhere. His imagination, indeed, ran riot, but whenever he endeavoured to picture to himself what was passing in Cairo or London, he arrived at conclusions which were not only unworthy of himself, but grotesque, as for instance when he likened himself to Uriah the Hittite, and insinuated that the British government hoped that he and his companions would be killed or taken prisoners by the Mahdi. In fact, except personal courage, great fertility in military resource, a lively though sometimes ill-directed repugnance to injustice, oppression and meanness of every description, and a considerable power of acquiring influence over those, necessarily limited in numbers, with whom he was brought in personal contact, General Gordon does not appear to have possessed any of the qualities which would have fitted him to undertake the difficult task he had in hand. . . . But, when all this has been said, how grandly the character of the man comes out in the final scene of the Sudan tragedy . . . no Christian martyr tied to the stake or thrown to the wild beasts of ancient Rome, ever faced death with more unconcern than General Gordon. His faith was sublime.'

Two major mistakes had been made, Baring concluded: his own in agreeing that Gordon should go up to Khartoum in the first place, and Gladstone's in not sending the expedition sooner.

These were the arguments and admissions of an experienced administrator, and yet it seemed to most people in England that in a vague, confusing and most moving way, the truth still lay with General Gordon. It was an open question as to whether or not Baring's calm deliberation had brought him any nearer to wisdom than Gordon's emotional and instinctive changes of policy. Baring's own behaviour had been a mass of inconsistencies: he had opposed Gordon's appointment and then had supported it, he had delayed in giving his backing to Zobeir until it was too late, he had advised the government to abandon the Sudan and had lived to see the day when he would become a strong advocate of its conquest.

Little by little as the years went by it became apparent that, from start to finish, Wolseley's expedition had been based upon misapprehensions, and that Gordon had seen this more clearly than anyone. It was never a question of merely getting Gordon himself away from Khartoum. Had Wolseley reached the garrison in time he must have realized that the Sudan could not have been suddenly abandoned; some sort of government would have to have been established. He would have been bound either to defeat the Mahdi or to come to terms with him. It was neither an honourable nor a valid policy to 'let the Sudan stew in its own juice', to allow the country to sink back into chaos.

There was one other man in Africa in 1885 who foresaw all this almost as clearly as Gordon. The Anglican missionary, Alexander Mackay, whom we must presently meet, wrote from Buganda: 'He [the Mahdi] slew General Gordon as chief of the Turks, and stuck up the English hero's head to be ignominiously handled by the Arab rabble, whereupon the English army ran away home, forgetting that they came to do what Gordon came to do, viz. rescue the garrisons of the Sudan. Mark the logic. Because the General could not do that, without an army, therefore the army could not do it either, although it had another general!' Lupton, an Englishman, was still in the hands of the Mahdi, but no steps were taken by the expedition to discover whether he was dead or alive, let alone to rescue him. In the same way Slatin had been abandoned, and so had Emin, still holding out in Equatoria, and so had the Egyptian garrisons now awaiting their inevitable fate— massacre—in Kassala and Sennar.

'But the English,' Mackay goes on, 'to the amazement of all the Arabs, and the bitter disappointment of all the Europeans and Egyptians, turned tail, no man knows why, and ran home leaving all the garrisons to the mercy of the murderers. Now the great provinces of Bahr-el-Ghazal and the Equator are merely a prey to the slave raids of the Dervishes of the Mahdi party. This desertion of the great Negro land, which Gordon governed once in the most humane manner, has been called in England "the leaving alone of a brave people to enjoy their freedom". Certainly the Dervishes [1] have thus been left alone to devastate the fairest part of Central Africa, that, too, by the English, who once said they were determined to stop the slave-trade there.'

Gordon's death appeared to close a chapter that was by

[1] The word 'Dervish' was widely used to describe the followers of the Mahdi, but is not accurate, for it was British soldiers' slang imported from the Middle East and India. Among the Arabs themselves the Mahdi's warriors were known as Ansar.

no means closed, but if England was in a mood for revenge it did not last very long. By April 1885 the public indignation was running down, and a new crisis on the North-West Frontier in India was filling the columns in the newspapers. Lord Salisbury, who defeated Gladstone in June and brought the Tories back into power, continued the evacuation policy in the Sudan. It seemed that the White Nile, like some recurring affliction that becomes acute and then, of its own accord, dies away, had vanished from British politics for the time being. But Gordon had raised issues in England that were fundamental, and emotions that were very deep. The struggle between Islam and Christianity was not ended, and Central Africa could not remain a void. A little group of Europeans still held on at the source of the river and they were determined not to fail.

Chapter 15

THE MAHDI'S GHOST

IN FEBRUARY 1885, less than a month after the fall of
Khartoum, the Mahdi retired across the river to Omdurman. He still professed his determination to conquer
Egypt and the world, and as a first step in that direction
he sent off a strong force of cavalry to harry Wolseley on
his passage down to Wadi Halfa. Yet there was an extreme love of sensual pleasure in the Mahdi's character,
and once the siege was over he seems to have abandoned
himself to it altogether. If we are to believe the Europeans who were his prisoners at this time the life he now
began to lead in Omdurman sounds like the Mohammedan
idea of paradise. He had grown enormously fat in his late
thirties, and in the privacy of his harem his concubines
attended him as though he were some great, sleek queen-
bee in the pulsating center of a hive. Each day his body
was anointed with sandalwood oil, and the patched *jibbeh*
of the Arabs was exchanged for drawers and shirts of fine
materials which were scented before he put them on. Anti-
mony was painted round his eyes to give them an added
lustre.

During the month of Ramadan, when an absolute austerity was enforced upon his followers, huge crowds gathered in Omdurman to await the Master's appearance at
prayers. But they had little notion of what was going on
inside the Mahdi's house. There he reclined on pillows of
gold brocade with some thirty of his women taking turns
to wait upon him: Aisha, the chief of his four legal wives,
pitch-black Negresses of the Nile tribes, copper-coloured
Abyssinians and little Turkish girls, rather lighter in colour
and hardly more than eight or nine years old. 'Almost

every tribe in the Sudan,' Father Ohrwalder says, 'supplied its representative.' They squatted upon the Persian rugs spread over the sand, some of them fanning the Mahdi with ostrich feathers, others massaging his feet and hands, and thus in a trance of pleasure, interrupted only by short councils of war, the hot hours of the day went by.

When the crowd outside became importunate at the long delay the Mahdi would bestir himself at last. He was helped up, red shoes were placed upon his feet, drawers and shirt were replaced by his patched *jibbeh*, his girdle and his turban; and so attired he proceeded through the shouting and adoring crowds to the mosque. As he went by women fell to the ground behind him and embraced his footprints, believing that by so doing they would cure their illnesses and ensure the quick and painless delivery of their children.

At times he would cross the river with a part of his harem and remain for a day or two in Gordon's Palace, but he rarely moved from Omdurman. Aisha, the chief wife, appears to have been the presiding genius of this lurid household. She had her own system of espionage with which she kept a check on the multitudinous intrigues about the town and her influence was very great. The wives of the principal Emirs made a practice of calling upon her when the Mahdi was absent from the harem.

Meanwhile in Khartoum a semblance of order was being re-established. After the first fury of destruction was over it was found that no great damage had been done and soon the dockyards were working once again. The remnants of Gordon's little fleet of steamers were salvaged and repaired, and at the arsenal the manufacture of cartridges and bullets went on as before. The lithographic press was put in order, and in the mint new pieces of gold and silver were struck with the Mahdi's imprint upon them.[1] Huge magazines were established on the river bank to house the goods that had been seized from the inhabitants, and mar-

[1] Egyptian piastres, Maria Theresa dollars and English gold sovereigns, part of a haul of £55,000 which was captured at Berber, also circulated. These last were known as 'cavalry money' because of the symbol of St. George and the dragon stamped upon them. As time went on there was also a good deal of counterfeiting in Omdurman, and not even the penalty of death could prevent it.

kets were set up for the sale of the grain and the cattle that were once again brought in from the surrounding country. The town, in fact, might even have had a prosperous look but for the utter misery of the conquered people. Many of them succumbed to an epidemic of smallpox soon after the siege, others died of starvation and maltreatment in the gaols, and every day new victims were brought for trial before the Mahdi's courts. It was enough for a man to be pronounced a 'Turk', an infidel, and any trumped-up charge then served to have him convicted, flogged and imprisoned. Hordes of spies and informers made any sort of life except that of abject obedience quite impossible.

Yet still greater numbers of tribesmen and their families kept arriving in Khartoum and Omdurman from the outlying districts along the White and Blue Niles, and through the hot months of March, May and June the exaltation of victory continued in the air. Messengers kept bringing news of the British retreat and of the weakening of the last two Egyptian strongholds that were holding out at Kassala and Sennar. The *jibbeh* was now not only a symbol of spiritual faith but of military infallibility as well. Primitive sheikhs who a year before had counted their wealth in flocks of goats now dreamed of leading armies into battle and of taking whole provinces under their control.

In the midst of these excitements the Mahdi died. There are several different accounts of his end. According to one story he was given poison by a woman he had outraged, and he is said to have lingered on for a week in agony before he died. Others assert that typhus or smallpox was the cause of his death, and no doubt his long months of debauchery left him little strength to resist disease, especially in such an insanitary place as Omdurman. Whatever the cause, it is certain, however, that he died there on June 22, 1885. He had survived Gordon by just five months.

Long before this the Khalifa Abdullah had been chosen, in preference to the members of the Mahdi's own family, as his successor. He was a member of the Ta'A'Ishi branch of the Baggara tribe, one of the poorest yet one of the fiercest of the nomadic groups in the West Sudan; a tall, imperious-looking man with a dark chocolate-coloured complexion much marked by smallpox,, a long prominent nose and a short beard turning grey. He limped a little from an old bullet wound in the thigh. In later years every possible epithet was attached to the Khalifa by those few of his European prisoners who were lucky enough to escape down the Nile to civilization: he was sly, suspicious, vain, quick-tempered, unbelievably cruel and despotic. Yet all agree that he possessed a certain ruthless charm, and there is no doubt whatever that he was an exceptionally shrewd and energetic man. It is said that he could neither read nor write, and he knew next to nothing about the outside world—he once asked Slatin if France was a tribe—but he was the kind of man who finds his way in politics through common sense, and he was no bad soldier in the guerrilla warfare of the Sudan. That he was brave goes without saying—all the Mahdists were brave—but he never succumbed to luxury as the Mahdi did. He lived grandly enough in the only two-storey house in Omdurman with a personal bodyguard and a retinue of eunuchs, and he was much addicted to harem life, but he continued to wear his greasy *jibbeh* and with the utmost punctiliousness he presented himself at the mosque five times each day to lead the tribes in prayer. He had joined the Mahdi when he was aged about 35, and from the first had been one of his most unswerving supporters. The fact that he controlled a powerful body of Baggara horsemen made it easier for him to rise to the office of Khalifa, and he strengthened his position by taking a daughter of the Mahdi as one of his wives. Already at the siege of Khartoum he had been nominated by the Mahdi himself as the heir apparent, and during the last debauched months of the Mahdi's life he is said to have dominated affairs entirely.

Abdullah moved very shrewdly through the early days of his rule. He made no attempt to diminish the Mahdi's name, but rather he sought to enhance it and to use it as a cover to strengthen his own hold on the tribesmen. He dreamed dreams in which the Mahdi appeared before him, exhorting him to continue with the holy war, and these dreams were recounted to the assembled Emirs and their followers in the mosque as though they were divine inspirations, direct commands from the Prophet himself.

The reputation that the Mahdi established for himself in his own lifetime was nothing compared to what his successor was able to do for his ghost. A tomb was built in Omdurman with materials brought over the river from Khartoum, its 80-foot dome visible from three days' journey away, and there the holy relics lay, perfumed with incense and surrounded by candles in a cool gloom. It was held to be a holier thing for a Moslem to visit this place than to go on a journey to Mecca. Before long pilgrims began to arrive in Omdurman from as far away as Samarkand and Bokhara in Central Asia, and even from Mecca itself.

Abdullah appears to have divined by instinct the first principles for establishing a tyranny. A threatened rising of the two rival Khalifas was quickly put down and the Mahdi's family was submitted to a steady and increasing humiliation. Others who might have disputed the succession, especially the more powerful Emirs like Wad el Nejumi, who had defeated Hicks in 1883, and who had led the assault at Khartoum, and Abu Anga, who had risen from a slave to command an army, were dispatched with fresh troops to the outskirts of the empire. At Omdurman itself the Khalifa concentrated his resources. The Baggara tribe, numbering about 7,000, was elevated into a ruling clique, and Yakoub, his elder brother by a different mother, was placed in charge of a rough and ready civil service. Soon almost every post of importance was held by a member either of Abdullah's family or of his tribe. They were loathed, of course, but they were also feared, and their very unpopularity had the effect of binding them more closely to the Khalifa.

All state wealth was gathered into the *Beit-el-Mal*, which now became a kind of universal storehouse for specie, arms and ammunition, booty captured in battle, grain, livestock and even slaves, who were chained like horses in a long line on the river bank awaiting sale. Slavery, of course, had been revived throughout the Sudan during the Mahdi's lifetime, and it was now expanded into a major industry.

On any day in the Omdurman market some fifty or sixty women and rather fewer men might be seen being offered up for sale. Their thin bodies as usual were rubbed with oil to give them a sleek appearance, and their owners recited aloud the pedigrees of their victims in the manner of auctioneers at a cattle market, stating that such and such a man was from the Dinka tribe, aged 18 or 19, the son of a chieftain, and so on. Women slaves were more in demand than men, and a black skin was preferred to copper-coloured. From 50 to 100 dollars (approximately £10 to £20) would be paid for a pretty young concubine, who would be obliged to undress and submit to the usual handling before she was purchased. It seemed to the European prisoners in Omdurman that most of the slaves accepted subservience as a domestic animal accepts it. They expected to live out their lives in captivity; now that the influences of the outside world had receded from the Sudan they had no other horizon. Father Ohrwalder noticed that women owners were more cruel to their retainers than men; it was no uncommon thing, he says, to see a disobedient slave gashed with a knife. Salt was sometimes rubbed into the wound, and other worse mutilations were inflicted as well. Equally fierce punishments were meted out by the courts to the Arabs themselves when they offended against the Mahdist law, and the only appeal against a judgment was to the Khalifa, who was not often ready to intervene; a great part of his personal wealth came from the confiscation of prisoners' property. In all important cases, such as mutiny, the Khalifa himself decided what the penalty should be (usually death by beheading) before the evidence was given to the court.

Ohrwalder estimated that, besides himself and the four surviving nuns of his ruined mission, there were about eighty Europeans or near-Europeans held prisoner in Omdurman, many of them Greeks who had been captured in the *Abbas* when Stewart was murdered. Some, like Martin Hansal, the son of the Austrian Consul, were taken in Khartoum; others, like the German, Charles Neufeld, were merchants who had hoped to trade in the Sudan and were engulfed by the Mahdist tide. Many of them pretended to be followers of the Moslem faith in order to save their lives, and were allowed to earn a living by manufacturing small articles of commerce and selling them in the bazaar. But it is surprising that any of them survived. Both Lupton and Slatin were kept in chains for months at a time and were constantly threatened with death. Eventually Lupton was put to work in the dockyards at Khartoum, and there he died, worn out by starvation and illness, in 1888. Poor Lupton. He was barely 30. More than any of the other Europeans in the Sudan he gives the impression of being overwhelmed by events which were much too big for him. Emin, who knew him as governor of the Bahr-el-Ghazal province, describes him as 'a mere figurehead'. Yet he was brave, and within his limits he was steady and unpretentious. He was survived by an Abyssinian wife and two daughters, who vanished at once into the precarious anonymity of harem life in Omdurman.

Slatin was more fortunate because he was useful to the Khalifa as an interpreter and as a kind of aide-de-camp in the Khalifa's entourage. Abdullah liked to play a cat-and-mouse game with him, sometimes throwing him into prison and sometimes treating him as a privileged intimate. The latter experience was almost as bad as the former, since Slatin, when he was in favour, was obliged to sleep outside the Khalifa's tent, run beside his horse at military parades and sit cross-legged before him during the interminable services at the mosque. When he eventually escaped Slatin remembered the cramp in his legs as one of the severest trials he had to undergo.

The nuns attached to Father Ohrwalder's mission were at first distributed among the Emirs and savagely tortured when they refused to become Moslems. Later on they were permitted to live with the Greek community and they managed to eke out a living by sewing *jibbehs* for the tribesmen. Naturally it was the dream of all the Europeans to escape one day, but they were divided by hundreds of miles of desert from the Egyptian outposts and nothing could be done without camels and guides which were almost impossible to obtain.

Omdurman, after the fall of Khartoum, developed into a considerable city. It stretched for six miles along the bank of the Nile; a great dun-coloured honeycomb of flat-roofed huts and filthy narrow streets that led on haphazardly to the central meeting-place beside the Mahdi's tomb, and the population is estimated to have risen to 150,000, perhaps even more. There was a constant stir of movement in the city; men and women of some fifty different tribes mingled in the streets, and caravans were continually arriving along the great trade routes that led in from Kordofan in the west and Berber in the north. There was even a desultory traffic in goods across the desert to the Red Sea and the southern borders of Egypt. Except for a line that ran under the river from Khartoum to Omdurman the telegraph was destroyed, and messages from the outlying provinces were delivered by camel-post. Beside the Mahdi's tomb a space about 1,000 yards long and 800 yards broad was set aside as a mosque. It was roofed over by enormous mats held up by forked sticks which gave the place the appearance of a forest, and here each day the followers assembled in thousands, sitting cross-legged with downcast eyes, to hear the Khalifa describe his dreams and inspirations. No Emir or sheikh of any standing dared be absent from these services; the Khalifa liked to have them all under his eye and a man's presence at prayers was a proof of his loyalty.

Khartoum was not allowed to continue for long as a rival to Omdurman. When Ohrwalder visited the city in April 1886 he found that most of the damaged houses had been repaired and some of the Emirs and richer merchants were living there in comparative luxury. A few months later, however, the Khalifa gave orders that the city should be evacuated, and the inhabitants were allowed just three days to get out. Gangs of slaves then fell upon the empty houses and levelled them to the ground. Gordon's Palace and the Austrian Mission Church were the only buildings of any size that were left standing, and the only industries that were permitted to survive were those being carried on in the dockyard and the arsenal. Khartoum after this became a ghostly and forbidding place with bushes growing out of the ruined walls and the desert sand took possession of the empty streets.

Now, once again, austerity was the rule. Money, the Khalifa declared, distracted men's minds from heavenly considerations and was an offence against the Prophet. This however was not a principle that applied to the Khalifa himself, for he soon grew very rich indeed. Something like a thousand slaves worked on his personal estates where large studs of camels and horses and herds of cattle were maintained. Five hundred men rode behind him in his bodyguard, and by the same process of despotic inflation some four hundred women were added to his harem. The principal wives were housed in separate establishments, each with her own retinue of slaves and eunuchs. As his power grew the Khalifa could endure only flattery. People coming to see him were obliged to advance on all fours, looking at the ground, and if they were wise they accorded him the same reverence that had been given to the Mahdi.

Abdullah never left Omdurman; he sat there in the centre of his political web with his Emirs around him, and he was kept very well informed by a spy-system that spread outwards from the city to the most distant provinces. Each day was like the last. He rose at dawn and proceeded to the mosque for prayers. He then returned to his house to sleep for two hours, and after a conference with his Emirs he rode forth in procession to review his soldiers on the outskirts of the town, his great black flag in front and his escort following behind. Like the Mahdi before him he was growing very fat, and a huge Negro was required to lift him into the saddle. Friday was regarded as a special day, and then as many as 50,000 horsemen would gallop towards the black flag brandishing their spears and shooting their rifles in the air. Breakfast followed, and after midday prayers the Khalifa spoke again in the mosque. Two o'clock found him back again behind the high walls of his house or conducting business in the *Beit-el-Mal*, and then more prayers at sunset, more speeches and announcements in the mosque. The evening meal was followed by the fifth and final meeting for prayers, and finally the Khalifa retired to his harem to be seen no more until dawn the following day.

It was theocracy of the crudest and most rigid kind, and no one can say it was entirely cynical. After all, the Arabs could now claim that they had killed five British commanders and had defeated two full-scale expeditions that had been sent against them. The most modern European weapons had failed to hold them back. They felt invincible and they can hardly be blamed if they believed that there was a divine providence behind it all. If, as Slatin says, the Khalifa encouraged every sort of sexual excess including homosexuality, he still enforced the Islamic law and made at least a serious outward show of piety. He followed the familiar path of tyranny, but it is still difficult to see what else he could have done if he was to retain his hold over such a wild and barbarous following.

Then, too, his isolation helped him. After Wolseley fell back to the Egyptian border (where his army was broken up and replaced by a defensive frontier force) very little news of what was going on in Omdurman and the White Nile provinces filtered through to the outside world. Of the 30,000 odd men in the Egyptian garrisons in the Sudan only a few thousand managed to return to the Delta. Major F. R. Wingate, whose star was rising as a brilliant young officer in charge of army intelligence in Egypt, gathered together such threads of information as were available from the statements of escaped prisoners and from captured letters and documents. But as yet no reliable European witness had found his way down to Wadi Halfa, and the British and Egyptian outposts there stood like lifeguards on the edge of a hostile sea where no ship ever sailed and where very little debris was cast up on the shore. Rumours of revolts and upheavals in Omdurman and the outlying provinces came in from time to time, but nothing was known for certain. The interior of the Sudan was almost as remote as Tibet.

In Europe at this time, and especially in England, there was a general disposition to regard the Mahdist state as an implacable evil—as evil as ever Lenin's Bolshevism was regarded in the nineteen-twenties or Hitler's Nazism or

Mussolini's Fascism in the nineteen-thirties and nineteen-forties. Mahdism, of course, was a far less serious affair, and it hardly affected the general current of events outside the Sudan. Yet the hostility towards it in Europe ran very deep. It was not only a question of Victorian power and self-righteousness smarting from a sense of unavenged defeat: it was felt that the Christian faith itself was defied by these murderous fanatics in the Sudan, and the Anti-Slavery Society in England lost no opportunity of spreading every fresh report of the Khalifa's brutalities. This was the atmosphere of war, when all things tend to become exaggerated and touched by propaganda. It was scarcely possible for any man, particularly if he was a public figure, to take a detached view, or to argue a case for the Arabs; to have done that would have meant being branded not as a liberal, not as a realist, but as a traitor. As in time of war communications failed, a heavy fog of censorship prevented the impartial facts from penetrating to either side, and ignorance was a wonderful breeding-ground for imagination. It is true that men like Slatin and Orhwalder tried to give correct accounts of their experiences when they eventually escaped from the Sudan, but as prisoners-of-war they were hardly likely to have discovered virtues in their gaolers or to have known all that was going on. When they came to write their books the memory of their own sufferings was very vivid in their minds. Even such authorities as Wingate were inevitably affected by these feelings, and in subsequent years works of fiction like A. E. W. Mason's *Four Feathers* continued to spread the notion that Mahdism was all savagery and unrestrained barbarism. This propaganda was very strong and has not even yet been mitigated to any great extent by the researches of European scholars who in recent years have had access to the Mahdist archives for the first time. One might find a parallel in the fact that, in our own times, some years had to elapse after the last two world wars before the British could bring themselves to think of the Germans simply as Germans and not as Huns or Nazis.

That the Mahdists were, by our standards, incredibly primitive, cruel, obsessed and ignorant is impossible to deny. Yet it must be admitted that the Khalifa did succeed in erecting a much more coherent state than his Christian contemporaries would allow. If this state had been governed entirely by greed, by inhumanity and by crude emotions it would not have continued as long as it did. There were factional rivalries at Omdurman and manoeuvrings for power such as occur in any dictatorial regime, but the bulk of the people were not crying out for liberation as the Europeans like to imagine they were. Towards the end of the Khalifa's reign there was no exodus of refugees from the Sudan; the general run of the people had a bearable existence which was certainly no worse than life had been under the Egyptians. Had the Europeans not intervened the Sudanese would almost certainly have continued to accept the Khalifa's rule.

Even as early as 1887, two years after the fall of Khartoum, the Khalifa could count himself reasonably secure. The Egyptian garrisons at Kassala and Sennar had been starved out and obliterated; on the Red Sea the British still had a tenuous hold on the port of Suakin, but all the rest of the Sudanese coast almost as far as Massawa had fallen to Osman Digna; and in the north Nejumi with an army of some ten thousand men was penetrating into Egypt in the neighbourhood of Wadi Halfa. The Khalifa now controlled an empire greater even than the Mahdi's; it was half the size of Europe. He dispatched a letter to Queen Victoria in England, summoning her to Omdurman, where she was to offer her submission and become a Moslem.

'Know that God is mighty and great,' he wrote, and he went on to remind the Queen of the fate that had overtaken Hicks, Gordon, and the other British generals in the Sudan: '. . . Thy soldiers thought only of retreat from the Sudan with discomfiture and defeat, whereof they have had more than enough . . . Thus hast thou erred in many ways, and art suffering great loss, wherefrom there is no refuge for thee save by turning to God the King, and entering among the people of Islam and the followers of the Mahdi, grace be upon him. If thou wilt do thus, and yield all the matter to us, then shalt thou achieve thy desire of perfect felicity and true repose, which is salvation before God in the blissful and enduring Dwelling, the like of which eye has not seen, nor ear heard, or heart of man conceived. But if thou wilt not turn from thy blindness and self-will, continue to war against the hosts of God thyself, with all thy armies and warlike equipment. So shalt thou behold the end of thy work. Thou shalt be crushed by the power of God and his might, or be afflicted by the death of many of thy people, who have entered on war with the people of God, by reason of thy Satanic presumption.'

Similar messages were sent to the Sultan of Turkey and the Khedive of Egypt.

The four Arab envoys bearing these letters presented themselves at the Anglo-Egyptian lines at Wadi Halfa and were sent on to Cairo where they were received by the Khedive. After some delay the documents were handed back to them with the verbal message that none of the three monarchs deigned to make a reply, and they returned to the Sudan.

The Khalifa's pretensions may have been absurd, and yet through these years Britain, Turkey and Egypt showed no signs of wishing to invade the Sudan again. There was even a very real fear in Cairo that the Mahdists might yet overrun the Delta, and by the summer of 1888 Nejumi, in fact, had advanced sixty miles into Egyptian territory. Nor was this all. The Khalifa was preparing to advance southwards as well. He had already subdued the Shilluk and the Dinka tribes above Khartoum and had overrun the Bahr-el-Ghazal province. Emin, the last of Gordon's governors to hold out, had retreated up the White Nile almost as far as Lake Albert, and in June 1888 the Khalifa decided to crush him. The *Bordein* and two other steamers with a line of barges in tow and a force of four thousand Arabs on board was dispatched from Khartoum with orders to ascend the rapids as far as Dufilé, and then continue to Buganda at the headquarters of the river. The last phase of the Moslem re-conquest of the Nile had begun.

Chapter 16

PARADISE REFORMED

AFFAIRS HAD been taking a strange course in Buganda through these years. All communications with the north had been cut off by the Mahdist rising, and the few scraps of news that reached the east coast at Zanzibar were mostly supplied by Christian missionaries. They had arrived at Buganda at the end of the eighteen-seventies in response to the letter which, it will be recalled, Stanley had written to the *Daily Telegraph* in 1875, and they had found Mutesa still securely on his throne.

Mutesa had become an extremely interesting man as he had grown older. He remained at heart a savage, and he was still capable at any moment of giving way to the most vicious and childish excesses: this was still Central Africa in all its fantastic primitiveness, and it was not possible for any petty chieftain to escape from its crushing limitations. Yet by 1877 when the missionaries arrived he had been for twenty years on the throne, and he had learned a great deal from the Arab traders at his court; he professed to believe in their religion, he spoke Swahili and some Arabic, he had adopted Arab dress, and had even acquired a semi-literate secretary who wrote his letters for him.

Important visitors were now conducted to the throne room through a bodyguard of soldiers dressed in red tunics and white trousers, and Mutesa himself on these occasions was to be found reclining among linen cushions on a Persian carpet, a jewelled sword at his side, and his Arab gown bound about his waist with a belt of silver and gold braid. He was a much quieter man, however. Self-indulgence had undermined his health and he now drank very little beer, never smoked, and allowed no one else to do so in his presence.

The Arabs had warned him about the real meaning of the Christian invasion. The missionaries, they say, would appear to be very humble at first, but presently they would ask him to confine himself to one wife, to liberate his slaves and pay them wages, and to desist from plundering women and cattle. If Mutesa refused to obey them the missionaries would call into Buganda other white men, politicians and administrators; and if these in turn were defied soldiers would arrive who would force the King to submit and perhaps depose him as well. All in all it was not such a bad forecast of the future, and Mutesa was intelligent enough to understand it.

Yet he needed the help of the Christians; he needed all the firearms and the modern devices they could bring him, and at the same time he saw that the missionaries at his court would serve as hostages, as guarantees against an armed invasion, whether from the Sudan in the north or from Zanzibar in the east. His best plan, therefore, was to make a show of friendship towards both sides, to play off the Arabs against the Christians, and thus he hoped to maintain his independence.

The missionaries were delighted with their reception. They presented their gifts (among other things they had brought letters from Queen Victoria and Stanley), and Mutesa professed the most lively interest in Christianity. Before long Bible-readings were being given regularly at the palace, and there was every sign that the King was breaking away from Islam. Mutesa did not actually agree to emancipate his slaves or reduce the number of his wives (who were now counted in thousands), but he did say he was perfectly willing to observe the Sabbath day, and he made no objection when the missionaries began to hold daily services in the little two-storey mission house they had built for themselves on the outskirts of the capital. The Baganda flocked to this new entertainment, and they were quick to learn. A printing press was set up to run off religious tracts in Swahili, and presently some of the younger pages at the court were making headway in reading. At the palace itself, meanwhile, Mutesa agreed to eject his witch-doctors and to submit to the missionaries' treatment for his illness (probably it was syphilis). He was an excellent patient and was soon able to walk again, a thing he had not been strong enough to do for many months. He also indicated to the missionaries soon after their arrival that there was nothing in the world he desired so much as a white wife, who would displace all the others, and that he was very ready to dispatch an ambassador to Queen Victoria in England, whom he acknowledged as a potentate quite equal to himself.[1]

It was all most encouraging.

One must pause here for a moment to consider the magnitude of the work the missionaries were undertaking. It was not only paganism they were attempting to displace, but the Moslem faith as well, and Islam was entrenched in Central Africa by this time. It had strong attractions for the primitive tribesmen, since it could be understood and practised by the simplest mind. There was no complicated initiation, no elaborate ritual, not even priests or a church were required: one could worship wherever one wished, inside the hut or in the open, alone or with the rest of the tribe. Already the Africans comprehended in a vague way the concept of God, and Islam merely demanded of them that they should acknowledge the authority of his prophet Mohammed. It was enough to declare 'There is no God but God and Mohammed is his prophet', and the pagan illiterate was accepted into a faith that offered him all kinds of advantages; he became a socially superior person inside the tribe, he received the protection of the Arab slave-traders, he was provided with a new code of living which did not greatly disturb his habits and which offered him the most dazzling pleasures after death. It is true the men had to undergo the operation of circumcision, but that was not

[1] Three Baganda envoys actually accompanied some of the missionaries on their return to England. They were taken to Buckingham Palace and the London Zoo, and eventually came back to Buganda with awesome stories about the size of the British capital, and the horse-drawn traffic in the streets. This, however, did not prevent at least one of the envoys from becoming violently anti-British later on.

regarded as any great hardship—in fact, it was rather intriguing to the primitive mind. Perhaps it was a little galling for the African to give up alcoholic drink—his daily gourd-full of *pombe*—but no one pressed him too closely on that score, and the other obligations of Islam, the avoidance of certain sorts of meat, the fasts, the daily prayers, hardly constrained him at all. It could easily have been that he delighted in the mystical gesture of prostrating himself towards Mecca, and the strict asceticism of the month of Ramadan, when no one may eat or drink during the daylight hours, was nothing very strange to a tribesman who was already living in a world of taboos and prohibitions.

The status accorded to women by Islam also suited the Africans very well, since they were accustomed to polygamy; Mohammed allowed a man four wives who were all inferior to him, and divorce was easy. Best of all, perhaps, was Mohammed's paradise, for it contained just those sensual delights that preoccupied the Africans here upon earth: a cool water-garden inhabited by beautiful women, the gratification of every physical want, and, by night, four houris to attend him in his square tent (it being understood that no one houri would be aware of the others' presence). This was just the sort of heaven that savage man might have imagined for himself.

The Moslem woman, of course, did not come very well out of the arrangement; she was merely instructed that on her husband's death she must veil herself upon his grave (for by then he was in the arms of the houris), and no specific paradise was promised for herself. But then women had never counted much above slaves in Central Africa, and through long-enforced habit they had come to accept their inferior position.

As for slavery itself (which the Africans had always practised), it was condoned by Islam. Mohammed made it a virtue to liberate slaves and he laid it down that Moslems should not make slaves of other Moslems, but there was no general condemnation of the practice.

Compared to these easy-going doctrines, Christianity presented a hard, uncompromising front. Its emphasis upon original sin and its dogma were difficult for a sluggish mind to master, and its prohibition of slavery and polygamy seemed to the tribesmen to be flying in the face of nature. The ethereal Christian heaven had very little appeal when contrasted with the sensuous Moslem paradise, and even the outward forms of Christianity were somewhat incongruous in this hot climate: the mosque had its graceful minarets, its great cool space beneath the rounded dome, its pleasant carpets to kneel on, and it harmonized with the landscape. But the severe lines of Christian architecture were alien to Africa. Even the western (and therefore Christian) clothes the missionaries wore—the tight jackets and trousers—must have seemed absurd to the Africans when compared to their own semi-nudity or the cool and comfortable Arab gown.

There was another obstacle before the Christians in Africa, and it was fundamental. Unlike the Moslems, who were all Sunnites, they were divided against themselves. Nothing is more strange in ecclesiastical history than the bitter conflict that developed between the Roman Catholics and the Protestants in Buganda through these years. Even the briefest glimpse of the careers of the Church Missionary Society representative Alexander Mackay and of his rival Père Lourdel, of the French White Fathers, gives one a startling insight into the tremendous religious fervour of the mission-workers of the time, their bravery, their bigotry and their utter determination. Mackay was a Scot, a blue-eyed little man with a genius for improvisation and for practical mechanics, and his faith in his God possessed him absolutely. 'Ah, poor Spain, and poorer Portugal!' he wrote home on his journey down to the Mediterranean. 'The loving Lord has given thee a sunny land with pretty mountain slopes, where every man in thee may sit under his own vine and lie in the shade of his own fig-tree. But the venomous blood of the Bourbons and the cursed leaven of Rome have undermined thy vital powers, and now thou art a corrupting mass, waiting maybe till, like thy fellow-victims of the East, thy sickness proves incurable, and thou wilt cease to be.'

Père Lourdel, who arrived in Buganda soon after the

Protestants, was not quite so forthright as this, but he too was a man of remarkable tenacity, and he was every bit as dedicated as Mackay was.

Mutesa quickly appreciated the advantages of this situation, and he seems to have enjoyed himself very much indeed. He liked to summon Mackay and Lourdel together to the court, and to provoke them into argument. The band of drums and harps was silenced, the wives and the courtiers gathered round, and all listened intently even if they did not understand. The following extract from Mackay's journal gives the flavour of these meetings:

'Prayers being over, I was asked to read the Scriptures as usual. I opened the book and commenced. The first sentence—"Ye know that after two days the Son of Man is delivered up to be crucified"—struck them by its accuracy of prediction, and hence its testimony to the divinity of the "Son of Man". I never got farther. Mutesa in his abrupt style, said to Toli (one of the courtiers), "Ask the Frenchmen, if they believe in Jesus Christ, why don't they kneel down with us when we worship Him every Sabbath? Don't they worship Him?"

'M. Lourdel was spokesman. He became all at once very excited, and said, "We do not join that religion, because it is not true; we do not know that book, because it is all lies. If we joined in that it would mean that we were not Catholics, but Protestants, who have rejected the truth. For hundreds of years they were with us, but now they believe and teach only lies." Such was the drift of his excited talk, in a mixture of bad Arabic, Swahili, Luganda and French.'

Then the Arabs would be brought in to put the case of Mohammed, and they contrived to vex Mackay even more. 'Terrific conflict with the Mussulmans again,' he writes. 'They blasphemed terribly against the assertion that our Saviour was Divine.'

Thus, even as early as 1879, and in these bizarre circumstances, three rival camps were forming in Buganda. The Arabs in the main were in favour of things continuing as they were. They were getting about a thousand slaves out of the country every year, and they were not at all appalled by Mutesa's brutalities. They continued to warn him privately that there could be only one end to the Christian invasion; the Europeans were 'land-eaters', sooner or later they would swallow him up. Mackay and Lourdel, on the other hand, continued to weaken themselves by acting independently; each built up his mission as rapidly as he could, each encouraged his followers to look upon the rival Christian faith as heretical and vile. This was a dangerous business among primitive people; they were liable to translate their hatred into action.

As their novelty wore off, Mutesa found that he liked his Christian guests less and less: just as the Arabs had predicted, they were forever trying to reform him and to prevent him from enjoying the exercise of his natural instincts—especially his instinct for human slaughter. He was also shrewd enough to see that, for the moment, the danger of his country's being invaded by white men was diminishing, and that therefore he was no longer bound to treat the missionaries gently.

Suddenly orders were issued that there were to be no more Bible-readings, or Christian services at the palace; the missionaries in future must devote themselves to more useful work, such as the repairing of guns and rifles for the King. Witch-doctors were re-admitted into the court and it was not long before their savage influence was felt. Executioners were posted on the highways leading into the capital. Like the thugs in India, they fell upon any unsuspecting man who happened to pass by, secured him in a forked stick through the night, and murdered him at dawn. On one particularly horrible day two thousand victims were tortured and then burnt to death as an offering to the spirit of Mutesa's father, Suna.

Mackay was crushed and disillusioned. 'Every day,' he wrote in his journal, 'there is a wanton slaughter going on of innocent victims. It is dark about 10 p.m. All is quiet, the last drum heard being the executioner's across the small valley, announcing that he has secured his victims for the day, and will spill their blood in the morning. Suddenly a sharp cry in the road outside our fence, then mingled voices; an agonizing yell again, followed by the horrid laugh of several men, and all is still as before.

' "Do you hear?" says one of our lads; "they have cut that fellow's throat—hee, hee, hee!" and he laughs too—the terrible Baganda grin of pleasure in cruelty.'

Could this be the same man who had so impressed Stanley, who had been so affable when the missionaries first arrived? He was 'a monster', 'a murderous maniac'.

Mackay and the other missionaries who had joined him now found themselves half-starved at Rubaga, Mutesa's capital, and the Roman Catholic priests were no better off. In their common adversity the two missions became more friendly, but they were practically banned from the palace during Mutesa's more violent outbursts of blood-lust, and the months went by in a steadily deepening atmosphere of superstitious gloom. To make matters worse, the war with King Kabarega, who was still ruling in Bunyoro, was resumed more fiercely than ever.

In 1884 the young Scottish explorer Joseph Thomson made his brave journey through Masailand and reached the northeastern shore of Lake Victoria. Then in October of the same year Mutesa died. Both these events might reasonably have been regarded as a good augury for the beleaguered missionaries in Buganda. Thomson had opened up a direct route from the Zanzibar coast, and it was now possible to reach Buganda in half the time taken by the roundabout journey along the southern and western shores of the lake; and presumably any successor to Mutesa would be an improvement. In fact, however, only evil was to follow. Mutesa at least had had his moments of enlightenment, and Buganda had enjoyed a kind of stability during his twenty-eight years on the throne. Mwanga, the 18-year-old boy who followed him as King, was an utter barbarian, who added sodomy and the smoking of *bhang*, or hemp, to his other vices. Mackay likened him to Nero.

It is interesting to compare the portraits of Mutesa and Mwanga which can still be seen in the royal burial ground at Kampala. Mutesa has a thin and nervous face, and it is dominated by his large, liquid, sensitive eyes. There is nothing sensitive at all about Mwanga, his features are dark and coarse, and there is something about him—a certain air of swashbuckling authority and of passion—which in-

deed makes one think of the Roman emperors at their
worst. T. B. Fletcher of the C.M.S. knew Mwanga during
the last years of his life, and describes him as having a
'weak and undisciplined mind'. He was 'nervous, suspicious,
fickle and passionate'. And yet, Fletcher continues, it is
only fair to remember that the young King was surrounded
by a bewildering number of rival factions at the court;
from every direction foreign forces were closing in on
him, the Mahdists from the north, Europeans from the east,
and the Arabs were everywhere. It was only natural that he
should regard the missionaries and the slave-traders as the
agents of these forces, and that he should have taken his
revenge upon them.

Bishop Hannington was the first victim. Hannington had
been sent out by the C.M.S. to take charge of the gradually
expanding chain of mission stations in East Africa, and he
decided to follow Thomson's route up from the coast.
Mackay tried unsuccessfully to warn him that this was very
dangerous; there was a tradition in Buganda that the country would one day be overwhelmed by foreigners entering
the country from the east. Directly he heard of the Bishop's
approach Mwanga gave orders that he should be stopped
and killed. Hannington had barely reached the north-eastern
corner of Lake Victoria when the local tribesmen murdered
him and obliterated his caravan.

After this, Fletcher says, 'Mwanga and his advisers appear to have lost all control of themselves. For two years
intermittent cruel persecution was carried on, and not only
those who professed the Christian faith suffered but also
the Mohammedans. Islam too has its roll of martyrs.'

It was the Arabs, however, who provoked Mwanga to
commit his worst atrocities. They had taught him to prac-
tise sodomy in the first place, and Mwanga burst into
a furious rage when he found that Mackay's younger followers, most of them pages at the court, refused to submit
to his perversity. Early in 1884 three of these children were
tortured and murdered by the King's orders, and in 1886
there was a holocaust. The pages were assembled at the
palace, and those who had become 'readers' at Mackay's
mission were asked to step forward. Some thirty or more

acknowledged that they were Christians, and were asked to renounce the faith. They refused and were burned alive in one great funeral pyre outside the capital.

It is astonishing that Mackay and his fellow-missionaries should have been able to arouse such heroic faith. At Gondokoro the Austrian Fathers had worked for eleven years among tribes that were only a little less civilized, and they had failed to convert even one man to Christianity. Yet here in Buganda, where Mackay and Lourdel had been established only since 1879, Christians could already be numbered in hundreds, and for many of them their religion was more important than life itself. Even the massacre of the pages failed to undermine their faith; they still came secretly by night to Mackay and Lourdel to receive their teaching and to pray with them.

But it was not a situation the missionaries could withstand for long. One after another they were ejected from Buganda, and temporarily took refuge on the southern shore of Lake Victoria. By the summer of 1888, when the Khalifa dispatched his steamers up the Nile from Khartoum, events in Buganda had degenerated into the wildest confusion. Mwanga was not the kind of man who could keep the three hostile political groups—the followers of Mohammed, the Roman Catholics and the Protestants—under control. Indeed he rather tended at first to throw in his lot with a fourth party—the pagans and the witch-doctors.

The story of the ensuing religious wars may have a certain melancholy attraction for the ecclesiastical historian, but few others manage to follow it with interest, for it reads like a badly written melodrama, and hardly anyone emerges from it with honour, or distinction. At first the Moslem party combined with the Christians, only to turn against them later on; and then we find the Roman Catholics and Protestants fighting amongst themselves. Mwanga, who is willing at any stage to turn Mohammedan, Catholic or Protestant, or to revert to his native paganism, is tossed back and forth from one party to another, and in every scene in this grisly and bloodthirsty tragedy a few more Baganda are butchered, a few more villages are burnt to the ground.

This, then, was the chaotic situation on the Upper Nile at the end of the 1880s: the Khalifa's expedition was pressing southward up the river from the Sudan, Buganda was moving rapidly towards civil war, and in Equatoria Emin, the last of Gordon's governors, was still helplessly waiting to see what the future would bring.

Chapter 17

THE WATERS OF BABYLON

EVEN BEFORE Khartoum fell Emin had been called on by the Arabs to surrender, and in 1884 like Slatin and Lupton, he had decided to obey. Nearly two years had passed since he had been visited by a steamer from the north, and only the vaguest rumours reached him from Khartoum; it was reported that Gordon with 'a large army and elephants' had entered the town, but of the actual progress of the siege he knew nothing whatever. In 1884 Emin had still hoped to escape down the Nile, or at any rate to make contact with the Egyptian garrisons in Bahr-el-Ghazal and Darfur, but as the months went by a steadily deepening atmosphere of despondency settled upon his little headquarters at Lado. His correspondence with Frank Lupton in Bahr-el-Ghazal faltered and then ceased altogether. 'It is all up with me here,' Lupton had written in his last message, and soon after this runners came in with definite news that the Englishman had been taken prisoner, and that one of the Mahdi's Emirs was now marching on Equatoria.

Emin's prospects of retreating southwards into Buganda were hardly better than his chances in the north. He had a large and unwieldy garrison with him (it numbered about 10,000 Egyptians and Sudanese, many of them women and children), and it was scattered over a score of out-posts on the Upper Nile, and the rare letters he received from the English missionaries in Buganda did not hold out much hope of his being able to get through to the east coast at Zanzibar.

Emin was not entirely alone with his soldiers and their families. Dr. Junker, the German-Russian explorer, fled southward from the Arabs and reached Lado early in 1884;

and presently they were joined there by another traveller, an Italian captain of the Bersaglieri, Gaetano Casati. These men, together with the educated officers on Emin's staff, formed a little oasis of civilized living at Lado, and they were not altogether unlike a group of survivors who had been shipwrecked on a desert island. 'We all of us dreamed of nothing but the steamer from Khartoum,' Junker wrote later on.

At first the situation was not really critical. The Arabs delayed their advance. Lado with its brick buildings and its neat streets remained quiet, and Emin and his staff, dressed in white uniforms, went about their work each day as though nothing had happened. But gradually the lack of supplies from the north began to take effect. A fire in Lado had destroyed most of the equipment which had been left there by Gordon and Baker, and there was increasing short-age of ammunition. It was in these circumstances that Emin, in 1884, with the agreement of his Egyptian officers, de-cided to surrender. But then he changed his mind. After all, he still had his two steamers, the *Khedive* and the *Nyanza*, stationed above the rapids at Dufilé, and the Arabs, pre-occupied with Khartoum, could hardly hope to overrun his whole province, especially if he moved his headquarters further up the river. Early in 1885 he left Lado with Junker and Casati, and journeyed some two hundred miles south to Wadelai.[1] 'This is to be our headquarters until better times,' he wrote, and at once he began converting the fort into a habitable town. Here at last, in 1886, a year after the fall of Khartoum, he received letters from Kirk in Zanzibar and Nubar Pasha in Cairo informing him of Gor-don's death and the abandonment of the Sudan. He was instructed to get his garrison out to the east coast as best he could since the Egyptian government could do no more for them.

But this was still an impossible proposition: Buganda was at war with Kabarega in Bunyoro, and even if this was not enough to block his path to the coast there was still no means of transporting his garrison across the thousand odd

---

[1] Wadelai was the name of a local chieftain. He was reputed to be so fat a boy could stand on his stomach while he was sitting down.

miles of virtually unexplored territory that divided him
from the Indian Ocean. Unless help was sent to them in the
form of ammunition, porters and transport animals they
could not move. Junker, however, was eager to make the
journey by himself, and with the assistance of Mackay in
Buganda he actually succeeded in reaching Cairo via Zanzibar at the end of 1886. For the first time since the fall of
Khartoum—indeed, since Emin had been cut off three years
before—the outside world had authentic news of the strange
little outpost of civilization that was still holding out in the
centre of Africa. Up to this point Emin and his men had
been conveniently forgotten in Europe, but now there was
an immediate stirring of interest, and perhaps a certain
feeling of guilt at the abandonment of Gordon had something to do with it. All at once the Press, the politicians
and the geographic and missionary societies were eager for
news. Who was Emin? How had he managed to hold out
when all others had been submerged by the tide of barbarism that had swept along the Nile? Could he be rescued? Dr.
Felkin, one of the missionaries who had visited Buganda
and Equatoria in the eighteen-seventies, was able to add to
Junker's information, and Dr. Schweinfurth and other explorers supplied further details as well; and the more the
story came to light the more fascinating it appeared to be.

Emin, it seemed, was an extraordinary man, this German
eccentric who had been brought up as a Protestant in Germany, but who changed his name in the Middle East and became a Moslem. Even Burton (now living out his last years
in Trieste) hardly mastered such a range of accomplish-
ments: Emin was a doctor of medicine, a botanist and orni-
thologist, a linguist who spoke French, German, English,
Italian, Turkish, Arabic, Persian, demotic Greek, and several Slavonic languages. Gordon had recognized his exceptional gifts as an administrator and had promoted him from
the post of medical officer to Governor of Equatoria
at a salary of £50 a month. By carefully cultivating the
ivory, coffee and cotton trade in his province Emin had
converted an annual deficit into a profit of £8,000. The
museums and scientific societies of Europe, it now appeared,
knew him very well; before he had been cut off he had sent

out thousands of carefully prepared skins of birds and animals, thousands of specimens of plants, and these collections had been accompanied by the most precise and
scholarly notes. In his neat microscopic handwriting Emin
had recorded in letters to Dr. Schweinfurth (in German)
and to Dr. Felkin (in English) all kinds of hitherto unknown facts about the migrations of birds on the Upper
Nile and its tributaries, about the languages and customs
of the tribes, about the rainfall and the geology of the country. He spoke, for example, of 'the great python africanus',
which the women in some tribes befriended, keeping it as a
pet in their huts, rubbing it with fat, and pouring fat down
its throat; and elsewhere there were other tribes where
poisonous snakes were caught and secured by a cord passed
through a hole bored in their tails. These snakes were
then placed near waterholes so that they would bite the antelopes coming down to drink and thus provide meat for the
tribes.

Then again in his letters he advocated the immigration of
Chinese into Central Africa, and he wrote of cannibalistic
regions where 'men who abstain from human flesh are the
exception', and of polygamy and domestic slavery. There
was nothing that did not interest this methodical and inquiring mind. He was forever on the move about his province, and his journeys were recorded in his journal with the
precision of a chronometer: '15 August. Monday. Time: 5
hours, 21 minutes a.m. started off. Crossed Luri. Break
from 9 hours 18 minutes a.m. to 9 hours 47 minutes a.m.—
Arrived Lado 10 hours 48 mins. outward march 4 hours
38 mins. (against 4 hours 58 mins. for the return journey).'

In 1886 Emin had been twelve years on the Nile and he
was aged 46. Junker described him as 'a slender, almost
spare man, rather above the middle height, with a thin face
surrounded by a dark beard and deep-set eyes which look
observingly through his spectacles. The shortness of his
sight compels him to strain his eyes and concentrate them
on the person before him, and this imparts a hard, and at
times almost furtive expression to his gaze.' His 'undeniably
Oriental stamp', Junker went on, was of considered assistance to Emin in posing among the Egyptian officials as a

Turk. 'Every Friday he was seen to visit the mosque, where he repeated the prayers enjoined—and on these and all other occasions he preserved an almost painful punctiliousness and great care in his dress.' Yet Emin was probably not a devout Moslem. 'Don't be afraid,' he had written to his sister in Germany long before. 'I have only adopted the name [Emin]; I have not become a Turk.'

He rose at six in the morning and went off on his hospital rounds. Then followed a long day's work divided between his studies and the ordinary routine of the garrisons. He sailed his steamers up and down the Nile, he experimented in the spinning of cotton, he used cowrie shells from the Zanzibar coast for coinage, he built boats in his little docks at Dufilé and Wadelai, he went on steadily collecting and classifying his skins and specimens, he cultivated fields of maize and vegetables, and he continued to amass his store of elephant tusks which were now said to be worth £60,000. As his supplies ran out he improvised: honey was used for sugar, beeswax for candles, and soap was made from a mixture of fat and potash. The soldiers' wives, their clothes in rags, simply reverted to their tribal custom of wearing skirts made from grass and leaves. It was a sort of Robinson Crusoe existence, except that here it was not one man but ten thousand people who had been given up for lost and forgotten by the outside world.

Not everyone liked Emin. His own soldiers seem to have treated him with the mocking and half-insolent respect that unruly schoolboys give to a weak and hesitating master. He did not give commands; he cajoled, he temporized, he entered into arguments. The soldiers obeyed him because it was the custom, because there was no one else to organize their lives. If they cared nothing for his scholarship and his superior cast of mind he was still a recognizable figurehead, and he had an Oriental acceptance of hardship that prevented him from breaking down.

Some of Emin's contemporaries found him very difficult. Casati was to write later that he had a prickly kind of pride and was never able to reach a clear decision. Gessi thought him 'a man full of deceit and without character, pretentious and jealous . . . a hypocritical person, ridiculously complimentary and cringing in his manner, and capable of deceiving the astutest man in the world'. In view of what was about to happen these criticisms are revealing. For the moment, however, they were hardly to the point. The important fact was that this singular and persistent man, by some strange means, was keeping a little flame of civilization alight in the centre of Africa, and now he needed help. Junker in 1886 had been able to send him a caravan of supplies from Rubaga, and he still very occasionally managed to correspond with Mackay in Buganda, but for the rest he was even more isolated than Gordon had been in Khartoum. The latest news to come out indicated that the Arabs were still threatening to invade Equatoria. When Emin had gone south to Wadelai the tribes had risen in revolt behind him, and in Lado a small Egyptian garrison was being besieged. Felkin received a letter from Wadelai dated July 22, 1886, and in it Emin declared, 'I am still waiting for help and that from England.'

After the failure of the Gordon expedition the British government was naturally reluctant to involve itself. Salisbury, the Prime Minister, took the view that since Emin was a German it was up to the Germans to assist him. But there were other forces in Britain outside the government which were deeply interested in the matter. William Mackinnon, the Scottish shipowner who had founded the British India Steam Navigation Company, saw here an opportunity for combining philanthropy with business. For ten years past his ships had been trading with Zanzibar, and with the encouragement of Kirk he had developed the idea of setting up a chartered company which would exploit the Sultan's dominions on the mainland. An expedition going to the rescue of Emin could very well further these plans by signing treaties with the native chieftains at the headwaters of the Nile, and by exploring the possibilities for trade as it went along. Mackinnon may not have completely committed himself to this project when he agreed to become chairman of the Emin Relief Committee, but he and his business friends certainly had it in mind, and they set about raising money with great vigour. Some £20,000 was collected (including £10,000 from the Egyptian government) and at the end of 1886 the committee was casting about for a suitable man to take charge of the expedition. One possible choice was Joseph Thomson, the explorer who had travelled alone from the east coast to Lake Victoria in 1880. He was a Scot, and the main support for the expedition had come from Scotland; he was young, and he was a determined traveller. But then there was Stanley also to consider. He was widely known, and his name would attract a good deal of support for the expedition. In the end it was decided that he should be sounded out.

Stanley at this time was lecturing in America, but he returned to England directly he received a cable from Mackinnon and agreed at once to go. From this moment the plans went forward rapidly. Stanley himself contributed £500 to the funds, and offered to raise further sums by sending back dispatches to his newspapers in England and America. Once again the appointments were upon a lavish scale: the best of stores were ordered from Fortnum and Mason, and a Maxim machine-gun, the latest thing in modern weapons, was added to a heavy cargo of rifles and ammunition. Stanley was embarrassed by the number of young gentlemen-volunteers who wanted to accompany him, and who were ready to pay for the privilege, and eventually nine men were selected. Junker and Schweinfurth, who met the party at Cairo on its outward journey, at the beginning of 1887, thought that it more resembled a staff embarked upon a military conquest than a private expedition into the interior. And indeed there was a great deal more involved here than the simple rescue of Emin. The full extent of Stanley's commitments has never been entirely revealed, but it is certain that he was under instructions from King Leopold as well as Mackinnon. For Mackinnon he was to open up a trade route to Buganda, and to prepare the ground for a British East Africa Company. For Leopold he was to explore the possibilities of annexing Equatoria to the Congo. Emin was to be offered posts with both these enterprises; either he could join the British East Africa Company and build up a new trading station on Lake Victoria, or he could continue to govern Equatoria on Leopold's behalf.

Then there was the question of the £60,000 worth of ivory which was said to be at Wadelai—it would come in very usefully as an addition to the expedition's funds. Finally there was Stanley's own share of the proceeds: in addition to his newspaper dispatches he planned to write a book about the journey, and the other members of the expedition were asked to sign an agreement that they themselves would publish nothing until six months after their leader's account had appeared. Business as well as politics had entered into African travel.

One cannot altogether blame Stanley for doing the best he could for himself. After all he was risking his life once more, and the writing of travel books was his trade. Yet there was a flaw in all these calculations and it was sufficiently important to cast an air of unreality over the whole adventure. That flaw was concerned with Emin himself. When Emin heard from Mackay in Buganda that a relief expedition was on its way he wrote to Felkin: 'If . . . the people in Great Britain think that as soon as Stanley or Thomson comes I shall return with them, they greatly err. I have passed twelve years of my life here, and would it be right of me to desert my post as soon as the opportunity for escape presented itself? I shall remain with my people until I see perfectly clearly that both their future and the future of the country is safe. The work that Gordon paid for with his blood, I will strive to carry on, if not with his energy and genius, still according to his intentions and in his spirit . . .

'Shall I now give up the work because a way may soon open to the coast? Never! If England really wishes to help us, she must try, in the first place, to conclude some treaty with Uganda [1] and Bunyoro . . . A safe road to the coast must be opened up, and one which shall not be at the mercy of the moods of childish kings or disreputable Arabs . . . It is therefore out of the question for me to leave, so I shall remain . . . Evacuate our territory? Certainly not.'

In other words this was Gordon all over again; it was

---

[1] There was a tendency to drop the name Buganda in favour of Uganda, and eventually Uganda was used to designate all the territory between the Sudanese border and Lake Victoria.

not 'rescue' that Emin wanted, but the political and military support which would enable him to remain where he was.

The letter was published in 1888 in a book called *Emin Pasha in Central Africa*, which was edited by Schweinfurth, but by then Stanley and his men had vanished into the interior and were completely out of touch.

There were other strange aspects about the expedition, and none of them boded very well for the future. To most people who consulted a map at the time it seemed obvious that the best path into Equatoria was the one that led directly inland from the Zanzibar coast. But Stanley was resolutely opposed to this, and neither Mackinnon in London nor Baring (whom he had met in Cairo) could dissuade him. Stanley wanted to follow an enormously roundabout route; he proposed to sail down to Zanzibar from Egypt, and having there picked up his porters, continue with them by sea around the Cape of Good Hope to the mouth of the Congo River on the west coast of Africa. He then planned to cross the entire continent from west to east, picking up Emin on the way. The reasons he gave for preferring this route appeared to have a certain validity, at all events on paper. His Zanzibar porters, he said, were bound to desert him if he marched them directly inland away from their homes, whereas if he landed them on the west coast they would realize that their only hope of survival was to remain with him until he reached Zanzibar. Like horses returning to their stables they would quicken their pace. Then, too, he could transport his men in boats for a thousand miles up the Congo River and this would bring them within 350 miles of Lake Albert, where he hoped to make contact with Emin. There was still another consideration: the Germans were now penetrating into East Africa, and the vast area to the south-east of Lake Victoria was regarded as their private sphere of influence. They would not be at all favourable to the passing of a British column through this territory.

A little reflection shows that there was not much merit in these arguments. The desertion of porters had not prevented other explorers (including Stanley himself) from getting through to the lakes from Zanzibar, and the expedition in any case was more or less bound to pass through the German zone.

It seems more likely therefore that Stanley's real reason for wanting to take the roundabout route was political. By coming through the Congo he pleased Leopold and furthered his own interests there. The Congo was his special field in Africa and he was determined to return.

Not unexpectedly he had his way. In February 1887 we find him very busy in Zanzibar. He visits the Sultan Barghash on Mackinnon's behalf and gets his approval of the British plans in East Africa. On behalf of Leopold he seeks out the notorious Tippu Tib, who by now had become the virtual ruler of all the area between the Congo and Lake Tanganyika. Stanley made him just such an offer as Gordon would have made to Zobeir in the Sudan: Tippu Tib was to become Leopold's Governor on the upper waters of the Congo, and at the same time he was to supply Stanley with porters from Central Africa who would carry ammunition in to Emin and then bring out the £60,000 worth of ivory. It required but three days for Stanley to complete these arrangements, and on February 25, 1887, he embarked on the *Madura* with 620 Zanzibaris and Somalis, his British staff and his new business partner, Tippu Tib. Three weeks later they all landed at the mouth of the Congo on the west coast, and the most ghastly of all Stanley's journeys began.

Like Gordon in Khartoum, Emin was aware in a general way that help was coming, but he was very much in the dark as to precisely where or when it would arrive. Like Gordon too he was heavily involved in his own affairs. He succeeded in raising the siege of Lado, and even managed to re-occupy a dozen of his forts and stations which had been abandoned to the Arabs. But there was no telling whether or not the Khalifa would attack again. King Kabarega in Bunyoro had also turned hostile. The Italian, Casati, who had been with him as Emin's agent for over eighteen months, was beaten up and tied to a tree. He escaped to rejoin Emin half dead and robbed of all his belongings. In Wadelai itself there were further disasters. The fort took fire one day, and although the ammunition was

saved it was necessary to rebuild the entire settlement.
Emin's daughter, Ferida, was still with him, but his Abyssinian wife had died and his own health was failing. One of
his eyes had grown steadily weaker, and he was now obliged
to hold a book within an inch or two of his glasses before
he could read. In a letter to a friend he wrote, 'We have
hung our harps upon the willows, and sit by the waters of
Babylon.'

Despite all this, Emin's situation was not nearly so desperate as Gordon's had been in Khartoum; he had food in
abundance, space to manœuvre, and his soldiers were seldom heavily engaged. But the long aimless days of waiting
were destroying discipline in the garrisons, and it was clear
that his little empire was beginning to disintegrate. In
February 1888, twelve months after Stanley had left Zanzibar, Emin went south to Lake Albert in one of his steamers
in search of news, but heard nothing definite. A letter for
Stanley was left with Mpiga, one of the lakeside chiefs:

'Dear Sir,
    'Rumours having been afloat of white men having made
their apparition somewhere south of this lake, I have come
here in quest of news . . . Be pleased, if this reaches you,
to rest where you are, and to inform me by letter, or one
of your people, of your wishes. I could easily come to Chief
Mpiga, and my steamer and boats would bring you here . . .
we could concert on further designs.
    'Beware of Kabarega's men! He has expelled Captain
Casati.
                          'Believe me, dear Sir, to be
                                  Yours very faithfully,
                                          Dr. Emin.'

With this Emin returned to Wadelai and the long silence
settled over the wilderness again.

It was broken suddenly and dramatically at the end of
April 1888: one of Stanley's lieutenants, Mountenay
Jephson, appeared in a steel boat at a station of Emin's
on Lake Albert, and he had tremendous news. Stanley
had actually been on the south end of the lake in December

and had just missed Emin there. He was now camped on the shore barely a day's journey away. Emin set sail at once in the *Khedive* to meet his rescuer.

The history of the European pioneers on the White Nile is very largely a theme of conflicting personalities—of Burton's opposition to Speke, of Stanley's to Kirk and of Gordon's to Baring. Even the alliances that are made, such as that between Stanley and Livingstone, have often an odd and fortuitous character. But nothing could have been stranger than the meeting that now took place in the gathering darkness on the western shore of Baker's lake.

There was hardly a single quality that these two men had in common. Emin was passive, subtle, studious, indecisive, evasive, meticulous, fatalistic and full of compromise. Before him stood a man who had no patience with fine shades of meaning, who openly proclaimed his contempt for collectors and scholars, who knew only one way of life and that was to march unflinchingly upon his set objectives. Emin, one feels, was the sort of character who would have been given the worst table in a restaurant, while Stanley, presumably, would have been led at once to the best place in the room. Stanley's world was compacted into a straight line, an arrow in the blue. Emin described a series of faint spirals in the dust. Where the one man responded only to himself the other was enveloped by his environment. It was the conflict of ambition and of a bull-like strength with a precise and cautious intelligence, and the issue between them was doubly complicated at this moment since their normal roles were reversed: Stanley, for once, was the one who stood in need, and Emin, the man he had come to rescue, was the stronger of the two.

Stanley had had a frightful time. Even his original journey down the Congo in 1876 could hardly match the horrors that had overtaken him since he had left the coast. His men were scattered over 700 miles of lethal jungle and half of them were dead. Nothing in the way of starvation, of sickness and of calamitous accidents had been spared them. For many months they had groped about like dying insects in the gloom of the Ituri forest where daylight scarcely ever penetrated, and the pygmies had taken a terrible toll among

Stanley's rescue of Emin Pasha ------ 1887-1889

the bare-footed porters by planting poisoned arrows in the ground. One by one Stanley had seen all his plans go wrong, and his white officers had come to hate him. Those that survived were to give lurid accounts later on of their leader's violent rages, of how he called one man a 'God-damned son of a sea-cook' and rushed upon him shouting, 'I'll give you a bellyful,' (while Tippu Tib and the Africans looked on); of how he threatened another, saying that he would write home and break his army career; of how at one stage he had told his native porters to take no orders from the other white men and to tie them up if they gave any trouble. Floggings of 300 lashes that were sometimes fatal had been a common punishment for delinquents along the march. And now, his hair turned white and barely recovered from a month of illness, Stanley had struggled up to the lake with the remnants of his expedition. Except for a little ammunition he had nothing to give Emin and no means whatever of rescuing him—indeed, he was dependent upon Emin for food and other supplies in order to keep his men alive.

Already, too, Stanley was beginning to have dark misgivings about the man he had come to rescue. Why had Emin not been waiting to receive him when he had reached the lake in the previous December? He had driven the expedition forward at a murderous pace, believing that every day was vital; but here was the Governor of Equatoria looking very spry and apparently in no real difficulty whatsoever.

Yet their first meeting on April 29, 1888, passed off very well. Stanley describes the scene in his *In Darkest Africa*: 'At eight o'clock, amid great rejoicing, and after repeated salutes from rifles, Emin Pasha himself walked into camp accompanied by Captain Casati and Mr. Jephson, and one of the Pasha's officers. I shook hands with all, and asked which was Emin Pasha? Then one rather small, slight figure, wearing glasses, arrested my attention by saying in excellent English, "I owe you a thousand thanks, Mr. Stanley; I really do not know how to express my thanks to you."

' "Ah, you are Emin Pasha. Do not mention thanks, but come in and sit down. It is so dark out here we cannot see one another."

'At the door of the tent we sat, and a wax candle threw light upon the scene. I expected to see a tall, thin, military-looking figure, in faded Egyptian uniform, but instead of it, I saw a small spare figure in a well-kept fez and a clean suit of snowy cotton drilling, well-ironed and of perfect fit.[1]

'A dark grizzled beard bordered a face of Magyar cast, though a pair of spectacles lent it somewhat an Italian or Spanish appearance. There was not a trace on it of ill-health or anxiety; it rather indicated good condition of body and peace of mind. Captain Casati, on the other hand, though younger in years, looked gaunt, care-worn, anxious and aged. He likewise was dressed in clean cottons with an Egyptian fez for a head covering.'

Five half-pint bottles of champagne were opened and they had a two hours' talk.

[1] Emin was actually 5 foot 6 inches in height. A ceremonial uniform which Stanley had brought from Cairo for him proved to be so big that six inches had to be lopped off the trousers.

Next day Stanley handed over the thirty-one cases of Remington ammunition he had brought and Emin, with his Sudanese soldiers parading smartly on the shore, conducted his guest aboard the *Khedive*. They then cruised pleasantly up the lake, and Emin, it seemed, was willing to talk about anything but the business in hand. 'I am unable to gather in the least what his intentions may be . . .' Stanley wrote in his diary, '. . . but the Pasha's manner is ominous. When I propose a return to the sea to him, he has the habit of tapping his knee, and smiling in a kind of "We shall see" manner. It is evident he finds it difficult to renounce his position in a country where he has performed vice-regal functions.'

There was some truth in this. Emin was carefully calculating his position. It seemed to him that no great future was awaiting him on his return to Cairo, whereas in Equatoria he was still master of the scene, or at any rate nominally so. Could he not, with Stanley's help, set himself up in Equatoria as an independent ruler, more or less? But then Stanley's expedition had been a great disappointment; he had brought so few supplies with him and such a weak and exhausted following. Then again what effect was Stanley's arrival going to have on his own half-mutinous men? For ten years or more they had made their homes here, and many of them had established harems and families. Perhaps the Egyptians would be ready to follow Stanley to the coast, but would the Sudanese soldiers wish to go, now that their homeland had fallen to the Mahdi? If they decided to stay Emin ought to stay with them. In fact, he wanted to stay. Why should he abandon to the Khalifa this green and flourishing land where he had worked so long?

On the whole, Emin thought, there was an excellent case here for delay. He did not reveal the weakness of his own position to Stanley, but instead raised doubts about Stanley's ability to get the garrison—all ten thousand of them with their wives and children—down to the coast.

Stanley said he could do it, but Emin still hesitated. It was perfectly clear that once they were on the march to Zanzibar Stanley would be ruthless in pressing onwards.

Everyone in Africa knew what happened to stragglers on his journeys.

All through the first three weeks of May the argument dragged on, and in Stanley's account of it in *In Darkest Africa* there is a rising note of irritation. Yet he could not afford to be too brusque with Emin at this stage, since the *Khedive* was constantly bringing supplies and clothes into his camp from Wadelai. He sought to put an end to the discussion by coming out with his two propositions for Emin's personal future: would Emin like to govern Equatoria on behalf of the King of the Belgians at an annual salary of £1,500, with £10,000 to £12,000 administrative expenses? Or would he like to go with his garrison to the north-east corner of Lake Victoria and there set up a new colony for the British East Africa Company? Even these offers failed to pin Emin down. He flatly rejected the Belgian offer, saying that after so many years of service with the Egyptians he could not change sides. The British offer he found more alluring, but still he would not commit himself.

In the end it was decided that while Emin, Casati and Jephson remained behind and sounded out the garrison on whether they wished to go or stay, Stanley should make the fearsome 700-mile journey back to the Congo River to gather up his rearguard. On May 24 he set off.

Even now it is hardly possible to read Stanley's account of this gruesome march without recoiling. It is like some dark Germanic legend in which all nature is twisted into monstrous shapes, horror is piled upon horror, and the gnomelike little figures of the pygmies dart in and out of the nightmare as upon a canvas painted by Hieronymus Bosch. There is a perpetual twilight in the forest, and in the matted foliage monkeys and parrots scream and chatter out of sight. Below, in the fierce heat of the slimy, gloomy undergrowth, trees grow horizontally for fifty feet or more in their hopeless struggle towards the light, and wasps' nests hang among long creepers from their trunks. Every man is an enemy in this submerged world. The African savage, suddenly surprised, raises his weapon instinctively, stands staring for an instant, and then vanishes like a ghost.

The picture that Stanley, perhaps unwittingly, gives of himself is of some wild and dangerous beast crashing through the vegetation, and that, no doubt, is the actual impression he did make upon the pygmies and the animals living there. The porters that Emin had loaned him had known hitherto only the bright landscapes of the lakes, and now their dark skins turned bluish-grey, a fatal colour for a Negro since it indicated death; and they did die in scores as the march went on.

Stanley's determination in the face of these disasters was tremendous, but he confesses that when he finally reached his rearguard on the Aruwimi River, a tributary of the Congo, he felt that he was going mad. A year before he had left here a party of several hundred men under the command of five white officers, who had instructions to follow him to Lake Albert as soon as Tippu Tib supplied the porters he had promised. But this rearguard had scarcely moved. Tippu Tib had naturally failed to produce the porters directly Stanley was out of sight, and now Barttelot, the leader of the party, was dead, murdered by one of his own men, another white officer had been invalided home to England, a third had vanished down the river, and Jameson, the second-in-command, was supposed to be drawing up somewhere in the rear. Jameson, it appeared, had actually been sending back to the west coast stores that he judged to be unnecessary, and among those stores had been Stanley's personal kit and his private hoard of delicacies from Fortnum and Mason. Stanley dashed off a furious letter to him saying that he was a demented idiot, and ordering him to report at once. There was no response; by now Jameson, having been made delirious with malaria, was also dead.

This left Stanley with Bonny, his one remaining white officer of the rearguard, and the remnants of his Zanzibari porters, most of whom were sick or half-starved. However, he managed to collect four or five hundred men who were able to walk, and half of these were still alive when he got back to Lake Albert in December 1888 after a six months' absence.

Here an entirely new crop of misfortunes was awaiting

him. There was no sign of Emin, Casati or Jephson, and presently letters arrived from them saying that they too had been overtaken by disaster while Stanley had been away. At Dufilé, the most northerly of the remaining garrisons, Emin's Egyptian soldiers had risen in revolt, apparently with some vague idea of capturing Stanley and his provisions on his return to Lake Albert and of setting themselves up as an independent force. Emin and his two companions had been seized and kept in close confinement for three months.

It was the Arabs who had brought the mutineers to their senses. All this time the Khalifa's steamers had been making their way up the White Nile from Khartoum. Early in October 1888 they had arrived at Lado, and soon afterwards three Arab envoys appeared at Dufilé with a demand that the Egyptian garrison should surrender. A violent panic had ensued. The three envoys had been murdered, Emin and his companions had been hurriedly released, and the mutineers, all thoughts of mutiny forgotten, had fled southwards, abandoning Dufilé and a dozen other posts to the enemy. The three white men were now slowly making their way back to Lake Albert in the hope of meeting Stanley there. Emin was still unable to say what his ten thousand soldiers and their families intended to do; half of them were now loyal to him and presumably in favour of escaping with Stanley to Zanzibar, half were still against him, and there was no real authority anywhere.

Stanley says he was shocked and disillusioned when he heard this news. Emin had given him the impression that he was in perfect control of his garrison, and was well able to withstand the Arabs in the north. Now it was apparent that he could do nothing of the kind. Equatoria as a coherent state in the centre of Africa had ceased to exist, and Emin himself was in no position to prevaricate or to dictate terms any longer. He was not much more than a refugee—the sort of refugee, one fancies, that Stanley would have half-preferred to find in the first place. He sent Emin a letter saying that he would give him just twenty days to get to the south end of the lake and then they would march for Zanzibar.

Emin replied that since Stanley would not wait, then goodbye. Nevertheless, he did turn up in Stanley's camp in February, and there was a reconciliation of a kind between the two men: Stanley agreed to wait a few more weeks until such of Emin's followers as wished to escape from Equatoria had joined them.

During March these people straggled down to the south end of the lake, and this perhaps for Stanley was the most maddening time of all. He had been prepared to accept women and children and even concubines as well, but their luggage he considered excessive. They brought with them grindstones, beer-jars, bedsteads, all their last pathetic movable possessions, and Stanley's Zanzibari porters were obliged to carry these bulky packages up the cliffs, 2,000 feet high, that divided his camp from the shores of the lake. The camp itself was soon seething with discontent, and bitter quarrels broke out between the Zanzibaris and the Egyptians. Emin, it seemed to Stanley, only added to the confusion, for he did nothing to assert his authority and every trouble-maker that was brought before him for punishment was sent away forgiven. He occupied his days with the 'frivolity' of his plant and bird collections. Jephson showed ominous signs of falling under Emin's listless influence, and Casati, surrounded by his household of native women, was plainly demoralized.

It is not difficult to imagine Stanley's frantic desire to break free from this coil that was steadily closing round him, and early in April the Egyptian officers gave him his opportunity. They were foolish enough to imagine that they could still overwhelm the white men and seize control of the expedition for themselves, and were actually stealing arms for this purpose when Stanley burst in upon them. The conspirators were assembled, disarmed and threatened with death—a sentence Stanley would certainly have carried out if he had been given the slightest provocation—and orders were given for the march to start at once.

By now some six hundred of Emin's people had arrived, and to these were added about a thousand of Stanley's men. The long column marched south towards the Equator, paused for a month when Stanley and Jephson collapsed with malaria, and then trudged on again. It was at this time that Stanley beheld the sight that he had only glimpsed some twelve months before: the perpetual snow on the crests of the Ruwenzori Range, the so-called Mountains of the Moon. The bank of clouds that hangs forever round the upper slopes (the Ruwenzori is one of the wettest ranges in the world), rolled back just long enough for him to see the topmost peaks rising to close on 17,000 feet into the sky, and that was one more landmark he added to the African map. On Lake Albert the two steamers, the *Khedive* and the *Nyanza*, and the remainder of Emin's followers were abandoned.[1]

All things considered the 1,500-mile journey down to the coast was less disastrous than might have been expected. By August the column had rounded the south-western shore of Lake Victoria, and at Usambiro they found the British missionary, Alexander Mackay, waiting to receive them with a quantity of stores that had been sent up from the east coast. Here they rested in the mission houses for nearly three weeks, and in October they pushed on again, leaving Mackay behind them. The Maxim gun cleared their way through belligerent tribes.

It is plain from Stanley's book that his relations with Emin had by now become almost impossible. Emin, hating the whole idea of being rescued, but unable to resist, was in a fretful and suspicious mood. At the halts he would do nothing but pore over his scientific specimens. On the march he would take only a small cup of coffee in the morning and fast all day until the evening. He avoided Stanley as much as he could and instead devoted himself to Ferida, his small half-Abyssinian daughter, who was carried in a hammock just ahead of the donkey which he himself rode. No doubt he made the most of his small advantages; after all, he was the chief trophy of the expedition, and Stanley could hardly afford to abandon him. Stanley's own feelings were a curious mixture. He seems to have been both irritated and attracted by Emin; he goes on and on about him in his book, he cannot leave him alone. Here, he says, is a highly intelligent man, a kind of Eastern *Guru* full of

[1] Both steamers eventually foundered.

courtesy and acceptance. But what a weakling! How his subordinates bully him, how he hesitates and delays! In all his years in Equatoria he neglects his marvellous opportunities for exploring, and instead he wastes his time with his ridiculous collections; a pathetic man with that Mohammedan fez on his head and the cataract in his eye. And in the end how ungrateful!

It is a pity that, except for a few brief notes and some cautious letters, we do not have Emin's account of this journey, especially in its later stages, for its conclusion is a strange imbroglio of vanity and wounded pride. Near the coast the column was met by a German expedition that had come out to look for them, and Emin was at first dazed and then delighted to discover that he had become a celebrity. On December 4, 1889, 2 years and 10 months after the expedition had left the mouth of the Congo, Stanley and Emin, accompanied by a group of German officers, rode on horseback ahead of the column into Bagamoyo to find the township bedecked in their honour, and four British and German warships in the harbour. A German garrison had now established itself at the port, and at 7.30 that evening the two travellers sat down to a champagne banquet, with a band from one of the German cruisers in attendance. It was an emotional and lively occasion, for both Stanley and Emin had long since been given up for lost, and now the great news of their arrival was about to break upon the world. Stanley indicates that he drank a great deal and feasted on the delicacies placed before him, and no doubt the others followed suit. Emin, delighted to be among Germans again, and overwhelmed at receiving a personal telegram from the Kaiser, made two speeches. He then got up and left the room.

It was thought that he might be feeling unwell, but some little time elapsed before a search was made for him. It was then discovered that, with his poor eyesight, he had lost his footing on a balcony and had fallen fifteen feet to the ground. The German hosts rushed out and threw water over him, but his skull was cracked and he lay unconscious through the night. Stanley waited a day while Emin was treated at the Bagamoyo hospital, and then on December 6, with the remainder of his men, crossed in a flotilla of war-ships to Zanzibar. From Zanzibar he sent to inquire about the patient, and Parke, the expedition's physician, remained in Bagamoyo to treat him. But Parke's attentions were not welcome in the hospital, and Stanley received no word from Emin—indeed, he never heard from him again.

There was, however, very little time for Stanley to brood on this unhappy parting, for by now the news of his safe arrival had spread around the world, and it was the rescuer and not the man he had rescued whom the public wanted to acclaim. He arrived in Cairo on January 16, 1890, to find the world was ringing with his name. Telegrams from Queen Victoria, the Kaiser, Leopold, the Khedive and the President of the United States. Warm letters from Mackin-non and his committee in London. Invitations to banquets innumerable. In a word, kudos galore. Stanley very wisely resisted it for the moment. He found 'a retired house' in Cairo, the Hotel Villa Victoria, and there on January 25 he began to write the account of his journey. Proceeding at the rate of twenty printed pages a day he completed two volumes in precisely fifty days, and then sailed off to the welcome awaiting him in England. He was now 50.

In Darkest Africa was published later in 1890 and was an immediate success in six languages. Then followed in the same year Stanley's marriage to the artist, Dorothy Ten-nant, the conferring of honorary degrees upon him by the Universities of Oxford, Cambridge and Edinburgh, the purchase of a house at Furze Hill, near Pirbright (where the names Stanley Pool and the Mountains of the Moon were given to a pond and a hillock in the garden), and later his lecture tours, his entry into Parliament, and finally, in 1899, his knighthood. The hunter was home from the hill, and the waif from Wales had found his place at last.

Critics were not wanting, of course. They pointed out that nearly half of Stanley's original force of 700 Zanzi-baris and Somalis were dead, that but 260 of the Equatoria garrison of ten thousand had managed in the end to reach Cairo, and that Emin, the principal object of the expedi-tion, had been abandoned with a broken skull in Bagamoyo. Even the £60,000 worth of ivory was reported to have been lifted from Equatoria by an Arab trader before Stanley had arrived there—at all events Stanley never mentioned it. In the light of these facts the expedition could hardly be said to have succeeded at all.

Three of the surviving white officers wrote books about their experiences, and the journals and letters of two of the dead men, Barttelot and Jameson, were also published. Not all the authors drew very friendly pictures of Stanley— it was his ruthlessness that was chiefly remembered, the touch of megalomania. Casati, the Italian, in after years was observed to clench his fists at the very mention of Stanley's name, and Emin, slowly recovering in Bagamoyo, broke off all connection not only with his rescuer but with the British as well. No one, moreover, was much disposed to admire Stanley's dealings with the slaver, Tippu Tib.

But these were small voices in a tempest of applause. The hazards of the journey had been very great; Stanley, it was thought, was the only man who could have brought the expedition through, and in 1890 he stood forth as incontestably the greatest of all living explorers, the chief discoverer of Central Africa. In the face of his achievements one could afford to overlook, at any rate for the time being, the fact that the White Nile, along its entire length, from Khartoum to the Great Lakes, had returned once more to the barbarism in which Speke and Grant had found it nearly thirty years before.

PART FOUR

The Christian Victory

Chapter 18

THE OPEN RIVER

*'I would think twice of an Englishman's view
of his neighbour but would trust implicitly
his account of the Upper reaches of the
Nile.'*

Washington Irving.

STANLEY'S EXPEDITION was the last of the great private
journeys to the Nile. By 1889 events in East and Central
Africa were no longer controlled by individuals but by
European governments, and the undisguised contest for new
colonies had begun. Barghash's shadowy empire that
stretched in theory from Zanzibar almost to the White Nile
may perhaps be likened at this time to some old-fashioned
family business which has managed to keep going for
years with its assets under-valued and its methods increasingly out of date. Sooner or later resolute intruders
were bound, as it were, to buy up a controlling interest in
the company, and then eject its helpless directors into a
comfortable and humiliating retirement. Something of this
process at all events occurred when Germany, under Bismarck, decided to penetrate the East African mainland
which the British and the Zanzibar Sultans had left uncul-
tivated for so long.

In 1884 Karl Peters, who in many ways is the German
counterpart of Stanley in Africa, made his celebrated raid
into Barghash's dominions, and he was a great deal more
persistent than Captain McKillop and Chaillé-Long had
been in 1875. Travelling inland from the Zanzibar coast
towards Kilimanjaro he persuaded a group of native chieftains to accept the protection of his recently formed Ger-

man Colonization Society. It was, as Professor Coupland has pointed out, cynical, farcical and effective; the chieftains could neither read nor write and they had very little idea of the real nature of the treaties they signed with their crosses. Peters alone was nothing in the world, but when Bismarck, like some powerful banker, decided to support him it was an entirely different matter. Barghash and Kirk in Zanzibar might protest that this was hardly less than a hostile invasion of an independent ruler's country, but they were powerless without the support of the British government; and this they did not have. The British had no wish to thwart the Germans; Khartoum had just fallen, Egypt was not yet settled, and England needed Bismarck's backing in her quarrel with the French in Africa. Gladstone professed himself to be very little disturbed when he heard of Peters's exploits in 'the mountain country behind Zanzibar with an unrememberable name'. 'If Germany becomes a colonizing power,' he declared, 'all I can say is "God speed her".'

The speeding in fact was done by Bismarck's warships. In August 1885 Commodore Paschen, commanding *Storch, Gneisenau, Prinz Adalbert, Elizabeth* and *Ehrenfels*, drew up his ships in line off Zanzibar, ran out his guns, and informed Barghash that within twenty-four hours he must acknowledge the Peters treaties on the mainland and enter into an agreement with Germany. Kirk, under instructions from London, was unable to interfere; indeed, he was obliged to lend his services to the Germans in conducting the negotiations, and by the end of the year an agreement was signed.

After this it did not take Britain and Germany very long to come to an amicable agreement for the carving up of the Sultan's empire. The Germans took the view that Barghash was entitled only to those areas where his authority was acknowledged, and those areas, they decided, included only the three islands of Zanzibar, Pemba and Mafia, and a strip of the mainland coast ten miles in depth and 600 miles long. The rest of the great East African plateau that swept for a thousand miles into the interior was

Central and East Africa Showing the Routes
of the Principal Expeditions

described as a legitimate 'sphere of influence' for the European powers to divide amongst themselves.

Colonel Kitchener, the British representative on the boundary commission (he had come south to Zanzibar from the Sudan), was almost as indignant as Kirk at this cynical appraisal of the situation, but he was instructed to accept it on behalf of the British government, and an official settlement was made in London in 1886: Barghash was allowed to keep his three islands and the coastal strip, and the rest of the territory that had been nominally under his control was divided roughly into halves—the area now known as Tanganyika falling to the Germans and the present-day Kenya being allotted to the British. The western boundaries of this huge appropriation were left undefined, and Buganda for the moment appeared to be anybody's game.

Kirk had now been twenty years in Zanzibar, and his policy had collapsed entirely. He had persuaded Barghash that, in return for the suppression of the slave-trade, he could rely upon the British to maintain his independence, and now that independence had gone forever. He had tried to induce the British to develop East Africa before the other European powers arrived, and nothing had been done. He had striven to keep the peace between Africans, Christians and Moslems, and now the Arabs everywhere were arming against the Europeans, and men like Peters, who for sheer ruthlessness put even Stanley in the shade, were teaching the Africans to hate white men as they had never been hated before. Even the slave-trade, profiting by the general confusion, showed signs of reviving.[1]

Early in 1886 Kirk was awarded a G.C.M.G., and in July he left on leave for England. No doubt he had a premonition that he would not be asked to return to Zanzibar, and in London this was confirmed. If he felt bitter he made no great parade about it. Coupland quotes a letter which he wrote to a friend in 1887: 'I may have to go back to Zanzibar. Lord Salisbury [who had succeeded Gladstone as Prime Minister] wishes it, but my return is disliked by Bis-

---

[1] The last known slave dhow in East African waters was captured in 1899, but the traffic was not entirely abolished in Zanzibar until 1907, and in Tanganyika until 1922.

marck, and he has quite as much to say in our political appointments as our own government.' This for the moment was perfectly true, at any rate as far as East Africa was concerned. Kirk's successor, Holmwood, also displeased Bismarck, and was soon removed. Kirk himself settled down to life in England and a directorship of the Imperial British East Africa Company which now, belatedly, was formed by William Mackinnon and his friends as a rival to the German company.

Barghash did not survive Kirk's departure for very long. It is scarcely surprising that these events had left him disillusioned and listless. He grew increasingly unwilling to conduct public business, and in March 1888 he died at the early age of 51. His younger brother, Sayyid Khalifa, succeeded to a throne that hardly counted in the new pattern of affairs in Africa, for by then the great European land-grab had begun. Essentially it was a race for the interior between Germany and Britain, and Buganda (which had been left out of the 1886 agreement) was the prize.

We need not here follow in detail the story of the final conquest of the country, for it belongs not to the age of exploration on the White Nile but to the politics of modern Africa. By 1890 the essential point was decided: in July of that year representatives of the German and British governments, meeting in London, agreed that the whole of Uganda should be ceded to the British as a sphere of influence.

Emin played a strange part in these events. He remained for four months in Bagamoyo recuperating from his fall, and his accident seems if anything to have increased his eccentricity and his deviousness. For a time no one could make out what it was he wanted to do—to return to Egypt or Europe, where he was loaded with honours from universities and learned societies, or to stay and finish his work in Africa. He negotiated with both the British and German companies, offering his services first to one side and then to the other. There was, however, no real doubt about the outcome. After so many years of exile and of living the life of a Moslem it had been an overwhelming thing for him to speak his own language again and to be

honoured by his own countrymen. He was deeply touched
by the telegram he received from the Kaiser, and when this
was followed by the award of a medal, the Second Class of
the Order of the Crown, with a Star, he was stirred by
all the pride and the patriotism of the colonial official who
suddenly, after many years of obscurity, finds himself mentioned in the Honours List. Now at last he was not alone;
the weight of personal responsibility which he had borne
for so long in Equatoria was lifted, and he had a powerful
protector behind him. When he had still not completely
recovered from his accident—he was partially deaf in one
ear and he had difficulty in swallowing—it was announced
that he had joined the Germans and would lead a new expedition for them into the interior. Among the British
there was a good deal of bitterness when this news was announced; after all they had not rescued Emin merely in
order to make his services available to the Germans. But
Emin could now afford to ignore his opponents. He was
soon entrenched in the German camp at Bagamoyo, and his
letters reveal that he shared in the general feeling of hostility towards the British there.

He bought an estate outside Bagamoyo, settled his daughter in the town under the protection of a guardian who was
instructed to teach her German, and by the end of April
1890 he was ready to lead his expedition inland. A German zoologist, Dr. Franz Stuhlmann, three German officers, and some seven hundred Africans were placed under
his command, and he was generously equipped with guns
and ammunition. His instructions were 'to secure on behalf of Germany the territories situated south of and along
Lake Victoria up to Lake Albert'. He was 'to make known
to the population there that they were placed under German supremacy and protection, and to break and undermine Arab influence as far as possible'. In other words,
he was to seize Uganda and the sources of the Nile before
the British could get there.

Soon after he had left the coast, however, he was informed of the new agreement by which Uganda had been
allotted to the British, and he was now ordered to confine
his activities to Tanganyika. But Emin decided to go on.

Who knows what visions were agitating his tired and failing mind? Perhaps he was incited to disobedience by Peters, whom he had met on his way up from the coast. Perhaps he dreamed of reuniting himself to his soldiers, whom Stanley had left on the Nile in Equatoria, and of again setting himself up in an independent kingdom there. Perhaps, like so many others before him, he was driven onward by an obsession for the vast unexplored spaces of Africa itself. At all events, having founded the town of Bukoba, on the western shore of Lake Victoria, he pushed on to the north, ignoring repeated orders to return to the coast. In 1891 he actually succeeded in making contact with his old soldiers at the south end of Lake Albert, but most of them refused to acknowledge him as their leader any more. Many of the men and their families were now dressed in the skins of wild animals, and had been reduced to a squabbling and disorderly rabble. After some weeks of useless parleying, Emin abandoned them and went on into the Congo. The Germans by now had disowned him, and the last months of his life are the pitiful story of a man possessed. He seems to have formed the fantastic notion that with the remnants of his little column he could cross Africa to the Cameroons on the west coast, and like Livingstone before him he held on doggedly to his scientific work, believing that, in the end, it would justify all his actions and compensate every hardship.

'Caught a red mouse at last!' runs one of the final entries in his diary. 'Collected twenty-five fresh species of birds; shot a young crocodile.' When smallpox broke out in his camp Stuhlmann was sent back to Lake Victoria with such of the men as could walk, and it was understood that Emin was to follow as soon as the sick had recovered. But it is doubtful if he would ever have turned back. In October 1892, two and a half years after he had left Bagamoyo, he kept his inevitable appointment with death in the depths of the Congo, some eighty miles south of Stanley Falls; a group of Arab slavers rushed him in his tent and cut his throat. He was aged 52. Another year elapsed before definite news of Emin's fate reached the outside world, and his murderers were hunted down and

executed by Belgian officers in the Congo. The bulk of his
estate (£5,200 had been paid to him by the Egyptian
government for his work in Equatoria) was left to his
daughter, and she was taken into the care of his relatives
in Germany.

Emin's certainly was the most intelligent brain in Central Africa since Burton's time. Harry Johnston, arriving
in Uganda as British administrator some years later, rated
him as one of the greatest of African explorers in the sense
that he tried to understand Africa and the teeming life he
found there, rather than to treat the country merely as a
blank space to be 'discovered' and delineated on a map.

At all events, he belongs to that small group of adventurers who opened up the White Nile to civilization, and
among the mass of new men who were now advancing on
the river only a few like Lugard could match their stature.
These new arrivals were soldiers and administrators rather
than explorers. They moved in groups and teams and wore
the uniforms of European governments. They did not
know to the same extent as their predecessors the crushing and yet captivating weight of loneliness in Africa.

The early pioneers were vanishing very quickly at this
time. The two missionaries, Mackay and Lourdel, were
buried in Central Africa within six months of one another
in 1890 (neither of them having ever returned to Europe),
and in that same year Burton died in the British Consulate
at Trieste. A large map of Africa hung above his truckle
bed together with an Arab inscription: *All things pass*.
Grant was buried in Scotland in 1892, and in the following
year Baker died among his sporting trophies at his house
near Newton Abbot. His wife, however, lived on for many
years, a spartan and determined old lady who would permit no fires in the house from May to October. The nephew,
Julian Baker, who had taken part in the Gordon relief expedition, eventually rose to the rank of admiral in the
British navy. Stanley alone among the great explorers survived into the present century. He died at his home in England in 1904.

One feels that all these people, with the exception of

Lourdel, would have approved very much of the final settlement of Uganda under the British in the eighteen-nineties. Lugard, the chief architect of the modern state, was a
man after their own hearts: he perceived his objects with
the utmost clarity and proceeded towards them with an astounding energy. Yet he was still only a young unknown
officer of 32 when he reached Uganda as an employee of
the British East Africa Company—by then established in
offices at No. 2 Pall Mall, London, with a capital of
£250,000—at the end of 1890. Within two years he had
built a chain of stations from Mombasa to the Nile (the
true route into Uganda, as Gordon long ago had foreseen),
had signed a firm treaty with Mwanga, had settled the religious wars between the Moslems and the Christians, had
defeated Kabarega in Bunyoro to the north, and had carried out the work that both Emin and Stanley failed to do,
namely the evacuation of the garrison from Equatoria.

It was an extraordinary achievement. Speke from his
grave must have looked on with admiration. Then too, Lugard was an even better propagandist than Gordon. When
the Company wished to withdraw from the territory he had
conquered for it on the grounds that the expense of its
administration was too great, Lugard returned to England and raised a public outcry.[1] In letter after letter to *The
Times,* in public speeches up and down the country, he declared that the garrisons he had left behind in Uganda
could not be abandoned, and that the valley of the Upper
Nile could not be allowed to return to its former chaos:
the British government must step in and take over the administration. Gladstone, once more in office, and with the
memories of Gordon and the Wolseley expedition vividly
in his mind, recoiled from the idea, but once again he had
the public, the Church and the Queen against him. In
1891 Victoria wrote to Rosebery, the Foreign Minister:
'The fate of Gordon is not, and will not be, forgotten in

---

[1] There was little or no revenue at all to be got from Uganda at this time,
and Kenya was still regarded as a hopeless wilderness. Lugard was asked
by one of his correspondents if there was no prospect at all that Uganda
would yield 'a gentle *Dividend*—There's magic in that word'. He was
forced to confess that for the moment trade hardly existed.

Europe, and we must take great care what we do. The difficulties are great, doubtless, in Uganda, but the dangers of abandoning it are greater.'

In the end she had her way. In April 1894 the government announced that Uganda was to become a British protectorate. By the end of the eighteen-nineties the Mahdists, who had advanced as far as Wadelai, were driven out, a mutiny of Emin's former soldiers was put down, and Mwanga, who had gone over to the Moslems, was finally defeated with Kabarega. This was the end of all serious opposition to the British at the headwaters of the Nile.

In looking back over the forty-odd years that had elapsed since Speke and Grant had first breached the defences of these primitive kingdoms, one is struck by the personality of Kabarega. If he has been neglected in these pages it is because the explorers' records of him—almost the only records available—are sparse and almost invariably hostile. No missionaries ever resided at Kabarega's camp; not even Emin, his one apologist, continued for long in friendship with him. Yet Kabarega rises above all others in Uganda as a guerrilla fighter, and as a brave and determined defender of African independence. He is the one man who continues on the scene from first to last: as a young warrior he saw Speke and Grant march into his father's capital near Masindi; he fought Baker, Gordon, Stanley and Lugard as well as Mutesa. He was nearly always defeated and yet he never gave up so long as there was the ghost of a chance of rousing his men to resistance. It was a hopeless struggle, of course, but he did not think it so. And thus it is a little sad that one Sunday in April 1899 the British should have tracked him down in his last stronghold in a swamp north of Lake Kyoga, and that both he and Mwanga, who had joined him in adversity, should have been captured and deported to the Seychelles. Their durance on the island was more prolonged than that of Archbishop Makarios in recent times. Mwanga died there in 1903, but Kabarega still lived on, and there is a photograph taken of him in his old age that shows him standing with a walking stick and wearing a frock-coat with a stiff white collar and a handkerchief tucked neatly into his pocket—a caged lion. Yet still the gaze of the eyes is direct' and fearless, and it is a fine and indomitable head such as one might expect to see cast in heavy bronze.

When Kabarega reached the age of 80, and it was judged that he could make no more disturbances for the white men in Africa, he was allowed to come home from the Seychelles. However, he succeeded only in reaching the source of the Nile at Jinja and there he died. The body was carried up to Bunyoro and entombed close to the battlefield where he fought Baker in 1872. The modern traveller passing by on the main road will discover it very easily; a grass and reed hut surrounded by trees and a hedge. It is somewhat dark inside, but one can descry upon the grave a dusty covering made of the traditional barkcloth and the skins of leopards—the fierce and untamable animals which are the symbol of the royal kings of Uganda.

In the Sudan also the old pattern had collapsed, and the new era of European domination—and of European vengeance—had begun. One might take the year 1889 as the turning of the tide against the Khalifa. In early August Nejumi was routed and killed with all his chief Emirs at the Battle of Toski, sixty miles inside the Egyptian border. With this the Mahdist threat to Cairo vanished forever. Meanwhile on the Red Sea Osman Digna was falling back under a new British assault, and there were heavy casualties among the Khalifa's men in a third campaign that was being fought against the Coptic Christians in Abyssinia.

These defeats might have been fatal to the Khalifa had he not been protected by the deserts of the Sudan, and there were other dangers threatening him as well. The country was becoming depopulated. Slatin, at a later stage, estimated that, of the original nine million inhabitants, about 75 per cent. were exterminated during the Khalifa's rule. The continual wars and the slave-trade destroyed many thousands every year, diseases such as smallpox and syphilis were endemic, and now in 1889 the country was overwhelmed by famine. Great areas of cultivatable land had been left idle while the Arabs went off to war or congregated in the capital, and in the province of Darfur, where the Khalifa had put down a revolt with the utmost brutality, wild animals had taken possession of the empty plains. And now there appeared out of the blue one of those periodic plagues of African locusts which turn the land into a desert overnight. The insects arrived in such myriads along the Nile they blotted out the light of the sun, and the little grain they left in the ground was devoured by another plague—this time of mice.

The catastrophe naturally fell heaviest upon the overcrowded inhabitants of Omdurman. People became so desperate with hunger they turned cannibal and ate young children; hundreds of emaciated bodies were to be seen lying in the streets or floating down the Nile.

It says something for the force of the Khalifa's character, and also for the virility and toughness of the Arabs themselves, that they were able to survive these disasters and to continue to rule the Sudan for another eight years. But after 1889 it was a process of gradual retrenchment. In 1891 Father Ohrwalder escaped to Egypt with two of the surviving nuns, and Slatin managed to follow him four years later. From these and other witnesses a fairly precise picture was built up of the Khalifa's dwindling defences, and the Egyptian army began to take heart again. It was now commanded by an enthusiastic group of British officers who had learned the tactics of the desert.

Meanwhile in England there was a rising agitation for another campaign in the Sudan. Revenge for the death of Gordon and the defeat of the Hicks and Wolseley expeditions was, of course, a leading motive. Alfred Milner's *England in Egypt* and the books of Ohrwalder and Slatin, with their revelations of the cruelties of the Arabs, aroused a humanitarian indignation; and in 1895 the Liberals were displaced by a strong Conservative government. International politics also pushed the British into action: in the general scramble for territory in Africa they supported the claims of Germany and Italy against the French, and it was feared (with good reason) that France was preparing to move into the Sudan. Early in 1896 the Italians were defeated by the Emperor Menelik of Abyssinia at Adowa, and it seemed possible that they might be driven out of

Africa altogether, unless the British created a diversion on the Nile. To all this was added the old (and empty) fear that the Khalifa might renew his attack on Egypt and the Suez Canal. Thus the conditions for an imperialistic war were very nearly everywhere fulfilled. Perhaps too, from somewhere out of the past the voice of Gordon could be heard: 'The Mahdi must be smashed up . . . Remember that once Khartoum belongs to Mahdi the task will be far more difficult; yet you will, for safety of Egypt, execute it . . .' You will 'be forced to enter into a far more serious affair'.

By 1896 the British were ready to enter into this far more serious affair: Messrs. Thomas Cook's fleet of pleasure steamers on the lower Nile was requisitioned, some ten thousand Egyptian soldiers and their British officers were assembled on the Sudanese border, and even Sir Evelyn Baring was eager for the fray. His protégé, General Kitchener, now aged 48, was appointed to the command of the expedition, and he had with him a group of young men who were already making a name for themselves in the world: Wingate, with his excellent intelligence service, Slatin, now a senior officer in the Egyptian army, the young sailor David Beatty, and later, the young soldier, Winston Churchill.

The ascent of the Nile from Egypt was a long business— not the few months that Wolseley required, but two years. This time there was to be no haste and no mistake. Only one battle of any importance was fought before Omdurman. In April 1898 the Emir Mahmoud, one of the most aggressive of the Khalifa's surviving generals, advanced down the Nile as far as Atbara to meet the oncoming expedition. On Good Friday Kitchener fell upon him with all the force of his modern artillery, and to the music of Scottish pipes, English flutes, drums and brass, the British and Egyptian soldiers stormed the Arab barricades. No quarter was given to the enemy during the assault, and before long some 2,000 of them were dead. Churchill relates that after the battle Kitchener 'rode along the line, and the British brigades raising their helmets on the dark, smeared bayonets cheered him in all the loud enthusiasm of successful war. For almost the only moment in the course of this story he evinced emotion. He was, said an officer who watched him closely, quite human for a quarter of an hour! And indeed, if anything could break this stern man's reserve, it should have been the cheers of the soldiers who had stormed the Atbara *zeriba*; for this was the most memorable day in all his life that had yet run out.'

A victory parade was held in the neighbouring town of Berber, and Kitchener rode forward on a white horse to take the salute. At the head of the parade came the defeated general, Mahmoud, a proud and handsome young man in his early thirties. Chains were riveted round his ankles, a halter was passed round his neck, and his hands were bound behind his back. In these bonds he was made sometimes to walk, sometimes to run, and when he stumbled his guards drove him on. The inhabitants of Berber and the camp followers of Kitchener's army jeered at the prisoner and pelted him with rubbish.

It was a barbarous incident and there was worse to follow. To be fair, however, one must remember that much harsher treatment would have been meted out to the British and the Egyptians had they been captured by the Arabs, and that colonial warfare in the nineteenth century with all its savagery never achieved quite the same refinement of cruelty that was practised upon many prisoners in the last world war.

Kitchener's attitude to these matters was a complex one, and Sir Philip Magnus has gone a long way towards explaining it by pointing out that, at this time, he was an extremely reserved and unpopular man—as unpopular as only driving personal ambition could make him. He was unmarried. Mary Baker, the 16-year-old daughter of Baker's brother Valentine, had fallen in love with him in Cairo in 1883, but whether or not he might have married her is unknown since she died in the following year while Kitchener was in the Sudan with the Wolseley expedition. In Cairo he was regarded as a snob; it was known that he frequented the great houses on his trips to England (and he dashed back there to get political support more than once during the campaign), but in Egypt he avoided the provincial homes of his officers and their wives, and preferred instead to meet wealthy Jews and Turks. He had no use for married men on his staff, and was ruthless in cutting pay and allowances. No excuse, however genuine, was accepted from his subordinates for even the slightest failing. Ordinarily his manner was surly. He showed no interest in the welfare of his soldiers and seldom spoke to them. As an economy measure he allowed very few doctors to accompany the expedition, and his attitude to the wounded Arabs was, to say the least, one of indifference: they were left on the battlefield to die. Yet it is also clear that Kitchener towered above his men in a way that few field commanders have ever done. He was greatly feared and admired as a man of dispassionate, machine-like efficiency. His drill sergeants paid him the compliment of growing 'Kitchener' moustaches which were long, thick and martial. His officers never dared to question his decisions. The General's private doubts and hesitations were revealed only to his superiors such as Baring, and with Baring Kitchener very carefully watched his step.

So now, stimulated by success, eager for loot and more battle honours, the expedition pressed on towards Omdurman. Early in the summer of 1898 they reached Metemma and there they found the trenches and graves that had been dug by Wolseley's soldiers when they delayed in their advance to Khartoum thirteen years before. By September 1, 1898, Kitchener was before Omdurman with a force of more than twenty thousand, which included many British soldiers as well as gunboats of the Royal Navy, 100 guns, and a vast supply column of camels and horses. It had rained heavily in the night, and through the clear air the soldiers saw the great dome of the Mahdi's tomb rising in the sky, and beneath it, on the uneven surface of the desert, a long shadowy line that looked as though it might be a *zeriba*, a defence-work made of thorns and the branches of trees.

Churchill describes the scene: 'Suddenly the whole black line which seemed to be the *zeriba* began to move. It was made of men, not bushes. Behind it other immense masses and lines of men appeared over the crest; and while we watched, amazed by the wonder of the sight, the whole face of the slope beneath became black with swarming savages. Four miles from end to end, and, as it seemed, in five great divisions, this mighty army advanced—swiftly. The whole side of the hill seemed to move. Behind the masses horsemen galloped continually; before them many patrols dotted the plain; above them waved hundreds of banners, and the sun, glinting on many thousand hostile spearpoints, spread a sparkling cloud.'

It was not thought that the Khalifa stood much of a chance; many of his 50,000 warriors were armed with nothing better than spears, his guns were obsolete and Baker's old steamers, *Bordein* and *Ismailia* (which blew up when she was laying crude mines in the river near Omdurman), were not really a match for the British gunboats—and in the event this optimism was perfectly justified. Had the Khalifa attacked at night or had he chosen to make his stand in the desert out of the range of the British gunboats it might have been another story. But he did neither of these things. Allah, he declared, had ordered that he must fight at Omdurman.

The Arabs were very brave. They attacked *en masse* at dawn on September 2, rushing straight into the British artillery fire, and Kitchener's rifles completed the work. 'No white troops,' G. W. Steevens, the war correspondent, wrote, 'would have faced that torrent of death for five minutes. It was not a battle but an execution.' Except on the left flank, where the 21st Lancers made a gallant, disastrous and pointless charge, the Arabs never succeeded in reaching the invader's lines; the dead and wounded piled up in mounds on the desert, and within an hour or two there were some ten thousand bodies lying there, while many thousands of others who were wounded, or simply demoralized, streamed back in a rout to Omdurman. Kitchener's casualties were about 400. The General watched the action on horseback, with his staff around him and the great red banner of the Egyptian army flying over his head. 'At half-past eleven,' Churchill says, 'Sir H. Kitchener shut up his glasses, remarking that he thought that the enemy had been given "a good dusting".'

There was a break then for lunch, and afterwards Kitchener, who had now added the Khalifa's black flag to his own, rode into Omdurman. Very little resistance occurred. Most of the tribesmen who had survived the massacre had decamped, and a great wave of joy spread through the city when it was announced that the inhabitants who had stayed behind (mostly women) were not to be killed. Slatin, who must have spent a grimly exultant day, was recognized and cheered. In the early afternoon Kitchener made his way through the mangled corpses and the dead animals (the British artillery bombardment had been very heavy and lyddite was used for the first time) to the Mahdi's tomb in the centre of the town, and here an accident occurred. Four British shells, fired in error, fell almost at the General's feet, and Hubert Howard, *The Times* correspondent, was killed.[1] Pressing on further through the maze of crooked streets in search of the Khalifa Kitchener arrived at last at the prison, and here he released Charles Neufeld, the German trader who had been captured twelve years before, and about thirty others who were shackled in chains. He then returned to the mosque, where he set up his headquarters. Slatin brought him word there in the evening that the Khalifa had escaped; on returning to Omdurman from the battlefield he had rested for two hours and had prayed at the Mahdi's tomb. Then at 4 p.m., the very moment that Kitchener had entered the town, he had mounted a donkey and had ridden away with one of his wives, a Greek nun (who was to be used as a hostage), and a few attendants. About 30,000 fugitives, including Osman Digna, who had come up from the Red Sea for the battle, had gone with him. British cavalry through the following days pursued the Khalifa for a hundred miles south of Khartoum before they turned back empty-handed. The Khalifa by then was well on his way to El Obeid.

In Omdurman Kitchener proceeded to establish the

[1] Kitchener liked Howard (who, incidentally, had ridden with Churchill in the charge of the 21st Lancers) but he had no love for war correspondents in general. Until overridden by Salisbury he refused to allow them to advance with the vanguard, and directly after the fall of Omdurman they were sent back to Egypt. Shortly before the battle they were kept waiting for a long time outside Kitchener's tent, hoping to obtain a statement from him. At length he emerged and strode through them saying, 'Get out of my way, you drunken swabs.'

honours of victory. The Mahdi's tomb had already been damaged severely by the bombardment, and now the body of the Mahdi himself was dug up and flung into the Nile—not, however, until the head was severed, and this was purloined by Kitchener as a trophy of war. He appears to have had the notion that he might have used the skull for an inkstand or a drinking cup, or alternatively that it might have been forwarded as a curiosity to the Royal College of Surgeons in London, and it was sent down to Cairo.

There was an outcry about this matter when it became known to the public, and not even the General's popularity in England (where he was idolized after Omdurman) was able to protect him from it. Queen Victoria was deeply shocked—she thought the whole affair 'savoured too much of the Middle Ages'—and Kitchener was obliged to write her a mollifying letter. Baring in Cairo meanwhile quietly possessed himself of the skull, and sent it up to the Moslem cemetery at Wadi Halfa, where it was secretly buried by night.

But these events were to follow later as part of the disillusionment and sense of anti-climax which usually succeeds a victory. In Khartoum during these first days of exaltation after the battle Kitchener had another function to perform which was much more to the public's taste. Not many relics of Gordon remained; the earthworks he had caused to be dug were still visible, the *Bordein* was captured, and the telescope through which he had gazed so often from the Palace roof was recovered in perfect condition from the arsenal. But at this moment Gordon's memory was very bright. On September 4 a picked guard of soldiers was drawn up in a square before the ruins of the Palace, and four chaplains conducted a funeral service. Gordon's favourite hymn, 'Abide with Me', was sung, the British and Egyptian flags were broken out from poles erected on the rubble of the roof, and after the two national anthems had been played, three cheers were raised for the Queen and three more for the Khedive of Egypt. The gunboats crashed out a salute from the river. Kitchener, standing in the centre of the square, was deeply moved. Eye-witnesses declared that his shoulders were observed to be shaking with sobs, and that, turning away, he was obliged to ask one of his officers to dismiss the parade. Afterwards he walked for a long time in the Palace garden below the stairs where Gordon had been killed. 'Surely he is avenged,' the Queen wrote in her diary when she heard of the ceremony. This was true of course. Yet one cannot help feeling that Gordon himself was the last man in the world who would have wished to be avenged, and that he would have obtained a much deeper satisfaction from the college that rose in his name when Khartoum was rebuilt—that same college which has trained the Africans who rule and administer the Republic of Sudan at the present time.

There remained one other score for Kitchener to settle on the White Nile, and it was urgent. Shortly before the battle he had received from England sealed orders which he was not to open until Khartoum was reconquered. On reading these orders now he discovered that he was to proceed upstream from Khartoum at once, for it was believed that a party of Frenchmen led by a Captain Jean-Baptiste Marchand had crossed Africa from the west coast and put themselves astride the river. They were to be dislodged.

It had been known for some time that the French had been planning this *coup*—and indeed the British had contemplated sending an expedition north from Uganda to head them off—but nothing had been heard of Marchand for many months. Now, however, within a day or two of opening his orders, Kitchener received first-hand evidence that the French party had actually arrived. On September 9 Gordon's old steamer *Tewfikia*, manned by unsuspecting Arabs who knew nothing of the fall of Omdurman, arrived at Khartoum from the White Nile and was immediately captured. The crew had an arresting story to tell. They declared that they had gone south a month before in company with another steamer, the *Safia*, to collect grain. Approaching the old Egyptian post at Fashoda, about four hundred miles up the river, they had been fired on from the shore by black troops commanded by white officers under a strange flag, and had lost forty of their number killed and wounded. They had at once retreated, and the *Tewfikia* had been sent back to Omdurman for reinforcements. In support of their story the Arabs pointed to the bullets that were imbedded in the plates of the *Tewfikia*: they were nickel-plated and of a small bore known only in Europe.

Marchand's 3,000-mile march across Africa had been a *tour de force*. Setting out two years before from Brazzaville with a dozen French officers and something over 100 Senegalese he had made his way past fantastic obstacles in the interior, and had arrived at Fashoda in July 1898, six weeks before the Battle of Omdurman. His objects were entirely political. He proposed to seize the valley of the Upper Nile in the name of France, to join hands with the Emperor Menelik in Abyssinia, to drive off or come to an agreement with the Khalifa, and above all to forestall the Kitchener expedition that was advancing up the river.[1] Hardly anything more provocative, more hopeless of accomplishment or more audacious could have been imagined. Yet it was done, and the French government was prepared to back the enterprise almost to the point of war—not war between Marchand's hundred-odd men and Kitchener's army on the Nile, since that would have been ridiculous—but war against Britain in Europe. No such dangerous crisis was to occur again until the actual outbreak of hostilities in 1914, and by then France and Britain were allies against Germany.

Salisbury had foreseen the danger twelve months earlier when he cabled Baring in Cairo ... 'if we wait another year we may find that the French have anticipated us by setting up a French principality at Fashoda. It is, of course, as difficult to judge what is going on in the Upper Nile as it is to judge what is going on on the other side of the moon ... but ... if we ever get to Fashoda, the diplomatic crisis will be something to remember, and "what next" will be a very interesting question.'

Just why Marchand should have chosen Fashoda as his goal, describing it as a vital point of communications on

[1] Marchand also hoped to meet another French expedition which had actually reached the Nile from the Red Sea some weeks previously. Finding no sign of him, it had already retired.

the Nile, is something of a mystery, for there were half a dozen other places up and downstream that would have done equally well. It was a miserable collection of square, flat-roofed houses on the river bank, and perhaps its only claim to fame was that it was the headquarters of the priest-kings of the Shilluk tribe. The climate was hot and malarial and for a long time the Egyptians had used the place as a kind of Devil's Island for life prisoners. All the early explorers from Baker onwards knew Fashoda and hated it. Romolo Gessi in 1874 wrote, 'It is said that anyone sent to Fashoda never returns. The climate is unhealthy, the air pestilential. . . .'

Kitchener lost no time in setting out. On September 10 he sailed up the river with five steamers, two battalions of Sudanese, one hundred Cameron Highlanders, a battery of artillery and four Maxim guns. Once again he was taking no chances. Three days later he came up with the *Safia*. The Arabs on board opened fire and were quickly shelled out of the river. On September 18 the British flotilla was approaching Fashoda, and Kitchener sent a messenger on ahead with an invitation for Captain Marchand to come on board the following day.

Up to this stage of the campaign we have seen Kitchener in a harsh and uncompromising light. Nothing however could be more admirable than the way in which he handled the explosive and delicate situation he now found before him. It was fortunate, of course, that he spoke French so well, and he was doubly fortunate in having to deal with a man of Marchand's stature and good sense; but even apart from this the General's performance was a model of diplomatic skill. He did not provoke the French by wearing British uniform, but appeared instead in an Egyptian army fez and under the Egyptian flag.

The opening round of courtesies was extremely well done. Marchand congratulated Kitchener upon his victory at Omdurman and welcomed him to Fashoda in the name of France. Kitchener congratulated Marchand on his splendid achievement in reaching the Nile, and added that he was bound to protest against his presence there. What did Captain Marchand propose to do? The Frenchman said he would fight if he was attacked and that he and his companions would die at their posts; and this would probably mean war between France and England. He would agree to nothing until he had further instructions from France. Kitchener replied that he himself had his instructions already, and they were perfectly clear: he was to take possession of the Upper Nile. But he was quite ready to leave Marchand undisturbed until he had communicated with the French government, and all facilities would be given by the British to enable him to do so.

It was a fair proposition and Marchand agreed to it. After an amicable lunch on board Kitchener's gunboat he went back to his camp, and there, in the afternoon, Kitchener returned his call. A Colonel Jackson who also spoke French, and who was given the title of 'Military and Civil Commandant of the Fashoda District', was landed with a contingent of men who raised the Egyptian flag and immediately began to set up camp alongside the French. Kitchener made a short reconnaissance upstream to the mouth of the Sobat River, where he established another garrison, and then sailed away.

It was now up to the two governments at home to settle the issue, but nothing could have looked less like a settlement than the fury of indignation that swept over France and England directly the news from Fashoda became known. It seemed to the British that the French had attempted to rob them of their victory by an underhand trick. Captain Marchand, they protested, would have been wiped out by the Mahdists if Kitchener had not won the Battle of Omdurman. What was this insignificant detachment of French adventurers compared to Kitchener's army? Salisbury described Marchand as 'an explorer in difficulties upon the Upper Nile'.[1]

To the French it seemed that this was one more instance of British greed and British bullying. The British had abandoned the Sudan after the fall of Khartoum in

---

[1] This was not strictly true. Marchand was surprisingly well provisioned and equipped. His men were provided with such things as mosquito nets which were unknown in the British army, they had cultivated a flourishing vegetable garden, and when they eventually evacuated Fashoda they left with the British a quantity of champagne and other wine.

1885. Marchand by his courageous march had taken possession of a part of the empty space, and now it belonged to France by right of prior occupation. The French had got there first, and if for the moment they were weak in Africa they were not weak in Europe. The French nation would fight for its rights.

Throughout the first weeks of October 1898 the French and British Press attacked one another with an extreme virulence, and Kitchener, returning home at the end of the month, provided an additional outlet for the fierce patriotism that was raging through England. A special train bore him from Dover to London, and Charing Cross Station was bedecked in his honour. He stayed with Salisbury in the country and then went on to the Queen at Balmoral. The public was delighted to see him honoured—it was part of their defiance of the French.

Fashoda itself continued for a time to be the quiet centre of this maelstrom. Marchand and Colonel Jackson, though vigilant, got along with one another very well, and the two camps exchanged provisions. In the middle of October 1898, Marchand was summoned by the French government to Cairo, and he was courteously received by the British at Khartoum; they gave him a banquet, showed him over the battlefield, and then sent him on his way to Egypt.

Conditions at Fashoda deteriorated immediately after his departure. Captain Germain, who had been left in charge of the French expedition, was a less accommodating man than his chief. In defiance of the agreement that had been made between the two sides he occupied the country of the Dinka tribe on the right bank of the river, and prevented the Dinka chiefs from making contact with the British. The French boat, the *Faidherbe*, was dispatched up the river beyond the limits that had been agreed with Kitchener. Jackson, with two gunboats under his command and much stronger forces, held his hand but protested repeatedly. By the time Marchand returned a situation that was reminiscent of Mackay and Lourdel and the rival British and French factions in Buganda had developed, and hostilities were almost on the point of breaking out. Marchand quietened the scene. At Cairo he had learned with bitterness—a bitterness so deep that in after life he never again referred to Fashoda—that the French were giving way.

Indeed they had never had a real choice. It was apparent by now that the Abyssinians did not intend to come to their help on the river—they had a loathing of those hot and foetid swamps—and no matter what happened in Europe the French position at Fashoda was clearly untenable. Then too, France herself, and the French army in particular, were ruinously divided over the Dreyfus case at this time. The British, on the other hand, were absolutely united upon the Fashoda issue.

At a Lord Mayor's banquet given for Kitchener in London on November 4 Salisbury was able to announce that the crisis was over; the French were willing to withdraw.

Early on the morning of December 11, 1898, the French lowered their flag at Fashoda to the accompaniment of a roll of drums and a flourish of bugles. There was a moment of slight tension when one of the French officers, in a passion of hurt pride, stepped forward and flung the flagpole to the ground. However, a communal breakfast of the two garrisons followed, and later in the day the British fired a salute as the French steamed away on their long journey home through Abyssinia (they preferred not to take the easier, shorter route down the Nile through British territory). The British flag was not raised until they were out of sight, and as a further gesture, the hated name of Fashoda was erased from the map. The village that exists today near the original site of the outpost is called Kodok. Marchand was given a tremendous reception on his return to France, but he was seen no more in Africa. He went on to China to play his part in the Boxer rising, and died in 1934 after a distinguished career in the First World War.

On March 21, 1899, in London, Salisbury and Cambon, the French Ambassador, signed an agreement by which the Nile valley was reserved to the British and the Egyptians, while the French were to be given a free hand to the west of the river. That same month a further agreement was signed between Britain and Egypt by which the two countries undertook to rule the Sudan together. Kitchener, as Gordon had suggested so long before, was appointed Governor-General.

By now the General was back in Khartoum and honours were falling thick upon him: a step up in the army list, a grant of £30,000 from Parliament and a vote of thanks from both Houses. Five thousand workmen began to rebuild Khartoum and seven thousand trees were planted to relieve the bareness of the new city. Kitchener was determined that the new Palace which was rising from the ruins of the old should be worthy of his office. Workmen were instructed to scour Khartoum for suitable materials. 'Loot like blazes,' Kitchener wrote to Wingate, 'I want any quantity of marble stairs, marble pavings, iron railings, looking-glasses and fittings; doors, windows, furniture of all sorts.' He also let it be known to the cities which were anxious to honour him in England that he needed no more ceremonial caskets or ornamental swords; he had enough already and would prefer plate, furniture and pictures for a private house that he intended to buy. Early in 1899 Baring came up to Khartoum for the first time, and he laid the foundation stone of Gordon College, for which Kitchener had raised £120,000 by public subscription in England. Soon afterwards a statue of Gordon himself, mounted on a camel, was placed in the principal square behind the Palace.

Both Baring and Slatin, who had been so much in Gordon's mind during the last months of his life, lived on into distinguished old age. Baring, elevated to the title of the Earl of Cromer, returned to England in 1907 and became a strong opponent of women's suffrage. He was chairman of the committee inquiring into the disastrous campaign at Gallipoli when he died of influenza in 1917, aged 76.

Slatin was awarded a knighthood after Omdurman and became Inspector-General of the Sudan. Later, as head of the Red Cross in his native Austria, he was warmly regarded for his humanity to Allied prisoners in the First World War.

Zobeir was allowed to return to the Sudan in 1899 and

he lived on to an extreme old age on his estates to the north of Khartoum.

Affairs in the Sudan, however, were not quite settled by the Battle of Omdurman: the Khalifa was still at large. A number of unsuccessful attempts were made to track him down in the wild country to the south of El Obeid, but it was not until October 1899, more than a year after the battle, that spies brought in definite news of his whereabouts. They declared that Abdullah, with all the principal Emirs who had survived, had established a camp near Jebel Gedir, some 400 miles south of Khartoum, and 80 miles to the west of the White Nile. This was the Baggara country where the Khalifa had been born, a place of dry hills and forests: a little to the north lay Abba Island, where the Mahdi had first declared his holy mission.

Kitchener dispatched a force of 8,000 men to Kaka, the nearest point on the river, and in November Wingate arrived to take command. In bright moonlight on November 21 he marched westward from the Nile with a flying column of 3,700 picked men, and on the following day caught up with an Arab caravan that was taking grain to the Khalifa's camp. It was annihilated within a few hours, and Wingate pressed on rapidly through a thick forest. On November 23 his scouts brought him word that they had found the enemy camp at a place called Um Diwaykarat, about half a dozen miles away.

It seemed probable that the Khalifa would stand and fight: his supply of grain had been captured, his pursuers blocked his escape-route to the north, and to the south and west lay nothing but waterless scrub. Wingate decided to attack at dawn. With the camel corps scouting on the flanks and the cavalry in front, the column moved off shortly after midnight, making as little noise as possible. At many places it was necessary for the men to hack their way through the forest, but by 3 a.m. the cavalry were within a mile of their objective and the infantry was now ordered to advance in fighting formation. In the distance they heard drums and horns sounding a warning in the Khalifa's camp, but these noises soon died away and the soldiers gained the grass on the rising ground without interference.

'At 5.10 a.m.,' Wingate wrote later in his report to Kitchener, 'in the uncertain light preceding dawn, our infantry picquets were driven in, and the indistinct forms of advancing Dervishes became visible.' The British machine-guns opened fire, and it was another Omdurman on a smaller scale. When the cease-fire sounded an hour later it was found that for the death of three of his men and the wounding of twenty-three others Wingate had gained a remarkable prize: a thousand Arabs were dead or wounded, and among the ten thousand-odd prisoners were 29 important Emirs, the Khalifa's eldest son and intended successor, and many women and children.

But it was on the battlefield itself that Wingate came upon a really awesome sight: '. . . only a few hundred yards from our original position on the rising ground, a large number of the enemy were seen lying dead, huddled together in a comparatively small space; on examination these proved to be the bodies of the Khalifa Abdullah, the Khalifa Ali Wad Helu [another of the original three Khalifas chosen by the Mahdi], Ahmed-el-Fedil, the Khalifa's two brothers, Sennousi Ahmed and Hamed Mohammed, the Mahdi's son, Es-Sadek, and a number of other well-known leaders.

'At a short distance behind them lay their dead horses, and, from the few men still alive—amongst whom was the Emir Yunis Eddekin—we learnt that the Khalifa, having failed in his attempt to reach the rising ground where we had forestalled him, had then endeavoured to make a turning movement, which had been crushed by our fire. Seeing his followers retiring, he made an ineffectual attempt to rally them, but recognizing that the day was lost, he had called on his emirs to dismount from their horses, and seating himself on his "furwa" or sheepskin—as is the custom of Arab chiefs who disdain surrender—he had placed the Khalifa Ali Wad Helu on his right and Ahmed Fedil on his left, whilst the remaining emirs seated themselves round him, with their bodyguard in line some twenty

paces to their front, and in this position they had unflinchingly met their death. They were given a fitting
burial, under our supervision, by the surviving members
of their own tribesmen.'[1]

Kitchener added these words to Wingate's report: 'The
country has at last been finally relieved of the military
tyranny which started in a movement of wild religious
fanaticism upwards of 19 years ago. Mahdism is now a
thing of the past, and I hope that a brighter era has now
opened for the Sudan.'

As the last weeks of the century ran out it did indeed
seem that a better future had opened up, not only for the
Sudan but for the whole valley of the Nile. Hardly forty
years had elapsed since all the upper reaches of the river
and the source itself were an unknown wilderness ravaged
by tribal wars and slavery, and now at every point the
civilized world was reaching into the centre of the continent. The slave-trade, if not absolutely dead, was dying
fast. The telegraph was restored, and in 1899 a permanent
channel was finally hacked through the Sudd. By a new
system of railways and steamers it was now possible for a
traveller to make his unmolested way along the entire
length of the river. Still another railway was being driven
inland from the east coast of Africa to Lake Victoria.

There had been fearful ravages, of course. The population of the Sudan had dwindled to a bare two million,
and in Buganda hardly a million inhabitants remained compared to the three or four millions in Grant's and Speke's
day. In some areas rinderpest had entirely wiped out the
herds of domestic cattle, and even worse plagues were soon
to follow. For many hundreds of miles the banks of the
White Nile were a desolation. In the light of this one was
permitted to wonder whether the price paid for civilization
was not too high. 'The Nile-land of today . . . ,' Harry
Johnston wrote at the turn of the century, 'is much of it
in sad contrast with its condition during Sir Samuel Baker's
government of the Sudan, and even during the silver age

---

[1] Osman Digna, the last remaining Arab leader at liberty, was captured
in the following January.

of Emin. . . . It is sad to think that the people were possibly happier [then].'

But by 1899 the nadir had been reached, and the incredible virility of Africa was beginning to assert itself again. Gladstone, who had died shortly before the Battle of Omdurman, might turn restlessly in his grave at many of the things the British had done along the river, but on the eve of the new century Queen Victoria, then in her penultimate year, could survey the scene with satisfaction. She ruled the river from the Mediterranean to the Mountains of the Moon. Egypt, the Sudan, Uganda—all were hers in fact, if not in name, and the Nile, for the first time in its history, was an open highway from Central Africa to the sea.

WITH THE exception of Winston Churchill, who defies all rules, the principal eye-witnesses of the events described in these pages are now dead. It is a great loss that this is so. How much one would have liked to have talked to Burton, Gordon, Emin and so many others, to have at least seen Livingstone with one's own eyes, and to have put so many questions to men like Kirk and Baring; to have asked poor Speke what really happened when he went out shooting on that autumn afternoon near Bath in 1864.

With such strong characters one is tempted to make comparisons and classifications. It might be suggested, for example, that some, like Livingstone and Gordon, were born great; others like Stanley and Kitchener achieved greatness, and others like the Khedive Ismail had greatness thrust upon them. But then there still remains another group—Burton and Emin are members of it—which fits into no category at all. A common hunger for adventure certainly bound them all to Africa, and one notes that so many of these men were Scottish, were the sons of clergymen, and were affected by, or took part in, the three great military events of the time: the Crimean War, the Indian Mutiny and the American Civil War. The desire to suppress the slave-trade and evangelize the African tribes, the profits to be made from ivory and the hope of discovering gold and other minerals, the collector's and the sportsman's instinct, the simple wish to be the first to break into new country—all these things drew the explorers on; and it has to be admitted that a great deal of effort was wasted on expeditions that set out to rescue men who did not particularly want to be rescued.

Islam in Africa also had a powerful influence upon the explorers. All of them to a more or less degree found that they had to come to terms with the Arabs, and most of them were obliged to take on, as it were, the protective colouring of Islam merely in order to keep alive. The Arab slavers led the way into the interior, and without their help few of the Christian travellers would have advanced very far. Burton was already enamoured of the Arab way of life when he reached Africa, and Emin, too, hovered in a strange Islamic-Christian twilight. Speke's journeys were based upon information given to him by the Arabs, Stanley entered into partnership with Tippu Tib, and Livingstone would have died much earlier had not the slavers more than once, and for long periods of time, come to his assistance. Baker judged it necessary to spend a year learning Arabic before he ventured southwards to the sources of the Nile, and later thought it nothing strange to take service under a Moslem prince. Gordon before the end made many compromises with Islam; he legalized slavery and would have set up Zobeir as Governor-General of the Sudan. There is also much evidence in his letters and journals that he respected the Arabs for their strong faith, and one feels that he resented Slatin's pretended apostasy, not so much on religious grounds, but because he thought it was venal and weak. Probably Kirk and Baring were the ablest in maintaining their independence—their Europeanness—but this was because they remained for the most part within their consulates and both were cautious men who held on firmly to their official connection with the Foreign Office in London.

Christianity, then, penetrated Central Africa under the cover of Islam, and it is remarkable that the Moslems took so long to realize what was happening to them. In the early days they were almost unfailingly helpful to the missionaries and explorers; they welcomed them as civilized companions in the vast wilderness of African barbarity. It was only later, at the end of the eighteen-seventies, when they saw that they were facing destruction—or at any rate subservience—at the hands of the Christians that they turned hostile. The Arabi rising in Egypt, the revolt of the Mahdi in the Sudan and the persecution of the Christian mission-

aries and their followers in Buganda, were the result. These
disturbances ended, as we have seen, in the crushing defeat
of Islam along the Nile, but it has proved to be only a
temporary defeat. Since 1900 there has been a steady resurgence of Islam in East and Central Africa, and at the
present time the Moslems are gaining more adherents than
are the Christians; as Roland Oliver points out, they are
winning 'the race—for the animist peoples of the world'.
Uganda, admittedly, is largely Christian now, but it will
soon be an independent state, and both Egypt and the
Sudan are already under Moslem rule. No prudent man,
however, would venture to say that this is the final end of
the matter. The conflict between the two religions—the East
against the West—appears to be a permanent part of the
African scene; it flows on, sometimes underground, sometimes above, as persistently and inevitably as the Nile itself.

But all this must not be allowed to diminish the splendour of the explorers' achievement in obtaining, within the
space of twenty years or so, the answer to a geographical
mystery which had baffled the world since the beginnings of
civilization. It must be remembered that they *walked* to the
sources of the Nile; the country then was just as primitive
and hostile as it was in prehistoric times, the harsh climate
had not altered, disease was probably just as prevalent, and
their scientific knowledge of the region was hardly superior
to that of the early Greeks and Romans. This was a sun-
burst of Victorian courage and imagination.

Central Africa, with its tremendous rainstorms and its
forest fires, its earthquakes, droughts and plagues, is a
mighty destroyer of the relics of the past, but such as remain have not been greatly overlaid by new civilizations,
and it is still a rewarding experience to follow the explorers' route from Zanzibar into the interior and then descend the White Nile from its source to Khartoum. At every
step of the way one is reminded of some phrase they recorded in their diaries, some old engraving or pen-and-ink
sketch that has survived, some moment of triumph or disaster in their wanderings, and a hundred years vanishes in
an instant.

Tornadoes, naval bombardments and the simple corrosion of the tropical air have devastated the Zanzibar waterfront, and it has been much rebuilt, but the general outline remains the same. One can still see through Burton's eyes the Arab dhows that have been washed in from the Persian Gulf by the monsoon, the Sultan's palace and the grey coral walls of the fort adjoining. A tall square house standing somewhat by itself on the left may appear to be just another house, but the initiate will know that Livingstone lived there before he set out on his last journey; and on going ashore he will make his way through the narrow streets to the old British Consulate which is now the headquarters of an East African trading concern. Here, if he is fortunate, he will be shown the upper rooms where Hamerton made so hospitable a home, where Speke and Burton stayed, where Kirk and Stanley discovered a mutual hostility and where Livingstone's body remained for a time before it was transported to England. Tippu Tib's house with its carved doorways lies only a little distance off, and in a grove of mangoes just outside the town the visitor will find the ruined walls of the harem that Barghash built for his wives shortly before he died. It must have been a grandiose place, but now there is a heavy monastic silence in the air, and it makes a pleasant contrast with the hot alleyways in the town where the rickshas still push through the crowd, and where, amidst a violent farrago of scents and smells, the exotic produce of the island—the paw-paws, sugarcane, limes, groundnuts, jackfruit, guavas, nutmegs, cloves, pineapples, coconuts and dried sharks' fins—is still laid out for sale, precisely as it was a century ago.

Beside Barghash's ruined harem a warm transparent sea washes up on to the beach of powdered coral that is almost as white as snow, and beyond it the green plantations of the island spread away. For most of the year a steamy heat envelops Zanzibar, and no matter how blue the sky there is always the oppressive feeling of an approaching thunderstorm in the air. In the evening, when the crowds emerge on to the waterfront for a breath of air, hectic sunsets break across the ocean, and presently the Southern Cross appears low down on the horizon. In the gathering darkness the boats in the harbour leave a bright trail of phosphorus in their wake. All this is very much as Burton described it.

There is a little museum in the town, and here one can see portraits of the Sultans, a folio of letters written by Speke, Grant and Livingstone, and the usual display of local arts and crafts. It is a good museum, splendidly arranged, and yet, as one passes by the showcases, one is aware that something is missing: the relics of the slave-trade. True, there is more than one picture of Tippu Tib on the walls, and in one corner a heavy pair of wooden stocks, much worn by the human limbs they once imprisoned, has been laid upon the floor. But Zanzibar wishes to obliterate slavery from its civic memories. The jungle has now overgrown the underground caves where the slaves were herded awaiting export overseas, and hardly a trace remains of the old slave-market which Grant described as 'a triangular space surrounded by rickety huts thatched with coco-nut leaves where the naked slaves sat silent as death'. The open square is there but it has been changed beyond all recognition. Upon one side the Anglican Cathedral rises up, and the bell tower with its explicit British clock is a very definite impediment to the memory of the terrible and lurid past.

The writer spent some time in going through the archives of the British Universities Mission to Central Africa which had its headquarters here as far back as 1864. In graceful and legible handwriting Bishop Steere and his successors kept a record of their daily lives, and here we learn that Livingstone's faithful companion Susi was baptized with the name David after the explorer's death, that 'Mr. Stanley arrived last night', that another British gunboat has come into Zanzibar with yet another batch of liberated child-slaves who are to be cared for by the Mission, that a Bishop has departed and another has arrived, that such and such was the order of the Easter service; and then again there are more entries about the slaves, their liberation, their baptism, their marriages and deaths. In page after page the entries continue through the years, and they impart a strong impression of the slow, uneventful passage of time, of the gradual subsiding of the island's life from the wild era of the slavers' caravans to the present days of tourist steamers in the harbour and the evening game of cricket in the park. It is a strange atmosphere. The theatricality of Zanzibar remains, but this is now a theatre without a drama.

At Bagamoyo, on the mainland, the effects are somewhat more pronounced. Here one is shown the window from which Emin is thought to have fallen when he reached the coast with Stanley in 1889, and on the river nearby one can still enjoy, with Burton, 'the deep dead silence of the tropical night, broken only by the roar of the old bull-crocodile at his resting-time, the *qua-qua* of the night heron, and the shouts and shots of the watchmen, who know from the grunts of the hippopotamus, struggling up the bank, that he is quitting his watery home to pay a visit to their fields.' The old caravan routes leading inland have long since been abandoned, but here and there along the way one comes upon old men who remember the slaving days very well. At Mpwapwa, which was an important staging post, one of Stanley's unfortunate companions lies buried, and Africans from some twenty or thirty different tribes are living in the district. These people are the descendants of slaves or porters who, on their way down to the coast, deserted the caravans or were left behind because of sickness. Like seeds scattered casually by the wind, they have taken root and somehow managed to survive.

From Mpwapwa one can strike north towards Lake Victoria across the Wembere Steppe, which is the route that Emin and Stanley followed, or take the more generally used road that leads to Tabora. None of this country is quite tamed as yet, for one still hears stories of cattle raids, of tribal feuds, of killings with the poisoned arrow, and of the 'lion-man', who is an idiot who walks on all fours in a mothy lion's skin, and who is trained to roar and leap, before an audience of witches, upon some wretched child, rending and finally killing it with a knife. The drunkenness which all the explorers speak about still persists in the villages, and it indicates that even now there is something lacking in life in this beautiful country, some fundamental discontent that leads to despair and hopeless idleness. It was here that Burton wrote that melancholy and monotony tend to descend upon human beings in beautiful places whereas in deserts this is rarely so. It is a point that strikes the traveller forcibly later on, when he reaches the hard and arid spaces of the Sudan. He may be less comfortable as he descends the river to Khartoum, but he will find that there is a stimulating quality in the air which is the reverse of the softness and the ennui that overtake existence on the equatorial lakes.

The house where Livingstone and Stanley stayed at Tabora has been faithfully rebuilt and converted into a kind of museum, with Arab muskets and other trophies on the walls. Someone had the notion of obtaining facsimiles of the dispatches that Stanley wrote here for the *New York Herald* after the two men had returned from Ujiji on Lake Tanganyika, and it is very strange to read the excited headlines in these surroundings: 'Dr. Livingstone Found'; 'The Famous Explorer in Good Health'. The words seem to arrest time for a moment, and it is not difficult to imagine Livingstone sitting under the mango tree which stands outside the front door, planning the journey that was to bring him to the source of the Nile at last, and being mercifully unaware that he would never reach it and that within nine months he would be dead.

Here too, or at any rate close by, Burton and Speke began their quarrel and Speke alone marched off to investigate the reports of a great lake in the north. Mwanza, the place at which he obtained his first sight of Lake Victoria, is now a modern port with European buildings on the shore, and villas and churches dotted about the rocky hills above, and there is a regular service of steamers to Uganda and Kenya in the north. Yet in the outlying villages nothing very much has happened since 1858: the mango trees originally planted by the slavers have now grown to a great height, and in their deep green shade the Arabs still sit cross-legged on the verandas of their black-brick huts. These are the thin, courtly, serious men with moist, brown eyes and a fringe of black beard round their faces, whom Burton liked so well. But once again the drama has gone; they trade no longer in slaves and ivory, but in such things as cotton cloth and plastic buttons and perhaps, occasionally, a little illegal rhinoceros horn, which is still regarded as a great aphrodisiac in the East.

From Mwanza gravelled and paved roads that roughly follow Speke and Grant's route lead on around the western shore of the lake to Karagwe, but of Bweranyange, Rumanika's old capital, little now remains. The traveller, coming over the brow of the hill, will see the sheet of water which Grant named Windermere because it so resembled the Lake District in England, and the mountainous country rolling away into Ruanda Urundi, but the slopes at his feet are empty. A dark hole in the ground with trees growing round it marks the site of Rumanika's court, and close by there is a curious circle of rusting iron objects thrust into the earth. On coming closer one sees that these are metal drums, broad spearheads, arrows, stakes with sprays like the spread fingers of a hand (probably for holding spears), and charming iron figures of cattle with iron horns. These are the ancestral symbols of the race and are said to date from Rumanika's time. But of the reed palace where the King used to meet Speke and Grant, and later Stanley, and the compound where they watched the war-dances in the moonlight, and the house of the fat wives, there is no sign whatever; these things, like the fictional scenes in a novel, have their reality now only in the records of the explorers. They were discovered only to be lost again.

Bukoba, the town that Emin founded on the western shore of the lake, is a green and cheerful place with quite a Corinthian reputation for lasciviousness; it is said that the women here are unusually kind and affectionate, and that there is a great demand for them among the native brothels of East Africa. Whether this be true or not it is a fact that the traveller here notices a certain lightening in the atmosphere: both men and women smile and wave as his car passes by, and the clothes they wear are brilliant billowing cottons. The dull scrub of Tanganyika is now replaced by wide green fields and plantations of bananas. The air is warm and damp—there are said to be two hundred thunderstorms a year at this end of the lake—and after the rain tropical butterflies make a patchwork quilt around the steaming puddles on the road. Presently jungles appear, splashed here and there by the scarlet flowers of the flame tree, and it is apparent that one has crossed one of the great migratory routes of the African birds—over a thousand species have been noticed—for they appear in myriads in the evening: great spiralling fleets of Abdin storks, egrets, fish eagles, pelicans, ducks and geese of many kinds, and the crested crane which cries as it flies, like a lonely Siamese cat. This is the threshold of Uganda.

Not much remains of Mutesa's capital at Rubaga. Its seven hills are now the city of Kampala, and his descendant, the Kabaka Mutesa II, rules (under the British) a world of Indian shops and cinemas, of railway yards and bus stations, of Christian churches and commercial crops of tea, coffee and bananas. Jet aircraft coming in from Europe will provide perhaps for their passengers a brief glimpse of the source of the Nile at Jinja, but Jinja is a place of bright brick bungalows like any other African colonial town, and the natural fall of the river from the lake is imprisoned in concrete.

One must go north from the source, following in the tracks of Speke, Grant, Chaillé-Long, Linant de Bellefonds, Emin and Gordon, and enter Bunyoro in order to see the river as they saw it. Even as late as 1959 it was difficult for a motor vehicle to follow the rough tracks into the Karuma Falls where the Nile begins its tempestuous westward course to Lake Albert. Samuel Baker and his wife, struggling back here after the disastrous Battle of Masindi, must have beheld the river with relief, for it is a lovely sight, a great white foaming rush of water past green islands. The hippopotamuses, rising to the surface in the whirlpools, look like knights in a disordered game of chess, and have not as yet been much disturbed by the new electric power-station on the bank.

For fifty miles below this point the Nile is barely navigable, but at the foot of the Murchison Falls it broadens into a quiet and softly-moving stream, with millions of little green cabbages, the *pistia stratiotes*, floating on the surface of the water. Here we are in the region of Gordon's and Emin's forts. Magungo, the first of these, lies on the left bank just above the junction of the river with Lake Albert, and has been much cut up by hippopotamus trails and by elephants coming down to the river to drink. But it is

Wadelai, the capital of Equatoria under Emin's rule, that one chiefly wishes to see. There is no road to Wadelai; one must proceed there either by launch (following the river about forty-five miles downstream from Lake Albert), or by bouncing across country in a truck. Choosing the overland route in the month of December, the writer found himself cut off from the river by a thick wall of coarse grass some eight feet high, which made the going very slow. There was no sign of a track, and the last village had been left far behind. Once or twice native women appeared, carrying water to their isolated huts, and on being asked the way had either denied that such a place as Wadelai existed or had bolted into the scrub. It was, then, a matter of some astonishment that a tall and nearly naked African now suddenly jumped up in front of the truck, and pointing with his black finger into the grass ahead, uttered a single, luminous cry: 'Emin Pasha'. No doubt this man's family had been here since Emin's time, and had somehow retained their memory of the name through nearly three-quarters of a century. Clearly too, he had reasoned that only some business connected with Emin or his ghost, could have brought a white man to this outlandish spot. At all events it was both startling and pleasant to be reminded thus of the continuity of things and, sure enough, the green sheen of the river with fields of feathery papyrus on either bank soon broke into view. But where was Wadelai?

A cairn of stones marked the site of the town, and upon it was a plaque with the words:

'Wadelai
Egyptian Station 1879–89
Headquarters of Equatoria
Under Emin Pasha.'

But the town itself had returned almost entirely to the jungle. All that was left of the orderly streets, the brick houses of the officials, the wharves and the gun emplacements, was a heap of reddish rubble hidden under the grass. Even the high walls and the ditch that once surrounded the garrison had fallen in and were now no more than a gentle undulation on the ground. It is much the same with all the other stations on the river; only at Dufilé, a little further to the north, where Gordon and Gessi assembled their steamers above the rapids, can you easily trace, among the borassus palms that have since sprung up, the general outline of the fort.

Here too, another change overtakes the river. Its rapids rush on into the dry wastes of the Sudan, and the Arab influence begins to make itself felt. The Sudd can still be a slight ordeal for a traveller even though he now passes through it on the deck of a paddle steamer with wire netting around him to keep the mosquitoes at bay. By the end of the first day—and from Juba it takes nearly three days to reach the clear water above Malakal—he will understand very well how Baker came to write 'during the dead calms in these vast marshes the feeling of melancholy produced is beyond description. The White Nile is a veritable Styx.'

To have been becalmed in this moist green wilderness must have been demoralizing; to have endured there the approach of death through starvation and fever as Gessi did, too horrible to contemplate. The papyrus reed when seen for the first time, or carved in stone upon some Egyptian monument, is a beautiful plant with delicate arching fronds making an hieratic pattern against the sky. But when it is multiplied to madness, hundreds of square miles of it spreading away like a green sea on every side, the effect is claustrophobic and sinister. The channels through which the steamer passes are often only forty or fifty yards wide, and so the passenger looks out upon interminable walls of interlacing stalks and they press upon him in imagination like the walls of a prison or a maze. Even the water in the channel itself is not clear, since within the last year or so that most prolific of aquatic plants, the water hyacinth, has taken hold upon the Nile. It reaches out from the banks in long floating filaments with a pretty purple flower, and although it is savaged and cut about by the steamers' paddles it never seems to die; rather, it strengthens its hold on the river from year to year and could, if unchecked, succeed in the end in blocking the stream once more as it was in Gessi's time.

The South Sudan, with its drifting sand and overpowering heat, has been even more ruthless with the relics of the past than Uganda has. When Winston Churchill, as Minister of Colonies, made this journey down the Nile in 1907, Gondokoro was still a name in the world, and he found there six houses, native huts, a telegraph station, a prison, a courthouse and a company of the King's African Rifles. Very little of all this now remains, and Baker's fort has vanished entirely. At Fashoda too, all traces of Captain Marchand's camp have subsided into dust, and there is nothing about Abba Island to suggest that it was once the cradle of the Mahdi's empire.

At Khartoum, however, there is more evidence of the past. The Mahdi's tomb has been re-erected at Omdurman, and the Khalifa's house has been converted into a museum. From here it is but a short drive to the battlefield, which remains virtually as it was in 1898—an uneven expanse of dry and rocky desert. The new city of Khartoum on the opposite bank of the river bears very little resemblance to the fortress Gordon knew. Even the General's statue has been removed in recent years, and one cannot be quite sure of finding the identical spot on the Palace stairs where he is supposed to have stood when he was stabbed to death. Yet from the roof the view is still much the same, and one sees more or less what Gordon saw: the low, mud-hut silhouette of Omdurman on the opposite bank, the desert spreading away on every side to become lost in mirages on the flat horizon, and at one's feet the Blue Nile coming in to join the White.

Here, more than anywhere, the river reveals its calm, slow, massive power. Already the main branch, the White Nile, has come two thousand miles from the centre of Africa, and it is so wide, so lake-like, so busy with barges and sailing boats, one finds it difficult to believe that the stream has still another two thousand miles to go before it reaches the sea.

But the Nile at Khartoum is something more than a great artery pumping life into the arid sand: it has a quality in time as well, something to do with the continuous movement of the water perhaps. One does not here feel so very distant from Wolseley's and Kitchener's soldiers making their way up from Egypt, or from the Khalifa's warriors, or from Speke taking pot-shots at the hippopotamuses in the reeds, or from Mrs. Baker washing her yellow hair in this same water, or from the Mahdi praying on Abba Island, or from Livingstone, Gordon, Gessi and so many others who, in their different ways, gave their lives for the river, or from Burton and Stanley who staked their reputations upon it, or even from Herodotus and Nero's centurions. The river binds them all together. Each of them was drawn towards it by an irresistible attraction, and it makes very little odds whether we think of the stream as it is in this present century or as it was in the age of Ptolemy. The Nile seems to be impervious to change. It flows on now, as it has always flowed, perpetually renewing itself from year to year and from century to century, a never-ending flood of warm, life-giving water that spans half Africa from the Equator to the Mediterranean, and it is still the mightiest river on the earth.

Asolo, Italy, 1960

ACKNOWLEDGEMENTS

THE ORIGINAL PLAN for this book was suggested to me by Mr. Ralph Dreshfield Q.C., the Attorney General in Uganda, and it was through his kind offices that I was able to consult the Uganda Government archives. I cannot sufficiently express my gratitude to him. Among others who discussed the work with me in its early stages and generously helped me later on were Sir Richard Turnbull, now Governor of Tanganyika, Professor Kenneth Ingham of Makerere College, Kampala, Mr. Rennie Bere, the Director of the Uganda National Parks, Sir Edwin Chapman-Andrews, Her Majesty's Ambassador at Khartoum, and Sir John Gray, the former Chief Justice of Zanzibar. Mr. H. B. Thomas, the authority on East African history, has, with the utmost kindness, spent many hours of work on the final text and has made innumerable corrections and improvements.

I am indebted to the Zanzibar Museum and the British Universities Mission to Central Africa for allowing me to see their records, and to Sir Henry and Lady Potter for their hospitality in Zanzibar. Mr. G. S. Holland, the chief draughtsman of the Royal Geographical Society, prepared a map which enabled me to follow the explorers' routes inland from Bagamoyo to Lake Victoria and thence down the Nile into the Sudan. Mr. Richard Waller accompanied me on that journey, and at every stage we were welcomed and assisted by District Commissioners and other government officials.

I also owe a particular debt to Mr. L. P. Kirwan, the Director of the Royal Geographical Society, to Mr. G. R. Crone, the Society's Librarian, and to Mrs. Dorothy Middleton, who allowed me to see a number of unpublished letters written to the Society by Burton and Speke, and who most kindly read this book in typescript. Mr. Richard Hill, of Durham University, and Mrs. Mary Bull of the Institute of Commonwealth Studies have also checked the manuscript, and to them, and to the London Library, who supplied most of the books listed in my Notes, I would like to express my warmest thanks. Brigadier J. H. S. Lacey, of the Institution of Royal Engineers, Mr. D. H. Simpson, Librarian of the Royal Commonwealth Society, Mr. D. Parker, of the Lands and Survey Department, Entebbe, and Dr. John R. Baker have most generously helped with the illustrations.

Finally I must acknowledge with gratitude the great assistance given me by my wife and by Mr. Richard Brain in preparing the index, collecting the illustrations and in editing the final text.

Extracts from this book have appeared in *The New Yorker*.

NOTES

HARRY JOHNSTON's *The Nile Quest* (Lawrence and Bullen, 1903) is one of the earliest attempts to give a connected history of the river, and it remains probably the best general introduction to the subject. But for a closer study one must turn, of course, to the books of the explorers. Most, if not all, of these are now out of print, and the early editions have become collectors' items in the second-hand bookshops. The principal works, however, can be found in any good general library as well as in the more specialized collections kept by such institutions as the Royal Geographical Society in London.

These publications are a pleasure to behold: splendid, massive works often running to two or three volumes, bound in solid cardboard and printed on thick, glossy paper with large type and wide margins. The illustrations are generally taken from the explorers' rough sketches which have been worked up into engravings and line drawings by professional artists in England, and the portrait photographs are of a standard which is commonly higher than anything seen at the present time. The maps, though often erroneous, are beautifully drawn and are either contained in a fat pocket at the end of the book or fold outwards in a solid sheet of linen. Many of the publishers have long since gone out of business, and indeed they would soon have become bankrupt had they attempted to issue such productions at the present time.

Some of the better-known books of this kind are Livingstone's *Last Journals*, Burton's *Lake Regions of Central Africa*, Speke's *Journal*, Baker's *Albert N'yanza*, Stanley's *Through the Dark Continent*, and Thomson's *Through*

Masailand. There are many others. Almost all are distinguished by a quality of writing which makes the study of this subject a delight.

Then there is a second class of books about African exploration and the Nile which are of much later date and which might be described as standard works, since they are the result of devoted scholarship in the present century. Of such are Coupland's *Exploitation of East Africa*, Allen's *Gordon and the Sudan*, Seaver's *Livingstone*, Oliver's *The Missionary Factor in East Africa*, P. M. Holt's *The Mahdist State in the Sudan*, and Miss Margery Perham's recently published *Lugard*. One must also mention here two earlier publications which are familiar to every enthusiast for the Upper Nile, Wingate's *Mahdiism and the Egyptian Sudan* and Harry Johnston's two lavish tomes, *The Uganda Protectorate.*

Gordon's letters and journals, the books of the various Europeans who were prisoners of the Mahdists in the Sudan, and the innumerable memoirs of missionaries, government officials and sportsmen, fall into still another category, since they were written for the most part after the explorers had completed their work and before the period of scholarship began. Most of these works are extremely personal, though none the less valuable for that. One might perhaps lump them together under the rather dull title of secondary exploration.

It is hardly surprising that in such a spontaneous spate of writing many gaps and superfluities should occur. Thus the big game hunters' books grow very tedious through their triviality of thought and endless repetition, while we still know very little indeed about the pre-history of the White Nile or even of the origins of the tribes that live there. There is a vast literature on the slave-trade and a corresponding dearth of books about the conflict of Islam and Christianity in East and Central Africa, which is now a much more lively issue and likely to continue so.

However, there is no aspect of the river, whether historical, geographical, anthropological, ethnological, zoological, botanical or geological, which is not touched upon by three periodicals which are published in Africa itself: the *Tangan-*

yika Notes and Records, *The Uganda Journal* and the *Sudan Notes and Records*. Being written mainly by government officials and others who have made their careers in East and Central Africa they give a picture of the country that can be instantly recognized as authentic.

It is then, from such books and publications as these, and from the personal experience of visiting nearly all the places here described, that the present work has been compiled. A more detailed reference to sources follows below.

Shortly before the publication of this book I received a charming letter from Mr. H. B. Thomas. In it he says, 'The problem of spelling African proper names has, over the years, substantially shortened my life.' Since so distinguished an authority can make such an admission I feel I need do no more here than point out that there has never been any general agreement on the subject. Is it Mohammed or Muhammad, or some other alternative? Should Bahr-el-Jebel, Bahr-el-Zeraf and Dar-es-Salaam have hyphens or not? Is it Zobeir or Zebehr, Mahdi-ism or Mahdism, Mtesa or Mutesa, Mruli or Mrooli? Should Dufilé take an accent? Is Kamrasi more properly Kamurasai? Most Arabists and students of African history will give you emphatic answers to these questions, but you will find that these answers differ from one another and often widely. This is an arena where personal preference seems to carry as much weight as scholarship and only common usage, whether accurate or inaccurate, can settle the matter in the end. In these pages I have used the spelling which seemed to be the most generally accepted. I do not claim accuracy. I only hope to be clear.

CHAPTER 1. Among recent publications Burton's life has been dealt with very readably and vivaciously by Lesley Blanch in *The Wilder Shores of Love* (Murray, 1954) and by Seton Dearden in *The Arabian Knight* (Barker, 1953), but his own books probably give the sharpest insight into his character and abilities. *Zanzibar, City, Island and Coast* (2 vols., Tinsley Brothers, 1872) is an excellent revelation of the author's peculiar cast of mind. It is very strange. He contrives to be pedantic, exuberant, malicious, learned and highly colourful all at the same time. The effect upon the reader is as if he were being rushed downhill by fits and starts—now the brakes, now full speed ahead.

Burton's account of the previous African journey he made with Speke to Somaliland is given in his *First Footsteps in East Africa* (2 vols., Longmans Green, 1856).

CHAPTER 2. Burton's *The Lake Regions of Central Africa* (2 vols., Longmans Green, 1860) and Speke's *What Led to the Discovery of the Source of the Nile* (Blackwood, 1863) fully describe the expedition to Lake Tanganyika, and its centenary in 1957 has been celebrated by a special number of *Tanganyika Notes and Records*. This last contains a remarkably well-balanced and informative sketch of Burton's life by R. C. H. Risley, and an appreciation of Speke by Professor Kenneth Ingham, of Makerere College. Sir John Gray, a former Chief Justice of Uganda who now lives in Zanzibar, also contributes an article on earlier trading expeditions into the interior, and the reader is furnished with a lucid map. Altogether this publication is a memorable achievement.

CHAPTER 3. Apart from such standard works as Johnston's *Uganda Protectorate* (2 vols., Hutchinson, 1902) and *Uganda* by H. B. Thomas and Robert Scott (Oxford University Press, 1935) there exists much information and useful speculation upon the early history of the three kingdoms, Karagwe, Buganda and Bunyoro, in the papers of J. Ford and R. de Z. Hall in *Tanganyika Notes and Records* (December 1947) and of Sir John Gray in the *Uganda Journal* (April 1935, September 1947, March 1951, September 1951). H. B. Thomas's paper 'Giovanni Miani and the White Nile' (*Uganda Journal*, April 1939), J. V. Wild's *Early Travellers in Acholi* (Nelson, 1954) and a note on Uganda history by Captain Hubert Foster of the War Office Intelligence Staff (*Foreign Office Correspondence respecting Zanzibar*, 1892, No. 242) have also been consulted.

But for a picture of the three kingdoms as they were in the early 1860's the richest sources, of course, are Speke's *Journal of the Discovery of the Source of the Nile* (Blackwood, 1863) and, to a lesser extent (it has a rather pedestrian pace) Grant's *A Walk across Africa* (Blackwood, 1864). These two books also give us the only full account of their great journey as far as Gondokoro, where they were met by Samuel Baker—an event he later described in his *Albert N'yanza, Great Basin of the Nile* (2 vols., Macmillan, 1866). Mr. and Mrs. Petherick in their *Travels in Central Africa* (2 vols., Tinsley Brothers, 1869) also give, though in an understandably aggrieved manner, an account of the two explorers' return to civilization.

CHAPTER 4. *The Nile Basin* by Burton and James M'Queen (Tinsley Brothers, 1864) was published, rather brutally, only a few months after Speke's death. In it Burton gives his account of the Bath meeting, and it follows fairly closely a second account he published later in his *Zanzibar*. Other references to his attitude to Speke at the time will be found in his wife's *Life of Sir Richard Burton* (2 vols., Chapman and Hall, 1893) and *True Life of Capt. Sir Richard Burton* by Georgiana M. Stisted (Nichols, 1896). Burton's new theory about the Nile arising from Lake Tanganyika was given in a paper read to the Royal Geographical Society on November 14, 1864. It is reprinted in *The Nile Basin*.

The Times of September 17, 1864, and of the days following, gives an account of Speke's death and the inquest, as well as its own comments on the affair. Mrs. Dorothy Middleton of the Royal Geographical Society has very kindly supplied a copy of Fuller's letter to the newspaper in 1921. H. B. Thomas has a paper on Speke's death in *The Uganda Journal* for March 1941.

CHAPTER 5. Dorothy Middleton's *Baker of the Nile* (The Falcon Press, 1949) is the most recent life of the explorer to appear, and has been consulted. The remainder of this chapter is based mainly upon his *Albert N'yanza*.

CHAPTER 6. Livingstone's three major works *Missionary Travels and Researches in South Africa* (1857), *Narrative of an Expedition to the Zambesi and its Tributaries* (1865) and *Last Journals* (1874)—each in two volumes and published by John Murray—have been consulted, together with Stanley's *How I Found Livingstone* (Sampson Low, 1872). The modern authorities on these last years of the explorer's life are *Livingstone's Last Journey* by Professor Coupland (Collins, 1945) and *David Livingstone, His Life and Letters* by George Seaver (Butterworth Press, 1957). Gaetano Casati's description of Stanley appears in his *Ten Years in Equatoria and the Return with Emin Pasha* (2 vols., Frederick Warne & Co., 1891).

CHAPTER 7. The quotation about the tribesmen on the Upper Nile is taken from *The Heart of Africa* by Georg Schweinfurth (Sampson Low, 1873). Thomson's comment on his wanderings occurred in a letter written just before he died in London in 1895 to his brother, the Rev. J. B. Thomson. There is an interesting note on Ernest Linant de Bellefonds and Stanley's appeal for Christian missionaries to come to Uganda by H. B. Thomas in *The Uganda Journal* for July 1934. For the rest this chapter is based chiefly upon Stanley's *Through the Dark Continent* (2 vols., Sampson Low, 1878).

CHAPTER 8. Sir Evelyn Baring's comments on Ismail are taken from his *Modern Egypt* (Macmillan, 1908) which is a valuable book for all events in Egypt and the Sudan from the eighteen-seventies onwards, to the end of the century and beyond. *The Great Canal at Suez* by Percy Fitzgerald (Tinsley Brothers, 1872) gives a brief account of the enterprise and its background, but a search of the contemporary newspapers who sent correspondents to the opening, especially the *New York Herald*, has proved rather disappointing. Somehow their many pages of fine print do not manage to convey the flavour of the day. One regrets very much that Lady Duff Gordon, who was then on the Nile, did not attend the celebrations, for she had revealing things to say about everything else she saw in Egypt. She is especially tart about Ismail and the plight of the fellaheen. Baker's expedition is fully described in his *Ismailia, a Narrative of the Expedition to Central Africa for the Suppres-*

sion of the Slave Trade (2 vols., Macmillan, 1874). It is almost as good a book as the *Albert N'yanza*.

CHAPTER 9. Coupland's *The Exploitation of East Africa 1856–90* (Faber and Faber, 1939) goes very fully into Kirk's career in Zanzibar and such matters as the slave-trade and the McKillop raid. Kirk's relations with Mutesa in Buganda are also discussed by Sir John Gray in the *Uganda Journal* for March 1951. A lively account of Zanzibar in the eighteen-seventies is given in *Uganda and the Egyptian Sudan*, written by the two missionaries, the Rev. C. T. Wilson and R. W. Felkin (Sampson Low, 1882). Winwood Reade's description of Cairo will be found in an introduction he wrote to Dr. Schweinfurth's *Heart of Africa,* and the quotation from Stanley is taken from his *In Darkest Africa or the Quest, Rescue and Retreat of Emin, Governor of Equatoria* (Sampson Low, 1890).

The Gordon bibliography is vast. Apart from Lytton Strachey's essay in *Eminent Victorians,* the principal books about him that have been consulted in the writing of this and subsequent chapters are Bernard M. Allen's *Gordon and the Sudan* (Macmillian, 1951), Wilfrid Scawen Blunt's *Gordon in Khartoum* (Stephen Swift, 1911) and his *Secret History of the British Occupation of Egypt* (Unwin, 1907), Cromer's *Modern Egypt, Colonel Gordon in Central Africa* edited by George Birkbeck Hill (de la Rue, 1881), *Letters of General C. G. Gordon to his sister M. A. Gordon* (Macmillan, 1888), the introduction to *The Journals of Major-General C. G. Gordon, C. B., at Khartoum,* edited by A. Egmont Hake (Kegan Paul, 1885), and Romolo Gessi's *Seven Years in the Sudan* (Sampson Low, 1892). Colonel C. Chaillé-Long's controversial references to the General are to be found in his three books, *Naked Truths of Naked People* (Sampson Low, 1876), *Three Prophets* (1884) and *My Life in Four Continents* (Hutchinson, 1912). Dr. Allen's *Gordon and the Sudan* contains a fascinating inquiry into the errors—especially the error about Gordon's heavy drinking—in Strachey's essay. He makes it clear beyond all reasonable doubt that Chaillé-Long was lying. The *Sudan Notes and Records,* Vol. X, 1927, contains some then unpublished letters of Gordon, and H. B. Thomas has a paper on 'Gordon's Farthest South in Uganda' in 1876 in *The Uganda Journal* for April 1938.

CHAPTER 10. All the books listed directly above have been consulted for this chapter, and in addition Dr. Wilhelm Junker's *Travels in Africa* (3 vols., Chapman and Hall, 1890).

CHAPTER 11. Cromer in his *Modern Egypt* and Blunt in his *Secret History* deal, from their opposite points of view, with the British occupation of Egypt. The Mahdi and his rising have been best described in one of the earliest books on the subject, Wingate's *Mahdiism and the Egyptian Sudan* (Macmillan, 1891). For a description of the Mahdi himself and his followers the books written by the two Austrian prisoners have been relied upon—Father Joseph Ohrwalder's *Ten Years' Captivity in the Mahdi's Camp* (Sampson Low, 1892) and Rudolf C. Slatin's *Fire and Sword in the Sudan 1879–95* (Edward Arnold, 1896). *Letters from Khartoum* by Frank Power, the British Consul and *Times* correspondent, (Sampson Low, 1885) is a fresh and revealing little book. It gives an intimate picture of life in Khartoum both at the time of the Hicks expedition and during the earlier part of the siege in 1884.

CHAPTER 12. Cromer, Blunt, Allen, Strachey and Frank Power in their books listed above, and Gordon himself (in his letters) all deal with the incidents leading up to Gordon's appointment and his arrival at Khartoum. The quotation from Winston Churchill is taken from his *The River War* (Longmans Green, 1899).

CHAPTER 13. The same authorities have again been consulted, though Gordon's own *Journals*, of course, give the best account of the siege.

CHAPTER 14. Wingate, as chief of intelligence in Cairo, made a long and careful investigation into the fall of Khartoum. He interrogated witnesses like Bordeini Bey, he attended the court martial which inquired into the matter in Cairo, he saw all the official documents of the Wolseley expedition and himself translated from the Arabic such of the Mahdi's papers as reached Egypt. The results of this long and painstaking work appear in his *Mahdiism and the Egyptian Sudan*, and in a paper he wrote for the *Sudan Notes and Records* in 1930. No two accounts of Gordon's death precisely agree. Even as late as 1899 the German trader, Charles Neufeld, in his *A Prisoner of the Khaleefa, Twelve Years Captivity in the Sudan* (Chapman and Hall), was flatly denying statements made by his fellow-prisoners Slatin, Ohrwalder and others. He denies, for example, that Gordon ever used a gun on the Palace roof but insists that he fought his way down into the garden, dispatching many of the tribesmen before he died. In the main the account here given follows Wingate. The quotation from the missionary, Alexander Mackay, is taken from *Mackay of Uganda* by his sister, published by Hodder and Stoughton in 1890.

CHAPTER 15. Slatin, Ohrwalder and Neufeld have all given first-hand accounts of life in the Sudan under the Khalifa, and Wingate has collated the intelligence reports up to 1890 in his *Mahdiism and the Egyptian Sudan*. Dr. P. M. Holt's *The Mahdist State in the Sudan* 1881–98 (Oxford, 1958) is a more detached study of the same subject, compiled largely from Arabic sources.

CHAPTER 16. The chief authorities consulted upon the closing years of the century in East Africa and Uganda are *The Missionary Factor in East Africa* by Roland Oliver (Longmans Green, 1952), *The Rise of our East African Empire* by F. D. Lugard (2 vols., Blackwood, 1893), and *Lugard, The Years of Adventure 1858–98*, by Margery Perham (Collins, 1956). Coupland's *Exploitation of East Africa* and *Uganda* by Thomas and Scott have already been mentioned. Harry Johnston's *Uganda Protectorate* also covers much of the same ground. Alexander Mackay's letters throw a great deal of light upon life in Buganda, and Mutesa's declining years. King Mwanga is dealt with in *The*

Uganda Journal by T. B. Fletcher in its issue of October 1936.

CHAPTER 17. Stanley's *In Darkest Africa, or the Quest, Rescue and Retreat of Emin, Governor of Equatoria*, the various books by his subordinates, and *Emin Pasha, His Life and Work*, compiled from his journals, letters, scientific notes and official documents by Georg Schweitzer with an introduction by R. W. Felkin, give us the fullest account we are ever likely to have of this expedition. Particular reference, however, should be made to *The Other Side of the Emin Pasha Relief Expedition* by H. R. Fox Bourne (Chatto & Windus, 1891), for it reveals the extent of the animosity towards Stanley that was aroused in England. Emin's life in Equatoria is also described in detail in a collection of his journals and letters translated from the German by Mrs. Felkin and published as *Emin Pasha in Central Africa* by George Philip in 1888.

CHAPTER 18. Emin's negotiations with the British and German East Africa Companies at Bagamoyo are mentioned in the *Foreign Office Correspondence respecting Zanzibar*, 1890, No. 37, and his death is recorded by Schweitzer in his *Emin Pasha, his Life and Work*. The Omdurman campaign is admirably described by Sir Philip Magnus in his *Kitchener, Portrait of an Imperialist* (John Murray, 1958), and the references to Kitchener in this chapter are largely taken from that work and from Cromer's *Modern Egypt*. Of first-hand accounts we have Winston Churchill's *The River War* (Longmans Green, 1899)—a fantastically early date for a living writer to look back upon—which surely must be regarded as a classic of war reporting and, among a number of other accounts, G. W. Steevens's *With Kitchener to Khartoum* (Blackwood, 1898). The Fashoda incident has been described on the French side with some understandable feeling, notably by Robert de Caix in his *Fachoda: La France et l'Angleterre* (Librairie Africaine et Coloniale, Paris, 1899) and Jacques Delbecque in his *La Vie du Général Marchand* (Hachette, 1936). Their view of the case has been integrated here with the accounts given by

Cromer, Churchill and, more recently, Sir Philip Magnus. Wingate's despatch describing the death of the Khalifa was published in the *London Gazette* on January 30, 1900, and a facsimile of the document has been most kindly supplied by Mr. D. W. King, the War Office Librarian in London. The quotation from Harry Johnston is taken from *The Uganda Protectorate*.

EPILOGUE. The Burton quotation is from his *Lake Regions of Central Africa*.

INDEX

Wilson, Sir C. Rivers, 211n., 231

Wilson, the Rev. C. T., 395

Wingate, Major F. R., 224-225, 271, 305, 306, 357, 369, 390, 396, 397, 399

Wingate, Orde, 176

With Kitchener to Khartoum (Steevens), 398

Wolseley, Sir Garnet (Lord), 220, 235, 237, 238, 255, 256, 261, 263, 269, 271, 272, 273, 274, 278, 289, 291, 293, 296, 305, 353, 356, 357, 358, 359, 385, 397

Zambesi River, 110n., 116

Zanzibar, 15-17, 19-23, 26, 31, 32, 33, 35, 36, 39, 48, 49, 50, 55, 58, 66, 69, 72, 90, 114, 115, 116, 117, 122, 123, 125, 126, 128, 130, 136, 143, 144, 153, 169-174, 187, 188, 189, 199, 208, 309, 310, 316, 320, 321, 322, 324, 325, 328, 329, 330, 334, 337, 341, 345, 346, 348, 376-378, 387, 392, 395

—Sultans of, *see* Seyyid Said, Seyyid Majid bin Said, Barghash, Sayyid Khalifa

Zanzibar, City, Island and Coast (Burton), 71, 91, 391

Zeraf, Bahr-el, 96, 158, 391

Zobeir Pasha, 196-198, 199, 202, 203, 205, 207, 233, 238, 239, 241, 246, 247, 248, 250, 263, 271, 272, 293, 329, 369, 375, 392

Created in response to the interest in the new Africa which has so recently and so dramatically sprung to the world's attention.

AFRICAN INDEPENDENCE

Contains a series of original and definitive articles on the geographical, historical and administrative backgrounds of the fledgling African nations, together with a frank assessment of the dangers and difficulties—both political and economic—that lie ahead.

Countries covered include: SENEGAL ● MALI ● IVORY COAST ● GHANA ● VOLTAIC REPUBLIC ● DAHOMEY ● NIGER ● SIERRA LEONE ● LIBERIA ● CAMEROON ● NIGERIA ● CHAD ● THE CONGO ● GABON ● CENTRAL AFRICAN REPUBLIC

Edited by Peter Judd

A LAUREL ORIGINAL   75c

"I'm afraid I can't marry you, because I shall never marry again."

There, it was said! And if Dacre was anywhere near as kind as she thought him he would let her return to her room without further argument. But it was then that she discovered Dacre wasn't so kind as she had believed and that he did want a further explanation!

"It's not just me?" he inquired quietly.

Dear God, she loved him! If anyone, it would be him. "No," she answered.

"Then why, Josy," he wanted to know, "do you think you will never marry again?"

Dear Reader,

If you enjoyed Belvia's story, *The Sister Secret,* published in November 1995 (Harlequin Romance #3385), you'll love Josy's story—told here in the exciting sequel, *A Wife in Waiting.*

Belvia and Josy Fereday are twins. Although they look alike, they are as different as chalk and cheese in personality: Josy has always been painfully shy, whilst Belvia—well, she isn't afraid of speaking her mind! But when sisters are in a tight spot, they stick together.

As we found out in *The Sister Secret,* Belvia has found her husband, and now Josy realizes that she is going to have to put her own disastrous first marriage behind her and stand on her own two feet. Luckily, Dacre Banchereau is there to help steady her....

Take a chance on Dacre, Josy—dare to dream!

The Editors,
Harlequin Romance

A Wife in Waiting
Jessica Steele

Harlequin Books

TORONTO • NEW YORK • LONDON
AMSTERDAM • PARIS • SYDNEY • HAMBURG
STOCKHOLM • ATHENS • TOKYO • MILAN
MADRID • WARSAW • BUDAPEST • AUCKLAND

ISBN 0-373-03416-4

A WIFE IN WAITING

First North American Publication 1996.

CHAPTER ONE

JOSY looked through a window of the cross-channel ferry and let go a shaky sigh. Albeit that she would be back from France by Christmas, she had made the break, had made that decision to leave the home she had shared with her father and, hopefully, to start a new kind of life.

Although she had to admit that she felt extremely nervous about what lay in front of her, Josy could not help but be pleased that she had made the decision she had—long delayed though that decison had been. In fact so delayed that it was still a wonder to her that Dacre Banchereau had waited all this while. Particulary since she had agreed to take the job for only six months. She realised she had the family connection to thank for that.

Abruptly she switched her thoughts away from that family connection, and mused instead on how few were the decisions she had ever had to make. She reckoned she could count them on the fingers of one hand.

Her first decision, though panicky, had been to stay home and keep house for her widowed father when she had left school. Some years later she and her twin, Belvia, had reached twenty-one and had come into an inheritance from their much loved mother who had died when they were sixteen.

Josy had bought a car, and decided also to purchase a horse. Dear, dear Hetty—it had been a wrench leaving her, but the next six months would go quickly, and Tracey up at the commercially run stables where Hetty was per-

manently housed had promised to look after her as if
she were her own, and Josy knew she could trust her.

Her lovely brown eyes clouded over as thoughts of the
stables inevitably triggered off other memories—memories she did not wish to dwell on but memories which
she could not always turn her mind from, memories that
returned so constantly to crucify her.

It had been up at the stables where she had met Marc,
a shy, unassuming Frenchman. Marc had worked there.
She had met him—and had made the biggest decision
of all. Last year in early June she had married him.

She choked down a knot of emotion. They had gone
to his parents in a village some miles from Nantes for
their honeymoon—but before they had been married
twenty-four hours Marc was dead. He had been killed
in a riding accident and had been dead over ten months
now—eleven in two weeks' time—and still she was
haunted by her own inadequacies.

She tried not to think about it, to concentrate on this
new life she had determined that she must make for
herself. She knew that she would never marry again, yet
at twenty-three she felt that she had to get out and start
to do something with her life. She did not want to go
on being her father's housekeeper. And, after the des-
picable way he had used her—but more outrageously her
sister Belvia—for his own devious ends, Josy felt she
owed him nothing.

It was partly for Belvia too that she had decided to
leave England for a while—Belvia, who had been so
wonderfully good to her. This was Belvia's first year of
marriage, and to Josy's mind her sister more than deserved that she did not have to worry about her. It was
important to Josy that her twin had this time with
Latham, her husband, completely worry-free.

Dacre Banchereau, Marc's cousin, a banker whom she had met only once, had been in England on business at the end of September and had made a courtesy call on her. Whereas her French was the schoolgirl variety, and all but forgotten through lack of use, Dacre had spoken English with barely a trace of an accent. And, when all her life she had been plagued by a most disabling and unwanted shyness, she had somehow found Dacre far easier to talk to than most other strangers she'd met.

It could have been, of course, that because he had been a guest in her home she had felt honour-bound to make something of an effort—good manners pushing her to invite him in and offer him refreshment.

All her inhibitions had been out in full force, however, when, glancing at her over the rim of his coffee-cup, he had enquired kindly, 'You are well, Josy?'

She did not like to have anyone's personal attention on her. 'Yes, of course,' she'd replied stiffly.

But, before she had been able to think up anything to say that would take his by now steady scrutiny from her, he'd replaced his cup in his saucer and remarked, 'You are very pale—do you get out in the air?'

'There's the garden. The shopping. The—the...' Her voice faded.

'You still have your horse at the stables,' he put in quietly, when she seemed totally stuck for words.

'Hetty. Yes,' she replied stiltedly.

'You manage to ride her every day?'

She did not want him questioning her; she wanted him to go. But he was a guest, was Marc's cousin and, though he was ten years older than her husband's twenty-five years, she knew from her conversations with Marc that there had been a bond between the two as of brothers.

'No,' she replied.

'Every other day?' Dacre suggested.

'No,' she replied again. And, to save him asking, Every week, every other week? went on, 'I haven't ridden at all since I came back—fr-from France, I mean.'

There followed a quite lengthy pause, and again she wanted the tall, good-looking Frenchman gone. But all at once, as she watched, she would have sworn that he lost some of his colour. There was certainly a trace of shock in his voice anyway when abruptly, bluntly, he questioned harshly, 'You are with child?'

'*No*! *No*!' she denied sharply, crimson colour staining her previously pale cheeks. 'I . . .' She turned her head from him, anguish again crucifying her. 'No,' she said once more, her voice a mere whisper this time. Oh, how she wished that she *was* with child—that she *was* pregnant. Oh, if only that were so then she would be rid forever of this torment of guilt at the fact that she had been unable to give herself to Marc.

'Forgive me; please don't be distressed!'

Josy came away from the torture of her memories to see that Dacre no longer appeared shocked, but was looking truly regretful that he had upset her.

'It—w-was a natural assumption, I suppose,' she managed to reply, her good manners holding up when what she wanted to do was to dash from the room rather than stay in what she felt was a strained atmosphere.

She flicked a nervous glance to the watching, observing, grey-eyed man. He seemed to be missing not a thing. Then suddenly, as she looked at him, he smiled a smile of such charm and ease that she stared at him in fascination and all at once forgot to feel strained.

'But you still like horses?' he commented in friendly fashion, swiftly changing the subject back to horses.

'Oh, yes, I love them.' She smiled shyly back, once more finding him easier than most to talk with. Then she saw a light of something almost speculative come into his eyes. It worried her a little.

But his expression was relaxed when unhurriedly he questioned, 'I wonder—and I hope you won't mind my asking—if you could help me?'

'Help you?' she queried. 'How?'

'It's to do with a couple of horses I own,' Dacre replied. 'I live in a very isolated area in the Loire valley—'

'You don't live in Nantes near your aunt and uncle?' she questioned impulsively—Dacre Banchereau had been there at the airport to meet their plane—she had assumed that he lived close by.

'My weekend home is a couple of hours' drive from Nantes, in a place near Saumur. During the week I live and work in Paris.'

'But—you were visiting Marc's parents the day Marc and I . . .' Her voice dried up. Oh, Marc, Marc, Marc. She should never have married him. If they hadn't married they wouldn't have gone to France, and he—

'I was at my weekend home on the day my aunt Sylvie and uncle Philippe received an early morning call from Marc, during which he told them he was coming home that day and bringing someone very special with him,' Dacre revealed, his look alert to the changing, shadowed expressions on her face. 'My aunt in particular was extremely excited. She had the strongest feeling that she was about to meet her future daughter-in-law.'

Josy had known about Marc's phone call, but not the rest of it, and while part of her did not want to hear any more there was another part of her that seemed to need to know more. She'd had plenty of time to think since Marc's death, and only now did she realise that, with Marc having loved horses even more than she did, horses had seemed to be their sole topic of conversation.

'Marc's mother rang you?' she asked.

'She had already phoned my mother, who, during the course of the conversation, said I was not in Paris but at home clearing up a few matters prior to starting a two-week vacation the next day. As soon as Aunt Sylvie had finished that call she rang me, insisting nothing would do but—because I was going away and would miss you and Marc—that I drive over to meet the woman who she was sure was her son's fiancée.' Dacre looked steadily at her for a long, long moment, and then commented, 'The surprise to all of us was that you were already his wife.'

'We didn't mean to hurt anyone!' Josy blurted out in an unhappy rush. 'Neither Marc nor I wanted a big wedding and—'

'My dear, you didn't hurt anyone,' he cut in to soothe understandingly. 'We who are of Marc's family knew of his preference for horses rather than human beings. When we met you we saw that Marc had been exceedingly lucky in that he had found someone with the same reserved temperament as himself.'

Lucky! How could Marc have been lucky? He had married her—and died. 'I . . .' she began, but felt choked suddenly and could not go on.

She fought desperately hard to get herself back together again, not to break down in front of this man who, for all he was of Marc's family, was a stranger, and as Dacre waited silently, watchfully and patiently she was grateful to him that, observing her emotional state, he gave her the time she needed in which to regain her control.

Then it was that he gave her something else to think about when he continued, 'To go back to the great help you could be to me. I live in a very isolated location, as I mentioned and, since I need someone to look after my horses, and with you loving horses so much—' He broke off. Then, looking at her with a steady grey gaze, he asked, 'I don't suppose you'd be interested in the job?'

'No!' she replied before he could draw another breath.

'It would be too isolated for you?'

'It isn't that,' Josy answered, and, realising that her manners had slipped and that her refusal had been too blunt, went on, 'I think I should like very much to live in an isolated area, but...'

'But you've no wish to live in France?'

It wasn't even that. 'I th-think I might like to live in France,' she told him honestly, and, starting to feel a mite panicky, added, 'But I couldn't come—I keep house for my father. He—'

'You're entitled to a life of your own, Josy,' he interrupted, and there was that something not to be put off in his tone that disturbed her.

'I know,' she replied, only just holding down her panic. 'But—but—I told you, I don't ride now. I've had nothing to do with horses since Marc died.'

For long, long moments after these words had left her Dacre Banchereau just sat silently looking at her. And then very quietly he let fall, 'Don't you think that you should?' She opened her mouth to say no, but, still talking quietly, he went on to state that just because Marc had died while out riding he would not have wanted her to deny herself the sport of riding which they had both loved, ending, 'And, talking of horses, are you now going to show me the stables where my cousin worked?'

'Stables?' she gasped, oblivious of his level-eyed gaze. She had avoided the stables like the plague since she had returned from France almost four months ago. 'I—I— I don't go to the stables! I haven't been to the stables since I got back!' she stated agitatedly.

'Then I think,' Dacre replied calmly, 'that it's time that you did.'

Josy stared at him, to her astonishment feeling quite angry with him. She, who seldom ever felt anything so positive as anger, realised that she felt astonishingly angry with him and his interference.

'I...' she began defiantly, and saw his grey glance go to the angry sparks flashing in her eyes—as if her anger surprised him as much as it did her. And as she remembered some of her own recent thoughts and feelings on the subject of the stables—only just lately she had started to wonder herself if she should try and do the self-same thing that he was suggesting—suddenly her anger fizzled out. Her sister had been little short of an angel—exercising Hetty every day for her, loving, protecting and caring for her. But many had been the times over the last week or two when Josy had thought that she wasn't being fair to Belvia—that she really should make an effort. 'D-do you really want to—to see where Marc worked?' she heard herself ask.

Dacre's firm gaze held hers. She then saw that steady look move over her pale, unblemished complexion, rest on her long fair hair with its hint of red, before it came back to her large, deeply brown eyes. 'Yes,' he said, looking straight into them. 'I really do.'

Josy clenched her hands tightly as she fought to find the courage she would need. She owed it to her dear twin, who had done so much for her, to be strong. She owed it to Marc—oh, my heavens, how she owed it to

Marc. And because of Marc, whose family had lost him, she owed it very much to this man Dacre Banchereau, who had loved him more as a younger brother than a cousin, to be strong and to do as he asked and show him where Marc had worked and been happy.

'C-could you—would you w-wait while I go and get changed?' she asked.

'Of course,' he replied kindly.

Josy left the room, but when she returned she had changed not from her everyday dress into a smarter outfit but—and it had taken all of her courage to do it—was wearing her riding clothes.

Dacre was on his feet. 'R-ready?' Josy asked jerkily, saw his glance flick over the long length of her legs in their well-fitting jodhpurs and had her answer when he joined her at the door.

They went to the stables in his car, and Josy silently owned to feeling all strung up and tense when, leaving him to follow, she went looking for Hetty. But the moment she saw her so, for the first time in almost four months, Josy felt something in her start to come back to life.

'Oh, Hetty, Hetty,' she crooned, the fact that Dacre Banchereau was but a yard or so behind her entirely lost to her as warmth for the horse flooded her heart. She hugged Hetty and laid her face against her neck, and Hetty whinnied in approval.

How long she stood there stroking the mare, a glow of loving about her, life entering her being, Josy did not know. But, her eyes still alight, some slight sound made her turn around, and then it was that she remembered Dacre.

She looked at him, felt shy, but because for the first time in an age she had experienced a small fraction of inner peace she just had to say a quiet, 'Thank you.'

And he understood, it seemed, for he just looked back at her, his eyes travelling over her expressive face. Then softly he hinted, 'It would be a pity not to put those jodhpurs to good use.'

In truth Josy was not at all sure why she had changed into her riding clothes, save that she always dressed like this when she came to the stables. But Hetty looked willing and eager, and as more life lit Josy's eyes so she found that she was asking, 'Will you wait?'

'I will wait,' Dacre confirmed solemnly, and the next she knew was that he was helping her to saddle up.

And wait for her he did, and when, with a hint of pink in her otherwise pale cheeks, Josy returned, he helped her unsaddle Hetty and attend to her before he drove Josy back to her home.

Outside her house she wondered if she should ask him in. But in the close confines of his car she felt shy again, and was not sure that she wanted him inside her home a second time. However, good manners being what they were, she was about to invite him in just the same when he got out of the car, came round and opened the passenger door. And as she got out and stood with him on the pavement for a moment he asked her to, 'Think about my suggestion, Josy. I need someone reliable to look after my horses.'

'I—' she began to decline.

'Think about it,' he urged. 'Think about it most carefully. If you feel you can come for only a short while— say six months—think about it.'

'I...' Again she was about to refuse.

'I'm hardly ever there. Some weekends I don't make it at all,' he informed her. And with a disarming smile added, 'I should feel happy to know that a member of my family was there.'

How nice he made that sound! 'I'll—er—think about it,' she heard herself promise.

And Dacre went away, and she did think about it, right until the next morning when Belvia came home from spending the weekend with a friend. Barely had she told her sister all about Dacre's visit when Latham Tavenner came looking for Bel. And then—staggeringly—Belvia, with an adoring Latham by her side, told her that they were getting married.

Josy gasped at the shock of that and later, when her sister told her all she had to tell her—including what their father had been up to in his endeavours to get Latham to invest in his company—there was no space in which to think about Dacre's suggestion that she go to France to work for him.

Five days later, as September gave way to October—and after a whirlwind of shopping and arranging—Belvia and Latham married. Belvia looked radiant, and Latham looked as if he could not believe that she had not only agreed to marry him but had just said so in church.

And, for Belvia and the love she had for her, Josy managed to overcome her shyness to be her bridesmaid—only Belvia and Latham being aware that because of her married status she was more matron of honour than bridesmaid.

Josy had never told her father that she had married Marc. In fact her father had never met Marc. She had wanted to bring him home one time, but her father was a snob of the first water and had looked down his nose at the idea of her bringing a mere groom into his home.

And Josy had thought too much of Marc to introduce him into such an atmosphere.

She'd no idea then, though, that because he was averse to meeting people Marc had opted for a simple life when in actual fact he came from quite a wealthy background. Only when they had been married and on their honeymoon flight to tell his parents of their marriage had Marc confided about the businesses his father owned, and the fact that he had no need to work at all unless he wanted to.

Her head was still filled with thoughts of Marc, and of Belvia and Latham and their wonderful happiness a week later. She also thought a great deal about her father and his treachery. And then she started to think too of Dacre Banchereau's job offer.

It would mean leaving her father to look after himself, but after the way he had behaved Josy felt little compunction about doing that. She had planned to leave home anyway when she and Marc returned from their honeymoon, though she had planned to look in on her old home daily to check her father's larder and his laundry. But, as Bel had said only a couple of weeks ago, 'Let him pay for a housekeeper.'

Suddenly it all seemed possible—if she dared. For Belvia, and for herself. It would mean leaving Hetty, but she was such a lovable mare that everybody wanted to spoil her—and would. And it would only be for six months—Josy was certain about that as she began to look on Dacre's offer as a lifeline.

She felt she needed to get away, to take stock, to make the break from her domineering father. What better chance? If she went to France there would be no way that he would ring her when he couldn't find something or other and expect her to come home and find it for him.

Some weeks ago she had started to think that she couldn't go on like this, that she must make more of an effort. Whilst still swamped by guilt, she was better than she had been, and over the worst of the shock, at what had happened, which had so rocked her.

Those first few weeks after Marc's death—his funeral, she and Belvia flying home and Belvia covering for her so that their father should know none of it—had passed for the most part in a traumatised haze.

It was only lately that Josy had begun to realise how much she owed her sister. Bel had at once dropped everything to rush to France to be with her, had supported her, and back in England she had defended her, been an avenging angel for her—and Josy knew that she would be forever grateful to her.

But Belvia was married now, and while there would always be a strong bond between them Josy realised that it was time to let go. She took a deep breath and at that moment determined that she would take up Dacre Banchereau's offer.

Then the phone rang, and to her amazement it was him! 'How are you, Josy?' he enquired.

'I'm very well,' she replied politely.

'Can I hope you have made a decision in my favour?' he asked, without further ado.

Josy took a shaky breath, but the determination of her decision a moment ago was still warm, and while her nerve held out, with a 'neck or nothing' kind of gulp, she told him, 'I should like to—um—take the job for six months.' The taut kind of silence that followed was equally unnerving—so much so that Josy found herself blurting out, 'I don't speak much French—well, hardly any at all, really.'

'That's no problem,' Dacre's voice came back charmingly in her ears. 'Would you like me to come for you?'

'Oh, no.' She at once rejected the idea. 'I can come by myself.'

'When?' he wanted to know, now that he had her acceptance of the job seeming to be impatient for her to start.

'I don't—er—can I let you know? I—um—haven't told my father yet.'

'You won't let him change your mind?'

'No, I won't do that,' she promised, and heard Dacre all businesslike as he asked her if she had a pen and gave her his telephone numbers where she could contact him.

In the event, however, over six months were to pass before Josy was able to keep her promise and leave England for France. To start with, her father was not at all pleased to hear that the streamlined running of his existence was going to be interfered with.

'I don't want to employ a housekeeper,' he snapped angrily.

Josy looked at him and thought of the many times she had given in to his likes and dislikes. She thought of the dreadful life he had given her mother. And she thought of his deviousness and—for only the second time in her life—she stood up to him. 'The house is going to get very untidy without one,' she told him.

'Did your sister put you up to this?' he snarled.

'Belvia's still away on her honeymoon,' she reminded him.

'You're horse-mad!' he attacked nastily—and the next day went down with a heavy bout of flu.

Josy rang Dacre. 'I'm sorry, my father's ill with flu. I don't know when I'll be able to come.'

'You've told him you're coming to France?'

'Yes—but... If you don't want to wait... I mean, it's only a temporary job, after all. If you want to get somebody else...' she offered, seeing her chance of going getting away from her.

'You're family—I'll wait,' Dacre replied.

Never had she known flu to last so long. She was still nursing her father well into November. 'Don't you think you should try to go into work?' she dared to hint.

'Latham Tavenner's had the nerve to send his accountants in!'

'That's natural enough, surely, since he intends to invest a tremendous sum in your company?' Josy suggested fairly.

'Well, they can do it without getting any answers from me!' he declared spitefully. 'If they ring tell them I'm indisposed.'

Josy rang Dacre Banchereau again in December. 'I should still like to come, but I don't feel I can leave my father alone over Christmas and New Year,' she stated.

'I'll see you in January,' he clipped, sounding not at all pleased, and put the phone down.

Only then, as she began to panic that the job was going away from her, did Josy realise that she really wanted this chance to change her life. Much to her relief, however, Dacre rang her on Christmas Day and seemed much more friendly.

'I wanted to wish you the best Christmas you can have,' he stated, and Josy started to feel quite warm towards him, knowing that he must have been thinking of Marc and realising that she must be feeling particularly low at being without him at this festive time.

She didn't want his sympathy, though. She was still weighed down by guilt—and didn't want to think about it. 'Thank you,' she replied. 'Have a good Christmas.' She had nothing more to add, so rang off—and oddly found that she was wondering in which of his two homes he was spending Christmas—and who with. He was a good-looking, virile, sophisticated man—it went without saying that he would not be spending it alone.

At one time such a man would have terrified her. But Belvia and Latham—sometimes with Latham's own sister, sometimes not—frequently urged her to dine with them, and the more she got to know her sophisticated and worldly-wise brother-in-law, the more she began to feel less constrained and more comfortable in a sophisticated man's company.

She made another call to Dacre in January, to tell him that she was having trouble finding a suitable housekeeper for her father.

'Please feel free to forget about your job offer if you feel I'm messing you about,' she ended, and prayed hard that his feelings about her being family would hold up—because by then, while still nervous to some extent, she had started to feel quite excited at the prospect of going to Dacre's home.

'You insult my French honour,' he replied—and she realised that he was teasing.

'Er—g-goodbye,' she said, and fancied that she liked his teasing.

It was in February that her sister took a hand in interviewing the next set of potential employees and decided that a stern-eyed Mrs Vale was ideal for the job of keeping house for their ill-humoured father.

'Mrs Vale has to give notice to her present employer,' Belvia said when they had seen her out. 'So I've arranged for her to start on the first of April.'

'Father will want to see her to give the OK first,' Josy told her lovely blonde-haired sister.

'Tough!' Belvia laughed. To Josy's mind she seemed to have grown more beautiful than ever since her marriage. 'I've told Mrs Vale that her salary will be paid monthly into her bank, and I'll arrange that since the old skinflint is likely to use "Can't afford it" as another excuse. Now, you just get on that phone to France. You still want to go, love?'

Josy nodded, and because she thought it only fair to Mrs Vale to stay with her for a couple of weeks she decided to give Dacre a date in the middle of April.

'And that's definite?' Dacre asked.

'Most definitely definite,' she replied, and laughed— and when there was a short silence on the other end realised that to hear her laugh must have surprised him as much as it had surprised her. She had laughed little lately. 'I—um—I'll make my own way,' she added quickly. 'Is there anyone I should see if you're not home that weekend?'

'I'll make a point of being there. And I'll also send you directions,' he answered, which she thought was very nice, and then, before he rang off, he added, 'Nina and César are looking forward to seeing you.'

'Nina and César?'

'Your charges,' Dacre informed her.

'Ah—um—it's all right that I'm taking the job for only six months?' she thought to ask, after all this while still anxious at the last minute.

'Perfectly all right,' he answered evenly, and, with nothing more to be discussed between them, bade her, '*Au revoir.*'

True to his word, directions for how to get to Saumur, and very detailed directions for how to get from there to his home, arrived—and Josy started packing.

She had decided to travel on a Friday, to stay overnight in Normandy, and to drive on to Saumur and from there to Dacre's home the following morning.

It was, perhaps, with the view that her father might be unpleasant to her on her last night home that Belvia and Latham invited themselves to dinner on Thursday evening.

'You've nothing to worry about, I feel sure,' Belvia told her confidently as they were leaving. 'I haven't met Dacre Banchereau, it's true, but his parents were at Marc's funeral and they seemed lovely people.'

Josy couldn't remember them. But that was not surprising. Apart from the fact that many, many other people had been there to pay their respects, she had been in deep shock, and little else had registered but that Marc was dead and wouldn't have been if...

Belvia hugged her tightly. 'I'll miss you.' She smiled— her eyes shiny.

Latham put an arm around his wife's shoulders and held her close to him as he in turn smiled at his sister-in-law and told her, 'Remember, Jo, any problems and we can be with you within hours.'

'I'll remember,' she smiled, but did not anticipate any problems, and said goodbye to them realising that Belvia had been right when ages ago—when Josy had started to surface from her shock about Marc—she had said that her uncertainty about everything would pass. Because never would she have thought that she would so much as contemplate the step she was taking now—not only leaving home and taking a job, but a job in a foreign country!

An announcement to car drivers over the cross-channel ferry's speaker system brought Josy out of her reverie. People started to move—they had arrived in France!

She had never driven on what she thought of as the wrong side of the road before, but after her first fifteen minutes of intense concentration she discovered that there was nothing to it. She had never had any problems with driving and, while confidence had never been her strong suit, she drove with confidence and care.

Josy found the hotel she had a reservation with—one Latham's PA had arranged for her—and went up to her room, feeling she would like to phone Dacre to say that she had arrived in his country.

Shyness and a feeling that since she would be seeing him tomorrow he would probably think her an idiot held her back. She had a meal sent to her room, and went to bed.

Josy was an early riser, and was up and on her way by eight on Saturday morning. This was it; this was the start of her new life. She had made the break from home, from her father. She would see how things went, and when she returned to England—if her nerve held out—she would see about finding somewhere else to live, see about finding another job.

The remainder of the money her mother had left her was still substantial but it wouldn't last for ever. She might find a live-in job looking after horses. She'd like that. She might even be able to have Hetty with her. She'd *have* to have Hetty with her, she decided with unusual determination. It sounded a bit grand but she would truthfully be able to tell any prospective employer that her last job had been looking after a stables in France.

Josy smiled at her temerity. Grief, she hadn't started the job yet—and Dacre had only two horses. But they were stables, weren't they? She decided there and then that she was going to be more positive.

Feeling more light-hearted than she had in an age, she motored on. When she came to the sizeable town of Angers, however, some of her new-found confidence took a dip. Saumur and surrounds, she calculated, were getting on for an hour's drive away.

She had no idea what time they had lunch in Dacre's household, but she did not want to arrive slap bang in the middle of it. And even though it was over six months since she had seen Dacre Banchereau she remembered him clearly—dark-haired, grey-eyed, tall, good-looking, mid-thirties and sophisticated with it . . . and, to be painfully honest, she was starting to feel overwhelmingly shy again.

Josy left her car in a cark park in Angers and took a stroll around town. She also, and not without taking a deep breath, entered a café and ordered what she thought was a sandwich, but—her French being as poor as she had supposed—it turned out to be half a French loaf stuffed with everything one could imagine.

She was too embarrassed to leave it—yet didn't know how to start it. Then suddenly she started to get cross with herself. This was her new life. She was a new person. Two-handedly she raised the filled French bread to her mouth and began her chewing marathon.

She arrived in Saumur some time after half-past two. At three-fifteen, Dacre's directions having been faultless, she pulled up outside his house. Though 'house', she rather thought, was a misnomer. For, endorsing her knowledge that Marc came from moneyed people, in her view it was more of a manor-house. It stood in its own grounds with parkland about and not another dwelling in sight.

She loved its splendid isolation and, wondering if she had after all made a mistake with the directions, she got out of her car with Dacre's instructions in her hand. Taking her glance from the white-fronted, many-windowed, two-storeyed building, she looked from the wide expanse of drive over extensive lawns with a small wood beyond, and then checked his directions again.

Then she discovered that she had not made a mistake, and nor did she need to check the paper in her hand, for a voice called, 'Josy!' She looked up at the sound of her name, and relief flooded through her.

'Dacre,' she answered, shyness taking her as the tall Frenchman, clad in trousers, shirt and light sweater, came from the house and over the gravel drive to greet her.

Her instinctive good manners pushed their way through her shyness, and as he reached her she extended a dainty hand to him—and then she realised that she was well and truly in France, when, ignoring her out-stretched hand, Dacre extended both his hands to her. 'Welcome to my home.' He smiled, his grey eyes taking in her hair, her face and her person, clad similarly in trousers and light sweater.

Josy felt his hands on her arms, felt him drawing her closer. She tried hard not to panic, and discovered as he came yet closer that even for a man with such an athletic build he had a surprisingly broad chest. Then she felt his skin against hers as unhurriedly he kissed first one of her cheeks and then the other.

She felt hot all over. Even while her brain registered that this was the way any Frenchman would greet someone whom he considered to be a member of his family she felt hot and in need of taking in great gulps of air.

She pushed him away, saw her action register with him, and then felt awkward and embarrassed and wanted the ground to open up and swallow her. From somewhere, though—and maybe it stemmed from her earlier decision to be more positive—she managed a smile. And as his hands fell away from her, she stated, 'I'm glad to be here.' And hoped that only she knew just how much the feel of his kisses to her cheeks had disconcerted her.

CHAPTER TWO

'YOU will be tired after your journey. We'll leave your luggage until you've had some refreshment, some lunch...' Dacre went on and, shy or not, Josy just had to interrupt.

'I had lunch in Angers,' she butted in to reveal, then added quickly, rather than cause offence, 'But I'd love a cup of tea.' Oh, grief, she was in France. 'Or coffee,' she as quickly tacked on.

'We drink tea in France, too,' he teased, his eyes alight on her worried look. 'I'm sure my housekeeper has the kettle already boiling.'

Josy walked over the gravel drive with him and she started to feel more relaxed—his teasing was responsible, she guessed.

'Your journey was without mishap?' he enquired conversationally as they went through the stout front door and into an elegant hall that had a beautiful mahogany staircase that seemed to go on for ever, and divided at the top to form a crescent-shaped landing.

'Yes, thank you,' she replied politely, and walked alongside him past various closed doors until they came to one which was open and which was clearly the drawing-room door. No doubt Dacre had been taking his ease in this room when he had heard and possibly seen her car arrive.

Before they could enter the room, however, a neatly clad lady somewhere in her middle fifties appeared from around the corner of the long hall. Dacre, with a mur-

mured 'My housekeeper' for Josy's benefit, waited for
her to approach and introduced her.

Josy was normally reserved in her greetings, but as
Agathe Audoin went a tinge pink, and as Josy recognised in the housekeeper a shyness which she herself had
always endured, it triggered in her a need to put a fellow
sufferer at ease.

'*Comment allez-vous, madame*?' she dredged up a
half-forgotten French 'How are you?' and even found
a smile to go with it as she stretched out a hand to the
housekeeper.

The housekeeper's reply was to smile, shake hands and
reply with a brief something in very fast French which
was totally incomprehensible to Josy. But as Josy turned
to glance at Dacre she saw that he was looking at her as
if arrested by something.

Before she could start to feel anxious about what that
something might be, though, he was giving Agathe some
instructions and, with a start, Josy definitely picked up
the words Madame Paumier—her own married name.

Agathe went on her way, and Dacre ushered Josy into
the superb, high-ceilinged drawing-room. It was exquis-
itely furnished with lush carpets and French antique
furniture.

'Agathe will not be many minutes with your tea,' he
commented, while at the same time indicating that she
should take a seat in one of the lovely high-backed chairs.

But as she went over to one of them and sat down,
and realised that he had just given Agathe instructions
about some refreshments, she realised too that Dacre
Banchereau was not a man to pretend that he had not
noticed something when he had. For no sooner had he
taken a seat opposite her, than, looking at her, he was

remarking, 'You seemed surprised, Josy, that I should refer to you as Madame Paumier?'

There was a question there, and Josy half wished that she hadn't come. Then she caught herself up short. Good grief! Was this the way to make a fresh life—to want to bolt at the first minor hurdle? To want to run for cover the moment someone said something that touched a raw nerve? Dacre wasn't to know of her guilt, nor of the fact that she had never felt married.

'I...' she tried. There had definitely been a question in his voice. She didn't know how to answer.

'Forgive me—perhaps I'm being insensitive,' he apologised, when he could see she was stuck for words. 'You're not wearing your wedding ring, I know, but—' he broke off, and, insensitive or not, enquired, 'Is it that you prefer to be known as Miss Fereday?'

'Er...' She was sorely tempted to grab at that suggestion. But suddenly, as she looked at him, she checked, halted when the words were on her lips to say that, Yes, that was it—that in this emancipated world she preferred to be known by her single name. Somehow, as she looked at him, looked into those steady grey eyes, she felt that she could not lie to him. He made her feel that she would be letting herself down if she did. She swallowed. He shouldn't be able to do that to her. He was nothing to her but a cousin-in-law—if there was such a thing—and yet he gave her a feeling that if she was going to make any kind of a life for herself then she wasn't going to make much of a start on it by being dishonest. Somehow she was going to have to be both brave and honest—and Dacre's steady gaze seemed to refuse to allow her to be anything less. 'It—isn't that,' she replied, realising that he was patiently waiting for

her to answer. 'I—just—er—don't feel as if I've ever
been married.'

'Oh—poor Josy. I'm so sorry. I didn't mean to cause
you pain,' he at once apologised. 'You were married for
less than a day and—'

'Please don't sympathise,' she interrupted. It wasn't
right—she had no right to his sympathy. She took a shaky
breath. 'I . . .' she began, with no clear idea of what she
was going to say.

But, as if realising that to talk of her brief marriage
was upsetting her, Dacre stated soothingly, 'Marc would
have been pleased that you came to me.' And she supposed then that he had known Marc far better than she
had.

'You must miss him,' she in turn sympathised.

'There was a ten-year age-difference between us, so
naturally I had different pursuits. But our mothers are
sisters; we shared the same blood and were close—' He
broke off at the sound of a trolley being wheeled along
the hall. 'Your tea, I think,' he murmured, and went to
open the door for Agathe.

He spent a few seconds in conversation with his
housekeeper before turning his attention back to his latest
employee to ask, 'Have you your car keys, Josy? Franck,
Agathe's husband, will take your cases to your room.'

Josy wanted to protest that she could do it. She had
after all brought her luggage from her room at home
and loaded up her car without help—her father having
been in a sulk. Not that he'd have done it anyway. But
Dacre obviously employed Franck to do that sort of
thing, and she had no wish to tread on anyone's toes.
She handed over her car keys.

'Are you having tea too?' she asked of Dacre, when Agathe plus car keys had gone and everything from the trolley was laid out in front of her on a low table.

'*Certainement*,' he accepted.

She picked up a most delicate china cup and saucer, sent up a prayer that she wouldn't spill it or, even worse, drop it, and poured out some tea. 'Milk?' she enquired.

'Why not?' he replied, and she realised that she quite liked this tea-drinking, milk-taking man, who was doing his best to make her feel at home. Miraculously she poured and delivered his tea without mishap. 'I can recommend my housekeeper's pastries,' he suggested, offering her an appetising plate of cakes.

'I'm still full from lunch,' she refused, and, remembering the gargantuan repast she had struggled with in Angers, thought it possible that she would still be full up come dinnertime.

She glanced from him to one of the three long windows from where she could see parkland and woods. 'It's idyllic here,' she murmured. Already the peace and tranquillity of the place where Dacre had his home were getting to her.

'You don't think it will be too quiet for you?'

She turned to look at him, and saw that he was serious. 'Never,' she replied quietly. 'I wonder you can ever leave here.'

'Paris has its attractions too,' he replied, and suddenly, as she wondered if he had a steady girlfriend in Paris, another thought struck her. 'You're not married, are you?' she asked, and all at once went a shade of pink. 'I'm sorry; I'm being personal.'

'Josy, my dear, you're part of my family,' Dacre answered straight away, seeing her embarrassment born of shyness. 'I should like very much for us to know each other better. So, please, you must ask anything you wish to know.'

She stared at him with direct honest eyes. He had successfuly sent any embarrassment on its way and she thanked him for that. And it was kind of him to say that, because she was part of his family he wanted them to know each other better. But she had always been reluctant with friendships, and didn't quite know how she felt about anyone getting to know her better.

Josy considered him seriously, her expression unsmiling. Then she thought of Marc and remembered how—if she could only wipe away the last twenty-four hours of their knowing each other—he had been her best friend, apart from Belvia. She felt that he would have urged her to be friends with his cousin—to get to know him better and, if she could, let his cousin know her better too.

So she smiled her rare smile. 'And—*are* you married, *monsieur*?' she asked mischievously, owning to feeling slightly staggered to find suddenly that she had an imp of mischief in her.

So too did the Frenchman appear a touch taken aback. But suddenly he smiled that smile that was so charm-filled and which she had seen once before in England. 'I am not married.' He answered her question on the second time of asking. 'Nor am I seriously involved with anyone at the moment.'

'Oh,' Josy mumbled, realising that the attractions in Paris he had spoken of must be its monuments: the Louvre, Notre Dame cathedral, the world-renowned nightclubs—all in direct contrast to his home here.

Then it was that she saw how Dacre had the best of both worlds. Undoubtedly he worked hard, but when his day's work was done there was always the Paris nightlife—and whether 'seriously involved' or not, it was without question that he did not relax alone. And when his week's work was done what better pleasure than to leave the enjoyment of the bustling capital and come home here, to this serene and beautiful place?

Her tea finished, she glanced opposite and saw that he had been studying her. She looked quickly away, to his teacup reposing on the table. He had finished too.

Casually he rose from his chair. 'Would you like to see your room?'

She went with him from the drawing-room and up the thickly carpeted elegant staircase. They reached the landing where there seemed to be an equal number of rooms going to the right as to the left. Dacre led the way to the right.

'I thought you would be comfortable in this room,' he commented when about four doors along he stopped, opened a door, and stood back to allow her to enter.

And that was when Josy knew that she was to be treated as a member of the family and not as an employee. The room she had been given was not the usual kind of stable-girl's room, she was sure, and her breath caught at the beauty of it.

More French antiques, in the shape of wardrobes, chests and a dressing-table, complemented the room. There was a four-poster bed draped in cream velvet with coffee-coloured, hand-embroidered tie-backs, that matched exactly the curtains at the windows. She turned on the ankle-deep cream carpet. 'It's beautiful!' she breathed. 'A lovely room.'

Dacre stared at her rapt expression for some moments. Then very quietly he stated, 'It is my wish that you grow to be happy here.' And as he turned to check on her luggage which had been brought up Josy felt quite touched by his words.

'Thank you,' she murmured, realising that while she was nothing like the mess she had been those first few months after Marc's death she still had quite some way to go before she could be happy, and that Dacre, a more sensitive man than she had recognised, had seen that.

'I shall leave you now to rest. We'll eat at eight, but come down to the *salon* as soon as you wish.'

Again she offered her thanks, but when he had gone she knew that she would not go seeking him out until it was time to take their evening meal.

She would have liked to take a look around outside, to say hello to Nina and César, but—she glanced at her watch and saw with surprise that it was already half-past four—she was reluctant to poach on any more of Dacre's free time.

He was in her mind a good deal of the time as she investigated a door leading off her bedroom. She saw that it was a cream-coloured bathroom with fluffy cream towels with coffee-coloured embroidered hems.

She returned to her bedroom, noticing that she had a splendid view from both of the long windows. She realised uncomfortably then that Dacre was according her every respect because she was his cousin's widow.

All too clearly he had a strong sense of family, and, in his dear cousin's memory, nothing was too good for Marc's widow. Worriedly Josy paced from one window to the other. It wasn't right. She hadn't been a wife to Marc, so how right could it be that she was being housed as such?

She could feel herself starting to get agitated, and in desperate need of something to do she unlatched one of her two suitcases and set to work unpacking.

When at last both of her cases were empty, everything she had brought with her either hung up or folded away, she had worked through her agitation and, since she had determined only that morning to be positive, she had found a plus in the fact that Dacre *needed* her.

He needed someone reliable, someone he could trust to look after his horses. He needed someone who would not be put off by the isolation of his home and, with that special discernment he seemed to have—that sensitivity—he had seen that she would do splendidly.

Starting to feel very much better suddenly, but still shy enough not to want to leave her room before ten to eight, Josy remembered that he had left her so she might rest. She did not feel in the need of a rest, but... She glanced at the phone in her room, thought about ringing Belvia to say that she had safely arrived but made herself resist.

Belvia had a different sort of life now and, although they were so close that they would think of each other often, Josy was determined that her sister should enjoy this first year of her marriage to Latham without having to think and worry about her the whole while.

Having been sidetracked, she thought again of how Dacre had greeted her—'You will be tired after your journey'. Who was she to argue? She found that she was smiling as she slipped off her shoes, rolled back the beautifully embroidered bedcover, climbed on to the double four-poster and lay down.

She had not thought that she was at all sleepy, but the bed was the last word in comfort. Her last waking thought was a scrappy reasoning that with the town of Saumur—with its picturesque château on the banks of the Loire, the longest river in France—not more than half an hour's drive away then the situation where Dacre

had his home was nowhere near as isolated as it would
have been before motorised transport. She hadn't decided whether she was glad or sorry about that when
sleep claimed her.

Josy awoke with a start to see that it was a quarter to
seven. Good heavens—and she was a poor sleeper! She
yawned delicately, and guessed that there must be something magical in the air around this delightful place. And
then she remembered that dinner was at eight o'clock,
and for someone who wasn't too fussed about eating,
especially after she had eaten enough at lunchtime to
last her all day, she was starting to grow hungry—it had
to be that magical air again.

She was in the bath prior to getting ready for dinner
when she suddenly found that she was pondering what
she would wear. Good heavens, it must be that magic
again—she could not remember the last time she had
worried about what to wear.

At ten to eight she had her long fair hair neatly
brushed, the smattering of make-up she wore neatly applied and, having opted for a fine wool dress of a deep
apricot shade, she was ready to go down to dinner. Unfortunately, having felt quite hungry at seven-thirty, she
now didn't feel hungry at all, and would have much preferred by far to remain in her room until breakfast-time.

At five to eight a mixture of good manners, which
decreed unpunctuality to be a sin—especially since
Madame Audoin might already have the starter ready to
serve—together with impatience with herself and the *un*-
positive person who was trying to weaken her made Josy
leave her room.

She owned to feeling a need to hold on to the mahogany banister as she made her way down the stairs,

and in need of clutching on to it when, perhaps some slight sound having alerted him, Dacre came from the open drawing-room door as she reached the bottom stair.

She was aware of his gaze on her as he moved towards her, and she forced herself to go on.

'Your rest has done you good,' he commented pleasantly.

'I went to sleep.' The words just seemed to slip out. 'I didn't mean to—f-fall asleep, I mean—but—' She broke off, feeling dreadful. Grief, here he was, a sophisticated man, and she was prattling on. She felt gauche, ridiculous—and wanted to go home. She fell silent.

He placed a hand on her elbow, guiding her to the drawing-room. 'Perhaps an aperitif before dinner?' he suggested.

'Oh, no,' she refused straight away. 'Thank you,' she remembered her manners. The idea of sitting—or standing, for that matter—in the drawing-room with Dacre, trying to make small talk as she sipped a pre-dinner drink was destroying.

'You don't drink alcohol?' he enquired, halting at the drawing-room door and, since he still had a light hold on her elbow, causing her to halt too.

Josy looked up into cool grey eyes and felt lost for words suddenly. Then with relief she recalled her earlier thoughts on the subject of punctuality. 'It isn't that. It's—well, I've no wish to be discourteous to you, but I shouldn't like to be rude to Madame Audoin either.' She took her eyes from his to consult her watch. 'It's eight o'clock,' she advised him.

He did not move, not for a second or two, but just looked down at her. Then as a warm light entered his eyes he murmured, 'You're very sweet.' And as he bent his head a little she had the strangest notion that he was about to drop a light kiss on her cheek. Quickly she pulled back but, before she could panic, and to show just how very wrong she had been, he agreed easily, 'We must not keep Agathe waiting,' and escorted her further up the hall. And Josy knew that he would have been amazed if he'd realised how she had misread what must have been no more than a small bow in acknowledgement of her reminder of his housekeeper's efforts in the kitchen.

The dining-room was furnished as superbly as the rest of the rooms she had seen. The dining-table was a long, long affair, but only one end had been laid.

Dacre saw her seated and took his own place, and then his housekeeper was there to serve them a delicious starter of various types of mushrooms that had been marinated in wine and spices.

'This is really good,' Josy could not refrain from commenting, her non-existent appetite suddenly reawakened.

'We grow a lot of mushrooms in this area,' he informed her pleasantly. 'But this particular dish is one I believe Agathe made specially for you, to make you welcome.'

'Oh, how kind,' she responded, and felt truly touched by the housekeeper's thoughtfulness—so much so that when the shy housekeeper came in to clear away their used dishes and to serve the next course, Josy plucked up courage and plunged into, '*Merci, madame, pour bons champignons.*' And, while she felt that her 'Thank you, madam, for the good mushrooms,' was woefully inadequate for such a splendid offering, she saw that the housekeeper, who had replied something which was too fast for her to comprehend, was looking very pleased.

'Agathe has requested that you use her first name,' Dacre informed her as the housekeeper departed.

'Then I shall,' Josy answered, and although she rather thought that any alcohol used in the recipe would have evaporated in the heat of cooking she was at a loss to know why else she should find she was beginning to relax.

She certainly felt more comfortable with Dacre than she would have thought possible half an hour ago, she mused as she took her first sip from the glass of wine he had poured to go with the lamb cutlets in pastry. It could have been because he had been telling her how France's national equestrian centre, the Cadre Noir, was situated locally—anything to do with horses tended to make her forget her inhibitions.

But, whatever it was putting her at her ease—either Dacre or the subject—when he was done she found herself mentioning, 'Will my car be all right where I left it?'

'I have garaged it for you. I will show you around tomorrow morning.'

'Thank you.' She smiled, and looked forward in particular to visiting the stables.

'You have been driving long?' he enquired.

'Since I was twenty-one. I'm sorry, that doesn't answer your question. Two years,' she added, and, having just told him she was twenty-three, continued, 'Belvia, my twin sister, taught me to drive.'

'You're not identical twins?' he asked, explaining, 'I'm sure one of my family would have mentioned it had that been so.'

Her eyes clouded over. His family would have seen her and her twin together at Marc's funeral. 'No, we're not,' she confirmed, and, forcing herself through a sad moment, added, 'We feature each other, but Belvia is blonde and beautiful.'

Dacre looked at her in some surprise. 'You surely don't imagine that you are not beautiful also?' he exclaimed, and she stared at him, surprised in turn. Did Marc's cousin think her beautiful?

She decided that she didn't want this conversation. 'Belvia was married at the beginning of October and—'

'She no longer lives at home?'

Josy shook her head. 'Not now. And I'm so happy for her. She didn't hesitate to come out when I needed her, when Marc—w-was killed.'

'His parents told me of the deep shock you were in.'

She didn't want to talk about that either—and then a sudden thought struck her. 'Will Monseir and Madame Paumier be visiting you here?'

'It is most unlikely,' he replied. 'Would it worry you if they did?'

She thought about it for a few moments. 'Only in so much as to see me might, perhaps, bring back memories of their son.'

'They have happy memories of him, Josy,' Dacre told her quietly. 'They have the happiest memory of all— that you made his life complete by marrying h—'

'*Don't*!' She couldn't take it. Oh, heavens, she was going to cry!

'Oh, *ma chère*. Forgive me.' Dacre's hand whipped across the table and he grasped hers firmly. Oddly, though, as he gripped her his strength seemed to pass from him to her, so that somehow Josy found that she had managed to conquer her fear of breaking down.

'It's all right. I'm sorry. I . . .' She pulled her hand away from his.

'It is nearly a year; I thought it might help you to talk about it,' her French host murmured compassionately.

She could never talk about it. Not that! Though perhaps Dacre, who had loved Marc too, might have a need not to shut him away as if he never had existed? 'Sometimes it's all right—other times...' She let it go, but was not totally surprised when he changed the subject.

'It is very remiss of me, but I've only just realised that we never got round to discussing your salary. I will—'

'Oh, I don't want paying!' Josy exclaimed. 'Grief, it's only a couple of horses—it's hardly work.'

He stared at her in amazement. 'But of course I must pay you!' he stated authoritatively.

Josy, for all that she was extremely shy, had a spark of spirit which on a few, albeit widely-spaced occasions in the past had ignited without any assistance or fore-knowledge from her at the most unexpected moments.

She pushed her chair back and was on her feet. 'I, *monsieur*,' she reminded him loftily, with something in her—she knew not what—objecting strongly to Dacre Banchereau talking so authoritatively to her, 'am family!' And with that, while Dacre, staring at her as if he couldn't believe it, got to his feet too, she left the room.

Josy went straight up to her room, and only when she was in that safe harbour did she sink down on the bed and, as if she couldn't believe it either, wondered, Had that been her? Had that been her timid little self?

She went to bed. My word, was there something magical about this place or was there something magical?

She had not expected to sleep well, but to her surprise she did. Even so, she was up at first light and was ashamed of her non-positive wish to be back home of yesterday. Positive—that was the way from now on. Dacre would be gone by tomorrow. In all likelihood he would leave for Paris today—and then she could settle down and enjoy being here.

On that thought she went and showered and, still thinking positive, donned jodhpurs and a fresh shirt and sweater. In the light of that lovely spring morning, she could hardly credit that last night she had haughtily bounced back at Dacre that she was family, thereby neither expecting nor wanting to be paid.

She left her room quietly and tripped lightly down the stairs and out through the front door. She breathed in the new spring day—it was good. Her boots crunched over the gravel as she went along the wide frontage of the building and, as quietly as she could, down the side of the large house.

There were a few outbuildings at the rear of the property, she observed—in fact a good many outbuildings—but no stables. Now where—?

'Going riding?'

She spun round. 'Oh, hello,' she gasped. Why, when she had been very conscious of the noise she had been making as she'd walked over the gravel, hadn't she heard him? She looked beyond Dacre and realised that he had come out a back way. 'I can't find the stables,' she owned up, glad to hear from the teasing sound of him that he wasn't holding her abrupt departure from the dinner-table last night against her.

'That's because they're a quarter of a mile away.' He smiled—it was almost a grin. Strangely her breath caught.

'Ah,' she said. 'Is my car garaged here?' she asked, pointing to a block of single-storeyed buildings.

'You wish to drive to the stables?'

'Oh, no. If you'll give me directions I'll walk. I just thought, with you saying you'd garaged my car, that it might be here.'

'Come, I'll show you.' And, so saying, Dacre took her over to the buildings and opened one of them up.

'Thank you,' she said on seeing her vehicle, glad to know where it was—not that she envisaged using it very much. 'If you could tell me where—'

'I'll come with you.'

'But it's early, and you haven't had breakfast.'

'Neither have you,' he replied and, teasingly, she felt sure—although she couldn't be entirely certain—he went on, 'What sort of "family" would I be if I allowed you to go on your own—on this, your first morning?'

'Should I apologise for my rudeness last night?' she wondered out loud.

'I shouldn't think so,' he replied, making her realise that she must have spoken her thoughts, and, leading her away from the outbuildings and along a newly gravelled wide path, he said, 'Should I, perhaps, have written to your father?' This time he seemed to be wondering *his* thoughts out loud.

'No!' she exclaimed unequivocally. The one letter she herself had received from Dacre had been addressed to Mrs M Paumier. Thankfully her father hadn't been around when it had arrived. Though if he had he would have written 'not known' on it and either forgotten it or posted it back.

'You sound alarmed.' Dacre made no pretence of not noticing.

'My father wouldn't... Er—what would you want to write to him for?' She changed tack.

'A courtesy, no more, on the occasion of your exchanging his roof for mine. Perhaps a note to assure him

that I'll take every care of my cousin's widow would still
not come amiss.'

'*No*!' she exclaimed again, more vehemently this
time—and at her tone he halted. Josy stopped too, but
as she looked at him so she saw from a quietly determined kind of look in his eyes that that heated no was
not good enough. He wanted more.

'You're afraid of something?' he enquired, calm where
she was far from calm.

'No, I'm not,' she denied; she didn't have to tell him
if she didn't want to.

'What, then?'

Damn him! Dacre had stirred her to anger once before.
She who seldom knew anger felt angry again. 'I've told
you I'm twenty-three—hardly at the age when you need
to write home to my parent to tell him I'm fine.'

'You don't think he'll be anxious about you?' Josy
thought nothing of the kind. So long as Mrs Vale's
cooking, cleaning and laundry service went on uninterrupted she doubted whether her father would give her
more than a passing thought. 'Have you phoned to tell
him of your safe arrival?' he pressed when she did not
answer.

'I'll write,' she answered shortly.

And she felt she hated Dacre Banchereau when,
looking her straight in the eye, he replied, 'Out of
courtesy so will I.'

'No—you mustn't!' she flared.

'So tell me why.'

Damn him—damn him to hell. 'Because—because...' And damn him some more. 'Because—save for
him knowing I've come to France to work with horses—
my father won't have a clue who you are!' she said

heatedly, two bright spots of angry pink colouring her
normally pale skin.

'You haven't told him you were coming to your husband's family? That the man you—?'

'No, I haven't.'

'Why?'

She wriggled; she writhed; she hated Dacre with a
vengeance. 'Because...' she ground out, recognising a
tenacity in him that assured her he was not going to let
the subject drop. 'B-because my father doesn't know I've
got another family,' she railed, 'that I've had a
husband—that I've been marr...' Her voice petered out—
she wanted her words back. Dacre's astonishment was
all too obvious.

'Your father doesn't know you've been married?' he
queried incredulously.

'And I don't want you to tell him either!' she erupted—
and was made to endure his scrutiny as he rocked back
on his heels and studied her for long, silent moments.

'Oh, sweet Josy,' he drawled at length, 'who would
have suspected that there was such depth in you, such
anger in you, such—' he broke off, and, looking at her
sparking brown eyes, chose his next words carefully 'such
deceit?' he ended.

It was that word 'deceit' that got to her—as she later
realised it had been meant to. But then all she knew as
her spurt of anger refused to die was that she could not
stand still under that charge. 'I didn't not tell him for
me—but for Marc!' she retorted.

'My cousin asked you not to tell your father?' he
questioned. 'I know Marc was reticent with people, but
surely—?'

'It wasn't Marc's decision.'

'Yours?'

Josy, quietly seething, looked at him. But, short of
her packing up and going home right this minute, she
could see that there was nothing to do but tell him.
Having got here, having spent a night under Dacre
Banchereau's roof, she discovered that she felt reluctant
to leave. 'You won't like it,' she told him tautly.

'I'll be the judge of that.'

Was he needling her on purpose? 'Very well,' she began
sniffily, 'since you must know—my father would not
have looked kindly on my marrying a mere groom.'

'Your father is a snob?'

In spades. She nodded. At one time she might have
tried to cover for her parent, but after his last devious
trick she felt she owed him little loyalty. 'I'm afraid so,'
she agreed, and as all anger drained from her added,
'That was obvious when I suggested bringing Marc home
to introduce him.' She paused as she remembered, but
after taking a shaky breath she went on, 'Marc and my
father never met. We got married with just my sister
there to represent our families.'

Dacre wasn't goading her any more either as he inserted quietly, 'You had a flat to return to over the
stables, I believe?' revealing that he knew some of their
conversation with Marc's parents that evening of their
wedding day.

'Yes. Belvia went and saw to everything when we got
back, and kept my wedding a secret when I told her that
I didn't want my insensitive father to know.'

'Is that the real reason why you do not wear a wedding
ring?' he wanted to know.

It was only a part of it—a very small part of it—but
she wasn't going to tell him that. She could not tell him
or anyone else her feelings—that realisation that because she had never been a wife she had no right to wear

it. 'It's as I told you,' she said, and went to walk on, and then found, when he placed a light, restraining hand on her arm, that he hadn't finished yet.

And that caused a flicker of annoyance to touch her, before he followed up with a cool, 'Didn't you know that Marc could have bought the stables where he worked if he'd so wished?'

'I didn't marry him for his money, if that's what you mean,' she retorted, and straight away something sharp and, thankfully, in French hit her ears as Dacre let fly with an exclamation indicating that clearly she had misunderstood him.

'Don't I already know that?' he bit out, reverting back to English. 'Don't his family know that, when you have refused all offers of financial assistance?'

'I have my own money,' she retorted stubbornly. She had replied politely not only to Monsieur and Madame Paumier's wish to see her provided for financially, but also to Marc's lawyers, who had written to say that she was a beneficiary of his estate. 'It's not a fortune by your standards, but my mother left me enough to be independent.'

Dacre looked at her long and hard, and then he charged toughly, 'Do you think you are being quite fair to Marc?' and Josy jetted into orbit.

'How *dare* you?' she raged, and, flinging his hand from her arm, regardless that she might be going in the wrong direction, she stormed away from him.

How dared he? she fumed. He knew absolutely nothing about it! She was going home. Dammit, no she wasn't. She would stick it out here if it killed her. This was her new life. She wasn't going running just because Marc's cousin was showing himself to be a brute of a man.

He'd be leaving today anyway—at the latest, tomorrow. She'd keep well out of his way meantime, and—with luck—perhaps he wouldn't show up again for another month.

Josy gradually came down out of orbit, to be faintly astounded that she had come so far out of her shell since she had arrived in France that she could feel and show the outrage of fury she had just experienced. Only then—aware that Dacre, no doubt silently thinking his own thoughts, was walking right beside her—was she able to accept that guilt over her part in her unconsummated marriage had made her rage, How *dare* you? at him. She had not been able to accept Marc as a husband, so how on earth could she accept anything that he as a husband had left her?

She was still feeling not too well disposed to the man walking with her when he enquired silkily, 'Have you always been shy?' And the oddest thing started to happen in her. Remembering her rage, her fury with him, her anything but shy How *dare* you?, even while she was still annoyed with him Josy felt she wanted to laugh.

She wouldn't, of course, though it was a fact that her lips twitched a little. She gave a small cough, just to show that he had no power at all to winkle out her sense of humour.

'One of these days I'm going to grow out of it,' she threatened solemnly, but could not resist a flick of a glance at him. To her amazement she saw that *his* lips were twitching.

A minute or so later a newly fenced paddock came into view, and after a short while they were at the stables and he was introducing her to two very well-behaved horses.

With a pang Josy thought of Hetty. But Hetty was being well looked after, and she was only here for six months. By that time—and already, if her spat with Dacre was anything to go by, the signs were good—she would be ready to take on the challenge of finding a job in England where she and Hetty could be together.

A feeling of near-contentment washed over her as she stroked and patted first Nina and then César. 'We'll saddle up, and I'll show you round this area,' Dacre decided after some minutes.

'I can go by myself,' Josy replied, thinking to exercise Nina first and then come back for César.

'You going shy on me again?' he teased.

'Where's the tack-room?'

They were out for about two hours. They spoke little as they walked and sometimes cantered their mounts, but up in the saddle Josy began to feel more and more at home, and as they cantered over fields and walked through woods—sometimes catching a glimpse of Dacre's stately house, sometimes not—so she realised it was common sense for him to ride with her this first time. Tomorrow she would be able to follow the same route, and soon, when she had found her bearings, she could start to explore other routes.

Her face was aglow with pleasure by the time they returned to the stables. But before she could dismount she saw that he had already dismounted and was coming over to her, looking up into her face. He looked pleased, she thought, but didn't know how *she* felt when he put up his arms as if to help her down.

She wanted to tell him that she did not need his help. But with her equilibrium fully restored after that lovely ride she hesitated. Somehow, especially after the way she had lost her temper with him—and she could still barely credit that that had been her—it seemed churlish and as if she were sulking over the comments he had made.

She cocked a leg over the saddle and leaned down to catch a hold of his arms—and just at that moment Nina did a sideways shuffle and Josy went pitching forward.

But Dacre caught her. He went a shade off balance but, his arms coming round her, he caught her and held her fast while he regained his balance. Josy had to lean her body hard against his so that she too could get her balance, and just as Dacre glanced down into her face she went scarlet.

He stilled, held her motionless as he stared, fascinated, as the colour rioted in her face. Her breath caught, her heart thundered, and as wild panic hit she felt that she was going to faint. She looked up into a pair of grey eyes that were watching her—and pushed him away.

Dacre took a couple of casual steps from her, and while she was a tangle of agitation, striving for calm, remarked, 'I've got a busy schedule; we'd better see about unsaddling.'

'I'll do it,' she promptly volunteered, and was amazed that when she was feeling so emotionally all over the place inside her voice should come out sounding so natural.

'They'll need feeding too, and turning out into the paddock.'

'I can do that too. It's what I'm here for.'

He consulted his watch. 'Would you mind?' he glanced up to enquire.

'Not a bit,' she replied, and was a lot relieved when, staying only to unsaddle his mount, he then went striding back along the path to the house.

Josy watched him go, and discovered that she was trembling a little. Oh, heavens, how she wished that he had left her to get down from Nina by herself. To help her off was a courteous thing to have done, of course, but oh, how she wished he hadn't bothered. She could still feel his body pressed against hers. It disturbed her—he disturbed her—and she didn't want to be disturbed.

CHAPTER THREE

Dacre had left for Paris by the time Josy returned to the house, and she was glad about that. Somehow he had a knack of causing ripples, not to say—and she recalled how furious he had made her—the occasional tidal wave in the still waters of her life.

Indeed, so unsettled had he made her—she didn't want any man's arms around her, even if she was fully aware that he had *had* to catch hold of her—she had taken her time in feeding, checking the automatic water supply, and grooming Nina and César before turning them loose in the paddock.

Not that there had turned out to be any need to rush back to the house, because, as if he'd known that she would not be in any hurry to go back but would return rather than offend Agathe, who might be preparing a midday meal, Dacre had sent a picnic. Agathe's husband Franck had pedalled up with it on the back of his bicycle while she'd been checking the water trough in the paddock.

He'd introduced himself and handed her the basket, and waited while she lifted the cover. 'Oh!' she'd exclaimed in surprise, the sight of a vacuum flask causing her to realise that the lunch had arrived. '*Merci, monsieur*,' she'd thanked him shyly.

She had been positively beamed at before he'd wished her, '*Bon appétit, madame*,' and cycled off.

There was an air of recent modernisation about the stable block she'd rather thought when, suddenly aware

that she was hungry, she'd gone to the washroom to scrub
her hands and had noticed the pristine condition of the
porcelain and piping.

Once outside again she'd taken her picnic basket over
to where a newish-looking, long wooden bench with a
back to it had been most conveniently placed. And,
seated with the paddock in front of her and lovely
countryside about, she'd begun to grow calmer again.
It was truly beautiful here.

Much later she'd investigated what else the well-
equipped tack-room housed, besides saddles and bridles,
and had spent an energetic hour or two polishing already
shiny leather.

When at half-past six she returned to the house she
recalled how Dacre had remarked on his busy schedule.
She thought that she could take it that he had only left
Paris in order to be at the estate when she'd arrived, as
he had promised he would be and had matters in Paris
that required his attention even on a Sunday.

As she expected, Dacre had left, and, feeling more
relaxed knowing that, Josy went up to her room, feeling
pleasantly tired and with nothing more strenuous in mind
than a soak in the bath,

However, she had no sooner entered her room than
she saw with a start that her car keys were on her
dressing-table, and beside them a note. Dacre had been
to her room.

   Agathe will serve you dinner at eight every evening
   unless you wish to alter that. If you have any problem,
   no matter how small, please contact me. Treat my
   home as your home.

In case she had forgotten to bring his Paris number

with her, Dacre had jotted down both his office number
and his Paris number. He had signed it 'D'.

That was when Josy decided that she definitely liked
her cousin-in-law. While he might wreck her equilibrium, and draw from her a person she hardly recognised, and while she might prefer it not to be that way,
and, therefore, appreciate his absence, it had been kind
and generous of him to tell her to treat his home as her
home. Josy, in an easier frame of mind, went and had
her bath.

There followed a week in which she made the acquaintance of two ladies from the village who came to
clean—Edith and Lilas—and also a fiftyish man by the
name of Georges, who gardened.

Between Franck and Georges, Josy had not the
smallest worry with the horses. For either they loved
horses too, or had had instructions from their employer,
because one or other of them was always there to help
her with Nina and César when she returned from exercising them. As, too, if she was overlong at the stables,
would one or other of them come cycling casually by.

She wanted to tell them that she was all right, that
they had no need to check on her, that she could very
well unsaddle the horses on her own. But she did not
feel that she could countermand any orders Dacre had
given, and, in any case, she knew full well that her French
was just not up to any involved conversation.

On Tuesday her twin rang. Josy was in the dining-
room enjoying her evening meal when Agathe came in,
and out of all that she said Josy picked up, '... telé-
phone, madame.'

Why her heart should suddenly beat faster at the
thought that Dacre was waiting for her to come to the
phone Josy had no idea, but she left the dining-room

and went out into the hall, where the nearest phone was lying off its rest on an antique table.

'Hello?' she said, feeling a mite shaky. And at once felt her equilibrium return on hearing her sister's voice.

'Are you all right?' Belvia enquired anxiously. 'You sound nervous.'

'I'm absolutely fine!' Josy replied, a smile in her voice. Aware that her sister would worry about her if she couldn't convince her, she added, 'I didn't know who was calling, but I'll admit I wasn't looking forward to trying to converse with someone in French.'

'I know what you mean. I don't know who answered the phone, but it was only when a string of French hit my ears that I realised I might have a few problems. I cheated, I'm afraid. I just said, *Parlez-vous anglais, madame*? I think I was told to hold on a moment, which I did, and here you are—so top marks to whoever it was.'

'It was Agathe, Dacre's housekeeper.'

'How is he—Dacre?'

'Oh, he went back to Paris on Sunday.'

'And you got there without any problems? I wanted to ring you on Saturday. Sunday and Monday too, come to think of it—' Belvia laughed '—but decided to let you settle in first. Coping?'

'Very well,' Josy replied. 'It's lovely here.'

She *was* coping very well, too, she realised, by the time Thursday rolled around. Not that looking after just two horses could be called work—as she had told Dacre.

She had started to feel relaxed too—unbelievably relaxed, given the few short days she had been here. Was it just the calm, the tranquillity of this lovely place in part of the valley of the Loire? Or did the fact that she had broken away from her father and his dominance play some part?

Whatever it was, when Friday turned out to be a dull, rainy day she went down to the stables to talk to Nina and César and to feed them and decided against exercising them. That afternoon she decided to take her car out of its garage. She drove in to Saumur, with its majestic fourteenth-century château built on a promontory and overlooking the lovely town below.

Yet, as lovely as the town was, Josy no sooner got there than she had a feeling of wanting to be back again at Dacre's home. She stayed long enough to purchase a picture postcard, however, and, taking an afternoon cup of tea, she addressed it to her father to advise him of her safe arrival. It only struck her how independent of him she had become when she suddenly found that she was thinking that perhaps she would consider writing a letter to him at some later date.

On her return Josy met Agathe, and they smiled and greeted each other and, as Hetty had been in her thoughts a lot that day, Josy went to the telephone and rang the stables.

'Tracey?' she enquired when the phone was answered.

'The same.'

'It's Josy Fereday. I'm in France. I wondered if Hetty was all right?'

'Never better,' Tracey assured her. 'Spoilt to death, of course, and missing her mum, but otherwise great.'

Josy felt a knife turn at 'missing her mum', but these six months would soon pass, and if Hetty really was missing her she could pop back to England for a few days to see her every now and then.

'You've got my number here if you need it?' she checked, and spoke to Tracey for another minute or so, then came away from the phone realising that, should she nip back to England for a few days to see Hetty, she had a decided aversion to returning to the home that she had shared with her father.

She was in her room getting ready to go down to dinner that night, with the same subject still on her mind, when it dawned on her that now that the break was made it was total. There was no going back. She knew then that whatever happened—even should she not be able to find a live-in job—she would never return to live in her old home. Suddenly she was starting to be the positive person she wanted to be. And she liked it. Then the phone in her room rang.

Startled, she stared at it. It had never rung before. Was Belvia phoning again? Had Agathe switched the call through? Josy went over to the phone and picked it up. 'Hello?' she said—and was all at once not positive about anything any more.

'You've had a good week, Josy?' Dacre enquired.

She felt breathless. 'Oh—yes,' she answered.

'With nothing to worry you?'

'No. Nothing.' She wished she could think of something to say—something positive—but could think of nothing.

'The horses are well?'

'Oh, yes. Yes, they are.'

'Then I will not keep you.'

Her brain sprang into action. 'Are you coming home tomorrow?' she asked in a rush.

There was a pause, a silence. Then he asked, 'You wish me to?' And Josy felt exceedingly embarrassed, and as if she had asked him to come.

'No,' she denied sharply. And, not knowing why the dickens she had asked—for it was no concern of hers what he did—she endured more agonised seconds of embarrassment, with no way to retrieve that sharp, No, while Dacre obviously considered if he wanted to make the trip from Paris or not.

Not, it seemed. Though she doubted whether her wanting him there or not made a scrap of difference when he at last replied, 'Then if you have no problems I will stay in Paris. *Au revoir*, Josy.'

'Bye,' she answered, and put down the phone feeling gauche and awkward, but overall generally glad that she would not see him that weekend.

Some of her new-found confidence had returned by Monday of the following week. On Thursday she again drove into Saumur, and on Friday she drove up to the Ecole Nationale d'Equitation, and watched in awe as the Cadre Noir put their splendid horses through their paces.

She was still reliving all she had seen in her room that evening. But as she started to get bathed and changed for dinner all thoughts of horses and anything else had gone from her mind.

She glanced nervously at the phone. Dacre had rung around this time last Friday. Would he ring again to-night? What would she say if he again asked if she wanted him to come home? In truth she had no idea. Somehow the positive side she thought she had found had started to waver again, and she didn't know if she wanted to see him or not.

Dacre had not rung by the time she was ready to leave her room. Nor did he ring while she was at dinner. Josy returned to her room knowing that he was not going to ring now. And why would he? It was his house; he could come and go as he pleased. And, in any case, she thought, recalling that last Friday he had as good as said that if the horses were well he would not keep her, he had only rung last Friday to check that Nina and César were all right.

When later she climbed into bed Josy had recalled a lot of other things too—among them how furious he had made her. She could only remember being so outraged once before—she had been fifteen, and had just witnessed her father striking her mother.

Josy slept very badly that night. She got out of bed early on Saturday morning, glad to leave it. The night seemed to have gone on for ever. She went to take a shower and, as if trying to outstrip unwanted thoughts that continued to pursue her, she hurried to the breakfast-room, had a swift breakfast of croissant, apricot jam and coffee, and went quickly the quarter of a mile to the stables.

As ever, both Nina and César were uncomplicated and glad to see her, as she was to see them. But for once, as she stroked and patted them and gave them an apple each to start the day, she could not lose herself totally in their company. Uppermost in her mind were still haunted thoughts of her abhorrence of physical violence—and her fear of it.

Sometimes she took the horses out together, riding one out and the other back, but that morning she felt filled with a restless kind of energy. To take them both would slow her down. She did a few chores and then, intending to take César out later, she saddled up Nina.

Josy was about two miles away from home and concentrating on anything but her riding when Nina stumbled in a pothole—and Josy fell off. Staring disbelievingly at Nina from her sitting position on the ground, Josy laughed ruefully. But she was yet more disbelieving when the well-behaved and lovable Nina, either thinking to have a game or perhaps thinking that she would be fed almost as soon as she returned home, took off.

'Well!' Josy exclaimed, watching helplessly as the horse cantered back the way she had come.

She was about to get up and start the two-mile walk back when she heard the sound of a light aircraft overhead. She watched it for some seconds, leaning back on her elbows. Then she lost interest. But, instead of getting to her feet as she had intended, she lay there, as if hoping that some of the serenity of her surroundings would rub off on to her. Either Georges or Franck would be there to look after Nina when she got home, she could guarantee.

Josy lay down, the sun warm on her face. She closed her eyes, but only for a few minutes as she tried to think of nothing and found that impossible. Thoughts of Marc penetrated. Dear Marc—she should never have married him. Guilt swamped her. Guilt she didn't need. Guilt she couldn't cope with. Think of something else.

An image of her father came to her, his face contorted with fury. She wiped him from her mind, and thought of Dacre Banchereau. But somehow she didn't want to think about him, either. He disturbed her, she acknowledged, and made herself think of Belvia instead. She thought of her sister's goodness, her caring, and began to relax.

'Josy! Josy!' She felt comfortable and didn't want to wake up.

But wake up she did—in a startled and terrified way. She had not been dreaming! Someone *had* been shouting her name! Barely realising that she had been asleep, Josy came to rapidly, to hear a volley of French in her ears, while at the same time she opened her eyes at the touch of an exploring hand in the neck of her shirt.

In an instant, even as she recognised that Dacre was somehow home, she was pushing him frantically away while at the same time yelling, 'Get away from me!'

'I was feeling for a pulse!'

'Don't touch me!' she shrieked, on her feet and moving backwards, her eyes fixed on his face. Vaguely she realised that he seemed paler than she remembered.

'I thought you were dead!'

'Well, I'm not!' she threw at him, her panic starting to subside; she had been mistaken—his colour now looked normal.

'I can see that you're not,' he retorted, and, with some utterance in French, added, 'My God—there's passion in you, Josy Paumier!'

Abruptly she turned her back on him. Passion she knew there was not. And, while she might have a legal right to be called Paumier, she knew that she was not morally entitled to that name either. And she was hating Dacre Banchereau that he could—even unknowingly—refer so easily to matters which were such an unhappy source of unrest within her.

She wanted him to go, to leave her in peace, but guessed that she should have known better.

'Come, here is César.'

She turned, noticed César for the first time, and realised that Dacre must have called him from wherever he'd left him. 'What do you mean—"here is César"?' she asked, belligerent in her trauma.

Dacre eyed her steadily, either assessing or not liking her tone—she couldn't decide which. 'Get on him,' he clipped—not liking, she realised.

'No!' she retorted. Nothing on God's earth was going to have her riding in tandem with him.

'I wasn't thinking of riding the horse with you, if that's what you're afraid of!' he snarled, clearly having read her mind.

And she didn't like that. But, more, she positively hated that word 'afraid'. And she hated him that he could suggest that she might be afraid of any physical contact with another human being—hated him so much that she wasn't thinking but only feeling when, furious with him for a second time, she charged past him like a flash, was up in the saddle and away.

Damn him; damn him to hell, she fumed as she set César to the gallop. Let *him* walk the two miles back. She hoped it came on to rain. A cloudburst would suit her nicely. A lightning bolt wouldn't come amiss either.

It did not come on to rain but remained a blissful spring-turning-to-summer day. Nor did Josy gallop César for long. Indeed, by the time the stables came into view she had slowed him to a walk and, her temper spent, she was quite bewildered to know what had come over her.

Franck was at the stables; he seemed relieved to see her, and she felt more guilt to think that although she had not meant to fall asleep, she had done so, causing him alarm when a riderless Nina had come home.

'I'm sorry, Franck,' she apologised, and guessed that he understood from her solemn expression that she was not too happy with herself just then. He smiled anyhow, and she thought that meant he had forgiven her when he helped her unsaddle César and look after him.

By the time both horses were attended to and were out in the paddock Josy had surfaced from the mind-numbing confusion of her behaviour to be dreadfully contrite, for, as she ceased trying to fathom the unfathomable about this new and fiery person her cousin-in-law seemed to cause to explode in her, so she began to think of matters from his side of things.

By the time Dacre appeared and neared where she was standing Josy was feeling very much ashamed of herself. Oh, heavens, leave alone the fact that the cousin he'd loved had been killed in a riding accident, Dacre must have wondered if history had been repeating itself when Franck had told him that Nina had come home without her.

He must have saddled up César straight away and come looking for her. Lord knew what his thoughts had been when, from high up on the back of César, he had spotted her lying there, still, not moving. Of course his first action before he did anything else on getting to her had been to check for a pulse in her neck, to see if she was still alive. And what had she done but shrieked at him like some demented fishwife?

Dacre was about ten yards away when, mortified, she moved in his direction. Inexplicably, considering the very vocal shrew she had been, she felt shy again. But, shy or not, it had to be done.

She approached him and stopped. He saw her, looked down at her from his aloof height and, without saying a word, carried on walking.

Josy stared after him; she wanted to call his name, to halt him, but that tedious shyness held her tongue captive. And that was when her new world started to shatter about her. His aloofness, his going by without a word said it all. Dacre wanted her to leave!

Her breath caught on that dreadful thought and she knew, for all that she had been there for only two weeks, that she did not want to leave. Her heart sank. She did not question the fact; she just knew that it was so. Just as she knew that she was too proud to stay anywhere where she was not wanted.

She went and checked the paddock. Nina and César were passing that part of the day in the plentiful supply of shade amongst some trees over at the far side. She went and washed her hands, after which, in a perturbed frame of mind, she started to walk back to the house.

Dacre was nowhere to be seen when she went indoors, but she hung around in the drawing-room for ten minutes just in case he came in. When he did not she decided to go up to her room to shower and change—perhaps she'd feel a shade more confident if she smelt less horsey.

She had just reached the landing at the top of the stairs, however, when a door a couple of rooms up from her own opened, and Dacre came from a bedroom which she assumed to be his. From the damp look to his dark hair she guessed that he had already showered and changed.

He saw her at once, and halted. And as warm colour seared her cheeks she knew she had to go on. She had no more idea of what she was going to say then than she had when she'd decided she must go and see him, but pride refused to let her stay where she was not wanted and forced her to go forward.

She drew level with him, saw that he was watching her with steady grey eyes, and blurted out, 'I expect you want me to go?'

He looked a degree startled, though his tone was calm as he replied, 'Go? Where?'

Was he playing with her? Involuntarily her chin tilted a proud fraction. 'I thought you might want me to leave.' She forced the words out.

Again she had to suffer his steady look. Then he asked softly, 'Why would I want you to leave?'

She stared at him, all large brown eyes. 'I thought—me leaving you to walk home and everything...' she managed lamely, joy starting to enter her being at the realisation that, by the sound of it, she had got it all wrong and Dacre hadn't taken exception to her behaviour.

'You are my family, Josy, are you not?' he answered, and to her delight smiled a smile full of charm as he teased, 'Do you not know that in families one is privileged to leave other family members to walk a solitary two miles home?'

'Oh, Dacre,' she murmured involuntarily. And, even though her mouth curved upwards in a smile which denied the apology, she said, 'I'm sorry.'

She saw his glance flick from her eyes to her smiling mouth, and observed the way he seemed fascinated by it—that was when she realised how seldom she smiled. No wonder he was fascinated. It was high time she lightened up. 'Well, don't do it again,' he ordered with a mock severity that made her want to laugh. He turned away, seemed about to go on his way, then turned back to enquire, as if it were his responsibility, 'Did you get down from Nina voluntarily or did she unseat you?'

'My fault alone,' Josy quickly assured him. 'I wasn't paying any attention to her or what I was doing when she stumbled and we lightly parted company.'

'You're not hurt?'

'Not even my pride,' she laughed, and it was true, and Dacre flicked one more glance to her mouth then turned abruptly about.

'Take a hot bath just the same,' he ordered over his shoulder.

Josy turned away and went to her room. She didn't want a hot bath, she thought rebelliously, and was under the shower when she paused stock-still to wonder what was happening to her. This wasn't her, not the Josy Fereday she knew, laughing, mutinous—her breath caught—alive!

She almost gasped at that last thought, but could not or would not work it out. She reached for her shampoo and drowned further thoughts by concentrating on washing her long strawberry-tinted fair hair.

She decided when lunchtime came around that she did not want to join Dacre for the midday meal. It was only the thought that she was likely to draw more attention to herself if she didn't appear at the lunch table that made her go.

And then she discovered that she need not have worried anyhow because Dacre was not there. By signs and bits of French Josy thought she had conveyed to Agathe that she would wait for *monsieur* before she began her meal, only to translate Agathe's admittedly slowed-down French to comprehend that Dacre would not be in to lunch, that *monsieur* was out seeing friends.

Whether Agathe had said *amis* for male friends or *amies* for female friends, Josy was sure she was not so interested that she wanted to find out. She was not very hungry, she discovered, but she ate what she could, since Agathe had troubled to cook for her, and afterwards she returned to her room to change. She felt restless again and, if Franck hadn't beaten her to it, she would go and muck out the stables.

Josy returned to the house at six-thirty and went straight to have the hot bath which Dacre had ordered earlier that day. She spent some time considering her wardrobe after her bath and opted for a plain, lavender-coloured dress that looked nothing on its hanger yet looked good on.

At five to eight she left her room, wondering if Dacre would be in to dinner or out again with his friends or, more likely, some lady-friend. No doubt he had lady-friends here as well as in Paris. Not that it was any business of hers. Not that she cared.

But, most oddly, Josy discovered that while at lunchtime she had not wanted his company she now would not have minded someone to chat with over a meal. Chat with? Grief, she had always preferred her own company!

She remembered thinking before that there was something magical—a magical air—about the place. It certainly had a lot to answer for. Any further thoughts on the matter, however, swiftly departed when it suddenly occurred to her that there might be more than Dacre for company. What if his *amie* was dining with them?

At one time that thought alone might have seen her hastening back to her room but—and again she hardly knew herself—while, admittedly, she had to pause at the drawing-room door to gather her courage together before she could open it, open it she did.

'Ah, Josy!' Dacre greeted her. And he was alone.

'I'm not late?' She knew she wasn't, but needed to say something.

'Not unless you insist on having a drink first,' he teased.

Oh, she did like him. 'No, thanks,' she replied, and silently owned to feeling a little breathless when, taking a light hold of her elbow, he escorted her to the dining-room.

Josy was tucking into a starter of mussels in parsley butter before she said another word. And then it was only in response to Dacre's, 'No sign of a bruise, I hope?'

For a second she wasn't with him. Then she remembered that she had come off Nina that morning. 'Not one,' she answered.

'You went back to the stables this afternoon?' he enquired conversationally.

'It's lovely there. Did you have that bench put there? It looks quite new.'

'You may blame me,' he invited with charm, and, oddly, her heart gave a little flutter.

'It's in exactly the right spot,' she murmured, and as a thought suddenly struck her she grasshoppered on to something else and said, 'I saw—this morning when I was—um—taking my ease—I saw a small aircraft go over. It wasn't you, was it?'

'There's an airfield quite close, and very convenient,' he replied, giving her a warm look, and she promptly ran out of questions. But not so he. 'You feel—um— settled in with us now?' he enquired.

Given that there seemed to be an uneasy restlessness growing in her, and given that in two short weeks she was losing sight of the Josy she had always been, she rather thought she had settled in amazingly well.

'Yes, thank you,' she replied politely, and found a smile for Agathe when she came in to remove their used dishes and to deliver a most appetising chicken casserole that was worthy of a much more splendid name.

Dacre poured some wine, and as Agathe left the room, enquired, 'Have you been homesick at all?'

In all honesty she had to confess that she hadn't— confess to herself, that was. 'My twin left home when she married—as I told you. Seven months ago now. So I've got used to her not being around much. But Belvia phoned me here. And I rang the stables where my horse is. I miss her a little,' she added.

'Hetty.'

'You remember Hetty?'

'*Naturellement*!' He smiled, but, a still kind of look came to him. 'You mention your sister and your horse.' He paused, and then asked quietly, 'Do you not miss your father?'

'I...' She hesitated, and all at once became aware that, having lived in the same house with her father all her life, not only did she not miss her parent one tiny bit but she seldom thought about him. 'You make me feel guilty!' she exclaimed.

'Because you do not miss him?' She nodded. 'Forgive me—that was not my intention,' Dacre apologised at once, and, looking steadily at her for a few moments, he quietly asked, 'Was he a good father to you, Josy?'

Yes, she wanted to say. Oh, yes, wonderful. But Edwin Fereday had not been a good father, nor did he deserve loyalty, and when she opened her mouth to lie to Dacre she suddenly discovered that she could not lie to him.

'No,' she mumbled, and decided to leave it at that.

Only she had reckoned without Dacre who, on hearing her reply, did not seem to want to leave it there. 'He—beat you?' he enquired, still in that same quiet tone.

Josy stared down at her plate and shook her head to indicate that she did not want this conversation. Dacre said nothing, but nor did he carry on eating. For all his quiet way of speaking it seemed he was determined on more of an answer than that. A silence stretched, and Josy debated leaving the table and returning to her room.

Then incredibly she heard her own voice say, 'Just the once.'

Startled, she could hardly believe that she had answered. She made a small movement prior to getting up from the table, but, in doing so, glanced up and across

to Dacre. He was sitting as silent as before. Silent—and
waiting. But there was something in the grey depths of
his eyes that was warm and encouraging—as if he knew
that there was more to it than her having been lightly
slapped for some childhood naughtiness.

And somehow Josy found that she had subsided back
into her seat. 'Tell me about it,' he requested, his voice
soft now, soothing. She stared at him. There was something slightly hypnotic about him. 'I am family, *petite*,'
he reminded her gently.

Some family confidences were best kept to oneself,
she decided. But as the seconds ticked by she replied,
'Th-there isn't a lot to tell.'

'How old were you?'

'Fifteen,' she answered, and, as the silence stretched,
added, 'He was always aggressive, my father.' She
stopped, yet somehow, as if a dam was starting to burst,
she did not seem able to stop. 'For the most part he
ignored us—me, Belvia and my mother.' Josy took a
shaky intake of breath, and the dam fractured a little
more. 'Then one Saturday Bel had gone swimming and
I'd been to my music lesson. And when I went home
there was an almighty row going on upstairs. I knew my
parents were having a fierce verbal battle about something. I—' She broke off; she couldn't go on.

'But it wasn't purely verbal?' suggested a quiet, barely
accented voice.

Again she shook her head. She didn't want to say any
more. 'I—c-can't cope with physical aggression,' she
whispered.

'But you did,' he gently prompted.

This time she nodded. And, as though speaking to
herself, found that she was adding, 'I didn't want to hear
them rowing. I went to the outer door. I thought I'd go

and meet Belvia at the swimming pool. Then I heard a thud, a slap, the sound of my mother crying out. I don't remember anything after that but I suppose I must have rushed up the stairs, because the next thing I knew I was in my parents' bedroom.'

Words were pouring from her now—pent-up words she didn't seem able to stop, released words. 'My father was hitting my mother. I charged in between them and he began hitting me—he sent me flying across the room.' She gasped then, almost as if she could still feel the physical pain, the mental scars she still carried.

She felt her hands taken in a warm clasp and blinked, and saw that Dacre was sitting on a dining-chair next to her and was holding her hands. She had no idea when he had moved from his seat opposite or that she had turned towards him.

'You're nearly there,' he murmured softly.

'I—don't—want to say any more,' she choked.

'There's not much more, is there?' he sensitively invited.

'No, I suppose not,' she acknowledged slowly. 'I'm—er—all right now,' she told him, realising only then that she must have sounded quite distressed, and that Dacre, as sensitive as she had thought him, had left his seat to try to give what comfort he could.

She pulled her hands from his hold and he let her go, and, after a glance at her pale face, he went back to where he had been sitting—and Josy made every effort to control how shaky she was feeling.

'You charged in between your parents, you said,' he probed quietly when it seemed that he judged she was up to continuing. 'And he beat you.'

For the first time ever in the eight years that had elapsed since that dreadful afternoon she revealed, 'I hit him too.'

'You hit your father?'

'He was hitting my mother. I think I must have flipped because I went for him again, and the next thing I remember, my mother was pulling me from him and getting her and me some space from him. She had just received a private inheritance, and for the first time in her life was independent of him,' Josy explained. 'But I had never seen her so angry, nor so determined, when she told him that if he ever laid a finger on me again—or her, for that matter—then, regardless of the damage such publicity would cause him and his business, she would sue him for assault.'

'Your father—he never hit either of you again?'

'He is, I'm afraid, a bully. And like all bullies he backed off when he could see that, mainly because of me, my mother really meant what she said.'

'Your mother—she was the opposite of him,' Dacre stated.

'She was wonderful,' Josy agreed.

'She died when you were sixteen,' he commented.

'Marc's parents told you?'

Dacre nodded. 'You were a very brave young woman to try to protect your mother the way you did.'

'Oh, I don't know about that. Being brave is doing something that terrifies you, don't you think?' And, not waiting for an answer, she said, 'I wasn't terrified; I wasn't even thinking.'

'You just raced up the stairs and got in between them.' Dacre smiled. 'All of which,' he added, his smile gone as his grey eyes stayed on her, 'has left its mark on you.'

'Oh, I don't...' she began to deny.

'Your reserve—'

'I've always been shy,' she butted in, and suddenly became aware that at one time she had been so shy that she would never have butted in on what anyone was saying. 'Well, I was till I came here.' She smiled a little self-consciously.

'You still are.' He grinned as Agathe came in again. 'Mmm, a little cheese before your pudding?'

When Josy went to bed that night she feared that she might lie awake for hours reliving yet again the horrors of that time eight years ago. Yet, strangely, she went to sleep almost as soon as her head touched her pillow. Her last waking thought was, What was it about Dacre? She had never told a living soul what she had told him— what was it about the man?

CHAPTER FOUR

JOSY still found it incredible in the week that followed that she could have revealed to Dacre all she had about her father. It seemed to her not only incredible but unbelievable, when that secret had been locked up in her for so long, that she had opened up and told him all she had.

She was still puzzling out how it had all come about. Perhaps she had given away a hint that she and her father were not close in her admission that she did not miss him. It had brought forth Dacre's intuitive question of, 'Was he a good father to you?' anyhow.

But, whatever, while nothing seemed to take away the heavy burden of guilt she carried over Marc, Josy owned that she felt better about that dreadful scene eight years ago since she had shared it with Dacre.

He came home again at the weekend, but Nina had a slight cough and, having isolated her in the end stable of the block of four, putting César at the other end, Josy was more interested in staying near to the stables than in staying around the house.

She did make it for dinner on Saturday evening, though. 'This is the first time I've seen you today,' Dacre remarked when, on the stroke of eight, in a white shirt and a floral skirt—the first things to hand after her brief shower—she went quickly down the stairs.

'Er—hello,' she greeted him, and knew her rush not to keep anyone waiting was the reason for her breathlessness when Dacre, his hands coming to her arms, drew her to him and kissed first one cousinly cheek and then the other. 'Have you been to the stables?' she asked as they walked to the dining-room.

'Several times,' he replied drily.

'Oh, I'm sorry. Did you want to see me about anything in particular? Nina's got a bit of a cough, you see, and in between checking on her I've taken César for several long walks to keep him away from her.'

'I'll get someone in to help you,' Dacre decreed promptly.

'There's no need for that!' she declared, giving Agathe a warm smile when she came in with a soup tureen and went out again.

'Why isn't there? I'm not allowed to pay you, so why shouldn't I be allowed to pay someone to make your day easier?'

'Franck and Georges are always about if I need them,' she retaliated, amazed to realise that she was arguing with him—she who would run a mile from an argument! 'And, anyway, I like working on my own. Not that it's work,' she added hastily, and received a disgruntled look for her trouble.

Josy did not linger after her meal but returned to the stables. She discovered she had company, albeit silent company on the way back. She wanted to apologise to Dacre if she had done anything wrong but, in all honesty, couldn't think of anything she should say sorry for.

'I think Nina sounds a bit better.' She found her tongue as they went into the house. 'But if you wouldn't mind I'd like the vet to take a look at her.'

'I'll arrange it,' he clipped out, and Josy went to bed, relieved that the vet would call but feeling very mixed up about Dacre.

She had a restless night, and was up earlier than usual on Sunday morning and down at the stables checking on Nina. She was in the middle of crooning sweet nothings in the mare's ears when a droll voice suggested 'Why don't you bring your bed down here?'

A smile started deep inside her. She did not like to be bad friends, and it sounded as though—whatever her crime had been—Dacre had forgiven her.

She turned about, her eyes laughing. She hadn't been mistaken; Dacre's good humour had awakened with him—she could tell from the slight upturn at the corner of his rather splendid mouth. 'I didn't wake you up—leaving...?' Splendid mouth! Grief, where had that thought come from?

'I seem to require as little sleep as you,' he returned pleasantly. 'I was in my study, leaving a message on the horse doctor's answering machine, when you went by the window. How is she?'

'Definitely better. But I should still like the vet to see her.'

It was Dacre who exercised César that morning, leaving Josy with Nina. He had soon returned and gone back to the house and it was nearing noon when he drove down with a man a few years older than herself whom he introduced as the vet. And, while Josy started to feel quite awkward that Monsieur Gramache had been called out on a Sunday, when the next day would have done quite as well, the vet examined the mare.

'I will leave you some medicine; she will be well again in two or three days.' The vet, clearly preferring the look of Josy to Nina, turned to her to smile. His accent was strong but his English good.

'Thank you.' She smiled in turn, and, having felt at ease with him when discussing Nina, was ready to retreat when his smile lingered on her.

'I'll drive back to the house with you, *monsieur*,' Dacre said curtly, authoritatively. '*Madame* Paumier will want to settle the horse.'

'I will call again on Wednesday, *madame*.' The vet smiled again.

Josy looked from him to a not-very-pleased-looking Dacre, then Nina coughed and she forgot both of them.

Nina was better by Wednesday, but Josy was glad to see when the vet arrived that Franck was busy near by, giving the already pristine food store another coat of whitewash.

'Would you like me to check both horses while I'm here?' the vet asked.

It seemed a good idea. 'I'd be glad if you would, *monsieur*,' she replied.

'My first name is Regis,' he hinted, with a winning smile.

'Oh, yes,' she mumbled.

'And you are?'

'Mmm . . .' It seemed utterly ridiculous not to tell him. 'Josy,' she answered. 'And that,' she said, pointing to the horse who was having a little trot in the paddock, 'is César.'

Regis Gramache made his examinations, pronounced both horses fit and, telling Josy of his very early start that day as they walked back from the paddock, hinted at coffee. Oh, grief, she had an idea that the vet wanted to have a little flirt; she had small idea how to handle it.

She looked over to the food store, where Franck was taking a breather and, knowing that the small kitchenette off the washroom was now thoughtfully equipped

by Agathe with the makings for coffee and tea, called
'*Café*, Franck?'

She made coffee for them both, and left the two men
while she went and took Nina down to the paddock.

Her sister phoned her that evening just for a chat, and
it was lovely talking to her. But it endorsed for Josy
again that she had made the right decision in leaving
England for a while. She knew Belvia was concerned for
her and she didn't want that. Josy wanted nothing to
worry her sister ever again.

Saturday, for no reason that Josy could think of, seemed
to take a long time to come around. Only when she heard
the sound of a light aircraft overhead early that morning
did she realise that she had been listening for Dacre
without being fully aware of it.

It need not necessarily have been him, she knew, but
she felt almost light-hearted when, getting down from
Nina after taking her out for a canter, she saw that Dacre
had come down to the stables.

'*Bonjour*, Dacre,' she greeted him, and he came over.

'We'll have you speaking it like a native yet.' He
smiled, took a hold of her arms, and, looking deep into
her large brown eyes, murmured, '*Bonjour*, Josy,' and,
his head coming forward, he kissed her cheeks.

'I—er—thought I heard your plane,' she commented,
stepping back, feeling slightly flustered.

For a few silent moments he studied her. 'And I heard
that you make pretty good coffee,' he answered.

'Ah,' she said, and as Franck appeared from nowhere
and Dacre handed him Nina's reins so that he could look
after her added, 'You've been talking with Franck.'

'Going to make me some?'

'Of course,' she said, and led the way to the kitchenette.

'You're going to have coffee with me?' he asked as he took his ease on a wooden chair while Josy got busy making some coffee. 'Or,' he tacked on as an after-thought, 'are you going to leave me to drink mine with my odd-job man, like you did the vet?'

'Oh, heavens—was I very rude?' she asked.

His answer was to laugh outright. 'Did you feel rude?'

She shook her head, looked at Dacre for a thoughtful moment or two, then, claiming *him* this time as a member of her family, confided, 'From one family member to another, I think I can tell you that I believed Monsieur Gramache had it in mind to have a little flirt with me—only—' she laughed this time; it was a self-conscious sound '—only, I don't know how to do it.'

She glanced across at Dacre, and at his stern ex-pression felt the lightness of her mood disappear. 'Did you not have other men-friends before Marc?' he de-manded—and she realised then that his stern expression stemmed from an annoyance that she, his cousin's widow, should be flirting with some other man—even though she hadn't been.

'No, I didn't,' she answered, and was awash with the guilt of all her daytime nightmares—she should never have married.

Dacre looked at her long, hard and, she thought, speculatively. Then, his expression clearing, he asked, 'Did you want to flirt with our friend, the vet?'

'Of course not!' she answered stiffly. And, with a spurt of temper she could not control, snapped, 'Why am I always confiding in you things I don't tell other people?'

He stared at her. Then he laughed, and she liked that about him, and immediately her temper cooled. She took two cups of coffee over to the table and he pulled a chair near to him for her to sit down.

'Perhaps—um—because I'm your—cousin?' he suggested.

'Yes, but...' She gave a shaky, shuddery, confused kind of sigh. 'Why you—and—and not Marc?' she asked, the question leaving her with difficulty.

'You didn't tell Marc of the emotional scars your father left on you?'

She wasn't aware that she had any emotional scars— save for her hatred of and disquiet about physical aggression, which she had in common with most other people, she would have thought. But it was only as she looked across at Dacre then that she began to wonder, Would she, like her twin, have grown more and more confident but for that traumatic and repressive incident with her father? Would she in fact, when she had left her teen years behind, have left her accursed shyness behind too?

She didn't think so, but it was also a fact that since coming here, since leaving her father's home a month ago, she was far less shy than she had been.

She came away from the complexity of her thoughts when Dacre, obviously thinking that he had given her long enough to answer, changed tack to enquire, still in that same quiet, unhurried voice, 'Your sister—she knew of the distress your father caused you when you were fifteen?'

'No one knew,' Josy answered, but felt able to explain, 'Belvia was doing exams at school—well, both of us were actually—but whereas I seemed able to hide anything that worried me Belvia used to shout out in her sleep when she was worried. She was going through a shouting patch when it happened, so there was no way my mother or I was going to add to her anxieties.'

'So you decided to keep it to yourselves?' he ascertained, paused, then asked, 'You never thought to tell her after your mother's death?'

'How could I? We both loved our mother dearly.'

'So—just as you had protected your mother that day, when you dived in between your parents, you protected your sister from knowing anything about it.'

'I couldn't tell her. It would have crucified Bel to know that my father had once—probably more than once, for all I know—physically assaulted our mother!'

'Instead, you let it crucify you,' Dacre commented gently. Josy didn't answer. She well remembered in the year that followed how she would hurry apprehensively home from school every day to check that her mother was all right. 'And after your mother's death you carried it alone—and couldn't even tell the man you married.'

She had thought he had forgotten his earlier question about her not telling Marc of her emotional scars. And only then did she realise the full tenacity of the man. She should have recognised it in the fact that he had waited months for her to come to France to look after his horses. She realised then that he had always intended to have an answer to that earlier question.

It irked her a little. 'No,' she replied shortly, 'I couldn't.'

'Why?'

Damn him and his quiet questions. She didn't want to answer. She wasn't going to answer. Indeed, she wasn't sure she knew the answer. She flicked a glance across to where he was tenaciously waiting and damned him again.

She thought about getting up, leaving him and going about her business, yet something stopped her. All at once it seemed to her that she had made a habit of turning away from the unpleasant things in life. But this was her new life, and hadn't she felt better for telling Dacre of her bullying father's actions that day?

'It all seemed so dreadful, so violent, so—sordid,' she pushed out painfully. 'Marc and I—we had a quiet, gentle relationship. We—' She stopped; she couldn't go on. 'I don't want to talk about it!' she said sharply.

Abruptly she shot to her feet and took her cup and saucer over to the sink. Ye gods, another five minutes of this seemingly bland probing and Dacre would have from her how her relationship with Marc had ended up anything but quiet and gentle!

She jumped, startled when, having not heard Dacre move, she suddenly felt a hand on her arm as he turned her about.

'Don't be upset,' he requested kindly.

His face was close—too close to hers. She didn't want to look into his eyes; she didn't want him looking into hers; she didn't want him to see the guilt that surely must be there.

'I'm not upset!' she lied, and, shrugging his hand from her, she did what she should have done some minutes ago. She marched out of there.

Dacre rode César a couple of times that weekend and, keeping herself busy, Josy saw very little of him. She felt quite relieved when he went back to Paris. With luck he'd stay there next weekend and she would have a chance to settle down again. In truth she was finding him most unsettling.

She had Marc much on her mind in the week that followed, and thanked his cousin not at all that he had stirred her memories of her husband. When she awoke on Friday, however, a sense of fairness awoke with her.

It would be their wedding anniversary two weeks today, and the day after—the anniversary of Marc's death—she would have him very much on her mind with or without Dacre's questions, she realised.

She was down in the stableyard when she heard the sound of a car and looked up to see Regis Gramache pulling up. Feeling a touch reluctant, because she wasn't totally comfortable in his company, she left what she was doing, and as he got out of his car and came towards her she met him halfway.

'I must have misunderstood you, *monsieur*,' she began to apologise. 'I didn't realise you would be coming to see Nina again.'

'Regis.' He reminded her of his first name when there was entirely no need. 'You did not misunderstand, Josy. I have not come to see either of the horses, but you.'

'Oh!' she exclaimed, and was stuck. Then, with relief, she saw Georges pedalling like fury down the path towards them.

'I came to ask if you would care to have dinner with me one evening?' he asked in careful English while beyond him she saw Georges get off his bicycle and pretend to do something with the back wheel. Oh, heavens, a straight no sounded a bit blunt and she could feel herself colouring up. 'I know you are a widow-lady now, but I know I could help you over your sad time,' Regis Gramache went on.

Really! There was arrogance—and arrogance. Dacre had it without conceit. But this man! 'Thank you,' she answered politely, 'but I prefer to take my meals at home.'

'You wish me to dine with you here?' he asked, and, niggled by him or not, Josy discovered that her confidence had grown and that she just had to laugh.

'I wish nothing of the sort, *monsieur*,' she replied, but her dignity was shot, though, amazingly, she found that she was the one in charge when she politely told him, 'Perhaps I may telephone you when I feel like entering back into the dining-out world?'

She wasn't sure that he fully understood what she meant, but she gathered he'd got the gist of it when, taking her right hand in his, and perhaps holding it a little longer than necessary, he shook hands with her. 'Until then, Josy,' he answered warmly, and went back to his car.

'*Café*, Georges?' she asked as they watched the car drive away. Had that been *her*? Had that truly been her? Had she really handled that situation which at one time would have caused her to die a thousand deaths?

Josy was feeling very much cheered when she awakened the next morning. She guessed it was a hangover from yesterday when she had dealt with the amorous vet, and when Georges, as if he had seen the vet's car, and in the absence of any other of her family being about, had chased down to the stables to watch over her.

She went down to the stables feeling very much warm and protected, and as if she truly was a member of Dacre's family. She heard a plane overhead and realised that, contrary to her opinion last weekend, she didn't mind if Dacre would be home this weekend. She was out riding Nina when her newly found sense of humour tickled her again. She didn't mind Dacre coming home! Grief, it was *his* home! He'd every right to be there.

He was in the paddock checking some fencing when she returned. He saw her and left what he was doing to come over. Josy quickly got down from Nina and stood waiting as he came over to her. Her heart ached peculiarly as she waited for him to kiss her cheeks in greeting, and she hoped that he would think the warm colour she felt storm to her face was merely from the exertions of her ride.

'Hello, cousin.' He smiled in greeting, his look taking in her large eyes, her warm colour.

'Hello, Dacre,' she answered, and although she was so used to him now, and so at ease with him that she had parted with one of her two deepest secrets, she suddenly felt astronomically shy. Oh, Lord, and she had thought that she was at last—at long, long last—growing out of it!

'Have you had a good week?' he asked, and while last Saturday she might have told him all about Regis Gramache's visit yesterday this Saturday she felt too constrained to do so. And in no way could she make him coffee and stay in the confines of the kitchenette and drink a cup with him.

'Very good,' she replied, adding hurriedly, not giving him chance to say another word, 'Would you excuse me? I w-want to check something with César.'

The fact that she seemed to have slipped back into the shy, stammering person she had been before bothered Josy, and she kept out of his way for the rest of the day. Good manners if nothing else, however, insisted that she join him for dinner that night.

Hoping to give her failing confidence a boost, Josy dressed with care that evening—and thought she espied an admiring glint in Dacre's glance as he pulled out her chair at the table for her.

However, she might not have been able to tell him that morning of Regis Gramache's visit, but there was nothing admiring in Dacre's look when, halfway through their starter, he revealed that somebody had.

'I heard the vet paid a call yesterday,' he commented conversationally, though there was something in his tone that warned her before she said anything that he was not best pleased about it.

'Oh, yes,' she answered non-committally, deciding that perhaps it might be best to keep her answers brief.

'He wasn't here long enough to check the horses, though.'

'He wasn't,' she agreed.

'Are you being deliberately obtuse?' he suddenly bit aggressively.

'You're obviously looking for a fight!' Josy retorted, surprised at herself.

Dacre seemed surprised too. He mastered his aggressiveness, anyhow, and more peacefully, if tautly, demanded, 'So tell me about it.'

For several seconds she stared mulishly at him. But was then weakened by the thought that he was after all Marc's cousin, and as such had taken it upon himself to see that she was looked out for.

'He came to see me.'

Whatever French expletive left Dacre she didn't understand it. She understood his English, though, when, switching rapidly to her language, and all aggressive again, he barked, 'He has the audacity to come courting you in my home?'

'Courting?' she exclaimed. 'Hardly that!'

'Tell me, then!' he commanded.

'He came to ask me out to dinner.'

'You're *not* going!' he thundered before she could blink.

'That's for *me* to decide!' she yelled back, and then suddenly collapsed into laughter.

'What's so funny?' her host icily wanted to know.

'You—me.' With difficulty she controlled herself. 'I'm sorry, Dacre. I've never been like this with anyone.' His icy look started to thaw. 'We have a saying in England, "wouldn't say boo to a goose", and I've always thought that about summed me up. But here I am—not for the first time, if I remember rightly—yelling my head off at you. I confess,' she added, her laughter now done with, 'that since coming here I hardly know myself.'

For long, long moments Dacre just sat and looked at her, and then, his fury gone, he commented quietly, 'Good.' Then Agathe came in.

Josy puzzled about that 'Good' during her waking hours. And it was as she was walking down to the stables on Sunday morning that she realised, on remembering the way she had been when Dacre had called at her home—why, almost eight months ago now!—that she had come a long way since then.

Then, much as she loved Hetty, she had been unable to face going up to the stables to see her. Dacre, within an hour, had changed that. Dacre had, in fact, been responsible for bringing about many changes in her life. But for him she might never have made the break from her home. She had, she realised, a lot to thank him for.

She was not, however, of a mind to thank him for any thing at lunchtime when she joined him at the lunch table, and he growled, 'You'll be wearing yourself and the horses out if you exercise them much more.'

So sack me, she felt like retorting, but, since he wasn't really employing her, and since he might well say, What a good idea, she of previous small retaliation held her tongue. 'They thoroughly enjoy it,' she replied calmly; but was honest enough to face up to the fact that, because Dacre was home she had deliberately kept them out longer. Somehow, and she could not pinpoint why, something was urging her to stay out of his way.

'Did you want to ride César?' she enquired.

'No,' was the clipped reply.

'You didn't—want me for anything?' she was unwise enough to venture.

'Not a thing!' he retorted sharply, and she hated, hated, hated him! So, OK, she couldn't think of a thing he might have come down to the stables to see her about either, but he could have been a little less blunt with his 'Not a thing!' reply.

With scarcely a word being spoken between them throughout the rest of the meal it was only good manners which kept Josy in her seat. Mutiny such as she had never experienced before was playing havoc with her, and she could hardly wait for the meal to end so that she could leave the table and take herself off somewhere.

At last she put down her napkin and, since she didn't think she could very well get up and leave without another word, she pushed back from the table and offered a defiant, '*Should* you need me for anything I'll be out on either Nina or César!'

Hostilely they stared at each other, but when she saw a minuscule movement at the corner of his mouth, as though he was hard put to it not to laugh, she turned abruptly away and made quickly for the door.

To her astonishment, however, Dacre had left his seat too and was at the door before her. She halted; he was blocking her way. She looked at him mutinously, and felt not one iota less mutinous when he drawled, 'Since you obviously work, think and dream horses, I'll take you to a performance of the Cadre Noir next week.'

And if you think I'm to be mollified by that you can think again, she fumed. Arrogant swine! 'Actually,' she told him loftily, and with no little delight, 'I've already been.' And had her ears assaulted for her trouble.

'Who with?' he snarled aggressively.

'By myself!' she retorted angrily. 'And very good company I was too!' With that she pushed past him and went up to her room to change. And if he hadn't gleaned from that that she preferred her own company to his, then tough!

By the time she had cooled down enough to realise that there was absolutely no earthly reason why he should want to mollify her anyway Dacre had returned to Paris.

Josy spent Monday and Tuesday hoping that for the next four and a half months or so—when her six months would be up—he would stay there. She found him too disturbing, too annoying, and much too much *too* everything else.

She owned that she had never felt so confused—and it was getting worse. Her sleep patterns were shot, and with the anniversary so close, if she didn't have Dacre on her mind, she had Marc.

On Friday night she dreamt of them both, and on Saturday morning she got up feeling drained and exhausted, and bogged down by feelings of inadequacy at the fact that she had been unable to love Marc as a wife should.

Josy went to the stables hoping with all she had that she and Dacre wouldn't strike sparks off each other this weekend. She didn't think she could cope with that. Then she found that she didn't have to—because he didn't come home that weekend.

She found that she was listening for his plane, and for a while alternated between being glad that he wasn't coming home and regretful. He worked hard—must do—and must want and need space to unwind to relax.

Oh, grief, was he fed up with her being there? Josy spent a worried ten minutes fretting about it before it dawned on her that if Dacre did not want her there then, family or no, it wouldn't take him long to find her somewhere else to live, even if it meant making a flat over the stables—and that triggered off thoughts of Marc, and she wondered if she was going mad.

Just as she also wondered why when at the beginning of the week she had hoped Dacre would never come home she was now missing him. Of course I'm not missing him, she contradicted. Nor did she care a jot that just because he'd got something heavy going on in Paris—undoubtedly with some stunning-looking female—he couldn't be bothered to stretch out a hand to the phone to tell somebody that he wouldn't be home.

Josy felt more mixed up than ever as, the weekend over, Monday gave way to Tuesday. She was still sleeping badly, and fresh guilt over Marc had appeared to haunt her.

On Friday—her wedding anniversary—she awoke so distracted that she felt that she had to go and visit Marc's grave. She attended to the horses early and, turning them out into the paddock, went to find Georges. In fractured French, with accompanying hand signs, she asked him to keep an eye on her charges while she drove into Saumur. Tomorrow, early, before Dacre arrived—if indeed he intended coming home that weekend—she would drive to Nantes.

It did not take her long to purchase a map and she returned home to take it up to her room. She opened it out, and judged that the journey would take about two hours. But, while she could see no problem in getting to Nantes, since she could barely remember Marc's funeral, let alone the place where he was laid to rest, she realised she might have a problem from then on.

It was still early—not quite eleven in the morning—when, leaving the map open on her bed, Josy decided to go downstairs and check in the library to see if there were any maps there that might give her more precise details of the Nantes area.

Somehow, too, she realised as she left her room, she was going to have to let Agathe know where she was going tomorrow. She couldn't leave for the day without telling her. Then she would have to arrange something about the horses.

She was halfway down the stairs when the front door opened and, causing her to blink and wonder if she had missed a day somewhere, Dacre came in.

She had halted, as had he. Then she carried on walking down the stairs just as Dacre, a weekend bag in hand, moved towards her.

'I didn't hear your plane,' was the first thing that came into her head as they met at the bottom of the stairs.

'How are you, Josy?' he enquired, dropping his bag to the floor and taking a hold of her arms, his eyes scrutinising her face.

'Fine,' she lied, knowing that she looked drawn and strained and, in fact, a wreck.

Dacre scrutinised her for a second longer, then the phone rang near by. He did not go to answer it immediately but kissed her cheeks and, causing her to stand motionless from the shock of it, she was sure that he pressed his warm cheek against hers.

Josy was still standing motionless when he let go of her and went to answer the phone. I've imagined it, she thought, but promptly came away from her surprise when she realised that Dacre, who had answered the phone in French, had switched to English.

'Josy is here now,' he advised, and the next moment he was holding out the phone to her.

Josy went forward and took the phone from him. 'Hello?' she enquired.

'Hello, love,' her sister answered, and suddenly Josy was fighting to hold back tears. 'Was that Dacre Banchereau?'

'Yes,' she answered, and hid her tears in a shy smile to him as he looked back before picking up his bag and starting up the stairs, clearly on his way to his room.

'He sounds nice,' Belvia commented.

'He is.'

'How's your weather?'

'Beautiful,' Josy answered, and felt tearful again when her dear sister, who needed no excuse to ring her, got down to the real reason for this particular call.

'Latham and I came back last night—from a few days away, actually—and I thought, if it's all right with you, that I'd come this afternoon and stay with you for a couple of days.'

Josy swallowed down a knot of emotion at her sister's thoughtfulness. She knew her twin well. What Belvia was really saying was, I know it's your wedding anniversary, and I know that it will be twelve months tomorrow that Marc died—and I'll be with you.

Her sister had been with her a year ago, and it had been her sister who had kept her from cracking up. And Josy felt that she had never loved Belvia more than she did then. But this was the first year of Bel's marriage too, and as Belvia loved Latham so much, and Latham absolutely adored Bel, it would be painful for the two to be apart and Josy could not let her sacrifice herself any more.

'Oh, Bel, I'd love you to come,' she answered, battling to keep emotional tears out of her voice, 'but I won't be here.'

'Where are you going?' Belvia wanted to know at once.

'To Nantes.'

'I'll come with you,' she promptly offered, and Josy fought with all she had to be strong.

'No,' she answered. 'I'm all right now—honestly I am.' And, although she would have dearly loved her sister's company, went on, 'If you wouldn't mind, Bel, I think I should like to go on my own.'

There was a small silence the other end, then Belvia, proving that she was as sensitive as ever, asked, 'You're sure, Jo?'

Josy was battling harder than ever to hold back tears when a few minutes later she put down the phone. And there was no way she wanted to go to the library to search for any detailed map. All she wanted to do was to get to her room.

Fearful that she might break down before she got there, Josy raced up the stairs, and reached the top just as the door to Dacre's room opened.

Swallowing convulsively, she went swiftly past him and into the privacy of her own room. Only it turned out to be not so private as she had thought, because before she could turn about and close the door Dacre, without stopping to knock, was there too.

'What's wrong, *chérie*?' he asked urgently.

'M-my sister, sh-she wanted to come and stay for a f-few days,' Josy stammered on a gasp of emotional breath, wiping desperately at a stray tear which had escaped her control.

Dacre came closer and caught hold of that hand. 'That's nothing to cry over, little one,' he murmured, leading her over to sit on the edge of the bed. 'Agathe will make up a room for her in no time.'

'Belvia isn't coming.'

'She's not?' he queried, sitting down on the bed beside her.

Josy shook her head. 'I told her not to. I couldn't let her. Oh, she's been so good—' She choked. 'You've no idea . . . Yet, even though she's married herself now, and is so happy, she's remembered that it's a year ago today that Marc and I married. A year tomorrow that Marc...' She couldn't go on.

'Shh . . .' Dacre soothed, and, letting go of her hand, he placed an arm about her shoulders and quietly held her.

They sat like that for some seconds, then Josy gave a shaky sigh, and suddenly became aware that Dacre had an arm around her. Her heart started to jump about; she thought it was panic. She pulled away from him and left the bed.

'I . . . I'm all right now,' she told him, and knew he didn't believe that for a minute when he looked at her long and hard.

His attention having been all on her, as he too stood up he half turned, and only then noticed the map spread out on the bed.

'Thinking of going somewhere?' he enquired evenly, evidence of where she might be intending to go spread out before him.

'I want to take some flowers to Marc,' Josy answered, and saw Dacre give a slight nod, though whether of approval or merely acknowledgment of what she wanted to do she couldn't tell.

She was left staring blankly at him for a moment or two, however, when he stated, 'I'll drive you.'

'I'm not going until tomorrow—and I can drive myself,' she declined.

'I don't think so,' he decided for her. And, when it looked as if she might object, added, 'Look at you, all huge-eyed from the stress you're under. Have you slept at all this week?' he demanded.

'I—I'm all right,' she replied, suddenly no longer feeling weepy, but starting to feel angry. My God, this man! 'I'm no longer the emotional wreck I was. I—'

'I know that!' he retorted. 'The change in you since that day I called at your home is quite dramatic. But,' he went on when she drew breath to try to interrupt, 'you still have some way to go. And whether you know it or not—and I know you're going to battle like hell to ensure that no one sees you in tears—I don't think tomorrow will pass without you feeling a little emotional. 'Which is why,' he ended, his mouth quirking up at the corners, 'for the sake of any of my fellow countrymen who might be out on the road tomorrow, I will drive.'

He had a point there, she supposed, refusing to smile. She guessed she would not be giving her driving her entire concentration. 'I want to be off early.' She tried for a small obstruction anyway.

'I'll fly you there if you like.'

'No, thank you,' she replied politely.

'We'll leave here at eight,' Dacre decreed, then gave her something else to think about when he added, 'I think Marc's parents would appreciate it if we called on them.'

In an instant any hostility she was feeling towards him disappeared. 'They know I'm here—in your home?' she gasped.

'They have known from the time you gave me a definite date for your arrival.'

'And they don't mind—about it being me who's come to look after your horses?'

'They're delighted that you agreed to come,' Dacre assured her. 'They saw how happy Marc was to be with you. How—' Abruptly he broke off as a gasp of pain she could not control escaped her. 'What have I said? What...?'

Josy swiftly turned her back on him. 'He...' she gasped, but she couldn't tell him. Guilt stormed through her—guilt that would not let her be. Desperately she strove to get herself together but, swallow down emotional tears though she might, they were again coming nearer and nearer to the surface, and she just had to confess. 'You know that battle you spoke of? Well, would you mind leaving—while...' she swallowed '...while I'm still winning?'

She heard Dacre move, but it was not to the door as she had hoped but over to her. She kept her back to him and felt him take a hold of her arms. However, he did not turn her to face him but, allowing her her pride, in case she had lost her battle and had tears on her face, he just held her quietly by her arms.

'You have needed this year to mourn, little Josy,' he told her softly. 'But after tomorrow, I think—for your own sake, and for the sake of your happy memories of Marc—you should try to live for yourself.' With that he placed a light kiss in her hair.

That kiss and what Dacre had said affected her deeply. She didn't panic at his kiss to her hair; she had no need to. It had been more reverential than anything else. And yet it disturbed her. As too did his remark that after tomorrow she should try to live for herself.

She wanted to do that; she really did. The only trouble was that she suddenly felt so confused; she didn't know where she was going, or wanted to go, or what she wanted to do—or anything else any more.

She was so tired that presently Vicki Baum's novel was some unintelligible jumble of meaningless words where she ought to make sense of an experience that seemed to do ... too him a ... many hours.

CHAPTER FIVE

JOSY owned to being in sombre mood when just after eight the following morning Dacre headed his car in the direction of Nantes. She had little to say, and the nearer they got to their destination, the further she shrank into herself.

'Perhaps this wasn't such a good idea,' Dacre commented when half an hour had passed with not so much as a word coming from her.

'I—need to... I want to go,' she answered, and with a great effort, aware that he had given Franck and Georges instructions about the horses, she forced some conversation. 'Nina and César will be all right, won't they?'

Dacre's answer was initially to touch her left hand resting in her lap in a reassuring gesture. 'Who do you think looked after them when you took so long to get here?' he asked lightly—and she really did like him.

They stopped on the way so that she could purchase some fresh flowers. Because Marc had liked yellow Josy bought yellow roses and mimosa, and a vase to put them in.

Dacre carried the vase when they left the car. She had been worried that she might not remember where Marc's grave was. But proving that while he had been unable to attend Marc's funeral Dacre had since paid his respects, he guided her straight to the well-kept grave.

Fresh flowers had already been laid there, so Josy guessed that his parents had been early that morning.

Save for going and filling the vase with water from a nearby tap, Dacre stayed with her while she arranged the roses and mimosa, and she was pleased to have him there. Just as, after some minutes of standing with her in silence at Marc's graveside, she appreciated his sensitivity when he walked back to the car, leaving her alone with her memories.

Josy was still racked by the guilt of her last memories, but she remembered how Dacre had referred to her happy memories of Marc. She choked on a dry sob but made herself remember those happier times. She remembered Marc's goodness, his gentleness, his winning way with horses. But most of all she remembered his shyness. It had been that shyness that had caused her to be drawn to him. Next to her sister he had been her best friend. Dear Marc, her best friend and . . . Tears stung her eyes, but she was glad she had come.

She walked back to the car. Dacre was standing by it. And she was taken out of the solemnity of her thoughts when, before she could open the passenger door, he came round and halted her by placing a hand on each shoulder. She felt herself begin to tremble but, made by him to stand still, she raised her face and found herself looking into a pair of serious, steady grey eyes.

'What . . .?' she questioned faintly.

'I have to tell you,' he began quietly, 'that my aunt and uncle were very comforted when I told them that you would be coming here today.'

'You rang them?'

He nodded. 'They've invited us to lunch.'

'Oh, Dacre,' she whispered, and pulled out of his hold. He had said something yesterday about calling on them— and if she thought about it she supposed it was better that he'd telephoned them in advance rather than they

should just drop in on them. But she didn't want to go—
knew that she didn't—not back to that house where...
She couldn't be that brave; she... Her thoughts fractured again.

She was Monsieur and Madame Paumier's daughter-
in-law—the wife, widow, of their only child. And, even
if she didn't feel like their daughter-in-law, Dacre had
said that they had been very comforted to know she
would be there today. Oh...was she to be forever a
coward? 'I don't think I'm very hungry, but...' She
bravely agreed.

Dacre murmured something soft and warm-sounding
in French which she didn't catch, and probably wouldn't
have understood anyway if she had. Then he was as-
sisting her into her car.

Monsieur and Madame Paumier greeted them most
warmly. 'Oh, how pale you are!' Sylvie Paumier exclaimed, and enfolded her in her arms, as too did
Philippe Paumier. In fact, Josy had more of a hug from
her father-in-law than she had ever had from her own
father.

Lunch was less of an ordeal than she had thought it
would be, and Josy guessed she had Dacre to thank for
the fact that, whenever Marc's name came up, he would
steer the conversation to light anecdotes about him.

Both Marc's parents spoke English, though neither
was as fluent as Dacre and sometimes got matters a little
back to front, which left it to him to come in with a
translation. He did so again when Philippe Paumier
brought the subject of money up. As well as her feeling
awkward about it, the more her father-in-law tried to
explain how Marc had wanted things, the more confused Josy became.

'I'm sorry, I don't understand,' she confessed, starting to feel a little hot and bothered.

'Don't be embarrassed, little one,' Dacre bade her. 'It is just that my uncle, because of the language difference, wants to be sure that you understand Marc's wishes and, incidentally, theirs. They say you've written to their lawyer refusing the provision Marc willed to you and mailed to his lawyer the week before your marriage, but—'

'Please, I can't. I never knew Marc had money. And...' her voice wobbled a bit ' ...I can't take it.'

'We are upsetting you. Oh, please forgive us,' Madame Paumier rushed in—and Josy felt worse than ever. It was they who should forgive her!

Josy felt quite desperate on the drive home. It had been a mistake to go and visit Marc's parents. She had pretended that she wasn't upset, of course. Because of their kindness to her, because they were Marc's parents, she had to pretend. They were going through a bad enough time as it was, without them thinking that she had gone away feeling worse than when she had come.

It was a silent drive back to the outskirts of Saumur. On the way to Nantes she had tried to lighten up; on the way back she felt too down to try.

'Thank you for taking me today,' she politely thanked Dacre when he halted the car at his home. She got out of the car and found that he was there on the gravel drive with her.

'You have had a bad year, *ma chère*,' he commented as he looked down into her troubled and expressive face. 'But remember that from tomorrow you are going to live for you—and not in the past.' Unspeaking, she stared at him, and he stretched out a hand and gave her arm a little shake. 'You'll remember?' he insisted.

Josy opened her mouth, hesitated, then promised, 'I'll remember,' and turned about and went indoors, leaving him to garage the car.

She went wearily up to her room. She had promised to live for herself. But what did that mean? When she had first come here she had thought it a start to a new life—a new life which would begin in earnest when she returned to England and, taking Hetty with her, got herself a job. But the thought of leaving this lovely and tranquil spot to start her new life suddenly didn't seem to have any meaning either!

Josy saw little of Dacre on Sunday. She exercised Nina and he came down to the stables and took César out, and returned to Paris before lunch.

That evening, needing some occupation, she wrote to her father—not that she thought he'd be too interested in how she fared. But, duty done, she then wrote to Tracey at the stables, in the hope that she might reply and give her more detailed information about Hetty's day-to-day welfare than—if she caught her at a wrong moment—she might over the phone.

On Monday Belvia phoned, and Josy chatted to her for a good ten minutes. And after that the week progressed, and Josy began to grow more restless and fidgety than she had ever been. She was still plagued by guilt over Marc, but for the first time she began to acknowledge that, since she could do nothing about it, that guilt was just something she was going to have to learn to live with.

The odd thing was, however, that, while she felt so restless during the day, at night she had started to sleep better.

She awoke on Saturday feeling at once refreshed, and at the same time, as she recalled that Dacre would soon be here, she began to feel totally mixed up.

I haven't got enough to do, that's my trouble, she mused as, full of energy, she got out of bed. She had thought once or twice lately of asking Georges if he wanted any help in the garden. But a combination of shyness and the fact that Georges kept the gardens immaculate without her help kept her silent. It was also a fact, though, that looking after Nina and César was very far from being a full-time job.

A short while later, showered and breakfasted, she made her way to the stables. Already the day was warming up. She decided against saddling up the horses and taking them out but instead fed them and turned them out into the paddock. There were a few jobs she could be getting on with, but for the moment she watched as they frisked to the tree-shaded side of their enclosed area. Only when she became aware that she was listening for the sound of a plane did she grow impatient with herself and go and do a few chores.

By lunchtime she had neither seen nor heard Dacre. So, she'd be dining on her own tonight, she thought. Well, that was OK by her. She hoped he enjoyed himself wherever he was.

Josy went to bed that night in a very mixed-up frame of mind. For while part of her had started to grow quite anxious in case Dacre was ill, or something of that nature, there was another part of her that said she didn't give a damn that some glamorous-looking female was keeping him in Paris that weekend.

On the following Wednesday she awakened and went to her window to see that an early morning mist had settled over the landscape. It had been like that yesterday. The mist didn't take long to clear, and by nine a sunny day shone from a beautiful blue sky with only the merest scratch of cloud. Already it was a steaming-hot day.

Since she didn't like the idea of leaving the horses in their stables all day, the best thing to do was to turn them out into their shady paddock.

That did not take very long, and by eleven, their stables spruce and ready for their return, Josy walked back to the house. She felt hot and sticky and headed straight for the shower. She was under it when such a weight of restlessness took her that she just knew that she could not spend the day idly.

She had been to the town of Saumur several times. It was quite close by. She decided that she needed to go farther afield and went looking for Agathe. '*Je suis* going to Angers, Agathe.' She smiled as she hoped to convey that she was going to Angers. '*J'ai déjeuner*, Angers,' she added, to let the housekeeper know she would have lunch out. 'Nina, César...' she began.

'Franck *ou* Georges.' Agathe understood at once and gave her shy smile, and Josy went to get her car out in the confident knowledge that Agathe would instruct either her husband or Georges to keep an eye on the horses.

A little over an hour later Josy reached the city of Angers, and, finding a car park without difficulty, she left her car and strolled about. But she had little thought as to what she was doing or where she was going. She felt lost and alone, and there was an empty sort of ache inside her—it had been there for a few days—though she was mystified to know what that ache was.

She ambled into the Habitat shop and had a look round, but there was such a restlessness inside her that she came out again and walked on.

This is ridiculous, she lectured herself, and, seeing a crêperie in the Rue des Poëliers, with chairs and tables outside, she made herself go and sit down. She didn't want very much to eat—a snack would do. She ordered a *galette aux tomates et fromage*, and while she was waiting for her tomato and cheese pancake to arrive she wondered about Dacre. Then, trying to think about something else, for Dacre had seemed to spend quite a lot of time in her head just lately, she concentrated her thoughts on Hetty. Then all at once she became aware that there was a shadow in front of her.

Expecting it to be the waitress, she looked up, and her mouth opened in astonishment. Dacre Banchereau was standing there! And, just like that, in that very moment, she knew staggeringly that she was in love with him!

Her heart pounded; there was a roaring in her ears. She did not merely like him, she loved him! She would have welcomed a faint. But she didn't faint, and since Dacre seemed content to stand there watching her open-mouthed expression she took it that it was up to her to say something.

'What are you doing here?' she gasped.

'About to join you for lunch,' he drawled, and, bending down, he kissed both her cheeks. Then, while she was still striving for normality—when she had an idea that nothing would be normal ever again—he calmly took the seat next to her and asked what she had ordered.

'Er—the cheese and tomato crêpe,' she answered, the empty ache that she had carried around with her since he had not come home last weekend suddenly, as if by magic, gone.

'We'll be starving by dinnertime but I'll have the same,' he remarked conspiratorially.

She smiled, wanted to laugh; she was happy just being with him. 'How are they managing in Paris without you?' she controlled herself to tease—and felt as startled by her comment as Dacre looked. Grief—when had she so far forgotten her shyness to be so light-hearted?

Whatever, suddenly Dacre grinned at her sauce. 'With difficulty,' he answered wickedly, and she couldn't help it—she just burst out laughing.

Then she saw that Dacre still had his gaze on her, and swiftly she controlled herself. 'Er—have you been home?' she enquired.

'Flew in a couple of hours ago,' he answered, and she quite desperately wanted to know how long he was staying. But she kept silent. 'Agathe mentioned you were visiting the city, and since I had an errand this way I thought I'd come and help my English cousin with the menu. But—I was too late.'

Oh, she loved him, she loved him, she loved him. She especially loved him in this mood. It seemed to match her own so exactly. 'Um—I hate to tell you this, but there was a translation in English.'

'You know,' he murmured conversationally, 'without too much assistance you could grow to be quite cheeky.' She grinned. He stared. And she wanted that this lunchtime should never end.

But end it did, as it had to, and Dacre walked with her to her car. 'See you at home,' she offered, feeling shy again but hoping that he didn't mind her calling his home her home.

Apparently he didn't, for he looked at her warmly. 'Till then,' he said softly, and kissed her gently on both cheeks, and then stood back.

'Bye,' she mumbled, and got into her car and turned the ignition. For the first few minutes of her journey she negotiated city traffic while at the same time wondering at the fact that, out of all the places she could have halted at to have a snack, she had chosen one on the route Dacre had been walking.

She had cleared the city traffic and was on a straight part of the road from Angers to Saumur when she had space to give most of her attention to the astonishing and unbelievable fact that she was head over heels in love with Dacre. She did not have to dissect it. It was just there. She loved him—and it was like no other feeling she had ever known.

Quite when on that journey back to Dacre's home her feeling of inner happiness began to fade she could not have said. All she knew by the time she halted her car was that there was going to be very little joy for her in this love for Dacre that had come uninvited and unasked for.

Josy left her car on the front drive and, feeling all over the place suddenly, got out, leaving it where it was, and, feeling in the need of some action, took a walk down to the paddock.

Nina and César trotted over to her, and she crooned to them for a while, then fell again to thinking of the love she had for Dacre, which was still there—this different kind of love—and which, she just knew, always would be there.

She had loved Marc, but not in this way. But, while admittedly the love she had had for Marc had been nothing like this all-encompassing love she felt for Dacre, she faced the fact that she should never love any man. She had loved Marc—and he had died.

Josy was standing by the paddock rail, deep in thought while trying to find peace of mind, when suddenly Dacre came striding towards her. She felt immediately jumpy. Oh, how dear he was; how she loved him—but oh, how she should not. Pain smote her, and as he drew level and halted she looked away.

If he had expected to see his laughing companion of lunchtime, or the shy but happy woman he had parted from in the car park, then it was patently obvious his expectation would come to nought.

Silently he studied her. 'What's wrong, Josy?' he asked abruptly, his glance fixed on her lifeless expression.

Her heart thudded painfully, and she felt that she would just about die if ever he had so much as the merest inkling of how she felt about him. 'Nothing,' she answered woodenly—and too late saw that she should have known him better than to think he would let her get away with that.

'Don't lie to me!' he objected sternly.

'I'm not lying!'

'Something's upsetting you!' He let go something angry-sounding in French, then calmed down to ask, 'What is it? In Angers you were—'

'We're not in Angers now!'

'You're unhappy here, then?'

'Of course not!' she flew at him, starting to grow angry herself. 'I love it here—you must know that I do.'

'So what happened between here and Angers?' he was back to demanding to know.

'I don't need this!' she exclaimed hotly, and went to turn away from him but, tenacious as she had known he would be, he wasn't letting her get away with that either.

'Will you stop trying to hide from matters that bother you?' he roared, catching hold of her right arm and swinging her back to face him.

'Take your hands off me!' she shrieked.

'Then tell me what's wrong!'

She'd die sooner. 'Why do you want to know?' she yelled, her panic momentarily clearing, allowing her to see that her only way out lay in attack.

'So there *is* something!' he exclaimed triumphantly, and, loving him, she wanted to hit him.

Furiously she pushed him away. His eyes glinted; he didn't like it. 'What do you want from me?' she cried in anguish.

And she nearly dropped when, his anger with her out of control, he bellowed, 'I want you to marry me!'

'No!' she gasped, horrified, her breath sucked in; he looked as shaken that he had actually said those words as she felt to have heard them.

He recovered first, however. 'The idea's so alien to you?' he asked toughly, the fact that she was horror-struck not lost on him. 'The idea of being my wife, the mother of my children—'

'*Stop!*' she screamed. 'Don't...' She couldn't take any more, but turned and ran from him. This time, perhaps because he judged it would do more harm than good to try to hold on to her a second time, he let her go.

Josy was still in a state of shock when an age later she came to to realise that she was sitting in an armchair in her bedroom but could not remember how she had got there.

What she could remember, however, was that Dacre had clearly stated, loudly enough for anyone around to hear, that he wanted her to marry him. Stars above! But, worse, he had spoken of children, so he wasn't interested

in a 'name only' type of marriage. And, remembering
the virile look of him, she wouldn't have believed him
if he'd said he was.

A shaky fifteen minutes later everything was still
whirling around in her head. Dacre had said nothing
about love—perhaps he didn't think that love was
necessary. His attitude would be just a convenient, I'll
be home at the weekend—mostly. Occasionally in the
week too. You just look after the horses—the babies too
when they arrive. Oh, God, she felt she really was going
mad. Babies! Heaven help her—she couldn't bear that
any man should touch her!

Josy was dragged out of the agony of her thoughts
when someone knocked at her bedroom door. She started
nervously, and then decided, since Dacre was more likely
to walk straight in than knock and wait, that it must be
Agathe.

She went and opened it—but it was Dacre. He was
serious-faced, watchful. 'Are you all right?' he wanted
to know.

Cracking up fast, she could have told him. 'Fine,' she
replied stiffly.

'You look dreadful,' he informed her. She wanted to
say, Thanks, but nothing would come out. 'Try to rest
in between now and dinner,' he suggested, not unkindly.

'I—' she began, on the way to telling him that she
would be giving dinner a miss that night.

'And after dinner we'll talk, you and I,' he cut in to
decree.

She didn't want to talk to him either. As she saw it
there was nothing to talk about. She had covered all that
needed to be discussed in that horrified, No, she had
given him in reply to his suggestion that she marry him.

Then she recalled his accusation that she tried to hide from matters. 'Yes,' she confirmed reluctantly.

He nodded. 'Try to rest,' he repeated, and walked away.

Josy went slowly back into her room. She caught sight of her face in the mirror. It was ashen. She decided, regardless of his repeated instructions to rest, that she'd had enough of her room.

Belatedly she remembered that her car was still parked out front. She left her room, but when she went out through the front door her car was not there. Dacre, she realised, must have garaged it for her.

She felt better for being outside, she realised, and unhurriedly walked down to the stables. It was early evening by that time, but Georges, working overtime as he sometimes did, was down there making a fuss of both her charges. She waved to him and he indicated that he would put Nina and César to bed for the night.

Josy walked back to the house, reflecting that it had been kind of Dacre to garage her car, kind of him to come to her room and check that she was all right, while at the same time she was fast regretting that she had agreed to have a talk with him after dinner.

What good would talking do? It wasn't as though he loved her; he would laugh his French socks off at any ridiculous notion that his reason for wanting to marry her was anything more than expediency. He had decided that it was time he did something about having a wife and children and she—already installed in his home—was trustworthy and already family too. What could be more convenient, more efficient?

She couldn't be sure that that was the way his thoughts went, of course. And since being here she had grown stronger than she had been, and in his home she had

been happier than she had ever expected to be again.
And, not least because she loved him and because of his
kindness, she owned that she owed him more than a horrified, No, by way of explanation for why she would not
marry him.

In her room she showered and changed, but the closer
it got to eight o'clock, the less she felt like eating, or
seeing Dacre again. She had no idea what explanation
she could possibly give him.

But, as panic began to bite at some unwanted honesty
within her that decreed she must either face him or return
to England, so her watch showed eight. And because she
loved him, and wanted to stay here with him, she found
the courage to go down the stairs.

At the sound of her footsteps Dacre came from the
open *salon* door, and, while she somehow managed to
keep walking towards him, inside she froze.

'Shall we go and see what delicious morsels Agathe
has prepared for us tonight?' Dacre offered.

Josy went with him to the dining-room. If that had
been his way of easing a taut situation, he need not have
bothered. She wanted to run; she shouldn't have come
down. Oh, why, oh, why had Dacre had to complicate
what—up until this afternoon—had been a wonderful
arrangement?

She took her usual seat in the dining-room, but Agathe
could have placed a dish of chaff before her for all she
was able to enjoy the housekeeper's superb cooking. She
felt apprehensive, on edge, and, while she didn't want
any sort of conversation with Dacre, she wanted anything that had to be said over and done with so that she
could go back to her room.

She barely touched her first course. She tried hard
with her second course, but found that to swallow any-

thing at all took a tremendous effort, and she jumped, startled, when Dacre said suddenly, 'Relax, Josy.' And she saw it was as futile to deny that she felt jumpy. She saw his glance go to her plate, and found her voice.

'W-would you apologise to Agathe for me, and—and tell her that I had a big meal at lunchtime?' she asked.

'*Certainement*,' he replied urbanely, having seen for himself just how much she had eaten at lunchtime and yet not batting an eyelid at her lie. 'Would you care for some wine?' he enquired.

'No, thank you,' she returned politely; he might think it would help her to relax, but she was more interested in keeping a clear head.

She was surprised none the less when, his meal not finished either, he all at once stood up. 'My dear, you look just as if you're waiting for Madame Guillotine. Shall we go and get this over?'

'Your dinner?' she protested, again wanting to run.

'Come.' He refused to prevaricate, and came round to her chair. Josy moved before he reached her and they went from the dining-room to the *salon*.

Josy moved further into the room. She wanted this over in two minutes flat. But when Dacre closed the door and indicated that she take a seat she knew it was not going to be that quick—or simple.

Yet as she sat down, and Dacre took a chair facing her and her apprehension deepened, so she determined that it *was* that simple—of course it was. If she wanted this over quickly then, since Dacre was saying nothing, it was up to her to get started—and finished.

She looked up to see that he was eyeing her steadily, took a deep breath and, on a panicking instant of courage, started off. 'I'm sorry if my...' words failed her for a moment '...my—if the way I said no this

afternoon was a bit abrupt. What I should have said—
well, fr-frankly—I was a bit—er—taken aback by your
prop—by what you said—was that I'm afraid I can't—
um—marry you b-because I shall never marry again.'

There, it was said! And if Dacre was anywhere near
as kind as she thought him he would let her return to
her room without further argument. Josy started to
breathe a trace more easily, and even put her hands on
the arms of her chair prior to getting up. But then it was
that she discovered that he wasn't so kind as she had
believed—and that he *did* want further explanation!

'It's not—just me?' he enquired quietly.

Dear God, she loved him! If anyone, it would be him.
'No,' she answered.

'Then why, Josy,' he wanted to know, 'do you think
you will never marry again?'

She stared at him—and would not answer. Nor could
he make her answer. There seemed to be a determined
kind of glint in his grey eyes—as if he knew that it was
more than that she felt it would be a betrayal of Marc,
of her love for her dead husband, if she married again—
and determinedly Dacre was waiting. But she could be
determined too.

Dacre waited silently, not moving but patiently resolved that she should answer his question. She started
to feel jumpy again, and flicked a nervous glance to the
door. Then she looked back at him. His gaze seemed to
have softened, and she loved him, and although what
she truly wanted to do was run, somehow—perhaps because of what he had said to her about hiding away from
things, or perhaps because her love for him was weakening her—she found that she could not run.

Nor could she sit still either. She got up from her chair,
and Dacre rose too—though whether from politeness or

in order to be at the door before her if she made a run for it she could not tell.

She did not make for the door, however, but turned to walk over to the windows. It was still light enough to see out, but she saw nothing of the view as she fought for composure to tell him what he insisted on knowing—what she had never told another living soul.

'Is it so painful, my dear?'

She had not known that he was so close. She turned. Oh, Dacre, she mourned silently, you've no idea.

'Yes,' she owned, even at that late stage hoping he would let her off the hook. But he didn't, and while she again toyed with the idea of trying to leave the room she realised that because she loved him and because he had, in a manner of speaking, proposed, she owed him more than that.

'You said—accused...' she began, made a faulty start, and began again. 'This afternoon you accused me of trying to hide from things that bothered me. Well...' she paused to take a shaky but controlling breath '...well, that's not true. You're wrong,' she managed.

'Come and sit down,' Dacre suggested, his voice quiet, his tone hypnotic—so much so that she allowed him to lead her over to a sofa, where he sat down with her and, turning to her, prompted softly, 'Go on. Tell me how I'm wrong.'

She looked at him and away again, could not bear to see the look in his eyes change. And after another shaky start she began, 'I've hidden from nothing, Dacre. Ever—ever—since Marc died I've been crucified by facing up to the... guilt that is mine, the guilt that I was to blame for—his accident, the guilt for...' her voice started to fade '...for his death,' she ended on a hushed sound.

She couldn't look at him. She didn't want to look at him, to see hate and loathing in his face that she had been responsible for the death of someone loved and of his family. She moved to get up—and found his hand had come to her arm as he held her still.

Then his other hand was coming beneath her chin, and he was forcing her head up, forcing her to look up into his eyes. She looked, studied those grey eyes so close, but—unbelievably—saw not a hint of hate.

'Marc was thrown from his horse, Josy,' Dacre stated quietly.

'No,' she denied, then changed it to agree, 'Well, he fell; y-yes, he did. But it was because of—m-me. Because I...' Her voice faded; she couldn't tell him that— nothing on this earth would make her. 'He wasn't thinking what he was doing. When he fell off Diamant he wasn't thinking what he was doing. We'd...' She couldn't go on.

Then she found that she didn't need to, for, looking absolutely thunderstruck, something pretty explosive in French was leaving him. 'Oh, my dear, dear Josy—have you thought for all this while that Marc's death was your doing?' Dacre questioned. And while she stared at him, a mass of agitation, yet with a heart that pounded to hear him call her 'My dear, dear Josy', he said, 'Did no one tell you—?' He broke off, totally incredulous.

'Tell me what?' she asked, but was too het up to wait for an answer as she rapidly explained, 'W-we were all in shock—upset. I know I wasn't taking very much in— any conversation was all in French anyhow. But I don't remember much of anything, save that Belvia—who knows about as much French as I do—was there. All I could think, and know, was that if I'd acted differently then Marc would not have been upset—and that made me responsible for him falling off Diamant.' She gave a shuddery, racked kind of sigh—and became aware that Dacre had his hands on her shoulders, and was giving her a little shake.

She looked at him, saw that his expression was stern, and could not bear his hatred of her for her part in Marc's death. But she was then snapped out of her emotional unhappiness when, giving her shoulders another small shake, he bade her urgently, 'Listen to me, Josy, and hear every word. You were *not* in any way, shape or form responsible for my cousin's death.'

'I was.' She refused to believe him. 'Marc fell off—'

'Marc couldn't have fallen off a horse if he'd tried,' he contradicted her. 'He was born knowing how to ride. He did it instinctively; he didn't have to think about it— it was second nature to him.'

'Yes, but—'

'From a very early age his father would just sit him on a pony and Marc and pony were as one.'

'But—'

'Josy, Josy, hear me,' Dacre cut in, and, pausing for a moment, an alert look there in his eyes, he went on, 'You were obviously having—um—honeymoon problems.' She coloured, but somehow managed to keep eye contact. 'But, believe me, that had nothing to do with the fact that that black-hearted stallion threw him.'

Her eyes widened. She didn't believe their 'honeymoon problems', as he'd put it, had had nothing to do with it. But this was the first time she'd heard that Marc had been thrown! 'Threw him?' she questioned.

'That's what I said. Nor was it the first time.'

'It wasn't?'

His answer was to stare at her stunned. 'Didn't Marc tell you?' he asked.

She shook her head. 'He never mentioned it. What happened? Was he hurt?'

'He was in hospital for weeks—months,' Dacre replied, and, his look on her softening, he went on, 'Oncle Philippe was determined to have Diamant put down then, but Marc wouldn't hear of it. He wouldn't believe the brute had bad blood. So my uncle stabled him while Marc recovered and went on a European convalescent trip.'

'He was still convalescing when he found work at the stables?' Josy questioned; there was so much she hadn't known about Marc—his accident, his wealth. 'But he had no need to work!' she exclaimed.

'He wouldn't have called it work. In all probability he refused payment. But it would have been natural to him to head for the nearest stables.'

'His accident with Diamant wouldn't have put him off,' she stated, remembering Marc's love of horses.

'It wouldn't have,' he agreed. 'Just as, when he returned to his French home, his parents knew that within twenty-four hours Marc would be risking his neck on that devil stallion again.'

'And Diamant threw him again?' she questioned.

'He did. Despite his father warning him, Marc couldn't wait. They went towards the woods...'

'I was with him.' Josy, hardly aware that she had spoken, took over. 'Marc took off at a gallop—and I lost sight of him.'

'They were in the woods when the stallion made up his mind that he didn't want anyone on his back. One of the estate workers was there when he saw the beast rearing and bucking—even an expert like Marc was having difficulty hanging on. Marc was killed when the horse forcefully slammed him into a low-branched, solid tree.'

Josy stared at him, wanting to believe that Marc being thrown had had nothing to do with her. But, having gone through a whole year of dreadfully disabling guilt, she was finding it difficult to believe totally.

'You're sure?' she questioned.

'Absolutely positive,' Dacre answered unhesitatingly. 'I went to see Émile Caillère—the estate worker—myself a few weeks after it happened.'

'Oh—Dacre!' she exclaimed tremulously; could she let go of this dreadful guilt? Dared she let go? Dacre didn't know about... But...

'Oh—Josy,' he breathed softly, in return. 'I am so sorry that on top of losing Marc you have so suffered by thinking you were to blame.'

From somewhere she found a smile—a watery kind of smile. In a moment she would go to her room and digest all that he had said. But first she just had to stay and say, 'Thank you, Dacre. Thank you for telling me all you have.'

'You should have been told before. It should never have been left this long,' he stated, adding, 'I can only assume that my aunt thought the deep shock you were in came from the fact that you had not only lost Marc but had been a witness to his accident.'

'That must have been it,' she agreed, and was ready to return to her room. 'Thank you again,' she murmured, her head crammed with all he had revealed, hope starting to break through. Dacre had sounded so certain. Could it really be as he'd said, that Marc's accident was totally unconnected with their 'honeymoon problems'? 'I think I'll—er—say goodnight now, and...'

She halted when once more he stretched out a hand to stay her. She looked up, startled, and was shaken to see that that look of determination was back in his eyes. 'We haven't had our discussion yet,' he reminded her.

'We've been talking for the last ten minutes!' she protested.

'We've been talking about a side-issue that came up—something you should have known about a year ago, and which just had to be cleared away—cleared from your conscience before we went any further.' He corrected any misapprehension she might be under that he was in any way satisfied with her reasons for stating that she would never marry again.

'I—you...' she choked. And when she could not go on she discovered that he could and—what was more—that once he and his tenacity got hooked into something there was not the smallest glimmer of a chance that he would let go.

'To return to the reason why you thought Marc was not concentrating on his riding,' he took up conversationally. 'The honeymoon problems you were having.' She stared at him as if hypnotised, and just could not believe it when, his hands coming to her arms just as if he was aware that she might at any moment bolt, he asked very quietly, 'Tell me, Josy, did you ever make love with him?'

Stupefied, she stared into his steady grey eyes, his question rioting around in her head. Disbelieving, she stared—and still couldn't believe that she had heard what she had heard. And then she came to a very rapid decision—she was getting out of here! Her defences, admittedly, were down, but no way was she going to talk to him about *that*!

CHAPTER SIX

JOSY did not make it as far as the door. As if suspecting that she would take off, Dacre was ready for her and held firmly on to her as she leapt from the sofa.

'Let me go!' she shrieked, panicking wildly.

'Shh—I'm not going to hurt you,' he gentled her, keeping her at arm's length, but his hold unbreakable. 'You've been very brave, but there are still matters to be aired—matters to be faced.'

'I've faced them all—and they're nothing to do with you!' she hurled at him furiously. This man—he made her *so* angry! So... So...

'I don't agree. They have everything to do with me,' he countered.

How he came to think that whether or not she had made love with his cousin was anything to do with him she failed to see. She fought desperately for calm but hurled at him heatedly, 'My bedroom secrets are my own!'

'Normally I'd say you were right, and that my question was a gross impertinence. But nothing is normal here and...' he hesitated '... and I think it's important to us that we have this—discussion.'

She felt panicky again. She didn't like that word 'us'. But with a great effort she managed to hold down her panic, and since she didn't like Dacre holding her, and since it did not seem as if he was going to let her out of the room in a hurry, she took a step towards the sofa, and he let her go.

121

Only when she was sitting down did he go and take the chair opposite. Josy did not look at him. She was his prisoner; he could do his worst, but not another peep was he getting out of her!

For long, long, tortured seconds she was aware of Dacre looking at her. Stubbornly she showed him her profile. A taut silence stretched, and strained seconds ticked away. And still she would not look at him.

That was until quietly, gently into that silence, Dacre answered his own question. 'I don't believe you did make love with him on your honeymoon night, little one.' And then he added, 'Nor do I think you gave yourself to my cousin—or to any man—before your marriage.'

Josy turned her head. Dacre's look was as quiet as his words. 'Th-that's still got nothing to do with you!' she exploded shakily, her eyes measuring, hopelessly, the distance of her sofa from the door in relation to his chair and capture.

'Oh, little virgin, I'm not blaming you,' he breathed softly, seeming to know for a fact from her answer that she was indeed a virgin. And that, combined with her guilt, rattled her into being unwary.

'Then you should!' she erupted.

'I should?' he enquired, his tone mild—whereas she was going out of control.

'Yes, you should!' she retorted agitatedly. 'I should never have married Marc! I wanted to live with him, but not as a wife.' Horrified at what she had just confessed, Josy stared at Dacre, unable to believe that he had goaded her to reveal that. She had no idea how she had expected him to look, but to her surprise, save for a steady sort of waiting look in his eyes, Dacre still wore the same quiet expression. 'You're—not angry?' she asked.

'I'm not angry,' he confirmed, and asked, 'Did you not love him?'

'Yes, of course I loved him!' she stated unequivocally. 'Next to my sister Marc was my best friend.'

'You loved him as a good friend—and not as a husband?'

'Welcome to my nightmare!' she invited, no longer wondering about the various emotions Dacre provoked in her—some so violent that they sent shyness flying. She was in love with him—and he and it had turned her world upside-down.

'So tell me about your nightmare,' he invited in turn. 'When did it begin?'

Josy stared at him. That was something she hadn't been prepared to share with anyone—not even Belvia— so why were words bubbling up inside her? She loved Dacre, yes, but he wasn't her best friend.

'Marc was my very good friend.' She was barely aware that she had spoken. 'I never felt threatened by him.' She didn't seem able to stop. 'Somehow it seemed that he was more shy of me than I was of him.'

'So, recognising his shyness, you spoke to him to try and make him feel more comfortable, more at ease in your country?' he suggested, surprising her that he seemed to know how it had begun.

'I—er—yes,' she admitted, and found herself going on, 'And, crazy though it now seems, we somehow got married without—er—passion entering into it.'

'You had a passionless engagement.'

'Well, we were only engaged for a month, and there was a lot to see to—getting the flat ready and everything.' She halted. 'Why am I telling you all this?'

He looked levelly back at her. 'Because it's important that you should,' he stated, and, perhaps because she did love him so much, as she stared at him Josy found that she trusted him to be right. 'So, feeling unthreatened by Marc, you married him expecting a passionless marriage, and—'

'I didn't even think about it that deeply. I told you, we were friends! We had a mutual love of horses; I just didn't think about anything else.' A shaky breath escaped her. 'But,' she added, 'I should have done.'

'You didn't think about the physical side of marriage?'

'It wasn't an issue,' she replied, her voice growing shaky as she remembered how it had been. 'I suppose, if anything, I just assumed—Marc and me being such good friends and everything—that everything would sort itself out—' She broke off, unable to go on.

'Take your time, *petite*,' Dacre encouraged.

'There's nothing more to say,' she replied in a whisper of a voice. 'Marc and I came to his parents after the marriage ceremony—and my life became a living nightmare from that day on.' Her voice faded away; she had nothing more to add and silence filled the room once more. She thought Dacre made a movement as though he would have come over to her—but something caused him to hold back.

But he did not hold back from wanting to find out more, however, and there was a deep sincerity there in his voice when he said, 'Josy, my dear, please believe that I am not merely prying for the sake of it when I tell you that I need to share more of that nightmare with you.'

'You don't!' she retorted, getting angry again. What did he want—blood? 'We married, and Marc became a stranger to me—how do you like that?' she snapped. 'I knew him as a quiet, shy, gentle person, and yet there he was—th-that night—a stranger. An aggressive stranger. T-tearing at my clothes!' she cried, distraught. 'Throwing m-me on the bed. Aggressive, brutal—I was terrified!'

'Oh . . .' In an instant Dacre was over by her side, on the sofa with her, an arm coming round her.

'*No*!' she hurled at him, angry, agitated, and barely knowing how much she'd revealed, how much she had kept to herself, pushing him away from her. 'You want to hear the rest of my nightmare—the months of torment I've gone through in coming to terms with my inadequacies, my frigidity that caused a man to ride into the woods the next day and get killed?'

'M—'

'*No*!' she raged. This had been pent up inside her for too long. He wanted to hear it—let him; perhaps then she wouldn't hurt so much. 'You want to hear how that night, our wedding night, Marc slept in the dressing-room while I—chaste in my bed, and glad, oh, so glad of it—wondered what on earth I was doing there, why on earth I had married Marc?'

'You—'

She refused to let him get in. 'That night, and every night since, especially in those early months that followed, I've lain awake wondering why I married Marc at all. Wanting to live with a beloved good friend no longer seems sufficient reason. So was it more that with sweet, kind, gentle Marc sounding me out about marriage, I saw it as the tailor-made excuse I needed for leaving home? 'My sister was still there, but I'd sensed that she was only staying because of me, that I was holding her back—that once I'd gone she wouldn't hang around and put up with any nonsense from my father.

So did I marry Marc merely to escape—only to find myself in a worse situation?'

'You bore all these nightmarish thoughts alone?'

'Who would I have told?' she charged.

'Your sister?'

'Have you *no* idea how I felt?' she exclaimed, her voice trembling in her agitation. 'Can you imagine what it feels like to face up to the fact that you're passionless, that you don't want passion, that you're cold to it? I froze that night! Have you any idea how I felt after what I'd done to Marc, and—because I'd as good as caused his death—how I needed to feel? How could I have confessed any of it to Belvia?' she hurtled on. 'I know her; we're twins—she would have found excuses for me. I didn't want excuses. I hurt, and it was right that I should hurt. But for me, Marc would be alive. Oh, I was so unfair to him!' she cried in an agony of distress—and did not know that Dacre had both her hands in his until he gripped them tightly.

'Shh...' he tried to calm her. 'Oh, Josy, Josy, little one, you've been in hell,' he murmured softly, and gave her hands a little shake, as if to get her full attention. She looked at him, all large eyes and ashamed, and, having got her attention, 'Josy, my dear, listen to me,' he urged, and when, suddenly feeling too exhausted to move, she just sat and stared at him, he stated, in a tone that brooked no arguing, 'It was not you who was unfair to Marc, but Marc who was unfair to you.'

Josy did not believe that. 'That's not true!' she argued bluntly.

But Dacre was not backing down and, with his grey eyes holding hers, suggested, 'There were a lot of things Marc didn't tell you—I think you'll agree?'

'I—didn't know he had a—moneyed background, if that's what you're referring to,' she answered, calmer now, if still inwardly trembling after her emotional outburst. 'And I'd like my hands back, please,' she added crisply, not sure that she liked this tough, let's-dig-out-the-truth man, after all.

'Nor did you know of the various properties he owned—some of which he willed to you,' Dacre informed her, letting go of her hands.

'He was a property owner?' she enquired, thereby unwittingly revealing something else she hadn't known.

'Nor did you know about his accident,' he went on.

'Not until you told me about it,' she agreed, and was in no way prepared for what was coming when, his grey-eyed look steady on hers, he set about proving that Marc had been unfair to her.

'So, since Marc could not have told you the result of that accident without revealing he'd had an accident,' Dacre resumed, 'I think it's safe to say that you had no idea that the accident left Marc—impotent.'

'Impotent!' she exclaimed, warm colour coming to her face.

'I'm afraid so,' he confirmed, trailing the backs of the fingers of one hand down the side of her flushed cheek. Hurriedly Josy pulled back.

'I don't bel... How—?' No, not how. It wouldn't mean very much to her if he went into detail. 'I can't believe you!' she stated immovably. 'That night—the night of our marriage—he came after me like someone demented!'

'My dear, my poor dear, if you knew more of men you might—' Dacre broke off, but went on to expound, 'From what you've said, I'm fairly certain that my cousin, realising certain duties were expected of him that night, forced himself to be aggressive in the belief that aggression might push him through the barrier of his impotency.'

'No!' she gasped faintly. 'I...' She still couldn't believe it. But, her head in an emotional whirl from all she had said and from what Dacre had revealed, she suddenly remembered something—and didn't believe him at all. 'You once asked me if I was pregnant!' she challenged, hitting his lies about Marc being impotent soundly on the head—but only to find that Dacre had an answer for that too.

'It was soon after his accident, while he was still in hospital, that Marc told me the result of that stalliion half killing him. I could only assume, when I met you and Marc said you were married, that the surgeons who repaired him had been mistaken in their diagnosis. 'Forgive me, *ma chère*—Marc was twenty-five when you married and, for all his reserve, he'd had an affair or two. And you, little one—so beautiful, so shy—are a very desirable woman.'

Her heart fluttered to hear Dacre say that she was beautiful, but while she wanted him to think her beautiful she didn't want him thinking her desirable. 'What's the way I look got to do with anything?' she questioned—a tinge belligerently, she had to admit.

'You're lovely, and so unworldly,' he replied, which in her view was no kind of answer. 'Whether the medical people were right or wrong, I knew in that moment of meeting you—without actually thinking about it—that if it was possible for any woman to restore Marc's manhood then you could—or maybe had. But a short while ago you confirmed that you had not, and I knew that the surgeons who put him back together again had been right—Marc was impotent.'

'You... He... Oh, Marc, poor Marc,' she mourned—
and that night she had screamed in terror!

'Poor Josy,' Dacre corrected her softly. 'You went
through all—'

'Did his parents know?' she asked, remembering how
she and Marc, avoiding eye contact, had gone down to
the stables without seeing either his mother or father the
next morning. 'About Marc...'

He shook his head. 'He couldn't talk to either of them
about it. I was more of an older brother he was able to
confide in.'

'And ... you're sure?' she asked.

'I'm sure,' he answered steadily. 'But if you, as Marc's
widow, would like a medical report, it would be no
problem for me to arrange confirmation for you.'

Josy gave a shaky sigh—and realised that she believed
him, and had for a few minutes believed him. 'That won't
be necessary,' she said quietly, and then, silently owning
to feeling very mixed up about absolutely everything and
needing very much to be alone so that she could sort
out her head, she asked, 'Do you want me to go back
to England?' Somehow, confusingly, it seemed that she
had just cut all ties as a family member.

She was relieved, though, when she saw a slow smile
come to Dacre's face. From that smile she gathered that
he would not be throwing her out come morning. Her
relief, however, was short-lived, and she gasped in shock
when he answered gently, 'Oh, no, *chérie*, I want you
to stay here in France—and marry me.'

Josy felt the colour rush to her face and then drain
away, and she stared at him in stunned amazement.
'Haven't you been listening to anything I've said?'
she exclaimed.

'I've heard every word,' he replied, calm where she was all agitation again.

'Then you *know* I can't marry you!' she erupted, on her feet and in panic. 'I can't be a wife—to any man! It wasn't only Marc who c— It was me too!' Dacre had risen as well, but while she was panicking wildly she saw that his glance was as steady as ever.

Dearly did she want to know what he was thinking. Then she decided that she didn't want to know at all because, when *twice* already she had as good as told him no, he stretched out a hand and, stroking a finger down the bridge of her nose, assured her gently, 'I'll wait.'

Josy saw that as a threat and bolted. This time Dacre let her go.

She had been in her room five minutes before the quagmire of her thoughts quietened down into a more sensible thinking pattern. Still in a daze, she ceased pacing the floor and went and sat down on the edge of her bed, all that she and Dacre had discussed still shooting through her brain.

He was tenacious, was Dacre. That whole conversation with him just now had only begun because he had been determiend to talk to her, to find out what her horrified 'No!' had been all about when he had first stated— no, bellowed—'I want you to marry me!'

She should leave; she knew that for a fact. Remembering his quiet 'I'll wait', remembering his tenacity, most definitely she should leave. And yet—she didn't want to. She didn't want to go. She loved him, was in love with him, and the thought of never seeing him again was truly, truly dreadful. So how could she leave? But how, with that threat hanging over her, could she stay?

Her head was in much the same whirl when she eventually got into her pyjamas and climbed into bed.

She had always enjoyed being alone—but she didn't want to be alone without Dacre. Her thoughts came round full circle for the umpteenth time. She wanted to stay; oh, how she wanted to stay.

In an attempt to get him off her mind she thought of everything else he had told her, and for the first time began to know a little peace of mind in one part of her life when she started to believe that it was not through her that Marc had died.

What with her having been in deep shock and French being spoken all around her, it was no wonder to her now that she had been unable to pick up on a word dropped here and there that might have resulted in her questioning and knowing that Marc had not merely fallen off Diamant through not concentrating, but had been thrown when that vicious beast had slammed him up against a tree.

Marc, poor Marc—there was so much he hadn't told her. Perhaps if she'd loved him more she would have asked more pertinent questions. Perhaps he would have told her of his wealth—even of his accident, maybe. Oh, if only he had. They'd been more well matched than he'd known. He impotent, she incapable of giving herself!

Dacre was in her head again before she went to sleep. But by morning, even though she awakened with his quietly spoken 'I'll wait' still sounding in her ears, she was calmer than she had been. Dacre could not *make* her marry him. Nobody could make her do that.

She showered and got dressed and went downstairs, thinking that perhaps Dacre would go off the idea of wanting to marry her. Perhaps he already had. But fate gave a gleeful laugh.

For just then, as she stepped down into the hall, Dacre appeared from his study and came easily towards her. 'Good morning, Josy,' he greeted her pleasantly, and to her astonishment scrutinised her face for a brief second then lowered his head and—when she thought a salute to both her cheeks might be on the way, though not strictly necessary since he had so greeted her yesterday— he instead placed a light kiss on nowhere but her mouth.

Electricity shot through her. Open-mouthed, she stared at him, but while her heart drummed and her lips still burned from the touch of his lips he did no more than place an arm about her shoulders and turn her in the direction of the breakfast-room.

'You must be as hungry as I am,' he remarked conversationally, not balking at making oblique reference to the way neither of them had finished dinner last night.

She pulled out of his arm as soon as she could without showing him how jumpy she was, but felt all over the place again. Was this the way it was going to be—the seemingly casual kiss? He had stated he wanted to marry her. Was this—a brief touching of lips, an arm light about her—his way of trying to break down her resistance?

'Ah, here's a letter for you,' he announced after he'd seen her seated and gone to his own chair. 'A female hand, I think,' he added, and, as if having satisfied himself on that account, he passed it over.

She took it from him and felt more electricity shoot through her when their hands accidentally touched. Oh, heavens, she'd be a nervous wreck if he didn't soon go back to Paris. 'Excuse me,' she murmured politely, and opened her letter.

'Not bad news?' Dacre fished for information, and, although she was as jumpy as the dickens, and all over the place emotionally, she was visited by another emotion when she discovered that she wanted to laugh at his blatant angling.

'It's from Tracey; she works at the stables,' Josy obliged, unable to hold back a smile. 'I wrote and asked her how Hetty was.'

'Hetty, your horse.' He returned her smile, his eyes on her mouth.

'Hetty, my horse,' she confirmed.

'And how is she?'

'Extremely well, apparently—but missing the titbit I usually have for her in my pocket,' she replied.

'You sound as if you're still missing her.'

'Well, she is rather special,' she defended.

And she grew all up-tight again when Dacre commented pleasantly, 'Like her owner.'

'You'll be going back to Paris today, I expect?' she said abruptly, her question coming out far more bluntly than she had meant it to.

But while she anticipated something equally blunt in reply—it was his home after all—to her surprise his reply was evenly spoken. 'I thought I might take a few weeks' holiday,' he answered.

Her glance flew to him. 'Here?' she queried worriedly, wanting with all she had nothing better, while at the same time her anxiety mounted at what she saw as more pressure.

'Here,' he confirmed, his eyes steady on hers.

'Oh,' she mumbled, and knew then that this—and he—was really, really serious.

When she went to the stables Dacre went with her. When she saddled up Nina he saddled up César. And while it was pure and utter joy to be out riding with him Josy also experienced inner conflict as she began to grow more and more worried.

Friday and Saturday followed a similar pattern—the light kiss at breakfast and Dacre's going down to the stables with her, riding with her—and Josy's nerves stretched. For, while her guilt over Marc had started to drain away and she had begun to feel as if a ton weight had lifted from her, she was still left with one very big problem—her inability to let any man get close to her.

Josy awoke on Sunday morning and her first thought was of Dacre. Oh, how she loved him. Why, oh, why had he got this idea in his head that he wanted to marry her? Why couldn't they go on as they were? Or, rather, as they had been going on.

She went down to breakfast. '*Bonjour*, Josy,' Dacre greeted her and, as he had the previous three mornings, bent his head and placed a light kiss on her mouth.

'*B-bonjour*, Dacre,' she answered, and as her nerves stretched even tauter she could not help but wonder if today would be the day she snapped—and screamed at him not to touch her.

All that day Dacre was kind and warm and gentle to her—and Josy was getting to a pitch where she wished more than ever to be back the way they had been.

'Shall we go to the *salon*?' he suggested after dinner.

'I've—er—a few things to do in my room,' she answered jerkily, and as a stern look came to his eyes, and she guessed that he was not best pleased, she said in a rush, 'Goodnight,' and left him.

Josy was up in her room when she faced the fact that she could not go on like this. For heaven's sake, she loved him and wanted to be with him. She wanted to stay in the *salon* talking with him on most any subject that came up, and for as long as he liked, but—how could she now?

And what of him? She owned that she had not given too much thought to what Dacre wanted. She supposed the reason was that she was still reeling from the fact that he had stated that he wanted to marry her—and would wait.

But she didn't want him to wait. No way did she want him to wait. He wanted a wife and, much though she loved him, that would never be her. He wanted children and, dear God, that would never, *ever* be her.

Yet was it fair that he should keep on waiting? But that was hardly her fault! She had told him no—what more could she do? Feeling bogged down by the weight of her thoughts, Josy went and took a shower. Oh, what was she going to do?

She had found no solution to the problem when, finished with her shower, she donned fresh pyjamas and got into bed. She thought she heard a door along the landing close, and realised that Dacre had left either the *salon* or his study and had called it a day.

She was still wide awake with her thoughts thirty minutes later, sleep light years away. He had to see that he was wasting his time waiting for her, didn't he? He hadn't, though, had he? In four days he hadn't. Oh, what on earth...? Surely she could do *something*?

Another half an hour went by with Josy tearing herself to shreds, not wanting to leave, by no means wanting to leave, but wondering if to do so was the only answer. Then suddenly, out of the blue, out of her utter desperation, she saw another way—and she was more awake than ever.

No way, no way! screamed her nerves. The very idea was preposterous; she just didn't have that kind of courage. Not even for him? queried a faint, wanting-to-run voice.

Oh, God, she couldn't. Just thinking about it made her tremble. Yet... She blanked her thoughts off—but they wouldn't go away. She made herself face them. She took a deep breath, and faced them.

Fact—Dacre wanted to marry her. Fact—she could not marry him. Fact—he said he would wait, but she knew he would have a lifetime's wait before she would ever marry him. And fact—she just couldn't do that to him. She had to find a way of convincing him that he was wasting his time in waiting—and there was a way. She swallowed down panic; it was that or the alternative—to leave.

But she loved him too much to leave. Did she, then, love him enough to go to him now, and let him see for himself that she could never be a wife to any man? Did she have that much courage?

Her mouth went dry at the thought—yet it wouldn't take too long. She could be back in her own bed in five minutes. She'd be distressed, of course, but she was distressed now. And did she love him or didn't she? There were at least another ten days of his holiday still to go and, from what he'd said, probably more. Was she for the next ten mornings and more to go down to breakfast in fear and trembling that his light kiss would turn to something more passionate, when she would lose control and start creating?

Unable to sit still, Josy got out of bed and began pacing up and down until, finally, she grew furious with herself and the pathetic person she felt herself to be. In the next moment she had grabbed up a robe and, shrugging into it as she went, left her room.

Her spurt of anger with herself, however, had vanished into thin air by the time she found herself outside Dacre's bedroom door. She went hot and cold all over and turned to go back to her own room, but then halted.

Just five minutes, that was all it would take! Probably less. The way things were going she was going to lose control any day now anyway—why not go in and get it over with now? She loved him, didn't she? Yes, and much too much to keep him waiting for a day that was never going to come.

A two-second burst of courage arrived. She grabbed it, taking one second to open Dacre's door and the other to step inside and close it.

The light was on; Dacre was in bed, reading. He looked up and her face went scarlet. She stayed by the door. Had she not felt rooted to the spot she would have turned and fled. But she couldn't move; every muscle and joint seemed locked.

In trauma—self-inflicted trauma—Josy watched Dacre's silent gaze on her, watched him as he closed his book.

'C...' The words wouldn't come. Dacre had his arms on top of the light coverlet; she could see his naked hair-roughened chest and just knew that he slept without pyjamas. Her insides somersaulted. She tried again. 'C-can I...?' She raised her eyes to his waiting, good-looking face. That thought, 'waiting', spurred her on. 'Can I sl-sleep with you?' she asked on one gasp of breath.

Silently, unspeaking, Dacre studied her panicking expression. But just as her every instinct started to clamour out that she should not have come, 'Of course,' he answered obligingly.

For several seconds her feet refused to obey her brain's instruction to go forward. But, after an agony of wanting to turn tail, Josy moved and approached the double bed.

Once more obligingly, Dacre moved over to allow her a half-share. She swallowed, but when her hands went to the tie of her robe she found that, for all that she was pyjama-clad underneath, she just could not take her robe off with him watching.

And she loved him more than ever when, for all the world as if he understood, he murmured, 'It's all right, *petite*,' and, turning from her, he placed his book down on his bedside table and put out the light.

By that time, though, she was shaking so much that she could barely get the hurriedly tied-up knot undone. Eventually she managed it, but only by telling herself that she was doing this for him was she able to remove her robe and find her way under the light coverlet.

Despite it being from her great love for him, though, it was still tensely, while keeping as much distance from him as possible, that she lay there, ramrod-stiff.

She felt him move, and was shaking so much by then that she knew he could feel it too. He came closer and, propping himself on one elbow, as if by some automatic radar, he placed an arm about her waist. 'Hush, little Josy, I won't harm you,' he promised softly. But she was beyond answering.

She could feel his arm, warm about her rigid, shaking body, and she loved him so much—and she wanted to cry at the thought that soon, out of her control, she would be fighting him from her.

Every one of her senses seemed heightened; she even felt the warmth of his breath as his face came nearer. She could feel his chest against her, and as panic tried to get a deeper grip—she froze. She clenched her hands tightly, her nails digging into her palms, when gently Dacre placed his lips over hers and kissed her oh, so tenderly, neither demanding nor taking, but a longer kiss than those of breakfast-time.

Then his mouth left hers, and he took his arm from across her, and Josy waited for the dreadful onslaught that was to come as he gently stroked the side of her face.

But the onslaught never came. For, even while Josy knew that at any moment now all hell was going to break loose in her as she fought a battle with fear and lost, to her absolute astonishment Dacre kissed her briefly just once more, and then breathed, 'Goodnight, little one,' and turned over—and went to sleep!

CHAPTER SEVEN

DAWN was breaking when Josy awoke, and for all of one second she didn't know where she was. Then she became aware of another human form lying beside her, and in a bound of movement, her heart pounding, she was out of that bed.

Snatching up her robe *en route*—no time to put it on—she went for the door. She did not stop running until she was safely in her own room, and everything that had happened—which she had to admit was very little—played back in her mind.

With the coming of daylight it seemed absolutely incredible that she, shy Josy Fereday, had from somewhere found the temerity to go and get into bed with a man!

Oh, not just any man—agreed. And she had asked his permission first. But, great heavens, had that been her? With the coming of day she could only gasp at her nerve.

Without a doubt there *was* something magical about this place. Three months ago she could never have seen herself acting as she had last night. Even a month ago she would have scorned the very idea—but a month ago, while now she faced the fact she had been learning to love Dacre, she hadn't known that she was in love with him, and being in love had made all the difference.

She sat in a bedroom chair, her knees to her chin, her arms around her shins. Love made all the difference . . . Her eyes grew dreamy as she remembered the wonderful tenderness of Dacre's kiss last night.

Strange that she hadn't been alarmed by it. Fearful, yes—next door to terrified wasn't perhaps overstating it—but that wonderful tender kiss had not alarmed her.

When the time came for her to go down to breakfast Josy was again wondering at her nerve. Grief, he had been naked! And she had not only lain in bed with him but—admittedly after hours of lying wide awake—she had gradually stopped shaking and had even fallen asleep for a few hours.

She left her room, not knowing how she was going to face him again after what she'd done, and with a cowardly part of her half wishing that he had decided to return to Paris and had already left.

But he had not gone to Paris, and, as if he had known the precise second she would leave her room, was there in the hall just as she stepped down into it.

She knew the futility of wishing that she would not go scarlet when she next saw him and went crimson when he greeted her softly, 'Hello, *ma brave*.' His eyes raked her flushed skin and, having called her courageous, he bent and kissed her.

'Er—g-good morning.' She struggled to find her voice.

Dacre smiled. 'Breakfast,' he decreed briskly—and so the day began.

And it was a good day—a day that seemed to Josy to be better than previous days even though they did much the same thing. Together they attended the horses, and together they exercised them, sometimes in silence and sometimes talking. Dacre seemed prepared to answer the smallest and the largest questions she asked, while in between he asked his own questions of her—even drawing from her the reluctant admission that she played the piano quite well.

'Why did I tell you that?' she questioned in amazement
as they returned to the house around four that afternoon
after a long walk across fields and through woods.

'You didn't—I dragged it from you, Mademoiselle
Modeste,' he grinned.

'Oh, well, that's all right, then,' she laughed and,
laughter in her heart, and in her eyes too, she thought
she had better make herself scarce before Dacre saw a
hint of how she felt about him.

He had mentioned having to check something out in
his study, and at the stairs she went to part from him.
'Shall we have dinner out tonight, *petite*?' His question
stopped her.

She looked at him, her lovely brown eyes larger than
ever. She opened her mouth, but couldn't think of one
good reason why she shouldn't go out with him. 'Agathe
will have already begun some sort of preparation for...'
some self-preservation instinct found a small objection
anyway.

He shook his head. 'She knew this morning that my...'
he paused, and she waited for the word 'cousin'. 'My
amie and I might dine out this evening.'

'Oh,' Josy mumbled. 'Yes, then.' And, remembering
her manners, she added politely, 'I'd like to,' and went
quickly up to her room.

The day had been super, but she was starting to get
agitated again. When had she stopped being his cousin
to become his *amie*—his friend? And that 'Shall we have
dinner out tonight?'—not 'Would you like to', or 'May
I take you', but more comfortable than that as if—as if
he thought of them as an item and wanted her to think
that way—'Shall we', as though whatever they would be
doing it would be together.

Josy tried to put her worries behind her as she got
ready that evening, but it wasn't easy. He was waiting,

she reminded herself. Beneath it all, beneath the friendly conversation, the companionship of riding together, of walking side by side, of being her friend, he was still quietly waiting.

'You wore that dress on your first evening here,' Dacre commented, when, wearing her dress of deep apricot, she went into the *salon*. It surprised her that he remembered, but he was such a charming friend to be with that night that the evening flew by—and she started to wish that it might never end.

'I shall have to stop eating like this.' She laughed at the frothy, creamy confection Dacre had ordered for her as their meal came to an end.

'I can't see that you've put on weight,' he returned. 'But you are looking much better than when you first came to me.'

She knew that he was right. Given that she had a pale complexion that never seemed to tan, she had a tinge more colour and, with Dacre having told her all he had of Marc's two accidents, her guilt seemed a thing of the past.

But Dacre's 'when you first came to me' began to get to her. When they returned home she left him securing the house with a jerky kind of, 'Thank you for the evening; goodnight,' and went to her room, reading the word 'waiting' in that possessive-sounding part of the phrase 'to me'.

By the time she had taken a shower and donned her pyjamas she found herself on the same emotion-tearing treadmill that she had been on last night. Only tonight, having spent a most wonderful day with Dacre, a new dimension had been added. She now knew that with all her heart and soul she wanted to marry him! Just as she knew with every scrap of logic she had that that could never be.

How could it? The moment he touched her, not as a friend but as a lover, she would go to pieces. She knew it as if it had been seared into her brain. And he was 'waiting'!

Josy had been sleepless in her bed for two hours with the agony she had gone through last night seeming intensified that night—perhaps because of the wonderful day she had spent with him.

Anger—with herself, with him, with her sleeplessness—she was tired, felt worn out, yet still couldn't go to sleep—was the prod she needed to get crossly out of her bed to go and do something about it. To go and get it over with once and for all!

This time, however, she went so fast that she didn't even wait to put on her robe, which made it just as well that when speedily, if quietly, she entered Dacre's bedroom she found his room in darkness.

She halted just where she was, knowing he was asleep and that she shouldn't have come. Her anger gone, she went to back silently from his room, and then discovered that Dacre wasn't asleep after all, and that he knew she was there. 'Come to bed, little one,' he instructed her in the darkness, his voice all soothing and calm.

Her throat went dry again, and for long, long seconds she couldn't move. Then, barely aware what she was doing, like someone in a trance, she quietly closed the door and went over to the bed.

Her nerves started to plague her with a vengeance when she slipped in between the covers. Without touching him, she could feel his warmth. But he had his back to her, and made no move to turn to her, and all of a sudden she was overwhelmed by the enormity of what she had done. Dacre didn't want her in his bed! To come in the way she had, to get into bed with him was an imposition!

Mortified, she went to scramble out but somehow got tangled up with the bedding—and then suddenly she became aware that the piece of material she held in her hand was not bedding, nor was it her pyjamas—it was the jacket of *his* pyjamas!

Oh, Dacre, I love you. She stopped trying to get out of his bed. He had been expecting her—must have wanted her in his bed—or why, when he was a sleep-in-the-nude type of man, was he suffering to wear pyjamas?

She lay back down, her shaking settling down to a more healthy tremble. Dacre still had his back to her, but he stretched backwards with his left arm to touch her.

'Try to get some sleep,' he suggested kindly, and while she quiveringly took from that that he was more interested in sleeping himself than in attempting to make love to her he took his arm away.

Josy lay for some while trying to figure him out. The virile look of him, the very fact of his sophistication, plus the added fact that he had so easily asked her if she and Marc had made love before they married ruled out the idea the he held any pious 'no sex before marriage' views. So why? Was it her? Did she put him off?

How could she put him off, though? He had spoken of marriage, of children... Mists of sleep snatched at her. She moved, turned over on to her side—and then discovered that she had turned over to face Dacre's sleeping back.

Oh, how she loved him. She stretched out a hand to touch him; somehow she seemed unable to resist it. He didn't move. She edged a little nearer, finding comfort, warmth in his nearness. Still he didn't move. She edged nearer still, until there was just an inch or so separating them. And she wanted to touch him, to hold him. Hardly daring to breathe, she placed a tentative arm around his waist. His hand was there; she touched it.

'Goodnight, Josy,' he said lightly, and, taking her hand in his, he gave it a light squeeze.

She gave a start, and for about three seconds held her breath. Then she mumbled chokily, 'Goodnight, Dacre,' and a few minutes later began to feel really drowsy. Without thinking, she took her head from her pillow and laid her cheek against the warmth of his pyjama-clad back. She hadn't known that sleeping with the one you love could be so wonderful.

She awoke to find that it was morning—and could not remember when she had slept so well. She had no idea of the time, but from the strength of daylight realised that she had slept way past her usual waking time.

She had the bed to herself and guessed that Dacre must have been up and about for an age. Her brain suggested that she should hurry back to her room, but she found she liked being in Dacre's bed. She touched the place where he had lain, and loved him so much that it was like a physical ache.

Then the sound of the door of the adjoining bathroom opening caused her mind to go a total blank. And when Dacre, freshly showered, a towel around his middle his only covering, stepped into the bedroom she didn't know where to look.

'I—er—slept late,' she choked, and was half out of bed, ready to dive for the door, before she became aware of her own thin covering.

'So did I,' Dacre answered conspiratorially, and at the smile in his voice she looked across to him. She looked to his eyes; there was a watchful kind of smile in them, and on his mouth. 'You looked so beautiful lying there that it seemed a sin to disturb you,' he added conversationally.

She didn't know how she felt at the intimation that he had been looking at her while she had been asleep. 'Yes, well,' she said, which meant nothing, but which she hoped passed for an answer as she measured the distance from the bed to the door. 'I'd—er—better go and...' As the words left her she moved from the bed.

She had only gone a few steps, though, when he enquired, 'No morning kiss for me?' and she halted, mid-flight.

She turned. Dacre had greeted her every morning with a kiss. And albeit that that kiss had always taken place downstairs, with both of them fully dressed, it seemed— after having invited herself to his bed—a little churlish to be—um—stuffy about it.

Josy moved a little towards him and was glad that he came and met her halfway. She looked at him and still wanted to run—but found to her surprise that, thinly pyjama-clad as she was, she wanted to stay.

'Good morning,' she greeted him, and when he made no move to kiss her she stared silently at him, her expression serious.

Still he did not move. There was about a foot separating them. His naked chest was so close that she could have touched it. Nervously she stepped closer—and then reached up and touched her lips fleetingly to his.

Josy pulled back and stared at him. He said nothing, neither threatening nor looking ready to embrace her. And all at once, while she stood there warily watching him and her heart started to pound, she knew that she wanted to kiss him again.

She looked at him silently waiting. Did he want her to kiss him again? He wasn't walking away, was he? Josy moved a few inches closer, her body almost touching his, and shyly, nervously, but mainly because she didn't seem able to stop herself, she again stretched up and placed her lips against his—this time for a little longer. And that was when, just as she was going to break away from him and hurry back to her room, Dacre moved.

Josy felt his arms come about her. But although she jerked back instinctively she didn't fight to break out of his loose hold. Feeling slightly amazed that though her heart was beating nineteen to the dozen she was still there, Josy stared at him all large-eyed and, she had to own to herself, apprehensive.

'Don't worry,' he breathed softly. 'It will be all right.'

Would it? She didn't think so! On past performance, when she thought of the terrified way she had fought against Marc's physical aggression, she was sure it wouldn't be so. Which was why she was further amazed to hear herself ask, albeit a touch shakily, 'C-can I—kiss you again?'

Dacre smiled. 'I'd like that,' he answered.

Solemnly Josy eyed him. She felt she wanted to kiss him—but she wasn't certain. Nor was she certain about anything else for a few seconds, because, without haste, Dacre was helping her out and, not waiting for her to kiss him, was all at once claiming her lips—in the first lingering kiss they had shared.

Her knees went so weak that she placed her hands on his waist to hold herself steady. She felt his firm male body—and let go of him as though burned. But she had no need to worry about falling over for Dacre's arms about her tightened, and suddenly, while realising that she had never felt so secure or at the same time so bewildered, Josy moved to pull out of his hold.

'Are you all right?' he asked, releasing her immediately, his eyes searching hers.

'I'm—not sure,' she replied honestly.

And Dacre, after a moment more of looking into her eyes, unexpectedly smiled, and teased, 'Then I suggest, sweet Josy, that you meet me downstairs for breakfast.'

'Oh, Dacre.' She laughed, and, feeling all light-headed suddenly, quickly went back to her own room.

Another wonderful day followed. They walked together, talked together, and, when they were taking their ease by a stream, Dacre picked a wild flower and tucked it behind her ear. Even as her skin tingled from his touch she loved him for the gesture.

They had dinner at their usual time, but as the meal drew to an end so she started to feel tense. A closeness seemed to have sprung up from nowhere between her and Dacre, and she was starting to realise that she liked that closeness. But still at the back of her mind was the knowledge that nothing was ever going to come of it.

'Do you want to share it with me?' Dacre's voice in the silence of her thoughts startled her, causing her to realise that he had noticed her change of mood.

She shook her head. 'No,' she replied, and, aware by now that he was unlikely to let her leave it there, added, 'I'm—er—feeling a bit—uptight.'

For long moments he eyed her steadily and, making her feel terribly guilty, looked just as if he thought her being uptight was all his fault. 'I'm sorry,' he apologised. 'I didn't want that.'

'Oh, Dacre,' she said quickly, and was so confused all at once. 'I think I need to be on my own—do you mind if I don't come into the *salon*?'

She looked into his eyes, but could tell nothing of what he was thinking. 'Of course not,' he said, and Josy left him—and knew that she would not be going along to his bedroom that night.

In fact, a few hours later, when she lay sleepless in her bed, she was beginning to wonder how she had ever

found the nerve to do what she had. And yet, she then
realised, she had truly liked sleeping with him.

Over the last few days she felt that she had got to
know him better than any man she knew. Talking to him
by day, sharing his bed by night—it was an intimacy she
enjoyed. But truly it couldn't go on like this.

A few more hours passed, with Josy loving Dacre and
knowing that he should never learn of it. She grew more
tense than ever, wanting to go to him while knowing that
never again would she go and get into his bed. Her nerve
supply had run out, leaving her wanting to go to him,
and anxious, and emotionally all over the place.

And then, just as she was about to hit rock bottom,
her bedroom door opened and closed. And into the
darkness, for all the world as if he knew she would be
awake, Dacre said softly, 'I couldn't sleep without you.'

A mixture of joy to have him near mingled with a
familiar apprehension. 'We—um—can't have that,' she
answered, and moved over to make room for him.

'Are you still feeling tense, *chérie*?' he enquired as he
joined her beneath the light coverlet.

'It's—nothing,' she answered.

'Sit up.'

'S-sit up?' she queried.

'I'll massage the back of your neck,' he offered matter-
of-factly.

'It won't do any good.' She had no intention of sitting
up.

'How do you know?'

'Oh—you!' she exclaimed, and loved him—and,
perhaps a little nervously, she laughed.

But sit up she did. She presented him with her back—
and braced herself for his touch. And, when it came,
like everything else there it seemed to be magical.

He applied firm but gentle pressure, and she wanted to lean against him. 'Undo your top,' he ordered lightly, and she was all quivering tension again.

'Why?'

'Because I can't get at you properly—and you've knots of tension all the way down your spine.'

He was probably right there. She felt tense all the way down to her toes. And, after several minutes of thinking she'd be hanged if she would undo her pyjama jacket, she found her fingers going to the fastening.

She knew that he was aware her jacket was undone when, with a small tug at the material, he had the freedom he needed to work with. She felt his hands, warm on the skin of her back, and thought she might faint from the shock of it.

'You've—er...' Her husky voice faded altogether; he'd got the most wonderful hands. 'You've—um—done this before?' she asked, after a moment or two of getting her breath back.

'You're my first patient,' Dacre replied, gently moulding her spine, his voice—so close.

'H-how do you know what to do, then?'

'I was once a weekend guest at the house of some friends. The only book they'd got that I hadn't read was one on this subject.' He paused, and added matter-of-factly, 'I'm glad I bothered to open it.'

Josy couldn't have answered him then if she had wanted to, because although his voice might have sounded matter-of-fact his hands were telling her something different. For, while he was still massaging her gently, those movements at her back seemed to her to be more caressing than massaging. She could be wrong, of course, but... 'I'm all right now,' she said on a choky kind of sharp sound.

His hands stilled. 'You want me to stop?' he breathed, and when she didn't answer he moved her long fair hair to one side and placed a gentle kiss on the side of her neck. She tensed. 'You're beautiful.' he murmured. 'Your skin is like silk.' She swallowed. 'And I'd like to feel more of it,' he stated gently.

'W-would you?' This wasn't right. She knew it wasn't right—so why wasn't she screaming? Why was she sitting there? Why wasn't she yelling?

'Let me take this from you,' he suggested, his fingers on her pyjama top.

'Wh-why?'

'Oh, *petite*!' There was a smile in his voice. But, if he thought she should know why without him having to tell her, he refrained from uttering it but said softly instead, 'Little darling, it's time to let go some of your modesty.'

'Is it?' she asked croakily—and had her answer in the way that gently, unhurriedly he removed her pyjama jacket from her.

She pulled her arms forward to cover her naked breasts, and swallowed hard as he traced the tenderest of kisses over her shoulders. Then, while she was still coming to terms with that tenderness, those kisses, that all over tingling inside her, Dacre's hands came around her waist. He gathered her closer, and as her back came into contact with his hair-sprinkled chest so she realised with a start of alarm, that he was not wearing a pyjama top either!

'Shh—don't be alarmed,' he gentled her when she moved, startled—and for long moments he held her like that, still, close to him, as if to allow her to get used to the feel of him.

Josy had never experienced such intimacy. But after a minute or so her jumpy nerves began to settle. Oh,

Dacre—she wanted to call his name, to tell him that what he wanted would never be.

She leaned back against him, a sadness in her heart. She did not doubt that this was as intimate as she would ever get with any man. Or was it? Suddenly, as his hands about her waist pulled her more against him, so those hands began tenderly to caress over her stomach. She swallowed as with whispering traces Dacre caressed upwards nearer her breasts.

'Keep breathing—I'll let nothing harm you,' he murmured in her ear, aware of her sucked-in and held breath. Gradually his hands found their way beneath her shielding arms, caressing beneath the guard they kept over her breasts, and then, as she stopped breathing altogether, his right hand moved up to her right breast, until—after an agony of suspense—he eventually held her breast captive in his palm.

'Dacre!' she cried.

'It's all right. It's all right,' he soothed, and, turning her, he released her breast and held her safe in his arms, quiet, up against his heart. 'Shh, sweet flower,' he soothed. 'You'll be fine.'

What she was, Josy realised, was totally bewildered. She had thought herself bewildered before, but that had been before Dacre had held her breast and her discovery—that she liked it!

Gently then he kissed her. And Josy wasn't sure about anything any more. 'If you want me to go you've only to say,' he breathed, his cheek against her cheek, 'but I'd very much like to stay.'

'To—sl-sleep?' she asked.

He paused before answering. Then, 'To sleep, little love,' he confirmed.

'Please stay,' she invited, and together they lay down.

And Josy liked that too. Dacre kept an arm about her and she rested her head on his shoulder. Whatever happened, she would always have these moments to remember.

'Goodnight,' she said.

'Goodnight, *petite*,' he answered, and placed a light kiss on her brow.

And that was when Josy discovered that she wasn't sleepy, and that, since it was unlikely that she would sleep with Dacre again, she wanted to know the feel of his skin. She took her hand from across his waist and raised it to stroke across his chest. She loved the warmth of him. She guessed he was asleep, and with feather-light movements so as not to wake him, she investigated his shoulders, his chest, her curious fingers exploring his manly nipples.

She found the hair on his chest intriguing, and had just obeyed an impulse to follow a line of hair down to where his navel met the waistband of his pyjama bottoms when Dacre's deep—and disturbed—voice sounded in the darkness. 'Sweet flower, I'm only human.'

Startled, she realised that he had been awake to every one of her exploring movements. 'G-goodnight!' she said jerkily, and hurriedly took her hand back to where it had been before.

Dacre was gone when she awakened in the morning. But she remembered with sweetness, not fear the way he had caressed her in the small hours, the way she had explored him. He had cradled her to sleep and it had been beautiful.

He was there to greet her when she went down to breakfast. 'No problems?' he asked when he took her, blushing, into the loose circle of his arms. She shook her head, realising that he was asking if she was this morning resenting his intimate caresses. '*Bon*!' he murmured, and, with a light kiss to her mouth that lingered perhaps a second longer than it should have, he started her day.

And it was another wonderful day. They rode together in the morning and walked together in the afternoon, and as Josy got ready to go down to dinner that night she realised that, their discussions having been many and varied, they had talked over far more matters than she had ever done with Marc.

With Marc it had been horses and horses to the exclusion of everything else. And while she had been quite content with that at the time—given that by mutual consent a non-physical relationship had been agreed upon—would a daily diet of nothing but horse talk have been enough to sustain her?

She felt guilty thinking such thoughts, but it was a fact that she felt far more mentally stimulated after her discussions with Dacre than she had ever done with Marc. Oh, she would always love horses, she knew that. Her love of animals—horses in particular—must be something she had been born with. Just thinking of Hetty made her want to see her. But...

Josy left her room, suddenly aware that since knowing Dacre, and not least since falling in love with him, she had become more mentally—and physically, if she was honest—alive.

She was having dinner with him a short while later when he looked across the table to her and excused himself from joining her in the *salon* later. 'I've a little business to attend to this evening—it could take a while.'

'Oh,' she murmured, and was about to add that she would have an early night when several things struck her at once. Did he mean that he intended to work in his study, or was he going out? And, if he *was* going out, wasn't it a funny time to be going out to do business?

Realising that she was in the throes of nothing more than jealousy, Josy forced herself to recognise that in the business world work did not cease on the stroke of five.

Hot on the heels of that thought came another far more unpalatable thought. Oh, dear heaven, Dacre would be going back to Paris soon to look after his business. She had just spent a week of being almost exclusively in his company—how on earth was she going to cope, not seeing him every day?

'You look a little downcast, *ma chère*. Is something troubling you?'

She shook her head and saw that he was silently watching. And if she had learned anything about him, about herself, in the week she had just spent with him it was that, somehow or other, she always ended up answering his questions. And, since she seemed totally unable to lie, she began, 'Well, to be honest—' and broke off.

'Your honesty is something else I admire about you,' he inserted—which threw her completely. He admired her! Well, something about her anyway. 'Why so sad?' he asked insistently.

'Well, not sad exactly; I was just—er—thinking that—er—this has been a very pleasant holiday...' oh, grief, it was his holiday not hers '...and that—er—I think I'm—er—I'm going to—um—miss you a little next week.'

Dacre stilled and just looked at her. Then very quietly he remarked, 'I think, *ma petite*, that that is the nicest thing you've ever said to me.'

While Josy went a little pink, and with his look still steady on her, he paused for some seconds. Then, as if encouraged by what she had just said, he proceeded to cause her to stare back at him speechlessly, her heart thundering, when he asked deliberately, 'Perhaps, my dear, you would invite me to stay with you tonight?'

She stared, knowing that he meant in her bed. And her first reaction was to say a very positive, No, no, no. Because from that steady, determined look in his eyes, and the way he had said it, she just knew that if she said, as she had last night, 'To sleep?' that he would tell her, No.

She opened her mouth to say, I can't, but with his grey eyes holding her steady the words just wouldn't come. Somehow he seemed to be willing her to say yes.

Her throat felt dry. 'I'm—scared,' she confessed huskily—and still his eyes held hers steady.

'I know,' he acknowledged calmly—but didn't seem ready to let go.

'Wh-what if I panic?' If? There was no question in her mind. 'Oh, I ca—'

'You won't,' he told her evenly.

'Yes, but what if I do? You'll—'

'We'll handle it,' Dacre soothed, and, with the smile she needed to see breaking, said, 'Stop worrying about it, little flower—just give me the yes I'm waiting to hear.'

She took a deep breath. 'Y-yes.' She gulped and, albeit nervously, gave him a weak smile.

'Josy,' he said softly, and just at that moment Agathe came in to tell him he was wanted on the telephone. 'Excuse me, my dear,' he requested, getting to his feet. 'It's a call I've been waiting for.' With that he left the dining-room.

There was a phone in the hall, but when Josy could hear no sound of his voice she guessed that he was taking the call in his study. It seemed a good time to return to her room.

First one hour dragged by and then another. She had to start with paced her room, and then showered, got into fresh pyjamas, and paced some more. Half of her wished that he would soon come, so she could get this over with. The other half of her wanted to call it off altogether. What if she panicked as she had with Marc?

Oh, God! She began pacing again, knowing that it wasn't a matter of not seeing Dacre next week when he went back to Paris. Suddenly she knew that if she lost control and it all went wrong then tomorrow she would have to leave for England. She had been fooling herself in thinking that she could stay.

She calmed down a little when she recalled the sweetness of the way he had gently cupped her breast last night. She hadn't panicked then, had she? Perhaps it would be all right. Even if she couldn't believe that it would be, perhaps it might. She clung on to that thought; the alternative—to leave—was too awful.

Yet she was saddened when she went and got into bed because by then she had accepted that leaving was her only choice.

All this—her going along to Dacre's room—had only started because she had wanted him to witness for himself that he was wasting his time waiting in the belief that she might marry him and be the mother of his children. She had, she must own, rather lost sight of that. But now, for his sake, it had to end. She loved him enough to do that. The worst part of it, though, was that whereas before she had hoped she might be able to stay she now knew that after tonight she would have to go.

It was around midnight when Dacre entered her room. He was tall, broad-shouldered, wearing a bathrobe and, on seeing his bare legs beneath, Josy knew he had on nothing else.

He stood there, his hand on the light switch. 'Forgive me for being so long. My business took longer than I'd anticipated,' he apologised.

'You must be tired,' she replied without thinking, and wanted to groan out loud at the realisation that he might think that that was some last minute suggestion that he should go straight to sleep. He did not answer but switched off the light and plunged the room into darkness.

Josy started to shake the moment he got into bed with her. 'Hey, I thought we had done away with all that?' he teased, and she loved him, and loved his teasing, and had no objection to make when he reached for her.

The arm he placed about her was uncovered, his naked chest near her hand. 'I n-need a light on,' she gasped.

'*Certainement*.' There was warmth in his voice, and she loved him some more that he wasn't cross with her, but at once took his arm from around her and, leaning to his side of the bed, switched on the bedside lamp. Then he adjusted the shade so that the room was shadowed—a mere subdued and subtle lighting—and turned back to her. He did not place an arm around her but, propping himself up, looked down at her.

'I'm sorry,' she apologised.

'Oh, sweet Josy,' he smiled. 'You're scared and worried, I know. But I'm no different from the man you've slept with these last three nights.'

'I know.' She tried to smile back but couldn't. 'But— it's d-different tonight, isn't it?'

He looked at her, and then moved further into bed with her. She could smell the recently showered smell of him as he leaned to her and gently kissed the side of her face. 'Only if you want it to be,' he assured her, and, placing a kiss to the corner of her mouth, added, 'Believe me, my dear, whatever happens, should you feel panic or fear, there is no way that I'll force myself on you.'

'Oh, Dacre!' she cried, and took one arm out of the bed so that she could touch his face. She knew then that he was telling her that there wasn't even the smallest likelihood that he would lose control and start tearing at her clothes as Marc had.

'Trust me,' he urged, and, taking hold of her hand, he placed a kiss in her palm.

Josy closed her eyes, and a moment later felt the warmth of him as he moved nearer. She opened her eyes and saw his dear face near, and she smiled, and when lightly he placed his lips over hers she took her other hand from beneath the coverlet and put her arms round him.

His back was warm, hard-muscled and all male. And, just as her hands had explored his chest last night, she stroked them softly over his back. Dacre broke his tender kiss to look at her. Then, seeming to enjoy her lips, he kissed her again, more lingeringly this time.

I'm not panicking, she thought, and stared solemnly at him when he raised his head again. 'You've—um—' She broke off to cough, her voice all choky and almost inaudible. 'You've got a nice back,' she told him huskily, and he kissed first one eye and then the other.

'And so, Josy, have you,' he answered, one hand somehow finding its way under the top of her pyjamas. She felt the warmth of his hand on her midriff and tensed. 'Relax, sweet flower, relax,' he murmured, and placed his lips over hers and gently kept them there while sensitive fingers stroked and caressed beneath her thin covering.

Subtly then, for with all her heightened senses she was aware the whole time, the tenor of his kisses gradually began to change. His kiss became firmer, longer, his hold that bit stronger.

His hands ceased their caressing movements on her skin, and the next she knew was that she felt one hand at the buttons of her pyjama jacket. He did not immediately unbutton it, though, but, as if asking her permission, first kissed her and then looked at her.

'As you said—it's—um—time I let go of some of my m-modesty,' she managed chokily.

'My brave Josy,' Dacre murmured, and undid one button and bent to kiss that place, and Josy gripped on to him but did not panic.

Nor did she panic when he undid the next button and parted the material and kissed the skin beneath. When the last button was undone he gently raised her, holding her to him while he took her pyjama top from her. Tender words in French left him then as he held her, her breasts naked against him.

And Josy clutched on to him. She felt shy; she felt nervous but, she realised, she trusted him, and something in her started to relax. She felt his hands caressing at her back. 'Oh, Dacre,' she murmured, loving him so.

'Don't be afraid, little one. I have you safe,' he breathed, and she wanted to kiss him—and had to tell him so.

'I want to kiss you.' She gulped—and could not believe the long, drawn-out shaky sigh that left him.

'I so hoped you would,' he invited, and, holding her to him, he lay down, drawing her half over him. 'Kiss me, sweet life,' he added.

She stared down into his eyes. 'I'm not very good at it,' she confessed.

'You will be,' he assured her confidently, and she gave a little laugh; incredibly, she wasn't shaking any more!

She lowered her head and placed her mouth over his. She felt his hands come to move her more over him, and swallowed when she felt the caress of his touch as he captured her breasts, found the hardened peaks, and moulded them to cause such delight in her that she wanted more.

'Dacre!' she gasped.

'You're all right—it's natural,' he assured her, just as if he knew all about the excitement that was starting to build up in her.

'Is it?'

'Oh, yes.' He smiled, and she loved him and lowered her head to explore his mouth once more.

She pulled back; he had a wonderful mouth. She felt hypnotised by it, and bent to him, kissing him, looking at him again, and, hardly knowing what she was doing, but somehow as if wanting to taste him, she touched his mouth with the tip of her tongue.

An exclamation in French escaped him and a spasm of movement took him. 'Did I do something wrong?' she asked.

'Sweet Josy, carry on like that and you'll soon be graduating with honours.'

'Oh,' she said, and buried her face in his neck—and liked what he was doing to her when he rolled her over and took over the kissing tuition.

She felt his hands warm on her back, warm on her breasts, but, having thought that she had broken through those high barriers of modesty, found that she was overwhelmed by shyness again when he pulled back his head so that he could see her nudity.

She tried to cover herself, and heard him laugh softly. 'You are a true delight,' he murmured, and lowered his head, and as her hands fell away he kissed first one breast and then the other—and a fire of wanting started to lick into life within her. She gave a gasp, and immediately Dacre raised his head. 'Josy?'

'I...' she managed—and had to tell him. 'I think—I want to... I think I want you!'

His glance stayed with her; she saw a smile break on him, and, every bit as if he understood her bewilderment, gently it was that he asked, 'Would you like to find out for sure?'

She knew what he was asking, and for the first time panicked a little. 'Help me,' she pleaded.

'Oh, my darling,' he crooned, and gathered her in his arms and held her quietly for long moments, and then gradually, and still quietly, he began to stroke and caress her to a higher peak of wanting.

Josy felt his hands, his fingertips, at her breasts, stroking them and peaking them to hardened points of perfection. She kissed him, and he kissed her. She kissed his nipples, and he moulded the exquisite pink tips of her breasts with his tongue and mouth.

She felt his hands at the waistband of her pyjama trousers. 'Dacre,' she whispered.

'I know, sweet darling—it'll be all right,' he soothed, and unhurriedly he undid the fastening, and as unhurriedly took her only covering from her.

She wanted her pyjamas back—but didn't want them. It was a warm night and the light bedcover had disappeared to the floor by that time. Shyness took Josy again when he lowered his head to kiss her belly and thighs. 'Dacre!' she cried in alarm, and he was back with her.

'Shh, sweet love, you're doing fine,' he encouraged, and gently kissed her. But as his kiss deepened so more fire shot through her and her body, and with no thought of inhibitions she wanted to get closer to him.

She pressed near to him, and felt shock ripple through her when she came up against the waiting masculine wanting of him. She backed away, clutching fiercely at him as she fought through another barricade of shyness and panic.

And Dacre was marvellous. For, just as though he understood that this was another giant hurdle for her, he whispered encouraging words to her, kissing her, gentling her, moulding her silken body, his sensitive fingers a whispering caress.

And as her inhibitions started to fade and it was all so wonderful she wanted to tell him that she loved him. But she knew she could not. So she kissed him, and as he caressed her so that fire that had never died started to burn more fiercely than ever.

She lightly touched his body, loved his firm hips. 'Stay calm, my love,' he breathed softly, and whispered his touch to her thighs—and she stayed calm while he came closer and she again felt his wonderful body next to hers. He moved against her and she could only wonder at this freedom—this wonderful, wonderful freedom—as with kisses and caresses he took her to yet new heights.

Their legs intertwined as his magical, sensitive fingers made her body sing, and she sighed in pleasure and in love; he kissed her. Soon, she knew, he would make her his, and as her whole body throbbed out her need for him she was no longer afraid.

CHAPTER EIGHT

DACRE had gone when Josy awakened in the morning. The sun shone brilliantly through her bedroom window and she opened her eyes to a feeling of contentment and joy. She moved over to the spot where Dacre had lain and put her head on his pillow.

She remembered his wonderful lovemaking, his tenderness, and loved him with the whole of her being. How caring of her he had been, how patient. Oh, that magical togetherness. And, joy of all joys, she wasn't frigid as she had supposed. Not with him—her love.

Josy closed her eyes as she recalled the exquisite pleasure of his sensitive lovemaking. She had tried not to cry out at the initial pain of sharing her untried body with him but had been unable to prevent herself from sucking in her breath.

'Oh, forgive me, my dear one,' Dacre had whispered, kissing her and caressing her and waiting until the spasm had passed. And only when he'd judged that she was over that moment had he caringly made her his.

Josy opened her eyes on that word 'caringly'. Did he care? Her heart started to hammer; he had said he wanted to marry her, hadn't he? Suddenly a riot of thoughts and questions began to bombard her, making it impossible for her to stay in her bed.

She headed for the shower, but those thoughts and questions followed her. Did he care for her? That question pounded again and again in her head.

She had found no answer, when, showered and dressed, she discovered that she was reluctant to go and seek him out. In a way, she supposed, without comprehending how it was possible after having lain naked with him through the night, there were still pockets of shyness in her.

She guessed that she might always be shy to some degree. You couldn't change overnight. But—and here her breath caught—what she had discovered overnight was that she could be—a wife! Her mouth dried at the thought. Dacre, with time, patience and understanding, had shown her that. The problem, admittedly aided by her inexperience and reserve, had been Marc's!

But she didn't want to think of Marc—poor, dear Marc—just then. Just then it was quite momentous enough to take on board the discovery of her own normality and—her heartbeats quickened—the fact that she could marry Dacre—if he still wanted to marry her!

She brushed her hair at the dressing-table but, brush in hand, a shadow came to her joy in that morning. Perhaps Dacre wouldn't want to marry her—not now; not now that he had lain with her. He wasn't like that, though; she ousted the doubt. Besides, she trusted him. And no man could be the tender, considerate way he had been with her last night and... But what did she know of men? Why had Dacre wanted to marry her? Perhaps he didn't any more?

A mental pain started to nip that was almost physical. But her mental anguish halted abruptly, all thoughts fleeing, when just then the handle of her bedroom door turned. Josy stared, hypnotised, unaware that she was on her feet. Then as the door opened and, not pausing to knock, Dacre came in she felt her face go scarlet.

He looked at her. Silently, his expression serious, as if he was weighing up her reaction, he studied her, and as shyness threatened to choke her she sought for some-

thing to say that would get her through this un-
comfortable moment.

'Good morning,' she managed, and hastily looked at
the carpet, wanting to die. Grief—not too many hours
ago she had been manifestly less formal!

She was not left to suffer miserably for long, however.
For, while she was still finding the carpet of utmost
interest, a pair of expensive male shoes entered her vision.
And the next she knew Dacre had placed warm, sensitive fingers beneath her chin. And was forcing her to
look at him.

He said something about '*très adorable*', but, made
to look at him, Josy couldn't miss seeing that the look
in his eyes wasn't cool or distant as she had feared it
might be. In those grey depths she could see nothing but
warmth.

'You are well this morning?' he wanted to know.

Was he teasing? She couldn't decide. 'Quite well,' she
replied.

'But you don't like me this morning?' he enquired,
and Josy, hearing something in his voice—she wasn't
sure what, but it was a tinge of something that suggested
that it bothered him that she might not like him—could
only speak the truth.

'I—um—think I've gone shy again,' she mumbled.

'You *are* adorable!' he smiled, and, his head coming
nearer, their lips met.

She felt his arms come round her as he gathered her
to him, and felt his body against her as he moved closer.
'Oh, Dacre!' she gasped as their kiss broke, and stared
at him in confusion and amazement. For how could it
be? Last night she had been a shy, unawakened virgin.
And now, this morning, Dacre only had to touch her
and she wanted him to make love to her!

'It's the same for you too?' he asked, and she mar-
velled again that he seemed to know exactly what she
was feeling.

'You too?' she asked shyly.

'Have you no idea what you do to me?' he asked,
keeping her in the circle of his arms, but with a smile
answered for her, 'No, I don't suppose you have.' Lightly
then he kissed her mouth. 'But,' he went on, 'we have
important matters to deal with today, to discuss.' And,
as if searching for more control, he decided promptly,
'I don't think, *ma petite*, that your bedroom, with your
bed looking so inviting, is the place where we should
discuss anything. We will go to the stables.' Not giving
her time to think, he dragged his gaze away from the
bed and hurried her from her room. Together they went
down the stairs. 'Can you wait for breakfast?' he asked.
'I have something I want to show you.'

'Of course,' she murmured, loving him with all she
had, and food of small importance.

She had thought that they would walk to the stables,
but once outside the house she saw Dacre's car waiting
there. Clearly to have got his car out of its garage must
mean that he had already been out or intended to go
out. He held the door for her and she got into the passenger seat, while she hid the sudden anguish she felt at
the thought that perhaps Dacre meant to take a drive to
the airfield. She didn't want him to leave—ever.

Josy tried to calm herself by making herself remember that Dacre had something he wanted to show
her. It must be good if he wanted to show her in a hurry.

It did not take long to reach the stables, but before
they got there Josy was deep into what else Dacre had
said. He'd said, 'We have important matters to deal with
today.' *We*, not him. She and him! She swallowed hard

on a suddenly dry throat. Matters to discuss, he had said.

Her head was in a whirl when Dacre halted the car in the stableyard. 'Someone's turned Nina and César out,' she guessed when, leaving the car, she saw that their stalls were empty.

'They're in the paddock.'

'I'm sorry—I'm late this morning.'

'Understandably late this morning,' Dacre qualified, and remarked, causing her to go a trace of pink, 'You didn't get to sleep until the early hours.' He paused, seemed to hesitate, then, looking down at her, he quietly asked, 'Any regrets?'

She looked into his eyes, loved him dearly. He had made her feel like a woman. And no matter what happened today—even should the matters they had to deal with, to discuss, be matters related to her returning home—then never would she or could she regret a thing. She was suddenly feeling too choked to be able to speak, and all she was capable of doing just then was shaking her head.

But it was the answer that Dacre wanted, for, placing an arm about her shoulders, he held her to him for a moment. 'Come, let's go and see the horses in the paddock,' he suggested, and with his arm about her shoulders they walked from the stableyard and round the corner towards the paddock.

They were almost up to the paddock rail, however, when Josy stood stock-still. Dacre halted too. 'There are—three horses there,' she said slowly.

'Are you sure?' he questioned—but there was no mistaking the hint of teasing in his voice. Josy glanced to him, but then her glance went swiftly back to the paddock where the third horse—the stranger in the camp—had picked up the sounds of voices and had

turned; and as the horse moved and started to trot over—
with Nina and César following—a feeling of gladness
entered her heart.

'Hetty!' Josy cried, and took off at a gallop herself.
Oh, Dacre, she thought; this, then, was what he had
wanted to show her. She met Hetty by the paddock rail
and leaned over and hugged and kissed her—and had
to pat Nina and César when they trotted over too before
returning to Hetty to croon, 'How did you get here?'

Then, having never forgotten him, Josy became aware
of Dacre standing right there with her. And it was he
who replied, 'You remember the business I had to attend
to last night?'

Keeping one hand on Hetty's neck, Josy turned to
him. 'Hetty arrived last night?'

'The phone call I took was to say that Hetty and
horsebox had made it as far as Angers,' he revealed, and
added enchantingly, 'Before I could come to you, *ma
petite*, I had to wait for the horsebox, and after that,
having transferred her to a stable, wait to check that she
had everything you would want her to have, and to stay
with her a while to make sure she was happily settled.'

'Oh, Dacre,' she said softly, hardly able to believe that
Hetty was here, that Dacre had brought her here—that
he had done all that last night. Her hand slipped from
the mare's neck, and as he fed the three horses a sugar
lump each and they trotted back to the shade, Josy asked,
'But—why?'

'Why?' he returned, his expression deadly serious as
he looked back at her. 'Why else, my dear, than because
I wanted you to stay?'

'Stay?' she queried, stunned, her heartbeats starting
to race.

Dacre glanced from her to the wooden seat where she
had so often sat watching the horses. 'Let's go and sit

down—I said we had important matters to deal with—
to discuss.'

Josy went with him to the seat, her heart thumping.
From the seriousness of his expression she had an idea
that the 'matters' were indeed very important. Oh,
heavens, she felt a bag of nerves, half fearing that Dacre
would tell her that he wanted her to go, but pinning all
her hopes on the fact that Hetty was there and that Dacre
had definitely said that he wanted her to *stay*.

Once they were seated Dacre turned to her, and Josy,
looking at him, wished he would smile. Though, since
her own smile seemed to have gone into hiding from the
sudden uproar of her emotions, she doubted if she would
have been able to smile back at him.

'Y-you said you—brought Hetty over because...' she
began when the feeling of tension in her became more
than she could bear, only to have her voice fail on her.

'I knew you were missing her.' Dacre, to her relief,
took over. But suddenly some of his solemnity faded as
he confessed, 'I didn't want you to have any reason to
return to England. Because, after all my efforts to get
you here, you might go—and never come back.'

Josy was totally fascinated by this insight into the way
his thoughts had gone. But while she stared—and her
thoughts all over the place—she tried to look deeper into
what he was saying, the best she could sort out was,
'Efforts?'

'Efforts,' Dacre agreed, and caught hold of her hand
as he confided, 'Dear Josy, I have not always told you
the truth, I'm afraid.'

'You lied to me?' She wasn't very sure how she felt
about that.

'Believe me, trust me, *petite*; I regard you too highly
to lie to you for any reason other than that which
necessity forced on me.'

She couldn't begin to understand what he meant, but, at a moment when she might have pulled her hand from his, the fact that he'd stated he regarded her highly caused her to let it remain there.

'Have you done lying to me, do you think?' she asked, a trifle drily she had to own—and loved him when that brought a wry smile to his face.

'How you have changed this past year,' he commented.

'I've grown more confident since I've been here,' she admitted. And because it was his due added, 'And I thank you for that.'

'You think it's all my doing?' Clearly he doubted it.

'Since knowing you I've rediscovered I have a temper. That I can get angry—'

'I noticed that!' It was his turn to offer a dry note.

'Anyhow,' she went on quickly, suddenly realising only then that his having stirred her emotionally way back in England—albeit anger—could only have been the start of her falling in love with him. 'Um...' She didn't want him guessing at her love for him. 'Why did you find it necessary to lie to me?'

'Because I wanted you here with me,' he replied unhesitatingly.

'But—but... But you asked me to come here months and months ago. You asked when you came to England— the end of last September—if I would help you by coming to look after your horses. You said you lived in a very isolated—' She broke off when it looked as though Dacre wanted to interrupt. 'What?' she asked.

'I shall tell you no more lies, my dear; we have come too far for that!' he wasted no time in replying. And, while her heart started to race, added, 'But, to confess to some old—um—untruths, I must tell you that at the time of asking you to come and look after my horses— while stressing the isolation of my home because I judged that somewhere isolated would appeal to you—I did not then—um—own any horses.'

Josy stared at him in amazement. 'You didn't *own* any?' She gasped. 'But...' She was lost. 'Would you mind explaining?' she asked, adding quickly, since her brain didn't appear to be coping very well, 'From the very beginning.'

Dacre looked at her for long, long moments, and then told her quietly, 'I should like to.' First, though, he raised her dainty hand to his lips and kissed it, while Josy fought to keep calm—and failed miserably. 'It began, my little love, when I went to meet Marc and his bride at the airport in Nantes.'

'Then?' she queried, his endearment causing her heart to palpitate, which didn't help her confusion at all. Apart from during that drive from the airport to Marc's parents' home, and perhaps for half an hour afterwards, she hadn't seen Dacre again for almost four months.

'I met you, dear Josy—and didn't know what hit me,' he told her quietly, his eyes fixed on hers.

What was he saying? Whatever, it was doing nothing for her fast-beating heart. 'You—er—didn't?' she enquired huskily.

'I didn't,' he agreed. 'There you were so very shy, so very beautiful, so unaware of your own beauty—I at once fell totally in love with you.'

'Y—' Her voice caught in her throat, and not a peep more would come.

'I couldn't then believe it myself.' He smiled.

'You were—um—infatuated, perhaps?' she found enough voice to suggest.

'That was the best I could hope for. But I knew even then that—as at some future date I started lying to you— I would be lying to myself to try to deny my love.'

Dacre had loved her! She could hardly believe it was true. She wanted quite desperately to ask if he still loved her, but she didn't have the nerve. Though, as she remembered his tenderness, his understanding with her last night, a smile of beginning to believe started to shine in her.

'You wanted to deny it?' she asked huskily.

'*Chérie*, I had to! You were my cousin's bride, the ink on your wedding papers barely dry. There was I, a man who would never agree to love from afar, in love with someone who had just committed the rest of her life to my cousin—a cousin I loved like a brother. I couldn't take it. I felt as if everything I'd worked for and enjoyed all these years was crumbling about me.'

'Oh, Dacre,' she murmured softly, stunned still, but her feelings all for him.

He seemed to like the sound of his name on her lips, for he placed an arm firmly about her shoulders before going on, 'I was so stunned at this emotion creating havoc in me that when I delivered you and Marc to his parents I stayed but a short while and—my vacation plans for the next day suddenly having little appeal—I flew off that night in an opposite direction, to a little-known Greek island. I needed to get right away—needed to think, needed solitude—and hopefully I would realise I had made a mistake.'

'H-had you made a mistake?' she just had to ask.

His arm about her shoulders tightened. 'No, *mon ange*, I hadn't. It was, as I knew, irrevocably there— there in the fact that your beautiful face and manner haunted me the whole of the two weeks I was away.' Tenderly he kissed her brow. 'I returned from Greece to discover that both my father and my office had been urgently trying to contact me—and that Marc, killed riding that beast, was already buried.'

'I'm so sorry,' she stated softly, in her love for him all her sympathy going out to him for the shock that news must have been to him.

Only to find that Dacre, in his love for her, had been more concerned for her, when he revealed, 'I was still taking in Marc's death when I enquired about you. You were in deep shock, my aunt told me. And as I started to grow furious that they had allowed you to return to England on your own Aunt Sylvie told me how your fiercely protective twin had flown over and had escorted you back.'

'Belvia was marvellous.'

'I'm so glad you had her,' Dacre commented on a heartfelt note. 'I wanted to come to England to see you then myself,' he confessed. 'I should have done. As soon as you told me of the misapprehension you'd been under, the guilt that had riven you, I knew I had been mistaken not to come. I could have told you of that evil-hearted stallion—that it was Marc's love of him and not inattention because of the terror he put you through on your wedding night that caused his death.'

'I don't remember much of what went on around me in those early days except for the guilt,' Josy owned. But she found a smile as she added, 'Thanks to you, that dreadful guilt started to fade, and has now gone.'

'Oh, I'm so glad, *chérie!*' Dacre exclaimed. '*Je t'aime,*' he breathed, as if he could not help himself, and as Josy realised that Dacre had just told her in French 'I love you', she raised her head—and their eyes met. 'Oh, my sweet, sweet flower,' Dacre whispered, and kissed her a kiss of such beauty that when he pulled back she could only look at him. She knew indisputably then that he loved her. She wanted to tell him that she loved him— just how much she loved him—but wretched shyness seemed to glue the words to her throat. 'So, to explain

everything, my heart, to explain the extent of my lies—
since I am never, ever going to lie to you again—I must
tell you that while still emotionally shaken that we had
lost Marc, emotionally shaken at the fact that the love
I had for you seemed stronger at that dreadful time, I
began to feel hypocritical. I began to feel that my reasons
for wanting to go to England were more that I just had
to see you rather than that I felt I had to come and offer
you my condolences.' Josy stared at him and he went
on, 'For that same reason I denied the need to phone
or to write to you. But four months later I could deny
my need to see you no longer.'

'You were in England on business,' Josy recalled.

'A lie, *mon adorable*,' Dacre confessed. 'No matter
how I tried, I couldn't get you out of my head. I just
had to come and see you. To invent being in England
on some business seemed a good cover.'

'I'd no idea!' she gasped.

And gently he kissed her. 'My poor Josy, how sad,
how unhappy, how pale you looked. It was like a knife
twisting in my heart to see you so. I could not bear that
it was so. I wanted you in France, where I could take
care of you.' He smiled then as he stated, 'I knew from
Marc's parents of your love of horses. To invent having
a couple of horses that I needed someone reliable to look
after was the best, if slender, chance I could think of to
tempt you at that time.'

'But I fell for it.' She had to smile too.

'Not straight away. But I thought I'd seen a spark of
interest, and, for all you'd refused, my foolish heart
started to pound at the thought that if the gods were
kind there might be a hope that I would see you
every weekend.'

'Oh, Dacre,' she whispered. 'It was like that for you?'
Her heart was pounding too, right at that very moment,

as it began to sink in how very much he must have loved her—and still did.

'You cannot know, *mon coeur*,' he murmured, and kissed her gently before, as if he wanted it all said and out of the way, he pulled back and resumed, 'Purchasing a couple of horses, making a paddock and transforming some old outbuildings into stables was the easy part. The hard part was learning patience.'

'You're not normally a patient man?'

'Not then, my darling,' he replied. 'But I was fully aware of your shyness, and knew how carefully I must go with you if I didn't want to ruin everything. I'd been to the stables in England with you, and had become more and more enchanted by you when, your inhibitions falling from you, I observed a loving, tender side of you when you saw your Hetty. You asked if I would wait while you went for a ride on her—and I knew then, my dearest love, that I would wait for you for however long it took.'

'You've—been—wonderful,' she had to admit, even if, unused to speaking so, she spoke the words shyly.

'I'm glad you think so,' he grinned. 'I have to admit, *petite*, that hope and frustration in getting you here were warring enemies in my long wait for you. You took over six months to come to me!' he accused, and Josy burst out laughing.

'I'm glad I came,' she told him.

'No more than I,' he told her sincerely. 'I've so ached for you. You'll never know the joy in my heart that day when I could no longer resist the urge to hear your voice and I rang your home—and you told me you would like to take the job.'

'I'd no idea!' she exclaimed huskily.

'*Naturellement*.'

Josy smiled at him, loving him with all she had as she explained, 'I think I was starting to come to terms with Marc's death when you rang. I was still nursing a whole load of guilt, I know, but I was also starting to take stock, and realising that I must do something about making a different sort of life for myself. I'd just decided that I would go to France for six months, and make the break with my father, when, right at that moment, you rang.'

'And I was so euphoric after that phone call. I wasn't to know then that I was going to have to wait, and to wait, and wait some more for you to come.'

'My father was ill—'

'In view of your severely shocked state I should have written to him telling him I would take the greatest care of you—but I didn't for fear he might devise obstacles to your coming to me.'

'Was that how you felt—thought?' she gasped.

'It was,' he owned. 'Already there were too many delays in your coming to me.'

'You rang me Christmas Day!' she remembered.

'I had to. I was near to despair. Thank God I didn't know then that I'd have to wait until April to see you. But you, darling Josy, rang in February to give me a definite date when you'd be here, and I told you that Nina and César were looking forward to seeing you when in reality it was me that was eagerly looking forward to seeing you—and I thought I'd better do something about brushing up my rusty riding skills.'

'You don't normally ride?' she exclaimed, amazed.

'I hadn't ridden in years,' he confessed. 'For you I endured that—and more. And then that April day— when I'd been at the window most of the morning willing you to arrive—at three-thirteen that afternoon my straining ears heard the sound of your car. I waited a couple of minutes, deciding to be friendly but casual. And then I saw you, and all I knew was that, starved all those months for a sight of you, I had a desperate need to touch, to hold you.'

'You did—you held my arms and kissed my cheeks.'

'I was aware my action worried you when you stiffened as I held you. It endorsed for me that if ever I was to gain my heart's desire with you, I must find still more patience.' He smiled into her eyes. 'You have no idea how difficult that became when, with each new part I learned about you, I fell deeper and deeper in love with you.'

'You—did?' she asked chokily, her heart thundering; he did love her. He did, he did, he did!

'How could I help it? As shy as you are, you recognised shyness in my housekeeper, and I witnessed how you overcame your own shyness out of a sensitivity to put Agathe at her ease. Is it any wonder that I am enchanted? That I wanted to spend more and more time with you, to form a friendship, to build on that friendship, to gain your trust and—should good fortune be with me—perhaps gain a little of your love?'

'Oh, Dacre,' she sighed.

And he smiled tenderly, and told her, 'But, as reserved as you are, I've seen you angry and spirited. I've seen you with an imp of mischief dancing in your eyes and, with a speeding heart, I've known delight in seeing you emerge from the darkness that engulfed you. But, *mon petit ange*, when the love in my heart became too much to hold in I had to realise my weakness in being too impatient and deliberately force myself to stay away from you.'

'You've stayed away from your home because of me?' she exclaimed, astounded.

'It is true,' he admitted. 'I've had to pretend I've had a lunch engagement elsewhere when there has been none. Or that I had something to keep me in Paris at the weekend, or even to make me leave here for Paris earlier than I'd intended, when there was nothing in me but a desire to be with you.'

'I didn't know!' she gasped.

'I fear it would have terrified you if you had,' he commented softly. 'Don't you see, sweet flower, that I had to allow you to come to me in your own time? My problem was that I have always been intolerant of delay.'

'You've been through a very bad time,' she realised.

'So too have you, little one,' he murmured tenderly— and it seemed the most natural thing in the world that they should cleave to each other and kiss.

'Oh, my dear!' she whispered as their kiss broke and they pulled back to look into each other's dear face. 'Has it been so very dreadful?'

'There were better moments than the dread that took me that Saturday when I came looking for you on César and met a riderless Nina halfway. I have never been so panicked or, when I saw you lying there motionless, so terrified. I thought you might be dead.' He smiled then as he went on, 'Only you weren't dead, but shrieking loud enough to wake the dead when I dared to touch you.'

'I'm so sorry,' she apologised.

'So you should be,' he admonished teasingly. 'There am I, fearful that I have lost you before I've won you one minute, then the next, when my attention is merely to feel for your pulse, you are turning on me in panic and yet—while I don't like at all the fact that there is panic in your eyes at my touch—causing me to fall deeper in love with you than ever by showing me yet more of your spirited side—when you ride off without me.'

She had to smile, but confessed, 'I wanted to apologise. Back at the stables I cooled down and ... But you came by and looked so aloof that I couldn't say a word. And then I had the dreadful feeling you wanted me to leave and—'

'Oh, sweet and wonderful Josy! To be aloof was all I could be. Otherwise I would have taken you in my arms.'

'Truly?' she exclaimed.

'Most truly. I had such a feeling of wanting to hold you—not sexually, *ma petite*. But, just as at other times I've felt a tremendous need to be near you, to sometimes stretch out a hand just to touch you, so it was then, when, still feeling shaken from imagining you injured or worse, I had to fight an urgent need to hold you.'

'Oh, I'm so sorry,' she apologised again, and Dacre placed a light kiss on the corner of her mouth.

'As for wanting you to leave, *chérie*—I had waited over six months for you to come to me; there was no chance I would let you go if I could help it.'

What could she do? She kissed him, and smiled at him as she confessed, 'If it's—er—of any—interest, I—er—well, the thing is, if I'm honest—'

'I want only honesty between us from now on, my own,' he put in quietly.

She gave him a warm smile and confessed, 'Well, to be honest, you were too disturbing to me.'

'Disturbing?'

'I think I was starting to be aware of you—um—in a way I had never been aware of a man before.'

'*Petite*!'

'Oh, I wasn't aware of what exactly was happening to me at the time. But now I think I can see that when last September you came to England, and you suggested I start riding again, and I definitely felt angry with you—

I think even back then I was aware of you as Dacre Banchereau rather than merely Marc's cousin.'

'Please, whatever you do, my flower, do not stop there,' he ordered.

Josy laughed, and as she began to appreciate how much Dacre loved her, how careful and controlled he had been in his love for her, so for him, she tossed away any remnants of shyness to tell him openly, 'You made me angry; you made me laugh. You even made me feel rebellious—something was very definitely getting to me about you. I even found myself telling you of matters that had been locked up in me since I was fifteen—things I'd never told another living soul!'

'I wondered about that,' he put in softly. 'Were you beginning to trust me in a way you had never trusted Marc; or was it that I was so unimportant to you that it didn't matter to you that you'd told me? Because of that, little one, I kept out of your way for most of the weekend—and even told myself I wouldn't come home the next weekend.'

'But you did,' she recalled.

'And felt most put out that you spent the whole time— or most of it—out with the horses,' he remembered too. 'Then, a couple of weeks later, I invited you to the Cadre Noir—and you, obviously enjoying your own company, arrogantly told me you'd already been.'

'Arrogantly?' she queried.

'I'm sensitive,' he grinned. 'I thought you'd been out with that damned vet!'

'You didn't! You were jealous?'

'As jealous as hell,' he agreed. 'Apart from the fact that Franck and Georges very soon grew to like the young widow from England very much, they also had instructions to watch over you like a favourite daughter when I wasn't here. So I was confident that no one would

worry you while you while you were on my property.'
And, smiling into her eyes, he murmured, 'So, having
overlooked the fact that there would be times when I'd
have to invite a vet here, I started to go quietly out of
my mind about him—about you—while at the same time
I was forced to acknowledge that the time for the—' he
broke off to search for the right word '—togetherness I
was trying to form with you was not yet right. I deliberately stayed in Paris the next weekend.'

'But you came home the following Friday,' she inserted quietly.

'I couldn't keep away. It was your wedding anniversary; I couldn't bear you to be unhappy and alone.'

'You came especally...?'

'Have you not realised yet how adored by me you are?'
he enquired simply.

'Oh, Dacre,' she cried weakly.

'You have suffered enough, little one,' he breathed,
and kissed her tenderly before he went on to tell her, a
humorous note entering his voice, 'And so have I. By
then I was loving you so much that I was having a constant battle to hold it in. I was starting to feel a nervous
wreck, scared that at any moment I might break, give
in, and ruin all I was hoping to achieve by taking you
in my arms and telling you how I felt about you.'

He *had* been through hell, she realised. 'Was that why
you didn't come home the next weekend?' she asked.

Dacre nodded. 'Did you miss me?'

Shyness, which she despaired ever being free of,
threatened to swamp her again. But with Dacre being
so open with her she wanted with all she had to be as
open with him. 'Jealousy isn't purely your prerogative,'
she told him—and saw a smile break from him that was
wonderful to see.

'You thought I was nightclubbing in Paris with—!' he exclaimed, with a grin. 'And were you jealous?'

'When I wasn't anxious that you might be ill,' she admitted shyly, and was kissed for that admission, but, fearing another battle with shyness should he question her about her jealous feelings, she swiftly reminded him, 'You flew down from Paris on Wednesday.'

'I was desperate for the sight of you by then,' he owned. 'I just had to obey a compulsion to come and see you—only you weren't here when I arrived. Agathe said you were in Angers, so I came looking for you.'

'You had an errand in Angers,' she reminded him.

'You were my errand, *petite*. I came only to find you.'

'Oh—Dacre!' she laughed. 'And you did find me.'

'Oh, I did. I found you impudent, saucy, delightful—and felt more in love with you than ever. Is it any wonder, *chérie*, that when I follow you home and find my laughing companion at lunch has gone, I should lose my control in the frustration of the moment and blurt out that I want to marry you?'

'I... What can I say?' she asked helplessly.

'Your look of horror said it all for you,' he stated. 'And,' he confessed, 'it terrified me too—until our discussion that evening, when I learned of the terrible burden—terrible and unnecessary burden—you had been carrying alone.' He held her warmly to him. 'By last Sunday, my adorable Josy, I was having to rethink my strategy. I knew by then of your conviction that you were frigid. But, while Marc's unfortunate behaviour had petrified you and had not helped you at all to overcome your natural modesty, I thought it was probable that your belief you were frigid stemmed not only from Marc's behaviour but also from your own fear of violence. I was very much aware, little one, of the dense barriers to be negotiated.'

'You've thought about me a lot,' she realised.

'Constantly,' Dacre answered. 'You, my dear, were very much on my mind on Sunday as I lay in my bed having given up my attempt to read as I wondered if my new strategy of being more in your company in an endeavour to make you feel more comfortable with me was the right one. You hadn't wanted to spend a companionable evening with me in the *salon* after dinner.'

'I was a bit—er—mixed up,' she confessed. 'I think it was starting to dawn on me that I couldn't go on the way I was, that I had to show you—since you wouldn't take my word for it—that there was no future for us together as a married...' Her voice faded, but her heart rejoiced at the wonderful all-loving smile that he gave her.

'And what a brave way you chose to show me, my sweet Josy,' he murmured. 'You'll never know the pounding in my head, in my heart when you came into my room and asked, '"Can I sleep with you?"''

'You thought me forward?'

'I thought you entirely enchanting. You had once said to me that being brave was doing something that terrified you, and I knew how brave and terrified you were.' His voice deepened emotionally. 'I also knew, sweetest love, that to come to me when you were so terrified, to be so brave, so courageous must surely have meant— and my heart, I confess, was bursting at the thought— that you cared for me.'

She smiled shyly, and could not deny it, and he gently touched her lips with his. 'And I also knew, as I invited you into my bed, that then, more than at any other time, I had to control my—um—masculine urges. I found that far easier,' he owned, 'when I felt your nerve-racked body shaking beneath my arm. All I wanted to do then was to ease that dreadful time for you.'

'You were thinking only of me—not yourself?'

'You are my life,' he breathed sincerely.

'Oh, what a lovely thing to say,' she sighed.

'It's true.' He kissed her.

'You said goodnight, and went to sleep,' she murmured dreamily.

'I said goodnight, but slept little,' he corrected her. 'I was fully awake at dawn when, like a rocket from a missile launcher, you shot out of bed and out of my room.'

She laughed; she had to—it was pretty much the way it had been. 'I couldn't believe in the cold light of day that I'd been so bold,' she confessed. 'And yet I came to your room a second time—and you were again kind,' she remembered.

'How else would I be, dear love? I was trying to get you used to me, used to small intimacies. I wanted you to feel less nervous of me. In short, I wanted you to trust me.'

Josy looked at him steadily. 'I think I did. I—in the morning I kissed you—'

'Without fear in your eyes,' Dacre inserted gently.

'You—expected fear when...?'

'Oh, yes. We were getting closer to each other. But on Tuesday night you didn't come to me, and I realised that the intimacy we'd so far achieved would be as nothing—that the chance to let you discover for yourself that you weren't frigid would be gone—unless I did something about it.'

'You came to my room. You said you couldn't sleep.'

'Nor did I sleep. I spent most of that night fighting, holding down the urge to kiss you awake.'

'I didn't know...'

'I went back to my own room before dawn. Then last night at dinner you said you would miss me a little next week when I returned to Paris, and I was sure it must mean that you cared a little for me. For my part, although I'm already busy rearranging my work schedule so that I can do more work here, I shall not be able to leave at all unless you come with me.' Her heart, which had been cantering and galloping in turns, picked up speed again to hear him intimate that he intended to spend more time in his country home but that when he returned to Paris he wanted her with him! 'I knew then, last night at dinner, that we—you and I—had reached a point of no return.'

'You—um—wanted to stay with me last night, you said.'

'And you said you were scared, and I couldn't tell you, precious darling, that I was scared too—because if it all went wrong I stood to lose you for ever.'

'Oh, Dacre.' She smiled lovingly at him, and trusted him so much that she just didn't mind at all if he'd guessed that she thought him something pretty special.

'You're lovely,' he breathed, and held her close up against him for long, loving moments. 'And I love you so very much,' he added huskily. 'Can you not now, my shy darling, tell me of your feelings for me?'

Josy was by then fairly certain that he must know of her feelings for him. But love, as she had realised, was a jittery taskmaster. So she gathered every scrap of courage and began, 'You asked me that day when we came back here after lunching in Angers what was wrong. I couldn't tell you then, but that day, in that café, when I looked up and saw you there so unexpectedly—well, that was when I knew that I—um—cared very much for you—' She broke off to swallow, and felt his arm about her tighten, felt the tenderness of his kiss to the side of her face.

'Go on, *petite*,' he urged, and, as if he knew that there was more, he bade her, 'Don't stop there.'

'Well, I was so happy then. But...'

'But?'

'I was on my way home when cold common sense doused me in icy water. What was the point in caring? Nothing was ever going to come of it. And then you were there, asking what was wrong—and horrifying me by saying you wanted me to marry you.'

'And now?' Dacre asked very quietly.

'Now?' She wasn't with him.

'Now you know that something *can* come of it—what now?' he asked, a kind of tension in him as he waited for her answer.

Oh, heavens, she loved him so. Josy took a deep, shyness-banishing breath.

There had been a few occasions in her life when some quality which she had little control over had reared up out of her frustration with her inadequacies and pushed her headlong through those stout bastions of reserve. Such an occasion happened then when, loving Dacre with her whole heart, she took a deep breath and answered, 'And now, I think, if it's all right with you, that I'd like very much—to marry you.'

'*Chérie*. My Josy! I adore you!' he cried. And, exultant, he added, 'I knew! Last night I knew you loved me! You do love me, don't you?' he demanded, his grey eyes burning fiercely into hers.

'Oh, yes,' she replied, quite unable to believe the utter joy on his face. 'I love you so much.'

He gave another cry of rejoicing. 'And you'll marry me?' he insisted, as if he couldn't believe his hearing when she had said that to marry him was what she would like to do.

'Oh, yes,' she whispered.

And Dacre heard, and, standing up, taking her with him, he embraced her in his arms. 'One kiss, maybe two,' he decreed, 'Then we must go and arrange a wedding.'

UNLOCK THE DOOR TO GREAT ROMANCE
AT BRIDE'S BAY RESORT

Join Harlequin's new across-the-lines series, set in an exclusive hotel on an island off the coast of South Carolina.

Seven of your favorite authors will bring you exciting stories about fascinating heroes and heroines discovering love at Bride's Bay Resort.

Look for these fabulous stories coming to a store near you beginning in January 1996.

Harlequin American Romance #613 in January
Matchmaking Baby by Cathy Gillen Thacker

Harlequin Presents #1794 in February
Indiscretions by Robyn Donald

Harlequin Intrigue #362 in March
Love and Lies by Dawn Stewardson

Harlequin Romance #3404 in April
Make Believe Engagement by Day Leclaire

Harlequin Temptation #588 in May
Stranger in the Night by Roseanne Williams

Harlequin Superromance #695 in June
Married to a Stranger by Connie Bennett

Harlequin Historicals #324 in July
Dulcie's Gift by Ruth Langan

Visit Bride's Bay Resort each month wherever Harlequin books are sold.

BBAYG

MILLION DOLLAR SWEEPSTAKES

You're About to Become a
Privileged Woman

Reap the rewards of fabulous free gifts and benefits with proofs-of-purchase from Harlequin and Silhouette books

Pages & Privileges™

It's our way of thanking you for buying our books at your favorite retail stores.

PROOF OF PURCHASE
HR-PP159
Offer expires October 31, 1996

**Harlequin and Silhouette—
the most privileged readers in the world!**

For more information about Harlequin and Silhouette's **PAGES & PRIVILEGES** program call the Pages & Privileges Benefits Desk: **1-503-794-2499**

 HARLEQUIN®